Covert Patterns of Modality

Covert Patterns of Modality

Edited by

Werner Abraham and Elisabeth Leiss

CAMBRIDGE
SCHOLARS
PUBLISHING

Covert Patterns of Modality,
Edited by Werner Abraham and Elisabeth Leiss

This book first published 2012

Cambridge Scholars Publishing

12 Back Chapman Street, Newcastle upon Tyne, NE6 2XX, UK

British Library Cataloguing in Publication Data
A catalogue record for this book is available from the British Library

ISBN (10): 1-4438-4059-9, ISBN (13): 978-1-4438-4059-0

TABLE OF CONTENTS

Contributors

Werner Abraham
Germanistische Linguistik
University of Munich
Schellingstr. 3/RG
80799 Muenchen
Germany
werner.abraham@lmu.de

Winnie Chor Oi-wan
A0725, School of Arts and Social Sciences,
The Open University of Hong Kong
Homantin. Kowloon
Hong Kong
winnie_chor@yahoo.com

Marco Coniglio
Humboldt-Universität zu Berlin
Institut für deutsche Sprache und Linguistik
Dorotheenstraße 24
10117 Berlin
marco.coniglio@cms.hu-berlin.de

Aslı Göksel
Boğaziçi University
Department of Western Languages and Literatures
Bebek, Istanbul 34342
Turkey
gokselas@boun.edu.tr

Gerda Hassler
Leiterstraße 10
14473 Potsdam
Germany
hassler@uni-potsdam.de

Dagmar Haumann
Institutt for fremmedspråk og oversetting
Universitetet i Agder
Postboks 422
4604 Kristiansand
Norway
dagmar.haumann@uia.no

Barış Kabak
Universität Wuerzburg
Lehrstuhl für Englische Sprachwissenschaft
Am Hubland
97074 Wuerzburg
Germany
Baris.Kabak@uni-wuerzburg.de

Michail Kotin
ul. Migdalowa 6/2.
65-001 Zielona Góra
Poland
mkotin@poczta.onet.pl

Elisabeth Leiss
Germanistische Linguistik
University of Munich
Schellingstr. 3/RG
80799 Muenchen
Germany
elisabeth.leiss@lmu.de

Ole Letnes
Institutt for fremmedspråk og oversetting
Universitetet i Agder
Postboks 422
4604 Kristiansand
Norway
ole.letnes@uia.no

Rui Marques
Dep.to Linguística Geral e Românica
Faculdade de Letras da Universidade de Lisboa
Alameda da Universidade
1600-214 Lisboa, Portugal
rmarques@fl.ul.pt

Pierre-Yves Modicom
3 rue des Etats Generaux
56700 Hennebont
France
pierre-yves.modicom@laposte.net

Zarina Molochieva
General and Comparative Linguistics
Universitätsstraße 31
93053 Regensburg
Germany
zarina.molochieva@sprachlit.uni-regensburg.de

Jiao Wang
402 Stamford Dr Apt 2A
Newark, DE
USA 19711
wangjiao.beijing@gmail.com

Foong Ha Yap
AG412 Department of English
Hong Kong Polytechnic University
Hung Hom, Kowloon, Hong Kong
Foong.Ha.Yap@inet.polyu. edu.hk

Iulia Zegrean
Dipartimento di Studi Linguistici e Culturali Comparati
Ca' Bembo - Dorsoduro 1075
30123 Venezia, Italia
iuliazegrean@gmail.com

Debbie Ziegeler
18 Rue de l'Arnède
Montagnac 34530
France
dziegeler@msn.com

PREFACE

This book goes back to the 44th annual meeting of the Societas Linguistica Europaea, September 8-11, 2011. The conference hosted the workshop on covert patterns of modality, convened and organized by the volume editors, Werner Abraham & Elisabeth Leiss.

We thank the organizers of the SLE conference and the SLE secretary, Bert Cornillie, for their excellent preparation and administration of both conference and workshop.

INTRODUCTION

WERNER ABRAHAM
UNIVERSITÄT WIEN UND UNIVERSITÄT MÜNCHEN
AND ELISABETH LEISS
UNIVERSITÄT MÜNCHEN

To answer the obvious question "What is covert modality?" we see reason to distinguish two sources: complex patterns of modality, yet undiscovered due to their complexity; and silent, or covert, modality.

1. The dual notion of 'covertness'

To illustrate what we mean by the first type, we refer to one very striking, but not so well-known, case of an undetected category, i.e. aspect in the Slavic languages, of which its discovery and earliest linguistic discussion is due to the German universal grammarian Johann Severin Vater (1808). Aspect, before being recognized by Vater as a grammatical category in its own right, was treated as a particular tense form in Russian grammar writing of the 17th century. This led to a very complicated tense system in Russian, comprising ten tenses (for more detail, see Leiss 1992: 28-30). In other words, the non-detection of aspect considerably complicated grammar writing for languages with elaborate aspect systems. Vater, however, was the first to see the principled difference: tense marks verb-denoted events in relation to the speech act time with several options known all too well from the study of Classical Greek and Latin, while aspect is an inherent property of the event and its inner structure in terms of features like the homogeneity vs. heterogeneity of its subparts. We see reason to also speak of yet undetected modality beyond the rather limited cases discussed in the literature (beyond, for example, Embedded Infinitive Questions/EQI, which have found the interest of relatively numerous authors). Clearly, such undiscovered patterns of modality may be due to different linguistic traditions, but also to the lack of sufficiently-defined functional definitions that are accessible, perhaps, in knowledge of languages not belonging to the mainstream fields of scientific discussion.

As a consequence, lack of knowledge about the degree and implications of complex coding may play a role.

In contrast, silent, or as we prefer to say, covert modality covers undisputed cases in the category of modality (expressed either by modal predicates such as the modal verbs in the Germanic languages, or by elements in the categorial status of adverbials and the notorious modal particles, the latter surfacing in a variety of genetically unrelated languages from Indo-European to South East Asian). Covert modality must be seen as possessing a dominant functional status. It must be a non-marked type of modality while at the same time it needs to share with overt modality principal properties that are at least necessary for identifying modality.

Let us make a case in point of different traditions to appreciate linguistic categories. To the extent that evidentiality and epistemicity are categories of modality, different linguistic traditions may be held responsible for the homonymy, or even the synonymy, of the two terms even in the narrow Central European traditions. Are they of one and the same category or not? Are they expressed in terms of grammatical or as lexical elements? The one position (represented, for example, by Leiss 2008) sees epistemicity as truth-value undecided and likewise as the exponency of evidentiality, and, furthermore, clearly, and fundamentally, severs lexical from morphological paradigmatic exponents, considering them to be foundationally different under Bühler's theory of *origo* (Bühler 1934/ 1982) and grammatical shifting as espoused by R. Jakobson)> However, the competing camp (e.g., Diewald & Smirnova 2010a,b) considers the two terms as conceptually different on several counts, but includes lexical exponents on a par with grammatical ones. Notice that, in a number of traditions of grammar writing, evidential languages such as those of the Baltic-Georgian-Turkish evidential belt are languages belonging to linguistic and cultural traditions that are very different from the Central European ones.

Misinterpretations may also be due to a lack of functional definitions as distinct from formal ones. If, for example, one looks for an equivalent of modal particles so frequent in, and so characteristic of, the Germanic languages and the Slavic ones, one is bound to go astray in looking for formal correlates – what one seeks is a functional correlate (in the case of German modal particles[1], truth value-challenging illocutive clausal

[1] Modal particles are often compared, or even put on a par, with adverbials. However, it is important to note that they do not have constituent status as adverbials do. Modal particles are grammatical elements that grammaticalized from lexicals with quite different types of parts of speech (lexical categories). Due

operators). The same holds for modal verbs at least as long as they are represented by larger paradigms as in German and Dutch and the Scandinavian languages, which seem to be quite rare in the remaining languages of the world.

2. A closer look at grammatical epistemicity and grammatical evidentiality

Let us cast a look at the complex encoding of verb modality. The following illustrations demonstrate that interrelationships of root and epistemic modality with other categories such as aspect, tense, mood, and person are often ignored since they are not thought to hold generally enough across languages. See, first, the disambiguation of modal verbs in aspectual contexts, the so-called Aspect-Modality-Link/AML (going back to Abraham 1989, 2005). [DMV=deontic (= root) modal verb reading, EMV=epistemic modal verb reading]

(1) a. X must be dying[-telic] ...*DMV/ EMV
    b. X must die[+telic] ... DMV/*EMV

In the context of an imperfective embedding the modality construal in (1a) turns out to be epistemic. The opposite modality comes to the fore under the telic non-finite embedding. Reasons and illustrations in other languages were discussed in Abraham (1989, 2001). Let us resort to this generalization by the deep 'Aspect-modality link'/AML. It appears that this interface property can be suspended by temporal and aspectual adverbials.

Another rather unexpected interface property holds under the change of person. Notice that *will* in German is a true modal verb sharing with all other MVs the telling polyfunctionality between DMV and EMV readings. Notice which English lexical translations ("pretend") we have to resort to to render the meanings of the German modal *will.*

---

to their constituent status, modal particles assume illocutive functions that adverbials never assume to the same degree and functional status. See Abraham (2002) for the fuller story.

(2) a.. Er will auf den Malediven gewesen sein
he will on the Maldives been be
"He pretends to have been on the M."
b Er muss auf den Malediven gewesen sein
"He must have been on the M."
(3) a. *Ich will auf den Malediven gewesen sein
I will on the M. been be
b. *Ich muss auf den Malediven gewesen sein
I must have been on the M. been be

Comparison of German (3a, b) with (2a, b) tells us that what is behind modality in these cases is reference to the speaker rather than to the clausal subject. Since speaker and subject are identical in (3a,b) yields implausible ontological readings – something that does not come to the fore under non-identity of speaker and subject as in (2a, b). Note, furthermore, that English *will* does not lend itself to the same conclusions since it has grammaticalized down to a mere temporal auxiliary without modal weight (see Abraham 2002 for a circumspect comparison of English, Dutch, and German modal verbs).

Comparing German examples as in (4) yields a clear differential with respect to modal force. Consider which source for the information delivered emanates from the uses of the three different modals, *müssen-must, soll-shall,* and *will-will* (with the reservation that English *shall* and *will* cannot be taken as full root modals). Notice that there is a tripartite possibility for considering the source for *p* as listed in (4a-c) (clearly reaching beyond Schenner's (2010) attempt at narrowing down types of evidentiality).

(4) a. Source = L - locutionary person (speaker)
b. Source = P - propositional person (subject of the sentence)
c. Source = I - illocutionary person (viewer/observer)

The division of three modals over *p* in (5a-c) illustrates this. Notice that we are speaking of epistemic readings/EMV only (which is enforced by the embedded past infinitival *gewesen sein* rendering speech act time later than event time, e>s – one of the prerequisites of epistemic readings).

(5) a. *Sie muss schon mal in Logroño gewesen sein.*
"She must have been to L. once before."
... source: speaker inference on validity of *p*

b. *Sie soll schon mal in Logroño gewesen sein.*
she shall before once in L. been be
"She is said to have been to Logroño before."
...source for validity of *p*: hearsay from third person(s)

c. *Sie will schon mal in Logroño gewesen sein.*
she will before once in L. been be
"She pretends to have been to Logroño before."
... source for validity of *p*: viewer/observer

Each of the epistemic readings in (5) has a concurrent evidential component. Clearly, the evidential component in (5) is expressed by reference to the source differential in (4), while modal force emanates from the lexical MV. Note that the latter is not independent from the type of source. There is obviously something like a cline of truth-validity reliability with the speaker on the least challengeable (=most reliable) and hearsay from third person(s) on the most challengeable (=least reliable) pole. While we have been attending to the fundamental status of modal force ever since Kratzer (1981, 1991), the differential demonstrated by (4)-(5) turns out to be due to the input of the different modal co-players that represent the modal sources. There are 3 different force assessments of the truth value of the proposition and 3 different sources of assessment involved. It is this differential that appears to be responsible for the distinction of the evidential function from the epistemic one. [For <L, P, I> see (4) above]

Fig. 1: Source of assessment and speaker's assessment MV – feature matrix

MV	Source	Reliability/Force of evidence speaker-assessed
sollen "shall"	[-L] [-P][+I]	middle
müssen "must"	[+L] [-P][-I]	high
wollen "must"	[±L] [±P][±I]	low
können "can"		(alethically) neutral(ized)

Obviously, (4)-(5) and the adjoining discussions (Abraham & Leiss 2008, 2009 – see the respective introductions and the single contributions in the two collections) have not convinced others working in the field. Diewald & Smirnova (2010a,b), for example, see reason to separate evidentiality and epistemics arguing that there are lexical evidential verbs in Modern Standard German/ MSG such as *scheinen* "appear, seem", *drohen* "menace, threat", *versprechen* "promise" (viz. *the weather promises/appears/threatens to turn bad/good*), which are not paired by corresponding epistemic lexicals. They also consider adverbials like *anscheinend, scheinbar, offensichtlich* etc. as evidential adverbs. Disregarding the quite critical assessments Diewald/ Smirnova (2010a,b) have received from Ramat (2012a,b) and Aikhenvald (2012) (and indirectly by Schenner 2010) we feel motivated to refer to (4)-(5) and Fig. 1 to emphasize how intricately assessments of evidentiality and epistemicity fuse in languages like German and how much modal force can be seen to depend on the interaction of the co-players in the assessment of modality as in (4). Unless evidential modality is circumscribed in terms of uniquely designated morphological paradigms, we will gain little beyond vagueness for categorial distinction of epistemicity and evidentiality.

Let us disregard in this discussion lexical representatives of modality. They are something entirely different – for example, for the very reason that distinctions of the type in (2)-(4) will never surface. What we have seen so far is that grammatically encoded epistemicity and grammatically encoded evidentiality are functionally equivalent. Why then should they be labeled as different grammatical categories in languages that have no independent evidential paradigm (counter to the languages belonging to the Baltic-Turkish belt or those that rely on sparse grammatical research such as South and North American indigenous evidential languages)? There are no good reasons to do that except for those that have to do with traditions in linguistic methodology and their covert persuasions.

In sum, to find correlates of the main exponents of modality, modal verbs or modal particles, we cannot rely on formal characteristics alone mainly for the reason that these categories do not surface even in single languages with equal reliability and paradigmatic classification. Consider the fact that root and epistemic functions do not surface until they are exposed to aspectual contexts (see (1) and the adjoining discussion).

On the general topic of undiscovered patterns of modality we addressed questions of different linguistic traditions and their disregard for combinatorial and implicatory contexts. Let us turn to the other main hindrance to successful discovery: the failure to watch for functional, instead of purely formal, properties and definitions.

3. The range of modal functions: Modal verbs and modal particles

If you look for an equivalent of modal particles/MP, you should not look for a formal correlate, i.e. for particles, but for a functional correlate. The same holds for modal verbs, which seem to be quite rare in the languages of the world.

Modal particles, not known to Modern Standard English (MStE), are modal elements of a different, and yet of a prototypical, kind. Their chief characteristic (in the Germanic languages except for MStE, which has lost all of this in its historical development) is that, used in assertive declaratives, they suspend the truth validity of the proposition; inserted in questions, they challenge the reason for the interrogative operator; and in imperatives, modal particles add a note of the speaker to the adhortative source of *p*. There are legions of literature on this topic, which are restricted, though, to the languages that possess this adverbial-like modal category.

One of the chief functional assets of modal verbs is that, in line with Bühler's *origo* set-up, the speaker is divided into a viewer/evaluator and a source. In contrast to functions inherent in some MPs, the hearer does not participate in the assessment of the truth value. The truth assessment for MVs is located in the speaker ('intransitive assessment of *p*', coined by Abraham, introduction to the 2009 Lisbon SLE-workshop on '"Theory of Mind elements in sundry languages", see Abraham 2012a). On the other hand, the function of MPs is that the speaker negotiates with the hearer the common ground on which the truth value of *p* is based[2]. On this process of gauging the reliability of the assertion of *p*, the hearer is taken seriously. His view of the truth value counts, i.e., the assessment of the truth value is located in two different persons, the speaker as well as the hearer ('transitive assessment of *p*').

In sum, to find correlates of the main exponents of modality, modal verbs or modal particles, we cannot rely on formal characteristics only, mainly for the reason that these categories do not surface across languages with equal reliability and paradigmatic classification. What we need are functional descriptions and definitions in order to find cross-linguistic equivalents of those functions that may not surface in form. When looking for equivalents of German(ic) modal particles, one should not look for formal correlates, i.e. for particles, but for functional correlates (such as

---

[2] One may also say that the speaker feels motivated to suspend his own truth assessment given that he expects the hearer to challenge his assertion.

the appeal of the speaker to the hearer described above). A similar methodology applies to modal verbs and their polyfunctionality (i.e., the conditioned shift between root and epistemic validity), the specific status of which seems to be quite rare in the languages of the world.

4. Overview of topics suggested for the present volume

In line with the issues discussed so far, this is what we suggested as main chapters to be discussed. See (6a-e).

(6) a. Aspect and tense and their respective features as building blocks of modality.
b. Covert epistemicity in evidentials, and covert evidentiality in epistemic modals.
c. Sources of illocutive force in subordinate sentences.
d. Covert modality in pronouns and applicative datives.
e. Modality in non-finite contexts such as root infinitives and infinitival relatives.
f. Is there epistemic modality on forms of implicative and otherwise covert modality links?
g. How marked or unmarked are covertly encoding modal links? What is the general status of (un)markedness in connection with modality?
h. Are all sentences modalized? Or are there island of non-modality in full sentences?

For all of the above points, there exist discussions in the literature already: some richer, others less deeply investigated, and a few only singularly touched upon. For example, Abraham (this volume on a typological survey of covert modality) comes to the conclusion that the forms *HAS/HAVE TO*+V and *IS/ARE TO*+V, which are typical of triggering modal functions in some Central European languages of Indo-European origin, appear to be restricted to the covert encoding of root/ deontic modality and to avoid the epistemic domain (compare also Bhatt 2006). Another of the latter type is the covert encoding of modality in languages without polysemous modals such as Russian, where deonticity is encoded by means of aspect (Kotin 2008).

Russian and other aspect languages are highly instructive, when it comes to understanding patterns of complex encodings in the domain of modality as well as in the domain of definiteness/indefiniteness. It teaches us how intricate and aspect-related these patterns can be. The effects of the interface between MV-semantics and aspect, as uncovered by Abraham (1989, 1991, 2001, 2002a) is summed up in (7a-b).

(7) a. MV + imperfective infinitive yield an epistemic reading
b. MV + perfective infinitive yield root/deontic reading

As in (7) where modality effects are triggered by aspect selection, definiteness effects are likewise triggered in aspectual contexts in (8). What we see is complex encoding of definiteness in languages without articles in terms of interfaced case and verbal aspect. The following Russian generalizations are owed to Gladrow (1972, 1978) and Birkenmaier (1977, 1979) and commented on in detail in Abraham (1997) and Leiss (2000):

(8) a. Imperfective verb + ACC yields an indefiniteness effect
b. Perfective verb +ACC yields a definiteness effect
c. Perfective verb + GEN yields a partitivity effect

Such patterns are difficult to detect – and they are not without exceptions as the root links can be overwritten by effects outside of the inner grammatical core of the clause. As we have seen there is good reason to suppose that complex encoding is an important topic in relation todomains of grammatical categories. Complex patterns of encoding seem to be especially prevalent in grammatical categories such as mood and modality, which include and presuppose other categories such as aspect and tense as building blocks. There are even intricate patterns of covert modality triggered by definiteness/indefiniteness effects (see example (13) below).

As for the issue of unmarked or marked modality: Since all sentences are made up of two essential components, the proposition and its illocutionary force, it appears correct to say that illocutionary force is mostly silent in languages such as English or German. However, it is regularly overtly encoded in Japanese, Thai, and probably a whole range of other East Asian languages. As for modality in matrix sentences versus dependent clauses, it seems plausible to consider dependent clauses to generally be devoid of their own illocutionary force. However, this has shown to be false. There are exceptions to that rule (Coniglio 2011, Abraham 2012a,b,c) to the extent that the entire class of dependent clauses is divided into two different subclasses on exactly the criterion whether or not they tolerate modal particles in German.

Finally, there is the question whether modality is ubiquitous in language (modality in pronouns and other non-verbal or non-adverbial categories) and therefore mostly undiscovered. This question boils down to asking whether illocutionary force is shared by categories other than (ad)verbal? If so, are there nevertheless islands of non-modality, such as specific dependent clauses? Are there more of these islands of modality in language? It appears that there is room for linguistic curiosity.

5. Evident patterns of covert modality

In what follows the focus lies on the verbal modalities of possibility and necessity that are not expressed directly by lexical or grammatical elements, but that come out from certain constructions by implication or implicature. To all appearances, covert modality comes at least and most commonly in a number of clear constructions in German and in English. See below (9a-g) for German (see also Holl 2010) and (10a-f) for English (Bhatt 2006). (9b) is not Standard (written) German, but is the only form available in the dialects; there is no simple *zu*-infinitival embedding in the South German dialects. Notice that *zum* is the dative fusion of case marking and the preposition. In earlier stages of German, the dative was also marked on the gerundial form of the embedded infinitive thereby yielding a nominal form the infinitive (capital *Lösen*).

(9) a. Die Aufgaben sind *(zu) lösen
the tasks are to (be) solve(d)
... indicating obligatoriness or possibility

b. Die Aufgaben sind *(zum) Lösen
the tasks are to (be) solve(d)
... indicating obligatoriness or possibility;
gerundial form: only South German dialects

c. die *(zu) lösen- (sei(e)n-)den Aufgaben
the to solve (being) tasks
“the tasks to be solved“
... indicating obligatoriness or possibility;
gerundive

d. Das Buch liest sich gut
the book reads Refl well
... middle construction indicating possibility

e. Die Farbe ist abwaschbar
the paint is off-washable
... passive modality of possibility

f. Das Glas ist zerbrechlich
the glass is breakable
... passive modality of possibility

g. Das Auto fährt 210km/h
the car rides 210km/hour
... generic reading; indicating possibility on the basis of conventional implicature[3]

The construal *IS TO*+V as such need not possess any of the modal meanings denoted in the right margin. What we want to exclude are local existential meanings such as the following ones. See (10a-c).

(10) a. im Kühlschrank ist (da) etwas zu trinken
in the freezer is (there) something to drink
... no modal reading, just local existential

b. *im Kühlschrank ist ein Bier zu trinken
in the freezer is a beer to drink

c. hier hast du etwas anzuziehen
here have you something to put on
... no modal reading, just local existential

Notice the difference with (10a): The local adverbial *im Kühlschrank* "in the freezer" reduces the modality implication to nil, the result being just an indication where something to drink is located. The same holds for (10c). (10b) receives no meaningful reading: the beer would have to be drunkin the freezer.. Obviously, all of this means that any indication of modal obligatoriness or possibility as in (9a) – and, by implication, in (9c) – depends on the agentivity of the subject. The <*x ist zu V*>-construction is a strong subject controller due, to all appearances, to the copula *ist* "is" as a one-place PATIENT adjectival and the preposition *zu* "to" as the passivizer

---

[3] See von Wright's alethic equations < N (*p*) $_{df}$= I (~ p) $_{df}$= ~ P (~ *p*)>, in words: '*p* is necessary' is as much as to say that 'not-*p* is impossible' is again as much as to say 'It is not possible that not-*p*' (von Wright 1968). The last equation is appealed to by (1g): From 'p is the case' follows that '*p* is possible'. While von Wright's "alethic (modality)" has come to be replaced terminologically by Kratzer's "circumstantial (modality)", von Wright's 'deontic (modality)' appealing to social laws and human commitments still stands terminologically and conceptually: <O (*p*) df = F (~ *p*) df = ~ P (~ *p*)>, in words identical to the alethic formalizations above (abbreviations: N — necessary, P — possible, permitted, I — impossible, O — ethically necessary, obligatory, F — forbidden, df= defined as, ~ - Negation). See also Table 1.

and potential AGENT binder. In the ensuing discussion we want to exclude this interpretation of existential localization, and we know now how to avoid it.

The following utterances are owed to Bhatt as illustrations of silent modality in English (Bhatt 2006).

(11) a. Subject *w*-relative infinitive
Tim knows how to solve the problem
= Tim knows how one/he **could/should** solve the problem
b. Object relative infinitive
Jane found a book to draw cartoons in for Sara
= J. found a book for Sara one **could/should** draw cartoons.
c. Subject relative infinitive
The man to fix the sink is here
= The man whose **purpose** it is to fix the sink is here
d. Subject infinitive
Sue went to Torino [to buy a violin]
= Sue went to Torino so that she **could** buy a v.
e. Subject *have-to*
Bill has to reach Philadelphia before noon
= Bill **must** reach Ph. before noon
f. Subject intransitive infinitive
Will is to leave tomorrow
= Will is **scheduled/supposed** to leave tomorrow
g. Object decausative infinitive
The stomach is (/has) to empty/to be emptied
= The stomach **must** be emptied
h. Subject unaccusative infinitive
The monument is to fall
The monument has to fall
= The monument **must** fall
i. Infinitival DP-relative
the man to fix the sink
= the man who is to fix the sink

Abraham (in this volume, typological survey of covert modality) posits the following general unifying feature for (9) and (11): <no modal reading unless the infinitival preposition *to* is involved>. Let us take *to* as a directional triggering a telic interpretation with respect to the fulfillment of the infinitival meaning: $\lambda x \lambda t$ (is(x) $\wedge$ fall(x) $\wedge$ t'<t, but it does not denote λx (□fall(x)). Where does the necessity operator come from? Abraham concludes that it is a conversational implicature – certainly not an ordinary implication or entailment.

What might be called the opposite of covert modality – i.e., non-modality despite an overt modal – is shown in (12) (due to Thalberg 1968; see also Nishiwaki 2012).

(12) a In those days, Brown **was able to/could** hit the bull's eye three times in a row.
. ... modal reading
b. Brown **was able to/could** hit the bull's eye three times in a row.
... non-modal reading under specific context (specific context for (12b): 'Yesterday, B. hit three bulls-eyes in a row. Before he hit three bull's-eyes, he fired 600 rounds without coming close to the bull's-eye; and his subsequent tries were equally wild.')

As to the existence of a link between definiteness/ indefiniteness and modality that we indicated above, we can only present an illustration (due to Nishiwaki 2012). See (13).

(13) a. Du musst ein Buch kaufen. Es **soll/muss**$_{\text{DMV/*EMV}}$ intellektuell sein
you must a book buy. it shall/must intellectual be
"You must buy a book. It will have to be an intellectual one."
.... DMV/*EMV
b. Du musst das Buch kaufen/kaufen. Es soll/ muss$_{\text{*DMV/EMV}}$ intellektuell sein.
you must the book buy. it shall/mustintellectual be
"You must buy the book. It is said to be intellectual."
...*DMV/EMV

The striking fact is the change between root modal and epistemic readings on the modal in the apodosis, which appears to depend also on the object focus marking in the protasis. The explanation can possibly be reached by establishing the notion of *common ground* (CG). See (14).

(14) a. In the protasis of (13a) the property (intellectual or unintellectual) of ***ein*** *Buch* "a book" is unknown in terms of its indefinite article. This leaves the decision on the book's property to be specified in the apodosis in terms of what its property **must** (not may) be, i.e. in terms of specifying an attribute or relative clause to *book*.[4]

b. In the protasis the property of the book is known by way of its definiteness. All that the apodosis can do is take over this property. This leaves it for the speaker to infer this property (from the options given: intellectual or unintellectual) yielding only the epistemic, or inferring, reading of *soll/muss* "must".

Given the knowledge of the speaker about the literary predilection of the buyer (i.e. intellectual literature) the decision on how to solve the ambiguity of the modals in the apodosis depends on the article of the object nominal in the protasis. Thus, in a way, one can say that the interaction between the article in the protasis and the modal reading in the apodosis is reached on the common ground of knowledge existing for the decision to be taken. To turn the direction of the argument around, one may also say that the epistemic reading in the apodosis salvages this common ground in that it does not take as a prejudice what has been decided on already in the protasis.

6. The contributions to this book in the light of the above

Our goal in this introduction was to make plausible different notions of covert modality, foremost verbal modality represented by modal verbs and illocutive modal coming in the form of modal particles. It appears imperative to sketch the parameters on which modality evolves overtly before turning to covert types of modality. Verbal modality (root, epistemic, evidential) and modality expressed by modal particles and adverbials are clearly distinguished by their scopes and category status (in terms of: circumstantial vs. personal/ dynamic modal source, information source and reliability, truth assessability by speaker – by hearer – by evaluator, modal force, speech act interaction). Clearly, again, the topic of covertly encoded modality and its conditions of occurrence depend greatly on the para-

[4] Alternatively, we might take the indefinite article as referring to a TYPE ('such a book') in contrast to the definite article which refers to a TOKEN representation ('this book'). The epistemic reading is invoked by the Token reference since it cannot be specified with respect to its properties.

meters of overt modality. It is along these cirteria that the present collection of articles is to be assessed.

The most complex range of modality is taken up by **Werner Abraham** in ***(Inter)Subjectification or Foreign Consciousness/Other's Mind Alignment as synchronic and diachronic concepts of change? Conceptualizations and data fidelity.*** The target in this paper is the concept of (Inter)subjectification/IS (Traugott 1989), clearly a notion that is meant to explain the rise of modality both in cognition and in diachrony. Abraham's claim is that IS is an epiphenomenon of Foreign Consciousness Alignment (FCA). In essence, FCA, originally developed within child psychology under the name of Theory of Mind, simply bundles several linguistic categories and techniques based on insights developed by Bühler, Peirce, Jakobson, Sperber & Wilson, and modern ToM work to become aligned with problems of mood and modalization. (I)S plays a determining role in the 'cognitively' grounded theories developed by Langacker and Traugott in describing and explaining linguistic change both in synchrony and diachrony: e.g., to explain processes of metaphorization or the emergence of epistemic meaning from prior full verb status and root meanings of modal verbs. FCA establishes links to the semantics of possible worlds and the wide field of hedging in a range of categories (not only in terms of mood and modalization, but also polarity mechanisms and indefinite pronominals (veridicality). The hitherto solidly standing notion of (Inter)Subjectification introduced for explanatory reasons in diachronic development is subjected to scrutinous analysis on the basis of FCA with the result that Subjectification may be an epiphenomenon of the wider, and more complex, notion of FCA. **Pierre-Yves Modicom** takes this up in his ***Shared knowledge and epistemic reductionism: covert semantics of the German modal particles*** arguing that German modal particles/MP are used to illustrate how types of covertness, epistemological and structural, interact with modality. Epistemicity and Theory of Mind ("distribution of propositional attitudes") are shown to be the core semantics of MP such as *ja* and *wohl.*

The cognitively complex matter of modal particles and modal adverbials is also addressed by **Marco Coniglio & Iulia Zegrean** in ***Notes on overt and covert modality in Italian and Romanian*** to the effect that not only do MPs occur in matrix clauses, but also in those subordinate clauses that possess illocutive power in their own right – something that covers but a small, but well circumscribable subclass of subordinate clauses.

The central problem of this volume, covert modal encoding, while taken up by each of the contributions, is attributed to different triggers by the different authors. In ***Covert patterns of modality in typological comparison*** by **Abraham** several European languages are scrutinized on their potential to express covert modal notions on the *HAVE TO* and *BE TO* patterns. The author's conclusion is that the modal notion (either necessity or possibility, or both, is due to the futurizing infinitival preposition, which seems indispensable in most of the languages (a generalization that does not seem to be covered by Modern Polish, where a *HAVE*+V construal without the mediating *TO* gives rise to modal readings, and what is more intriguing, even to epistemic modal readings; see also Leiss (this volume). **Coniglio & Zegrean** conclude that overt and covert expressions of modality in Italian and Romanian are fundamentally different notions – something that is seconded by Abraham to the extent that given his typological findings no epistemicity surfaces in covertly encoded modality expressions. Abraham's *Epistemic Non-finiteness Gap Hypothesis* (Abraham 2001) appears to be at the bottom of this phenomenon.

One topic widely covered in the literature is to what extent the notions of epistemicity and evidentiality should theoretically, and can empirically, be separated as distinct concepts. **Dagmar Haumann & Ole Letnes** argue in ***German wohl – an evidential?*** that both the German modal particle *wohl* and Norwegian *visst* (cf. the German cognate *gewiss*) display covert evidential properties albeit strongly dependent on contectual support. The distributional differences between *wohl* and traditional evidential adverbs are taken to follow from the presence vs. absence of referential features which raising operations that target the left periphery ultimately feed upon.

It is part of the important empirical findings about covert modality that the latter can be triggered in aspectual contexts (Abraham 1989). Both **Zarina Molochieva** in ***Covert Modality in Chechen*** and **Gerda Haßler** in ***Indicative Verb Forms as Means of Expressing Modality in Romance Languages*** put this to the test in Chechen and Romance. The distribution and the semantics of the inceptive suffix *-d.ala* in Chechen depend on the valence and Aktionsart thus showing that aspect as well as Aktionsart provide an entry point for the rise of covert modality. In the Romance languages, imperfect(ive) verb forms may indicate double deixis, allowing the speaker to refer to a source of the communicated information without, however, naming the source. These uses can be explained by the general affinity between aspect and modality that is manifested in the case of the imperfect as metonymic bridge from imperfectivity to epistemic modality – an insight that has also been found to hold for Slavic languages ever since their oldest historical stage, i.e. Old Church Slavonic (Kotin 2008). This interesting interface claim is extended by **Elisabeth Leiss** in

Aspectual patterns of covert coding modality in Gothic and Old High German. In the "aspect period" of the Germanic languages the root modalizing function was triggered by perfective infinitives. Gothic and Old High German, still representatives of this aspect-driven period, demonstrate the way in whichthe verbal perfective prefix *ga-* elicits covert root-modal readings – an insight that has remained widely unnoticed in the pertinent philological literature on Germanic. Leiss goes so far in her paper to uncover covert epistemicity effects in Gothic and Old High German, triggered by intricate patterns of aspectual selection. The main claim is that the covert coding of modality is strongly prevalent in aspect languages, whereas overt modal encoding explodes as a consequence of dissolving systems of verbal aspect. On a similar note, **Michail L. Kotin** observes in ***Impersonal dative constructions as covert root-modality patterns*** an interesting, but likewise explanatory shift between personal and impersonal dative constructions in Russian resolved by aspectual contexts with respect to modal possibility or obligation/ necessity. Kotin even proposes that this is a prototypical pattern of covert modality. Some of these sentences are even incompatible with additional modal signals. While the personal dative construction displays an obligatory overt modal, the impersonal dative construals without an overt modal nevertheless express modality under strong restrictions on the selection of verbal aspect. Most impersonal dative constructions select the imperfective aspect of the main verb or a non-lexical equivalent.

Rui Marques' in ***Covert modals and (non-)implicative readings of too/enough-constructions*** strikes on von Wright's (1968) observation that the notion of modal possibility is deducible from a declarative of fact, most prominently if the fact declarative is generic. Marques derives the same modal notion in complement clauses of the *too* or *enough* operators, which are said to have a hidden, since only implied, existential modal verb expressing possibility. Marques' conclusion is similar to Melis' (2012) observation about the implicit modal notion of sufficiency in a number of seemingly unrelated linguistic phenomena. It is worth comparing the latter as well as Marques' observation with Mortelmans & Vanderbiesen's (2012) conclusions about similar implicit modal notions in construals of the type *(you had) better*+infinitive/past participle in several Germanic languages.

A quite different approach in this overview on exponents of covert modality is **Aslı Göksel & Barış Kabak's** discussion ***Covert modality and perspective shift*** on emotional perplexity triggered by an otherwise innocent construal in the past and with the second personal singular functionally boiling down to an imperative in an otherwise third person reportive narrative. The authors propose that the covertness is unraveled by the overt use of the second person pronoun, one of whose functions, in the otherwise pro-drop language Turkish, is the encoding of a shift of perspective. The components of the perplexive are cumulatively forced to have an interpretation that lies outside their canonical use in the time of utterance. This appears to indicate a shift of deixis in the sense of Bühler's (1982, 2011) sense of *origo* shift.

Regarding the important question whether covert modality appears also in non-verbal contexts, in ***Towards a composite definition of nominal modality***, **Debbie Ziegeler** questions the presence of covert modality in nouns and noun phrases, bringing to light the fact that specific and non-specific or generic nouns are encoded alike in many languages, a fact which leaves open the possibility of ever finding overt coding for nominal modality. She notes, however, that in some creole and English contact dialects, nominal modality may be represented by the fact that non-specific nouns are left unmarked for countability, an observation which leads to her hypothesis that there is an intrinsic relation between the ability for a noun to be enumerated and its factuality status. The derivation of nominal modality is seen as an intersection between, on the one hand, nominal reference and identifiability, and on the other, the measurability of the noun referent, invoking compelling questions for a more precise definition of modality itself.

References

Abraham, Werner 1989. Syntaktische Korrelate zum Lesartwechsel zwischen epistemischen und deontisch/volitiven Modalverben. *Groninger Arbeiten zur germanistischen Linguistik (GAGL)* 30 :145-166.

—. 1991. Modalverben in Germania. In: Iwasaki, Eijirō (ed.): *Begegnung mit dem Fremden: Grenzen – Traditionen – Vergleiche, Akten des VIII. Internationalen Germanisten-Kongresses, Tokyo1990*. Band 4: Sektion 4, 109 – 118. München: Iudicium.

—. 1997. The interdependence of case, aspect, and referentiality in the history of German: the case of the genitive. In: A. van Kemenade & N. Vincent (eds.). *Parameters of morphosyntactic change*, 29-61. Cambridge : Cambridge University Press.

—. 1999. Über allgemeine Zusammenhänge zwischen Präpositionsinfinitiv, Futur, deontischer Modalität und Perfektivität: lokalistische Allativität. *Sprachwissenschaft* 24: 361-405.

—. 2001. Modals: toward explaining the 'epistemic non-finiteness gap'. In: R. Müller & M. Reis (eds.) *Modalität und Modalverben im Deutschen*, 7-36. Hamburg: Buske [Linguistische Berichte: Sonderheft 9].

—. 2002. Modal verbs: epistemics in German and English. In: Sjef Barbiers, Frits Beukema & Wim van der Wurff (eds.) *Modality and its interaction with the verbal system*, 19-50. Amsterdam: Benjamins [Linguistik Aktuell / Linguistics Today; 47].

—. 2004. The grammaticalization of the infinitival preposition – toward a theory of 'grammaticalizing reanalysis'. *Journal of Comparative Germanic Linguistics* 7/2: 111-170.

—. 2005. Event arguments and modal verbs. In: C. Maienborn & A. Wöllstein (eds.) *Event arguments: Foundations and applications*, 243-276. . [Linguistische Arbeiten 501]. Tübingen: M. Niemeyer.

—. 2012a. Illocutive force is speaker and information source concern. What type of syntax does the representation of speaker pragmatics require: "constructions" or deep structural analysis? In: W. Abraham & E. Leiss (eds.) 2012: 67-108.

—. 2012b. Sprecherdeixis und Merkmaldistributionsdifferential deutscher Modalitätselemente. *Deutsche Sprache* 40(2012): 72-95.

—. 2012c. Satzabhängigkeit und Fremdbewusstseinsabgleich. In: Johan Brandtler, Stefan Huber, David Håkansson & Eva Klingvall (eds.) *Discourse and grammar. Essays in honor of Valéria Molnár*, 1-27. Lund: University of Lund, Sweden.

Abraham, Werner & Elisabeth Leiss (eds.) 2008. *Modality-aspect interfaces. Implications and typological solutions.* [Typological Studies in Languages 79]. Amsterdam: John Benjamins.

Abraham, Werner & Elisabeth Leiss (eds.) 2009. *Modalität. Epistemik und Evidentialität bei Modalverb, Adverb, Modalpartikel und Modus.* [Studien zur deutschen Grammatik 77]. Tübingen: Stauffenburg Verlag.

Abraham, Werner & Elisabeth Leiss (eds.) 2012. *Modality and Theory Mind elements across languages.* [Trends in Linguistics. Studies and Monographs 243]. Berlin: Mouton de Gruyter.

Aikhenvald, Aleandra 2012. Review of Diewald & Smirnova 2010a. In: *Studies in Language* 36/ 2.

Birkenmaier, Willy 1977. Aspekt, Aktionsart und nominale Determination im Russischen. *Zeitschrift für Slavische Philologie* 39, 389-417.

—. 1979. *Artikelfunktionen in einer slavischen Sprache. Studien zur nominalen Determination im Russischen.* [Forum Slavicum 34] München: Fink.

Bhatt, Rajesh 2006. *Covert modality in non-finite contexts.* [Interface Explorations 8]. Berlin: Mouton de Gruyter.
Bühler, Karl [1934] 1982. *Sprachtheorie. Die Darstellungsfunktion der Sprache*. Stuttgart: Fischer.
—. 2011. *Theory of language*. Amsterdam: John Benjamins.
Coniglio, Marco 2011. *Syntax der deutschen Modalpartikeln. Ihre Distribution und Lizensierung in Haupt- und Nebensätzen.* [studia grammatical 73]. Berlin: Akademieverlag.
Diewald, Gabriele & Elena Smirnova 2010a. *Evidentiality in German: linguistic realization and regularities in grammaticalization.* [Trends in Linguistics: studies and Monographs 228]. Berlin: De Gruyter Mouton.
Diewald, Gabriele & Elena Smirnova (eds.) 2010b. *Linguistic realization of evidentiality in European languages.* [Empirical Approaches to Language Typology 49]. Berlin: De Gruyter Mouton.
Gladrow, Wolfgang 1972. Sprachliche Mittel zum Ausdruck von Determiniertheit/Indeterminiertheit. *Zeitschrift für Slawistik* 17, 647-656.
—. 1978. *Die Determination des Substantivs im Russischen und im Deutschen: eine konfrontative Studie.* Leipzig: Verlag Enzyklopädie.
Holl, Daniel 2010. *Modale Infinitive und dispositionelle Modalität im Deutschen*. [studia grammatica 71]. Berlin: Akademieverlag
Kotin, Michail L. 2008. Aspects of a reconstruction of form and function of modal verbs in Germanic and other languages. In: W. Abraham & E. Leiss (eds.) 2008, 371-384.
Kratzer, Angelika 1981. In: H.-J. Eikmeyer & H. Kieser (eds.) *Words, worlds, and contexts,* 38-74. Berlin: de Gruyter.
—. 1991. Modality. In: A.v. Stechow & D. Wunderlich (eds.) *Semantik. Ein internationales Handbuch der zeitgenössischen Forschung*, 639-650. Berlin: de Gruyter [Handbücher zur Sprach- und Kommunikationswissenschaft 6].
Leiss, Elisabeth 1992. *Die Verbalkategorien des Deutschen. Ein Beitrag zur Theorie der sprachlichen Kategorisierung* [Studia Linguistica Germanica 31]
—. 2000. *Artikel und Aspekt.* Berlin, New York: De Gruyter [Studia Linguistica Germanica 56].
—. 2008. The silent and aspect-driven patterns of deonticity and epistemicity. A chapter in diachronic typology. In: W. Abraham & E. Leiss (eds.) 2008, 15-41.
—. 2012 *Sprachphilosophie.* 2nd edition, Beriln: Mouton de Gruyter.

Melis, Chantal 2012. The category of sufficiency. Paper presented at the conference „Modes of Modality", University of Munich, May 10-12, 2012.

Mortelmans, Tanja & Jeroen Vanderbiesen 2012. The comparative in German CMSs: besser, lieber, eher. Paper presented at the conference „Modes of Modality", University of Munich, May 10-12, 2012.

Nishiwaki, Maiko 2012. Modalverben und der Ausdruck von (In)Defininitheit – unter besonderer Berücksichtigung von sollen. Tagungsvortrag Funktionen der Modalität. Meeting „Modalität im Deutschen" Munich May 10-11, 2012.

Ramat, Paolo 2012a. Review of Diewald & Smirnova 2010a. In: *Linguistic Typology* 16/1: 169-177.

—. 2012b. Review of Diewald & Smirnova 2010b. In: *Linguistic Typology* 16/1: 177-183.

Schenner, Matthias 2010. Embedded evidentials in German. In: G. Diewald & E. Smirnova (eds.) 2010b *Linguistic realization of evidentiality in European languages*, 157-185. [Empirical Approaches to Language Typology 49]. Berlin: Mouton de Gruyter.

Thalberg, Irving 1969. Austin on abilities. In: K.T.Fann (ed.) *Symposium on J.L. Austin*, 182-205. New York: Humanities Press.

Traugott, Elizabeth Closs 1989. On the rise of epistemic meanings in English: an example of subjectification in semantic change. *Language* 65: 31–55.

Vater, Johann Severin 1808. *Praktische Grammatik der Russischen Sprache in Tabellen nebst Uebungsstücken zur grammatischen Analyse, einer Einleitung über Geschichte der Russischen Sprache und die Anordnung ihrer Grammatik und Berichtigungen der heymschen Sprachlehre.* Leipzig: Crusius.

Wright, Georg Henrik von 1968. *An essay in deontic logic and the general theory of action*. Amsterdam: North-Holland.

PART I:

THE ARCHITECTURE OF COVERT MODALITY

(Inter)Subjectification or Foreign Consciousness / Other's Mind Alignment as Synchronic and Diachronic Concepts of Change? Conceptualizations and Data Fidelity

Werner Abraham

Universität Wien und Universität München

Abstract: The concepts of (Inter)Subjectification/(I)S and of Theory of Mind/ToM or Foreign Consciousness Alignment/FCA (or Other's Mind Alignment) are contrasted and evaluated with respect to their potential for descriptive adequacy and explanative efficiency in synchronic and diachronic linguistic change and their methodological grounding. (I)S plays a determining role in the ‚cognitively' grounded theories developed by Langacker and Traugott in describing and explaining linguistic change both in synchrony and diachrony: e.g. to explain processes of metaphorization or the emergence of epistemic meaning from prior full verb status and root meanings of modal verbs. The concept of ToM / FCA was developed within child psychology and has recently been employed to grasp processes of modalization as the creation of *common ground* (CG) between speaker and hearer (Abraham 2009, Leiss 2008; Abraham & Leiss 2011) and their diverse possible world anchors. In essence, FCA simply bundles several linguistic categories and techniques based on insights developed by Bühler, Peirce, Jakobson, Sperber & Wilson, and modern ToM work to get aligned with problems of mood and modalization. After presenting definitions and sample illustrations the conclusion is drawn that FCA handles cases of description and explanation in processes of epistemization and, more generally, modalization far better than assumed by proponents of (I)S and simple speaker orientation (Narrog 2010) in contexts described by modern theories of rhetoric, dialogue and discourse sciences. FCA establishes links to the semantics of possible worlds and the wide field of hedging all sorts of categories (not only in terms of mood and modalization, but also polarity mechanisms and indefinite pronominals (veridicality) – it is, thus, anchored solidly in methodologically well calibrated areas of modern linguistic and psychological research allowing for direct links to syntax, semantics, and a systemically analytic pragmatics.

1. Conceptualizations

Research on subjectification is diverse.[1] Currently there are two clearly dominant conceptions of subjectification in linguistics, one by Langacker (1990, 1998, 1999), and another one by Traugott (e.g. 1989, 1995, 2003), disregarding Nuyts (2011, 2012) who, to all appearances, does not take grammaticalization and the history of languages as a point of departure in his discussions). According to Langacker's initial characterization, subjectification was "the realignment of some relationship from the objective to the subjective axis" (Langacker 1990: 17). He later re-defined it as "a gradual process of progressive attenuation," in which "an objective relationship fades away, leaving behind a subjective relationship that was originally immanent in it" (Langacker 1998: 75f). Langacker's definition is placed within a specific model of grammatical description, viz. Cognitive Grammar. The focus is on the event and the role of event participants. Langacker transfers his definition based on synchronic insight to the diachrony of English modal verbs. Traugott's approach, in contrast, is based on pragmatics and the historical analysis of semantic change in context. According to Traugott, subjectification is "the mechanism whereby meanings come over time to encode or externalize Speaker/Writer's perspectives and attitudes as constrained by the communicative world of the speech event, rather than by so-called 'real-world' characteristics of the event or situation referred to" (Traugott 2003: 126). In other words, subjectification involves "meanings [being] recruited by the speaker to encode and regulate attitudes and beliefs" (Traugott 2010: 35). Importantly, a dimension of intersubjectification has been added, i.e. the process whereby "meanings come over time to encode or externalize implicatures regarding Speaker/Writer's attention to the 'self' of Addressee / Reader in both an epistemic and a social sense" (Traugott 2003: 130). Intersubjectification presupposes subjectification.

In two more recent proposals, Narrog has put forward a model that combines subjectification and intersubjectification in the dimension of speaker orientation (Narrog 2005, 2007). De Smet & Verstraete (2006) have also contributed to Traugott's line of thought about subjectivity and subjectification, by distinguishing between 'ideational' subjectivity and 'interpersonal' subjectivity and drawing a new distinction between pragmatic and semantic subjectivity. Narrog's thrust – and principled, though always diplomatically phrased, criticism of the concept of subjectification – goes

[1] This chapter has profited from discussions with Elisabeth Leiss and Debbie Ziegeler. Thanks are also due to Sonja Zeman, Munich, for formal help.

in the following direction. First, he aims at discussing modality and speaker involvement not only with respect to one single categorial class – as, in Traugott's case, modal verbs and in particular, the emergence of epistemic readings from their root originals. Second, he makes the determined attempt to base all modal verbs on "will" as the most fundamental distinguishing element between different kinds of modality.[2] A sentence like (1),

(1) They *must* be afraid of us.

has two interpretations (following to Narrog 2010: 393). It either denotes the imposition of the speaker's, or a third person's, volition, in the sense of 'speaker/3rd person wishes/demands/orders that the state-of-affairs [= <they are afraid of us>] is brought about' such that the root/deontic interpretation is yielded; see (2b) below. The second interpretation is that it denotes an assessment of a present state-of-affairs, i.e. 'speaker concludes that they are afraid of us'; this is the epistemic interpretation; see (2c). In this way, the basic idea is that in deontic uses of modals an element of will is present, while it is absent in the case of epistemic interpretation. Modalities where, at least by strong tendency, an element of will is present are labeled 'volitive', while those where it is absent are labeled 'non-volitive'. Once this distinction is extended beyond deontic and epistemic, bouletic modality (*wish, want*, German *wollen*) will also be classified as 'volitive at the hands of someone else but the speaker / subject', and evidentiality and dynamic modality (*can, be able to*) as 'non-volitive' with respect to the speaker / subject'. Dynamic modality, denoting physical and situational possibility, is independent of the subject's/ speaker's volition. See (2a-c) for an account of this.

(2) a They *must* be afraid of us.
b $\lambda x\ \lambda y \lambda e \lambda s \lambda t$: *muss/soll/darf*(x,e,s<t) ≡ *will*(y,e(x,s<t))
c $\lambda x\ \lambda z \lambda e \lambda s \lambda t$: *muss/soll/darf*(x,e,s=t) ≡ *will*(z,e(x,s=t))

(where 'e' for 'event denoted by the embedded infinitival, 'x,y' for 'event participants' (and, by implication, verbal actants/arguments), 'z' for 'speaker of the utterance', 's' for 'speech act time', and 't' for event time')

[2] Narrog (2011) uses "mood" indiscriminately from "modality". For him modal verbs in their entirety are instances of mood, while he makes no attempt at distinguishing the two terms. A similar position is taken by Rothstein&Thieroff 2010.

Notice that the shift between root and epistemic modality hinges upon the time relation between s and t. If s=t holds, a root denotation is excluded; vice versa, roots require s<t. Moreover, epistemics disallow agentivity, or any theta role characterization, on the subject or speaker of the matrix verb. We shall return to this in connection with what are necessary and satisfying conditions for modality.

In her 2010-paper, Traugott surveys syntactic constructions typical of subjective expressions. See (3) (Traugott 2010: 33).

(3) a raising constructions, in which the "speaking subject" differs from the syntactic subject (Benveniste's "sujet d'énonciation" vs. "sujet d'énonce"): *She's going to give a lecture.* vs. *There's going to be an earthquake.*
b illocutionary uses of speech act and mental verbs: *recognize the Senator from California*
c epistemic modals: *That must be wrong.*
d concessive: *while*
e focus particles: *even*
f discourse markers: *besides*

Traugott's starting point for thinking about subjectivity was Lyons's characterization of subjectivity: "The term subjectivity refers to the way in which natural languages, in their structure and their normal manner of operation, provide for the Locutionary agent's expression of himself and his own attitudes and beliefs." (Lyons 1982: 102)

It appears essential at this early point of the discussion to set Langacker's notion of *subjectivization* apart from Traugott's *subjectification.* While Langacker transfers his notion prematurely to the emergence of epistemicity in the diachronic context of modal verbs without any solid documentation of the historical phenomena – quasi as "if things have developed in diachrony they must have in this and no other fashion" –, while Traugott bases her findings on phenomena in Old and Middle English, there is a very profound and noteworthy sense to his usage. Sentences are considered subjective (= not accessible for immediate and direct truth evaluation) even on their declarative form in the sense that, at least in most of the Western European languages, there is no adding the type of verifiability of the declarative (*I think / believe / have seen myself / have heard / have witnessed* etc.). In other words, we abstract from such performative qualifications – which may play an important role in specific cultural environments. In Japanese, for example, on detecting all of a sudden that my purse is no longer in my back pocket, to declare that "my purse was stolen" – something that is beyond my verifiability in the first place. Such a statement may deeply offend my companions. Statements like these receive an objective meaning only if implemented by something like *I think / believe / have seen myself / have heard / have witnessed* etc.. It is this sense of Langacker's concept that will stay totally out of the ensuing discussion.

2. First comments on the role of subjectification in the diachronic development of modal verbs

I think the first conceptual weakness can be found in this last part of Narrog's definition. We would say that dynamic modality has to have some overlap with any non-dynamic modality as it is not something entirely different. Given the possible-world semantics that we invoke for modality, any of the scalar modalities can be defined in terms of the quantitative contribution possible worlds provide: subjective modalities refer to fewer such worlds in which the modal force is valid than less subjective or totally objective, solidly and subject-independently pregiven, modalities.

The second bias I would like to posit is to be concluded from the following modalized example.

(4) a *Er* wollte auf Santorin gewesen sein.
he would on Santorin been be
"He pretended to have been on Santorin."
b **Ich* wollte auf Santorin gewesen sein.
I would on Santorin been be
"I pretended to have been on Santorin."

(4b) does not make sense unless the speaker (= subject, in this particular case) is detached from the evaluator, as would be possible in a dream situation. Without such displacement, or person split, (4b) will not make sense.[3] Any solely speaker-oriented explanation will not come to grips with such data.

---

[3] Notice that the English translation with *pretend* cannot render this unacceptability of the German modalized sentence. This is for the reason that English *pretend*, other than the German modal *will*, does not carry the person-link that the German volitive modal does. *pretend* is unambiguous with respect to any paradigmatically signaled grammatical person, whereas German *will* implies a split between subject, speaker, and evaluator.

A third area of modality in which Narrog's – and any of Traugott's, Langacker's or Nuyts' (inter)subjectification concepts – have not even been tried for their applicability is the class of modal particles/MPs – of which any of the Germanic languages has an abundance, just like German. MPs cannot be captured by the defining components that have been applied to MVs (Kratzer 1988). I shall return to this.

Finally, and quite generally, it is not clear to what extent occurrences of covert modality are accounted for by subjectification and the mere speaker-orientation scenario. Yet, the empirical facts are overwhelming. Take alone Bhatt (2006) with his book-length discussion of covert modalities on *have to* and *be to*. See examples in (5)-(6).

(5)	a	He has to come tonight.	– obligation reading
	b	He has a book to read.	– obligation and possibility reading
	c	the man to do this work	– purpose/obligation reading
(6)	a	This is (to do/)to be done tonight.	– obligation reading
	b	the man to do this	– purpose/obligation/ possibility reading

No epistemic readings are available in (5)-(6).[4] Subjectification, it appears, needs a lexical item to subjectivize in the course of linguistic history to develop a more subjectivized reading. In covert modal reading, however, all one has to go out from is the entirely non-modal possession verb *have* and the copula *be*. This abstracts totally from the fact that subjectification appears to involve gradual development of modalities of all medial sorts including prominently epistemics. Covert modality in the *have / be to* construals, however, only implies root modality, i.e., deontic and possibility readings – no epistemics. Why is subjectification, or speaker-orientation, totally suspended in cases of covert modality? There is an obvious answer to this, we believe.

---

[4] The history of the (semi)-modal *have to* seems to suggest a root modal (deontic) sense that was well-founded within the contexts in which it first arose (cf. Ziegeler 2010). It is often recognized as an (overt) emerging modal (see, e.g., Krug 2000). Furthermore, Ziegeler (p.c.) points out to me that there is evidence of epistemic usage of *have to* appearing in the OED Online (very recent though). It seems to appear also in related expressions like *you've got to be joking*. However, this does not affect our conclusions with respect to (5)-(6). Notice that, as we've pointed out before in (8) and (16) below, the embedded infinitive is in the continuative form (*to be joking*). As a rule, the modal reading follows the aspect of the embedded predicate (Abraham 2002, 2005).

3. What is the contribution of the concept of (I)S to a theory of grammaticalization?

I take the syntactic scenario sketched by Abraham (2003) and van Gelderen (2004, 2009, 2011) to be basic to any empirically grounded explanation of grammaticalization processes. All steps sketched in this scenario entail processes of categorial reanalysis and the manipulation of semantic features (in the sense of minimalism). Subjectification may refer to feature manipulation; it has nothing to do with the accompanying syntactic change.

One of the examples proposed to be typical of grammaticalization and gradual (inter)subjectification is the rise of the honorific *–mas-u* in Japanese (Narrog 1997, 2010: 387; Traugott & Dasher 2002: 241). Table 3-1 sketches the diachronic steps assumed to lead to the present purely honorific (i.e., lexically non-referential) grammeme.

Table 3-1: Historical emergence of the honorific suffix Japanese *–mas-u* ("" for etymological conjecture).**

Full verb status	Lexical meaning	Grammaticalizing step	Honorific feature
+/***mawi-ir-as-uru*	+/allow to come	+humility	+
-	-	+	+
-/*–mas-u*	-	-	+

Table 3-2: Historical emergence of the honorific German pronominal *Sie* (formal "you").

Paradigmatic pronoun status 3pl	Non-paradig-matic status 2sg/pl	Anaphoric meaning	Dialogue-deictic meaning	Grammati -calizing step	Pluralis "maiesta -tis" / honorific feature
+	-	+	-	-respect	-
+	-	-	+	+	+
-	+	-	+	+respect	+

Instead of assuming that subjectification took place as Traugott and Narrog do, the simple table tells the story in much simpler terms: All that remained in the process of phonetic erosion, delexicalization, and losing full verb status in favor of suffixal status is the honorific feature. Whether the trigger to this development needs to be called '(inter)subjectification' or not is of no necessary avail. Compare the German *Sie* in Table 3-2 as the respect-signaling address form developing from the prior 3rd person plural *sie*: Why would we call that 'subjectification' – in fact, no one has ever done so (Simon 2003a,b , Nübling 2010).[5]

Another case in point is the development of modal verbs in Germanic. Traugott and Langacker, the leading proponents of subjectification as a mechanism in meaning change, have treated modal verbs as prominent examples of grammaticalization and subjectification. Their research counts as a benchmark in this area. Langacker's account, in particular, makes crucial reference to the 'force-dynamics' model of modal meanings espoused by Talmy (1988) and Sweetser (1982, 1990, among others). The diachronic changes from MV as full verbs to modal auxiliaries in the history of English posited by Langacker can be summarized as follows (partly following Narrog 2010: 389):

Table 3-3. Subjectification in the history of the English modals according (but not literally) to Langacker [EMV = epistemic modal verb (reading), DMV = deontic (= root) modal verb (reading), s = speech time, e = event time].

Stage	Semantic change	Corresponding change in the history of English modals
I > II	domain of force shifts from physical to social	change from main verb to modal verb: V→ Aux
I > II	diffusion of source and target of potency	change from main verb to modal verb: V→ Aux As to the change from $s<e$ to $s=e$: If *e* = 'event' this should be a state or process, in the case of epistemics
II	maximal diffusion of source and target of potency	change from deontic to epistemic meaning: $s < e \rightarrow s=e$ Time reference wrt. Speaking and Event time is the key identifying feature of the two different modal classes, EMV vs. DMV

5 Needless to say, not all phenomena of grammaticalization need to be triggered by, or linked to, subjectivity/subjectification, but it is often a by-product of grammaticalization. However, just with honorifics subjectivization appears a clear guiding candidate – but it is not, as our two patterns in Tables 3-1 and 3-2 show beyond doubt.

II+III	potency comes to pertain to the evolution of the [speaker's] knowledge of reality	development of present-oriented epistemic meanings: s=e
II > III	conception of directed potency loses profiled status	modals become grounding predications: modality operating upon embedded predicate

Stage I > II in Table 3-3 only applies to deontics, as far as I can see. The change from $s < e$ to $s = e$: if e = 'event', shouldn't this be a state or process, in the case of epistemics?

Syntactic change from full V to Aux in the history of English (see Abraham 2002; disregarding the change of valence/governance direction from OE leftward-governance to ME rightward-governance): the MStE full verb does not leave VP to reach its final surface position, in contrast to all other North and Continental West Germanic languages, but in line with Romance). See (7).

(7) a MStE:

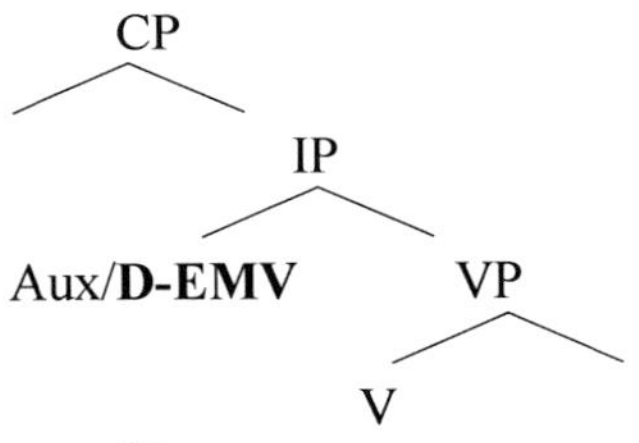

b German:

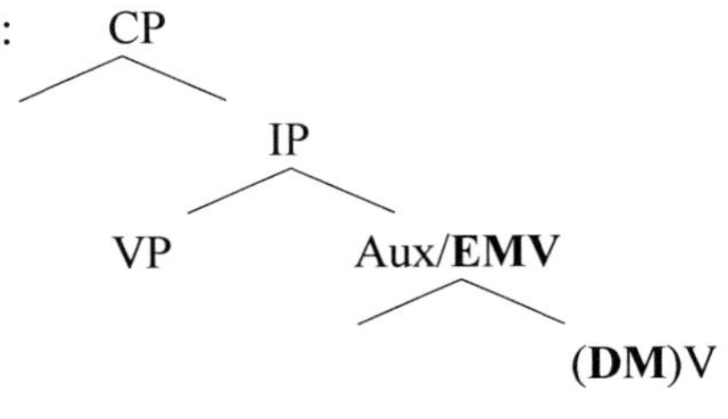

The underlying differences between MStE in (6a) and German in (6b), for example, are considerable. MStE has no non-finite forms of MV that could appear in VP. Consequently, there are no embedded MVs. Needless to say, with no VP representation no full verb status exists (suspending the gerundial function). English MVs only have grounding (no profiling) status – i.e., they contribute to modality incorporation into the verbal complex (contra Narrog's argument of separate adverb scoping for MVs; Narrog 2010: 5). Thus, English has undergone considerable erosion of form and, in consequence, of function, for MVs, much farther than German. In German MVs, the original full verb status is syntactically still preserved (existence of non-finites, consequently embeddability). Their original aspectuality as preterit presents still shows on the fact that aspect of the embeddings leads to a root/epistemic differential (Abraham 1986). American English reduces the root function of MVs a lot more than British English (Abraham 2002) with the result that *have to, be permitted to, be supposed to* etc. are used for the root readings almost standardly and that epistemic or temporal uses prevail. Notice, finally, that (7b) tells us that E-readings of MV occur only finitely ('Epistemic non-finiteness gap'; Abraham 1986, 1991). In other words, EMV cannot be embedded and, as a consequence, cannot be construed non-finitely (for the same result, at least for German, see also Erb 2001).[6]

Semantically, modal verbs in German are perfects or preterit presents originally. The fact that, instead of a weak d/t-suffix for the past, the singular and plural stem vowels display the typical shift (3rd or 4th strong paradigm) of strong pasts attests to this most clearly. See (8a-e) for the bi-phasic componential analysis of perfectives and (8f-g) for illustrations [t = temporal point; t(s) = speech act time; t(e) = event time].

(8) a MV(e) ≡ {(incremental phase(e) followed by) result phase(e) event-operating on the specific modal source}
b where the incremental phase is implied
c where only the result phase is denoted
d where the root-MV-denotation, on the strength of denoting a result phase, is situated in the future: MV(e,s,t, source) ≡ {(s<t(e)) for all modal sources}
e binary event phasing of any MV in its root reading – as for (8f) below:

t(s) < t(e)

---

[6] As often also in German, in English there can be embedding of epistemic non-finites; e.g., in a conditional sense: *That would have to be correct then* – Ziegeler (p.c.) is sure that similar, live examples can be found on Google. The question is always, for one, how frequent they may be. Notice, however, that, if finiteness is the guiding logic to the epistemic finiteness gap generalization, the question with the latter example then would be where the finiteness of the semi-modal should be located – which is not all clear in this illustration.

f |>>>>>>>|------------| for <e> embedded by MV such as *die*; see below, (8f) vs. (8g).
The doctor must die. ...
DMV/*EMV – no epistemic reading on *must* due to the embedded perfective verb *die*
t(s) = t(e)

g ~~~~~~~~~~~~~~~~~~ for <e> embedded by MV such as *be dying.*; *The doctor must be dying.* ...
*DMV/EMV – no root/DMV reading on *must* due to the embedded imperfective form *be dying*

Roots are control clauses – the external argument appears in each of the semantic phases, while epistemics are raising constructions with but one homogeneous phase allowing for only one external argument. The old perfect(ive) status of the Germanic MVs in their (Lightfootian) pre-modal stage is reflected in the modern variant distribution with perfective vs. imperfective embeddings. See also the summary in (25) below.[7]

Let us return to subjectification as a trigger to the modal change. Langacker's concept is novel in relating facts in the development of English modals to a cognitive theory of language description. The suggestion that the attenuation of the role of the grammatical subject is an important aspect of the semantic development of English modal verbs is intuitively plausible, even if he does not support it with historical data.

The most detailed account of change in modal meaning in terms of the concept of subjectification is to be found in Traugott & Dasher (2002: ch. 4) with analyses of the history of *must* and *ought to* (see earlier work on the topic in Traugott 1989; Nordlinger & Traugott 1997; Goossens 2000, amongst others). Traugott posits three stages based on concrete historical semantic shifts. See Table 3-4 and Table 3-5.

[7] As to clearly syntactic restrictions, Aijmer (1978: 164) claimed that epistemic modal auxiliaries in English do not occur in restrictive clauses, but that they do in non-restrictive relative clauses. Aijmer has not offered illustrations supporting this claim, nor has she offered a logical account. Maché (2011: 80f.) shows that German allows for EMVs in restrictive relative clauses.

Table 3-4: Sequence of semantic shifts from observations on historical structure for *must* (tracing Traugott & Dasher 2002: ch. 4).

Stage	Categorial status	Meaning of *must*	Historical period	Subjectification of speaker	'Dynamic force' direction
I	V	Ability + permission	OE	-/+	↓
II	MV/Aux-like	Obligation: Deontic	Late OE	+	↓
III	MV/Aux-like	Epistemic added → polyfunctional	Mid-ME	++	↓

Table 3-5: Sequence of semantic shifts from observations on historical structure for *ought to* (tracing Traugott & Dasher 2002: ch. 4).

Stage	Categorial status	Meaning of *āgan-ought (to)*	Historical period	Subjectification of speaker	'Dynamic force' direction
I	V	Possession	OE	-	↓
II	MV/Aux-like	Obligation: Deontic	Late OE	+	↓
III	MV/Aux-like	Epistemic added → polyfunctional	Early ME	++	↓

Now note how speaker and, consequently, subjectification come into the picture in the development of *must.* Concerning *must*, at stage II, Traugott & Dasher (2002) observe the emergence of more subjective deontic uses, when "no social, religious, or other normative force is specified or implied" (Traugott & Dasher 2002: 125). That is, similar to Langacker, it is the nature of the *modal force* (as well as *dynamic force*; see Sweetser 1990, Talmy 1988 etc.) that is taken as an instantiation and a measure for subjectification at this stage.

First, the deontic/obligation meaning is seen as subjective since the speaker who obliges someone, in which case the deontic modal "has been preempted to the subjective self of Speaker/Writer" (Traugott & Dasher 2002: 125). Second, (inter)subjectification at stage III comes in, when examples of the epistemic sense start not to "invoke general opinion [...], nor are they contextualized in logical reasoning [...], but simply express the speaker's confidence in the inference being made at the moment" (Traugott & Dasher 2002: 129).

With respect to *ought to*, a partially parallel subjectification process is observed: Initial uses expressing obligation at stage II are weakly subjective "in that the speaker is merely reporting an obligation which is imposed by a conventionalized, accepted set of rules and expectations (such as the Church or the Law)" (Traugott & Dasher 2002: 141). Later on in this stage, examples are found "that suggest that the speaker is identifying with these values, and is presenting him- or herself rather than society as the force behind the obligation" (Traugott & Dasher 2002: 141; Narrog 2010: 390). The epistemic reading of *ought to*, however, is apparently not as far subjectified as in the case of *must*, since "more strongly subjective examples grounded in the speaker's personal expectations rather than those of a wider group are rare" (Traugott & Dasher 2002: 142; Narrog 2010: 390).

Quite clearly, the development of epistemic meaning is conceived as the most typical instance of subjectification in modal meaning. The development *deontic > epistemic* has often been cited as part of the tendency to recruit general denotations into increasingly subjective semantics (Traugott & Dasher 2002: 149, 281; Hopper & Traugott [1993] 2003: 92; see also Diewald 1999 for the diachronics of the German modal verbs and, especially their epistemic readings). According to Traugott (1989: 37), by Tendency III (see Tables (3-4) und (3-5) above) the modals "acquired epistemic meanings that are primarily focused on the internal world of the speaker's belief and knowledge states."

It is important to note that Traugott (as well as Langacker, Sweetser, and others) sees the *type of force and the source of the force* expressed by the modal as a factor in semantic change in modals. However, she also places a careful and reticent note on this by stating that "there are reasons to doubt that the forces and barriers metaphor is a key to the semantic development of either deontics or epistemics. [...] [T]he lexical sources of the modals show little evidence of the semantics of forces and barriers." (Traugott & Dasher 2002: 111). We place such statements in the context that even the proponents of subjectification cast doubts on the trigger of the development of epistemics out of deontics/root modal meanings by invoking *type of force and the source of the force* expressed by the modal as a factor in semantic change in modals. Put less diplomatically, the line of argument is either circular, in that subjectification is driven by some kind of (dynamic) modal force, or vice versa (which does not make it less circular); or none of the triggers, dynamic force or its source, has the potential for explanation, in the first place. We shall argue later, that the latter is indeed the case since no observable data or their evident distributions are adduced to support such conclusions.

What appear to prepare a more solid ground for the subjectification line of argument are indications that contexts for change from *deontic* to *epistemic* imply that impersonal constructions and wide scope generalized deontic necessity (Traugott & Dasher 2002: 127, 130; see also Diewald 1999 for a similar reasoning on the development of the modals in German). Such factors clearly imply the attenuation of the role of the grammatical subject, and also a diffusion of the source and target of the modal force. In other words, Traugott and Dasher 2002 include pragmatic factors concerning the internal development of deontic and epistemic modalities that show how far the Speaker/Writer has preempted the modal expression to the subjective self. It appears appropriate to say that it is these pragmatic factors which are central to Traugott's concept of subjectification rather than anything else, and that the attenuation of the role of the subject is merely a factor in the concrete case of the subjectification of the modals (Narrog 2011: 391-92).

4. Data failed to be observed and considered in the context of the subjectification trigger of verbal modalization

Let us first turn to *ought to*, which plays a major role in the line of argument espoused by Traugott & Dasher 2002. *ought* cannot occur without the infinitival preposition *to,* while all other modal verbs never take, and never have taken, an infinitival preposition to embed verbal infinitives. Furthermore, *ought* is a weak past form, which, again, is foreign to all of the modal verbs: They are preterit presents by form and meaning, and they are strong verbs originally – a fact which they still strongly betray. By contrast, *ought* is a weak (*-t-*) form OE *āgen*, Old High German *eigan*, Gothic *aih-*, the pre-Germanic being reconstructed as **aih* as preterit participle of a preterit present (Kluge/Seebold 1989: 168). Furthermore, if the pre-modal meant "have, possess", it is not easy to see whether, and why, the assumed modal type and (dynamic) force was the trigger for the emergence of its modal meaning. There is doubt, beyond all that, that *ought to* never developed a full-fledged, frequently and unambiguously recorded epistemic meaning.

4.1 A brief report on the history of *have to*

One might conjecture that the epistemic meaning of *ought to* would be less subjectified perhaps because the modal may be less frequently used overall. There appear to be those that, when questioned, claim they had never heard of *ought to* in the first place. What is clear is the evidence from earlier states provided by Dekeyser (1998).

As for the historical development of *ought to*, meanings of indebtedness, in specific contexts, have been documented to have arisen out of meanings of possession in Middle English (Dekeyser 1998: 111-116):

(9) a An *ahte to* geldanne penningas fif hund
"one *owed ?=? had* to pay five hundred pence"
(c950 *Lindisfarne Gospels* Luke vii.41 OED: X: 990)

b My fader *had not to* pay to the maister of the ship for the fraught
(c1440 *Gesta Romanorum* xxiv, 90. *Harleian Manuscript)*

We can distinguish 4 stages with context-induced steps of grammaticalization (Heine & Kuteva 2002: 86; its application to the history of *have to* as an original interpretation as well as the examples (from the OED) come from Ziegeler (2010):

Initial stage: *have* already used in pre-infinitival position, with infinitive in attributive function.

Bridging stage: purposive meaning emanating with obligation reading; see (10a).

(10) a We sal pray [...] specially for all thas that haves the gude counsale of the lande for te kepe
"[...] who have the good counsel of the land to keep"
(1370-1450 *Bidding Prayer* III *in Lay Folks Mass Book,* 69.10)

Switch context: possession objects switch to non-possessable ones giving way to obligation reading that become more central: possession of an act to be undertaken. See (10b) as compared with (10a).

(10) b We sall pray especially for the person or for the vicar of this kirke that has youre saules for to kepe.
(1370-1450 *Bidding Prayer* III *in Lay Folks Mass Book,* 68.21)

Conventionalization stage: Erstwhile post-modified NP objects were replaced with infinitive-clausal objects. From this followed that obligation modal functions were the only construals available. The complement extended rapidly into intransitives and inanimate subject referents. With obligation usually implying unwillingness on the part of the subject referent, the obligation meaning of *have to* was reinforced by narrowing down to indicate adversity in many cases. See the ensuing illustrations (11).

(11) Such an editor too, would have to set his face against slander, & the depravity of taste which his nauseous aliment induces
(1897 T. Jefferson *Letters* 14 June in *Writings* (1984) 1178)

4.2 Distributional and componential properties

There is, of course, another source that offers itself readily for a parallel to the diachronic growth of the modal meaning of *ought to* deriving from its original meaning. This is the covert modal meaning, or implication of it, that MStE *have* possesses.

(12) a This *has to* be brought to the attention of all.
… passive obligation reading
b We *have to* bring this to the attention of all.
… active obligation reading

Furthermore, since transitive *have* has a strong lexical link to the copula *be* (Benveniste 1966, Kayne 1999) – see (13) below, the same covert modal meaning arises from the copula as in (14). Recall that there are languages that have no *HAVE*-lexical to use in the possession sense, and much less to use grammatically (such as Russian or Classical Latin); their way to render possession is by *BE WITH* (Classical Latin *esse apud* + DP_{ACC}; Russian "with me": *u menya (jest') (eta) sobaka* 'with me/next to me.GENITIVE is (this/) a dog' – "I have a dog; this dog is mine", where the copula may be left out only in the present tense, but must be inserted in the past and future with the auxiliaries *byla/budet*; see Kotin, this volume, 2012). The *HAVE*-replacive construction appears to be pervasive in the world's languages (shared also by Japanese: *kanojo-ni-wa kodomo-ga imasu* 'she.DAT.TOP-child.NOM-be' = 'with her are children' = "she has children").

(13) λxλy: have(x,y) ≡ be(y, with(x))

(14) a This is (*for him) to be brought to the attention of all.
passive obligation reading

b This is (for him) to bring to the attention of all.
ECM obligation reading

All this is to indicate that *ought to* is not a modal verb originally – neither by form nor by meaning. It cannot be included into the paradigmatic derivation process of the modal verbs – again neither according to their form nor their original lexical and grammatical meaning. We will argue that the original pre-modals as preterit presents carried perfective aspect which embodied the very core of the modal trigger by denoting event bi-phasicness (incremental phase followed by result phase). *ought (to)* never was one of these original perfectives. And, what is even stronger as a devaluating argument, *ought* stems historically from the possession verb *HAVE*. MStE *have* (as well as *be*) always brings forth the modal meaning with the help of the infinitival preposition *to* – it never does it without *to*. We shall adduce major attention to this data fact and draw the pertinent crucial conclusions from that.

Another data set that has been totally overlooked in this context of accounting for the modal trigger of overt and covert modal construals comes from Gothic. As Streitberg (1910) notes in his elementary book on Gothic, while control verbs embed infinitivals in modern Indo-European languages, the pertinent verbs in Gothic can only embed perfective predicates. See the non-modal intensional verb *sokjan* "seek", German 'suchen', which, in order to embed a lexical infinitive, looks for lexicals prefixed by perfectivizing *ga-* to yield modal meanings (Streitberg 2000: 127)[8]. See the following examples from Classical Greek and Old Church Slavonic (Kotin, this volume), which attest to this scenario provided by Gothic. It might be correct cross-linguistically, at least for languages that have a solid aspectual paradigm as do Classical Greek, Old Church Slavonic, and Modern Russian.

[8] We infer: It follows from Gothic *sokjan* meaning something like "seek" and *gasokjan* "find" (Streitberg 2000: 127) that what *sokjan* actually means in relation to *gasokjan* is "go finding, seek to find, be on one's way to find". *sokjan* is an inchoative-causative, as *jan*-verbs often are, and *gasokjan* is the resultative (usually, unless represented by *ga*-derivates, are strong verbs; see Modern German transitive *sprengen – sprengte* vs. intransitive *springen – sprang – gesprungen*).

(15) a καὶ διὰ τοῦτο ἐδίωκον οἱ Ἰουδαῖοι τὸν Ἰησοῦν,
& through the same pursued.AOR the Jews (the) Jesus,

ὅτι ταῦτα ἐποίει ἐν σαββάτῳ.
because such did on Sabbath
(John 5, 16)

The Aorist *ἐδίωκον* formed from *διώκων* means either (i) "make run/flee, put to flight, drive away", or (ii) "run swiftly in order to catch a person or thing, run after". But it may also be rendered by (iia) "press on": figuratively of one who in a race runs swiftly to reach the goal; or (iib) "prosecute (in a hostile manner); finally, (iii) "in any way whatever to harass, trouble, molest one", also "pursue, seek after eagerly, earnestly endeavor to acquire". The same translation from Old Church Slavonic sounds as:

(15) b И сего ради гоняху Иисуса Иудее и искаху убити
I sego radi gonyachu Iisusa Iudeye i iskachu ubiti
And therefore prosecuted Jesus Jews and sought kill.PERF

Его, зане сия творяше в субботу.
Yego, zanye siya tvoryashe v subbotu.
Him, then these did on Sabbath

"And for this reason the Jews prosecuted Jesus and planned to kill Him, so they did on Sabbath."

And the Russian synod translation is:

(15) c И стали Иудеи гнать Иисуса и искали убить Его
I stali Iudei gnat` Iisusa i iskali ubit′ Yego
And began Jews prosecute Jesus and sought kill.PERF Him

за то, что Он делал такие [дела] в субботу.
za to, chto On delal takie [dela] v subbotu.
for that, that He did such [deeds] on Sabbath
"And the Jews began to prosecute Jesus and planned to kill Him for what He had done on Sabbath."

The embedded infinitive for "kill" has to be a perfective form. Any imperfective renders the whole ungrammatical (Kotin, this volume). This shows that there is a very solid, cross-linguistic generalization behind our conclusion about the link between modality triggered by a matrix V and a perfective infinitival, as presented in (16b) below.

Assembling the above data together with the previous ones we have the following Old German(ic) constellation for achieving modalization in a verbal complex:

(16)	a	V_{FINITE} + *TO* + $V_{INFINITIVAL}$	for any embedding and embedded verb
	b	V_{FINITE} + *ga*-$V_{INFINITIVAL}$	for any embedding verb; *ga*-V stands also for lexical perfective verbs
	c	MV_{FINITE} + $V_{INFINITIVAL}$	for a embedding modal and any(?) embedded verb
	d	*HAVE* + *TO* + $V_{INFINITIVAL}$	for any embedded verb

What we do not have is this.

(17)	a	*V_{FINITE} + $V_{INFINITIVAL}$	for any embedding and embedded verb
	b	*V_{FINITE} + $V_{IMPERFECTIVE\text{-}INFINITIVAL}$	for any embedding control or raising verb
	c	*MV_{FINITE} + *TO* + $V_{INFINITIVAL}$	for a embedding modal and any(?) embedded verb
	d	**HAVE* + $V_{INFINITIVAL}$	for any embedded verb

The most striking distribution is the opposition between any controlling or raising verb with the indispensible mediating *TO*/embedded perfectivizing prefix, on the one hand, and MV which never takes the mediating preposition *TO*, on the other hand. The second fact deserving prominence is that there is covert modality triggering as for *HAVE* (and, in MStE, *BE*). The same holds for other Germanic languages as well as Romance (Bhatt 2006, Abraham 2011). I suggest that these facts not only be incorporated in seeking the solution to the question where the modal meaning comes from. What is more, I will show that they are the key to the solution and that all other suggestions, foremost the idea about subjectification, are epiphenomena to the proposed solution.

Undeniably, setting apart the modalizing triggers for *ought to* and the real modal verbs strengthens – in the present case of Traugott's discussion about *must* – the cause for subjectification to the extent that, if MVs and *ought to* should have different triggers, any common explanation might appear to be the better one. However, this is a fallacious conclusion. Notice that *ought to* functions as a modal only with the infinitival preposition *to* – *ought* by itself is meaningless. Assume we are successful in adducing modal force to the directional preposition *to* – as in fact we will do. In this case, and leaving all other considerations aside for the moment, MVs without *to* and *ought* WITH *to* may have in common the futural component all modals share. See (18) – and recall the facts from Gothic where non-modal verbs of seeking and trying afford the embedded verb to be perfective.

(18) a MV + V → modal meaning
b *ought* + *to* + V → modal meaning
c V_{seek} + PERFECTIVE-PREFIX-V → modal meaning

Compare also (16) and (17). What we appear to have is an at least necessary, if not satisfactory, condition to trigger modal meaning: the directional preposition *to* (German *zu*, Scandinavian (*till*) *a,* Romance *à*) or perfectivity on the embedded verb. This by itself settles the question whether or not the case of *ought to* has a modal trigger different from that of the true modals. And we may assume that one of the two prerequisites for the modal trigger, either directional *TO* or a perfectivizing component is present in MVs silently. But we had assumed this in the first place given that MVs emerged from preterit presents, i.e. from perfectives. See (19) repeating (8) above. ["e" for 'event meaning'].

(19) a MV(e) ≡ {(incremental phase(e) followed by) result phase (e) event-operating on the specific modal source}
b where the incremental phase is implied
c where only the result phase is denoted
d where the MV-denotation, on the strength of denoting a result phase, is situated in the future: MV(e,s,t, source) ≡ {(s<t(e)) for all modal sources}

It will be clear from (19d) why MVs became temporal auxiliaries in several languages: *shall/will* in English, *skal* in Scandinavian, *sol/sal* in Old and Middle High German, *zal* in Dutch. The original strong verb paradigm that MVs were part of still shows in the plural as distinguished from the singular: *skullen* in Scandinavian, *sullen* in O/MHG, *zullen* in Modern Dutch. This is the quadruple stem change for the third strong verbal paradigm (cf. MHG *binden* – *band* – *bunden* – *gebunden* for "bind").

(19) is to be added to (18) as a list for what are the necessary criteria for modalization. We shall of course return to the implications of (19) in

more detail. See the ensuing chapter. Note, however, that what we have reached is the position that, given the obviously diverse developments of *must* and *ought to*, subjectification need not be taken as the only common property of the two modal lexicals.

5. The aspectuality of modal markers in their root readings

The reading of deontic modals was characterized as biphasic, whereas epistemic modal verbs were taken to be monophasic (e.g. Abraham 2005a, b). This is a fundamental property to lay aground everything that we claim has explanatory value for the emergence of modality. However, just this is put to doubt by Narrog (2010). He claims that it is not entirely clear whether this holds for the modal verbs themselves or as a unit together with the proposition. The author sees grounds to believe that deontic and dynamic modal markers (incl. modal verbs) themselves are stative, that is monophasic. Epistemic modality at a low level (e.g. *it is possible that*) may be stative as well, but at a high level it has no aspectual event structure of its own, that is, it is neither biphasic nor monophasic. Obligations, necessities, and permissions (deontic modalities), abilities, desires and circumstantial possibilities (dynamic modalities) are all semantically states. Etymologically, the English and German modal verbs derive from preterit-present verbs, which denoted a present state resulting from a past event.

(19) above may lead to the conclusion that modalization is triggered by the interplay of MV and the embedded predicate. This in turn might imply that the modal verbs by themselves lack something that the verbal control or raising complex includes.

Now, according to Prokosch (1939: 187f.), obligations, necessities, and permissions (deontic modalities), abilities, desires, and circumstantial possibilities (dynamic modalities) are semantically all states. Etymologically, the English and German MVs derive from preterit-present verbs (like the Latin inchoative *cognōscō* "learn" → *cognōvi* "I have learned = I know"). Based on Prokosch 1939, Narrog 2010 correctly argues that MVs denote a present state resulting from a past event. However, how can he align this with the claim that Prokosch's pre-Germanic **motan* 'have space', **sculan* 'owe', *agan* 'own', *cunnan* 'know', *magan* 'be strong, have power', *willan* 'want to' have a clear stative meaning? Narrog's line of argument is that the pre-Germanic modals do not imply that the two phases required for perfectives as resultant states are still states (cf. *frozen* or *shocked*).

The following examples, (20a-d), contribute to just this conclusion drawn by Narrog (2010: 5). Narrog claims that the sentences show that *müssen* in its deontic sense is compatible with adverbs of duration, but not with time limit adverbs. He concludes that in their deontic use these predicates are stative. Recall that adverbs of duration such as *ten hours long* resist co-construction with perfective predications. Adverbs of time limitation such as *for ten hours* are incompatible with imperfective predicates. ["≈" means 'compatible with'; „≠" means 'incompatible with'; the second parenthetic equations in the sentences (a-d) yield the conditions for the grammaticality result; DMV = deontic/ root modal reading of MV, EMV = epistemic reading.]

(20) a **Zehn Stunden lang* muss er den Berg besteigen. **MV/*EMV**
zehn Stunden lang [er$_i$ muss [PRO$_i$ den Berg besteigen]]
Er$_i$ muss [zehn Stunden lang [PRO$_i$ den Berg besteigen]]
10 hours long must he the mountain climb
(Perfective V-induced limitation ≈ limitation Adv)
'*He has to climb the mountain for ten hours.'
(terminative V ≠ duration Adv)

b *Zehn Stunden lang* muss er warten. **DMV/??EMV**
ten hours long must he wait (Imperfective V- induced
'He has to wait for ten hours.' duration ≈ duration Adv)
'He has to wait for ten hours.'
(non-terminative V ≠ limitation Adv)

c *Innerhalb von zehn Stunden* muss er den Berg besteigen.
within 10 hours must he the mountain climb
DMV/*EMV
(Perfective V-induced limitation ≈ limitation Adv)
'He must climb the mountain within ten hours.'
(terminative V ≈ limitation Adv)

d **Innerhalb von zehn Stunden* muss er warten. ***DMV/*EMV**
within ten hours must he wait
(Imperfective V-induced duration≈duration Adv)
'He has to wait up to ten hours.'
(non-terminative V ≠ limitation Adv)

Apart from the fact that Narrog 2010 rates both (20a) and (20d) acceptable German sentences – which is evidently false – he construes two alternative structures for each sentence: one in which the adverb is in the scope of the modal verb, and one in which conversely the modal verb is in its scope. See as an example the two grammatical glosses for (20a). However, since this distribution fails for two of the entire set of illustrations, i.e. (a) and (20d), cannot be held through for all four illustrations, the conclusion Narrog draws fails also. The examples do not confirm that time limit adverbs, which require perfectivity, can only modify the embedded proposition and not the modal verbs. The modal verbs themselves cannot only be compatible with duration for the simple (cognition-theory claimed) reason that MVs are grounding predicates; i.e. they fuse with the embedded verb for scoping operations. MVs cannot be rated separately for adverb-scoping operations.

We might test Narrog's assumption by using MVs in their status as full verbs – i.e. without embeddings.

(21) Finite MV embedding (non-finite) MV:

a Er *muss* das 10 Stunden lang *können.*
he must.FIN this can.INF
DMV/$^{??}$EMV for *muss*
DMV/*EMV for *können*

b Er hat das in 10 Stunden *können müssen.*
he hat.FIN hat can.INF must.INF
DMV/*EMV for *müssen*
DMV/*EMV for *können*

(22) Finite MV embedding V + (non-finite) MV:

a Er muss die Trompete 10 Stunden lang blasen$_{\text{IMPERF}}$ können.
he must the trumpet 10 hrs. long blow can
DMV/$^{?}$EMV – untelic V ≈ durative Adv

b *Er muss das Ei 10 Stunden lang ausblasen$_{\text{PERF}}$ können.
he must the egg 10 hrs. long outblow can
*DMV/*EMV – telic V ≠ durative Adv

c *Er muss die Trompete in 10 Stunden blasen$_{\text{IMPERF}}$ können.
he must the trumpet in 10 hrs. blow can
*DMV/*EMV – untelic V ≠ limiting Adv

d Er muss das Ei in 10 Stunden ausblasen$_{\text{PERF}}$ können.
he must the egg in 10 hrs. outblow can
DMV/$^{??}$EMV – telic V ≈ limiting Adv

(23) Finite MV embedding V:

a Er muss die Trompete 10 Stunden lang blasen$_{IMPERF}$.
DMV/$^{?}$EMV – untelic V ≈ durative Adv

b *Er muss das Ei 10 Stunden lang ausblasen$_{PERF}$.
*DMV/*EMV – telic V ≠ durative Adv

c *Er muss die Trompete in 10 Stunden blasen$_{IMPERF}$.
*DMV/*EMV – untelic V ≠ limiting Adv

d Er muss das Ei in 10 Stunden ausblasen$_{PERF}$.
DMV/$^{??}$EMV – telic V ≈ limiting Adv

This is what the distributions in (23a-d) tell us about MVs and their syntactic functions. See (24).

(24) a There is no adverb-scoping difference.
b Non-finites never receive an epistemic reading.
c Finites may receive an epistemic reading, but when they do the embedding predicate must not be perfective/telic.
d (22) and (23) have identical readings: This means that in (22) MV fuses semantically and syntactically with the likewise embedded full verb (which means it is 'grounding' in Langacker's sense).
e (d) implies that MVs have no scoping separate adverb-scoping effects (contra Narrog).
f All distributions together tell us that there is a strong tendency towards non-finiteness constrained to modal root readings ("epistemic non-finiteness gap"; see Abraham 1986, 1991).
g All distributions together tell us that there is a strong tendency towards root readings triggered by perfective aspect on the embedded predicate, whereas epistemic readings are triggered by imperfective aspect on the embedded predicate ("Aspect-Modality link"; see Abraham 1986).

6. Theory of Mind – Foreign / Other's Mind / Consciousness Alignment

We understand modality (and, partly, mood) in ways that are determinedly different from subjectification based in Traugott's sense. See Table 6-1. The best one can say about the differences is perhaps that whatever can be said in terms of a differential is what a Westerner speaking an Indo-European language can say. And this is: Mood is laid away for the morphological expression of the (past and present) subjunctive, while modality covers origo-related shifts of speaker and hearer and the *common ground* that needs to be established between speaker and hearer in all of their communicative dealings.

Table 6-1: Mood-Modality differential (based on von Wright 1974, Portner 2006, Rothstein & Thieroff 2010)

Definition: Speaker	Mood	Modality	Speech act
does not warrant the truth of *p*-utterance: relies on report of p by others / truth in others' worlds	Present subjunctive		
lays claim on self-intended *p*-realization in worlds not at his disposal at any time	Past subjunctive		
hedges truth assignment to *p* by subjecting speaker's (and/or the grammatical subject's) disposition to *p* to another person's / evaluator's commission or the committing potential of objective forces (for *müssen, sollen, dürfen*)		DMV	
does not warrant the truth of *p*-utterance: relies on inference of his own or objective laws wrt truth of *p*; may imply Bühler's *origo*-speaker shift	EMV		

Table 6-2: Mood-Modality differential

Definition: Speaker	Mood	Modality	Speech act
does not warrant the truth of *p*-utterance: relies on inference of his own on various data input wrt the truth of *p* or on objective, universally accepted knowledge ('objective epistemics')	Evidential		
hedges the truth of *p*-utterance: negotiates truth by seeking CG with addressee (*ja, doch, schon*); invoking accessible worlds ('veridicality')		MP	
does not warrant the truth of *p*-utterance: negotiates with addressee the truth of *p*-utterance; implication of speaker displacement		Sentence tags(?)	
operation on utterance aiming at various subsequent linguistic actions involving the addressee			IMP, INTERROG, DECLAR, EXCLAM

We may want to draw the topical conclusion from Figure 1 with respect to where subjectification, or subjectivization, is involved:

(25) Subjectification involvement in the four main categories of modality:

a **DMV – Modality:** hedges truth of utterance of *p* based on various (Kratzer's 1981) sources of (committed) dispositions – **Subjectivization from proto-Germanic full verbs? (root modality ← lexical Possession/Ability)**

b **EMV – Mood:** hedges truth by invoking possible worlds on assessing *p* (Objectivity vs. subjective beliefs and inferences) – **Subjectivization!/? (← Objective epistemics)** c **Evidentiality – Mood:** does not warrant the truth of *p*-utterance: relies on inference of speaker's own on various data input wrt the truth of *p* or on objective, universally accepted knowledge ('objective epistemics') – **Subjectivization !/?? (← Objective epistemics)**

d **MP – Modality:** hedges the truth of *p*-utterance by negotiating truth of *p* by seeking CG with addressee (*ja, nur, denn, doch, schon*); invoking possible worlds ('veridicality') – **Subjectivization?? (← Addressee involvement/CG)**

We also understand modality in ways different from the rather simple-layered speaker-orientation discussed at length by Narrog (2010). The best plea for an understanding which reaches a good distance further than the mentioned ones is perhaps Rumsey's early denial of claims extended by Benveniste (Rumsey 2003: 184; taken from Narrog 2010: 392 fn. 5) in the context of denying attributing subjectivity chiefly to one category, namely person:

> "[It] is a mistake to see [subjectivity] as grounded in any one area of grammar, be it the category of person, modality, spatial deixis or whatever. It does seem to be the case, however, that there is a certain set of functionally interrelated grammatical categories which play a leading role in this respect. These are the ones which are indexically grounded in the speech situation, presupposing the roles of speaker and addressee, and shifting in their reference and predicational value according to who is doing the talking and who is the addressee." (Rumsey 2003: 184)

Yet, despite this insightful comment on simple-grounded attempts such as by Rumsey, it is astonishing that no Bühler (1936/2010), Peirce (1871/1984, 1982-2000), or Jakobson (1957/1971) have found their way into the new attempts at what has been discussed in much profounder ways almost a century earlier. This includes their early attempts at speaker and addressee orientation, the inclusion of the self, the distinction between speaker and evaluator, the shift between distinct speaker selves, the displacement of speaker to evaluator and back, and to the origo theory espoused by Bühler (1936; latest English translation of 2010 with a new preface placing Bühler's early insights in a modern context).

The following components are indismissible for an understanding of ToM / FCA in our sense:

(26) a the appeal to a *common ground* (CG) to be reached between speaker and hearer;
b CG is under constant updating and optimization while speaker and hearer are dialoguing;
c appeal to a semantics of possible worlds ('veridicality');
d the diagnostics of the source of root and epistemic modal meanings;
e epistemics arise through grounding in fewer possible worlds to be appealed to by the speaker.

Modality as paradigmatically classified in Table 6-1 above is defined by two fundamental components. See (23)-(24) as well as down to (27) below.

(27) a The involvement of speaker as well as speaker shifting/multiple displacement are necessary, but not satisfying, conditions for modality characteristics.
b The speaker's truth validation to p is put at the disposal also of the addressee for the purpose of reaching *common ground* between speaker and hearer. This is both empirically grounded on modal verbs and modal particles). By contrast to (26) above, this is a satisfying condition: truth value suspense – i.e., the speaker negotiates the truth applicability to each discourse step with the addressee in an oscillating, discourse-completing procedure.
c The two modality conditions in (23) and (24) are interacting in such a way that speaker displacement as an indismissible condition makes an appeal to different possible worlds which bear on constrained truth conditions characteristic of different speakers (and hearers).
d Modal particles/MPs are the most typical representatives of modality in that they all involve speaker-shift as well as truth suspension on the speaker's side in favor of a CG to be reached in a permanent, oscillating alignment process accompanying, and incrementing with, the entire dialogic discourse. To all appearances, tags come the closest to the interacting function of MPs.
e Modal verbs/MVs, by contrast, are split between modality-like and mood-like characteristics. Root modals / DMVs, while sharing with MPs source, type, and strength identifications and, consequently, possible world semantics, lack the alignment process instantiated as CG through FCA. They do not make use of the origo scenario.

f On the other hand, epistemic modals, EMVs, appeal to possible worlds as well as to speaker-shift/displacement (i.e., they do make essential use of Bühler's origo scenario).

As shown in Tables 6-1 and 6-2 and discussed in (26)-(27) above, Mood has fundamental possible world components also. There is an overlap between Mood and Modality, at least from the Indo-European linguistic point of view, to the effect that root modal verbs and their epistemic counterparts are classified diversely. In languages other than the Indo-European ones (African languages (Robert 1991, 1995); Berber (Galand 2003, Taine-Cheikh 2010); Coptic (Depuydt 1993, Reintges 2010); Oceanic (François 2003)) aspect, in particular the Aorist as a consecutively chaining procedure in narratives, appears to be part of TAM and Mood (Robert 2010).

7. FCA on modal particles, modal root, and epistemic verbs

The most important notions FCA makes use of are the notions of discursive disposability and discursive *common ground*. *Common ground* means that speaker and hearer reach a common set of possible worlds in which their assessments of p or $\neg p$ are alike enabling them to proceed in their discourse with an optimum of mutual understanding. *Common ground* is achieved by discursive disposability. This means that the speaker signals to the hearer that he is prepared to negotiate the truth assumption he conveys with his statement p or $\neg p$. The notion of discursive disposability is fundamentally different, and independent from, assertivity, since the latter notion excludes that the addressee may always accept or reject the truth of p or $\neg p$. Discursive disposability holds equally well for entailments and presuppositions. Notice at this point that it cannot be the assertoric force of declaratives that makes them disposable. This bears a crucial consequence for our FCA-scenario. In modalized assertions – that is, in declaratives in which the assertoric force is hedged by modal verbs or adverbs – the speaker's commitment to the truth may be signaled to be weakened through the modal context, thus making it possible for the hearer to accept or challenge the proposition. See this illustrated by the communicative exchanges in (28) and (29) (from Brandtler 2011: 89-90, fn. 1.).

(28) A: *Maybe* John wants to be alone.
B: Yeah, you're right; let's visit him tomorrow instead.

(29) A: John *must* feel awfully alone these days.
B: No, that's not true. / Are you sure?

Let us not try to decide whether or not the modal expressions *maybe* and the epistemic *must* are equivalent in their modal force and implications with respect to speaker and hearer. What is certain, however, B's different responses make clear what precisely he reacts upon. In (28), B reacts only upon *p* without the modal adverb *maybe*, probably because it is the more relevant portion of A's statement. An appropriate reaction to A's entire modalized utterance would have to include B's assessment of *maybe(p)*, probably something like *I don't know: he may feel too lonely after all.* Likewise in (29), B's reactions to A's utterance are of unequal discursive fit. "No, that's not true" can only refer to *p* without the epistemic *must*, since the speaker's inference expressed by *must* can hardly be truth-assessed negatively. Likewise, *"Are you sure?"* is inappropriate in the same sense, but to a lesser degree since the speaker's inference on personal criteria may at least be put to doubt. A better discursive fit would be – provided we maintain the refuting reaction – something like (toward A) *I don't agree: probably not – after all, he got married last week. I don't agree: probably not* operates on the epistemic inference expressed by *must*, not on *p* alone, and *after all, he got married last week* provides the reason for B's refutation.

The gist of all this is that the proposition is one thing to react to, and the entire modalized utterance is something else in the sense that modal expressions like *maybe* and *must* have a hedging impact on the assertoric operation on the proposition in the sense that the hearer is invited to co-assess its validity. Notice that the aim pursued by the speaker is to establish a *common ground* with beliefs and knowledge appealed to on the hearer's side.

In what follows we discuss four categories all of which involve Kratzer's (1981) fundamental criteria of verbal modality (modal source, type, and force): MV, epistemic adverbial, evidential adverbial, and modal particle, with the aim to show that no two share all of the features attributable to them. Let us claim the following.

(30) a Epistemic modal verbs/EMV denote a twofold deixis: according to the source of p, and another one according to the speaker's assessment of p.

b Haider *soll* betrunken gewesen sein
(with p = *Haider ist betrunken gewesen*)

c *soll*(p)

Source of p — <3rd person>

Sp-assessment[9] — <distance wrt p-truth>
<relative assertion of truth of p>
<average probability wrt p>

We take as a point of departure a slightly modified model of Davidson's (2004) threefold distinction of mind awareness (see Leiss 2008) as in (31) below.

(31) Davidson's 'Mind awareness triangle':
Foreign/3rd persons' knowledge awareness

Speaker's knowledge (= *I*'s) (= *I*'s) awareness

Addressee's knowledge (= (= *your*) awareness

"Foreign/3rd persons' knowledge awareness" may also be understood as "social/objective/intersubjective knowledge". The following model in (32) modifies Davidson's mind awareness triangle in Jakobson's shifting sense (see also the pertinent reference in Bühler's *origo*-scenario as in Abraham 2010): The speaker's role is divided into that of a viewer's (observer's) evaluating source and the evaluator (on the basis of the speaker's evaluating source) himself.

(32) Leiss' 'Other's mind awareness triangle' (Leiss 2008) referring to modality expressions (Evidentials, DMV, EMV, MP; possibly adverbials of modality).
Evidential function of epistemic modal verbs/EMV: cf. *Sterne müssen ferne Vergangenheit darstellen* "Stars must represent a far past".

---

9 The features are listed with some modest measure of redundancy, at this point of the discussion.

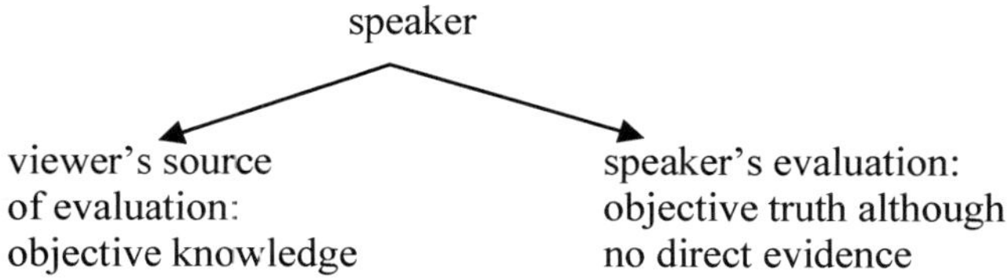

The model in (32) will be taken up again and illustrated in (38)-(39). Following (32) various modality utterances can be characterized with different sets of features. See (33)-(40) below.

(33) a Epistemic adverbials/epAdv unfold but a simple deixis – one where the source branch of (30c) is missing.

b Haider ist *wahrscheinlich/vermutlich* betrunken gewesen.

c

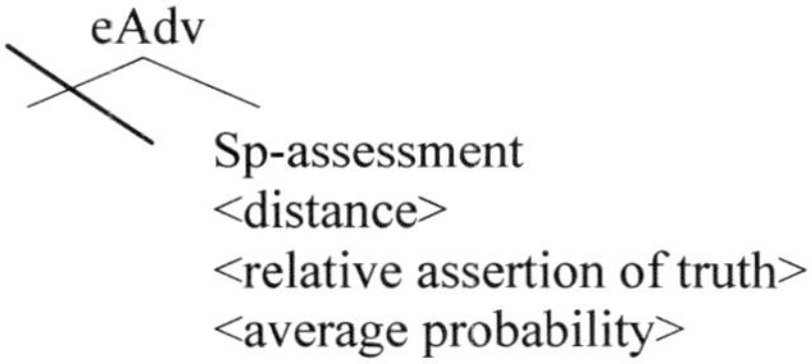

(34) a Evidential adverbials/evAdv likewise unfold a simple deixis – one where the speaker deixis is missing.

b Haider ist *offensichtlich* betrunken gewesen.
(with p = *Haider betrunken gewesen sein*)

c

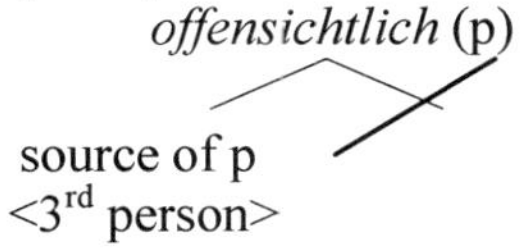

(35) a Modal particles/MPs denote a different deixis in the following sense: Speaker makes an estimate about the knowledge awareness of Addressee while letting the Addr know about this estimate and giving him a chance to relativize, or correct, this estimate about p. In this sense, the feature(s) under Sp-assessment are richer than those for EMV given according to the source of p, and another one according to the speaker's assessment of p.

b Haider ist <u>*ja*</u> betrunken gewesen
(with p = *Haider betrunken gewesen sein*)

c *ja* (p)

Sp-assessment of knowledge shared between Sp & Addr
<distance wrt p-truth>
<relative assertion of truth of p>
<average probability wrt p>

<+unified knowledge awareness> <–unified knowledge awareness>

Thus, MPs unfold a twofold deixis in the sense of (35c). The general insight is that MP serve the highest theory of mind mark (speaker deixis mark = speaker's assessment of Addressee's assessment), this to the extent that MPs – and only these as opposed to MVs and, even more so, E-adverbials – induce an interaction between Sp and Addr to achieve a *common ground* of beliefs and knowledge, without giving explicit lexical expression to this exchange. To all appearances, no other category does this in the same direct way; and, what is interesting typologically, no language does this, to all appearances, in the same deictic, discourse and *common ground*-related, way – i.e., any language that does not possess the MP-category (see Abraham 1991, 1995).

A similar view can be cast on the MV-differential as in (36) for grammatical epistemicity and evidentiality in German:

(36) a Sie *muss* schon mal in Logroño gewesen sein.
b Sie *soll* schon mal in Logroño gewesen sein.
c Sie *will* schon mal in Logroño gewesen sein.

There are 3 different assessments of the truth value of the proposition and 3 different sources of assessment involved. See the generalizations in (37a,b) and the illustrations in (30)-(35).

(37) a **Modal verbs:** the speaker is split into an evaluator and a source. The hearer does not participate in the assessment of the truth value (truth disposability / suspension). The assessment of the truth value is located in the speaker (**'intransitive' assessment**).
b **Modal particles:** the speaker negotiates the truth value with the hearer (truth disposability / suspension / hedging), where the hearer is taken more than seriously – his view of the truth value is taken into account to yield some *common ground*, i.e., the assessment of the truth value is locatable in two different persons and

their common belief denominator (Abraham 2011) (**'transitive' assessment**).

(38) a Michail *muss* schon einmal in Logroño gewesen sein.
b Michail *will* schon einmal in Logroño gewesen sein.
c Michail *soll* schon einmal in Logroño gewesen sein.
d **Ich *will* schon einmal in Logroño gewesen sein.
viewer necessarily ≠ Sp

As sketched earlier in (32), the kind of speaker role split relating to (38) is illustrated in (39),

(39)

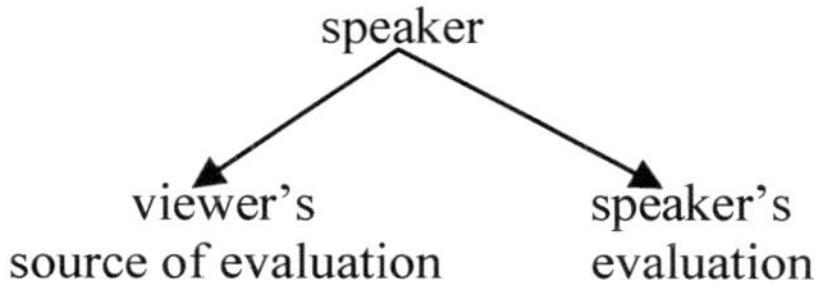

where (i) subject ≠ viewer / Reichenbach's ‚r' / speaker, and where (ii) (38d) is uninterpretable unless speaker „I" is depersonalized (as in a dream where the dreamer steps beside his self and observes himself as another person). Let us, then, distinguish between:

(40) a Source = **P**ropositional person (subject of the sentence)
b Source = **L**ocutionary person (speaker)
c Source = **I**llocutionary person (evaluator, source of modalization)

This yields the following distinctions based on the feature categorization in (40a-c).

Table 7-1: Source of assessment and speaker's assessment

MV-lexical	Source	Assessment of evidence by speaker
sollen	[–L] [–P] [+I]	middle
müssen	[+L] [–P] [–I]	high
wollen	[–L] [+P] [–I]	low
können	[±L] [±P] [±I]	neutral(ized)

So much for overt modality expressions. Let us now turn to covert modality expressions. It will be seen – at least for the sample expressions with *HAVE TO* and *BE TO* – that covert modality by far does not cover the space that overt modality covers. The most striking result is that modal epistemicity does not surface.

8. FCA on hidden modality

Hidden modality has to be part of our discussion because, as we shall see, modality emerging from lexicals that have no modal denotation is not accountable in terms of subjectification. See our (14a) above: Why would root modality be more subjective than the non-modal lexical verb from which modality is implicated? Furthermore, why does epistemicity, the declared subjective mood, not derive from hidden modality phenomena? Let us first clarify what we might understand 'hidden modality'.

8.1 What is covert modality?

We may want to distinguish two types of covert modality:

- complex patterns of modality yet undiscovered
  and
- silent, or hidden, modality (covert modality in the narrow sense)

Let us discuss the first type first. Modality in languages without polyfunctional, paradigmatically classified modals (Slavic, Romance, East Asian) is often encoded in one of the following ways (Abraham 1986, 1991, 2005; Kotin 2008, Leiss 2002 as well as others) and is often encoded in complex ways.

(41)	a	MV + imperfective infinitive	yields epistemic readings
	b	MV + perfective infinitive	yields root/deontic readings
		(Abraham 1991 and later, especially 2005)	

This type of complex encoding in turn yields definiteness effects in languages without articles such as Russian (Leiss 2000, 2002; Kotin 2006):

(42)	a	Imperfective verb	+ ACC	yields indefiniteness effects
	b	Perfective verb	+ACC	yields definiteness effects
	c	Perfective verb	+ GEN	yields partitivity effects
	(Leiss 2000)			

Now recall (13) repeated here for convenience as (43).

(43) a MV + V → modal meaning
b *ought* + *to* + V → modal meaning
c V_{seek} + PERFECTIVE-PREFIX-V → modal meaning

Recall also the fundamental insight that E-readings correlate with s=t (speech act time equal with event time), while root meanings cannot be correlated with other than s<t (event time in the future of speech act time). Consider (44a, b) with non-modal vs. modal matrix verbs.

(44) a Er wünscht/ist gehalten dies *(zu) erreichen.
he wishes/is committed this (to) achieve
… **DMV(VOL-OBL)/*EMV**
b Er will/muss dies (*zu) erreichen
he wishes.MV/must this (to) achieve
… **DMV(VOL-OBL)/ EMV**

What is striking is that the full lexicals as in (44a) never have E-readings, in contrast to MVs as in (44b). There is one obvious conclusion to draw from this: The bridging preposition *zu* (English *to*) cannot be responsible for the type of modal polyfunctionality that characterizes MVs. Furthermore, the *will*- or *must*-component responsible for modality cannot be what is represented denotatively in *wünschen / gehalten sein* "wish / be committed", in the first place. As a consequence, we want to say that directional *zu* is just a necessary, but not a satisfying condition of modality. Future projectivity denoted by *zu* lies aground of modality, but it is itself not making a verb modal in the exhaustive sense as MVs do. Moreover, two more conclusions appear to be appropriate. One is that if MVs express root modality the meaning of futural *zu* is understood in the first place, while it has to be added for full lexicals as *wünschen* and *gehalten sein* in (44a). The other equally obvious conclusion is that the modal component alone, represented lexically in the full lexicals in (44a), cannot provide the epistemic condition, i.e. 's=t'. The relation between full "modal" lexicals and MVs is asymmetric: Verbs selecting directional-*zu* embeddings miss the epistemic denotation, whereas MVs, necessarily without directional *zu*, integrate both 's<t' and 's=t', i.e. their polyfunctional potential. This opens a direction to look for another trigger of epistemicity – one that lies outside the component differential of MV.

8.2 How is epistemic modality triggered other than by subjectification?

Epistemicity is possibly a very simple procedure as an alternative to the root-modal reading. The trigger is grammatically rooted. See (45a-d).

(45) a *Er* muss darin liegen. ... DMV/EMV
he must therein lie
"He must lie therein."
b *Er* mag nie aufgeben. ... DMV/EMV
he may never give up
"He is not willing to ever give up."
c *Es* muss daran liegen. ... *DMV/EMV
it must thereon lie
"It must be due to."
d *Es* mag nie gelingen. ... *DMV/EMV
it may never succeed
"It may never be successful to."

The subject in (45a) has the potential to execute the committer's volition, while the subject in (45c) (in its expletive function) does not. Likewise, with the lexical predicate shifting from agentive to static, the reading for (45c,d) is more likely epistemic. No doubt, this differential is also triggered by the non-agentive verb and the non-agentive context triggered by *daran* as compared with *darin*, which does not exclude an agentive reading of the sentence. My claim is that this is all that lies at the bottom of epistemicity deriving from root modals: the fact that the subject is not in the position to execute a committing / volitional act. Expletive subjects such as that in (45b) are one such non-agent archetype.

Needless to say that, given the subjectification model and most of the other observations with respect to the historical emergence of epistemic modals, this is a strong claim. I see no reason to withdraw it given also the following reasoning. Expletive *es* came to appear late in Old High German and beginning Middle High German. My claim is the general conclusion that E-readings were late in the history of Germanic languages is wrong to the extent that the temporal correlation with the emergence of expletive *es* (English "there") (and, by implication, the emergence of thetic sentences) has never really been investigated. It may turn out that (46) is all that is to say with respect to epistemicity and its occurrence in the history of Germanic languages.

(46) a no E-reading of an MV unless non-agentivity of its subject argument
b no E-reading of any V unless s=t
c no E-reading of an V unless it is a true MV
d $^{?}$no polyfunctionality of a V unless it is an MV in the sense of the modal paradigm in Germanic (full verbs never project polyfunctionality)

If both (2a-c) and (8) hold – repeated here for convenience as (47a-c) and (48) – , then the fact that '*HAVE TO* V' only has the deontic reading, whereas *BE TO* has both the deontic and the possibility reading receives a solution.

(47) a They must be afraid of us
b $\lambda x\ \lambda y \lambda e \lambda s \lambda t$: *muss/soll/darf*$(x,e,s<t) \equiv$ *will*$(y,e(x,s<t))$
c $\lambda x\ \lambda z \lambda e \lambda s \lambda t$: *muss/soll/darf*$(x,e,s=t) \equiv$ *will*$(z,e(x,s=t))$
(where 'e' for 'event denoted by the embedded infinitival, 'x,y' for 'event participants' (and, by implication, verbal actants/arguments), 'z' for 'speaker of the utterance', 's' for 'speech act time', and 't' for event time')
(48) a $\lambda x \lambda y$: *have*$(x,y) \equiv$ *be*$(y,$ *with*$(x))$
b where: *have* is a lexically empty transitive verb
c where: *be* is a lexically empty unaccusative verb

What (48c) means is that its subject (theta role) in the hidden-modal construal is 'X is to (be) V(-ed)' is that of a direct object (theta role). *BE* selects adjectives and nominals. Adjectives select PATIENTS and possibly other low-hierarchy theta roles, never AGENTS. Given Bech's verb categorization, *BE* selects only verbal forms in the second and third status (infinitives with the infinitival preposition and past participles; Bech 1955/1983). The participial selection needs to be that of a perfective verb, at least in German (stative/adjectival participle can only be formed from perfective verbs). Thus, we may generalize as in (49).

(49) a *BE-TO-(BE)*-V(*-ed*) is selected for unaccusative properties open for both AGENT reading (of the underlying transitive active clause) and the (unaccusative) PATIENT reading. This creates an ambiguity between Agentives or Patients/Recipients of commitments; thus, the deontic/ committed reading of the active base as well as the passive, adjectival/property reading is available.

b *HAVE-TO*-V is selected for agentive readings only; thus, only the deontic reading is available.

This settles the question why *HAVE-TO* only triggers deontic/obligation modality, whereas *BE-TO-(BE)*-V(*-ed*) has both the deontic and the possibility reading. This is clearly a fully syntactic account without any hedges set up in pragmatics or semantics.

8.3 Is modality marking ubiquitous?

Is modality ubiquitous in language (modality in pronouns, etc.), and therefore mostly undiscovered? If yes, are there nevertheless islands of non-modality, such as dependent clauses (syntactic islands: failing extraction)? Are there more of these islands of modality in language?

Unmarked modality may be the norm in some languages like the European ones. However, all sentences are composed of two indismissible parts: the proposition AND its illocutionary force or speech act type. Illocutionary force is silent in languages such as English or German; it is as a rule overtly encoded in Japanese (Tanaka 2011) and probably a whole range of other languages.

Speech act functionality and marking are constrained across syntactically dependent clauses. Modality functions may be distributed differently in matrix sentences versus dependent clauses: Dependent clauses are generally devoid of their own illocutionary force. However, there are exceptions to that rule, which are very instructive (Haegeman 2006, Abraham 2011, Coniglio 2011).

8.4 The main phenomenal inventory of silent modality

The following list arrays German examples, in which nothing hints at modality in an explicit way.

(50) a Die Aufgaben sind zu lösen.
the tasks are to solve
... indicating obligation or possibility

b die zu lösen- (seien-)den Aufgaben
the to solve (being) tasks
„the tasks to be solved"
... indicating obligation or possibility

c Das Buch liest sich gut.
the book reads refl well
… middle construction indicating possibility

d Die Farbe ist abwaschbar.
the paint is off-washable
… passive modality of possibility

e Das Glas ist zerbrechlich.
the glass is breakable
… passive modality of possibility

f Das Auto fährt 210km/h.
the car rides 210km/hour
… indicating possibility on the basis of conventional implicature

The following utterances are owed to Bhatt as illustrations of silent modality (Bhatt 2006; for German see Holl 2010).

(51) a *Tim knows* [*PRO how to solve the problem*].
… *should*-deontic, *could*-possible/able

b Jane found [a book [PRO to draw cartoons in]] for Sara.
… *should*-deontic, *could*-possible/able

c [$_{DP}$ the man [$_{REL}$ PRO to fix the sink]
… *should*-deontic, *can/could*-possible/able

d Sue went to Torino [PRO to buy a violin].
… *should*-deontic, *could*-possible/able

e Bill has to reach Philadelphia before noon.
... *should*-deontic, *could*-possible/able

f William is to leave tomorrow.
... *should*-deontic, $^{(*)}$*could*-possible/able

g The stomach is to empty.
... *should*-deontic, **could*-possible/able

h The monument is to fall.
... *should*-deontic, **can*/**could*-possible/able

On our search for hidden modality, we have run these sentences through several languages. Table. 8-1 illustrates some of the findings.

Table 8-1: Hidden modality in adjunct-object complement infinitive: factive *know / wissen Tim knows [PRO how to solve the problem]* ≈ *should*-deontic, *could*-possible/able

Germanic	English VO	+
	German AuxOV	-/$^{?}$gerundial
	Norwegian VO	-/no gerundial
Romance	Italian VO	+
	French VO	+
Slavic	Russian VO	-
	Polish VO	-
Georgian	split ergative VO	-
Chinese	isolate VO	-
Japanese	agglutinative OV	-
no such syntax of (P-)infinitival embedding except for English and dialectal gerundial in German; complement-object complement infinitive partly possible: German, Norwegian. Syntax of infinitival embedding found in Slavic, but no modality implication – modality only via finite predicate, if at all. No infinitival embeddings in Georgian. Chinese needs overt modality encoding. No infinitivals in Japanese, its quasi-finite weak modality due to perfectivity (futural eventivity) of Japanese verbs.		

There is an interesting restriction in Norwegian holding for negation (Kerstin Eide, p.c.):

(52) a not (*a*) V
b – *(*a*) V

In negated sentences, the infinitival preposition is optional, whereas in non-negated ones it is required. I leave it at that in the present context.

8.5 Summary (on the basis of Table 8-1)

There appears to be a class of futurizing and, by that property, equally modalizing morphological elements. This class contains:

(53) a the directional 'infinitival preposition', English *to*, German *zu*, Romance *à*, Scandinavian *å*

b The auxiliary *HAVE* denoting a property of the subject of *HAVE* – however, why does *HAVE TO* not have the possibility reading, in contrast to *BE TO*?? See (41a,b) above for a possible answer.
c The directional 'infinitival preposition' and *HAVE / BE* cooperate in achieving the futural, and modality, denotation.
d The root modality meanings achieved by heeding conditions (45)-(47) remain vague as compared with the 6 paradigmatic meanings of the Germanic MVs. They are restricted to NECESSITY and POSSIBILITY. We might want to speak about the basic modality categories constituting in the evolutional-diachronic "modal proto-soup/modale Ursuppe" (Abraham 2010), from which all subclasses of today's modality distinctions, as represented in the paradigm of German modal verbs and the inventory of modal particles emerged in the course of time and by mutual dissociation.
e Transitive *HAVE*(x,y) is composed of, and lexically equivalent to, intransitive *BE(y)-WITH*(x), where x carries the prototypical attributing-to-dative (case) theta role (Kotin, this volume: 'something is with him.GEN (for/to) do(ing)'). Is this to be seen as the functional bridge between the prepositional futurity/modality trigger in Indo-European and the attributive modality trigger in Turkish?
f All of the considerations in (45)-(49) are totally independent of the embedding constraints of prepositional infinitivals in the different languages discussed here. One suggestion for such constraints is the failure of a variety of languages to relate infinitival form to gerundial, i.e. by nominal function of verbal form. Recall that exactly this relation is apparent in German dialects, but not in the standard language. In contrast to some of the Indo-European languages listed, however, the gerundial / nominal form is very obvious in Turkish. AND: Such embedding grammars seem to have nothing to do with Greenbergian typological classifications (OV, VO, let alone more detailed ones such as German [[Fin[[V]]] vs. English [S[Aux[VO]]]).
g Exception to the two morphological conditions discussed above is taken by two types of languages: isolating Chinese and agglutinative Japanese, the main reason being that no morphological agreement relation is encoded on the predicate; from this follows that no verbs in infinitival form exist distinct from finite ones.

h Japanese taking exception to the very existence of infinitival verbal forms excels in another way: almost exclusively, Japanese verb stems are perfective. Due to their bi-phasic event structure (incremental phase followed by resultative phase), perfectives denote the future enactment of the event expressed. This alone appears to give rise to (albeit vague) modality notions on most Japanese sentences (Iwasaki 2002: ch. 13; Tanaka p.c.).

8.6 (Too?) Strong generalizations for covert modalization

We list the properties found so far.

(54) a Silent modality exhausts itself in root modality – no epistemics are triggered in hidden modality: Is there an obvious reason for this? (*will/might* ***have to***, *will* ***be to*** *(be) achieve(d)* – non-finite (embedded) forms preempt epistemicity because epistemics presuppose s=t).

b Silent root modalities cover no more than possibility and necessity – the „modal proto-soup“ (= von Wright's (1973) modal logic; generalization by Fritz 1997).

c Implied/implicatured modality follows the epistemic gap for non-finites postulate: finites ≠ non-finites.

d Classificatory efforts for MVs fail on modal particles – quite another modal phenomenon entirely (*common ground*, hedged truth evaluation, veridicality) , unrelated to modal root verbs.

e Types of tags (Addr-oriented) ≈ types of MPs (seeking *common ground* between Sp and Addr)?

8.7 The emergence of modality in synchrony and diachrony

How is the modal reading of the examples of silent modality triggered? We have unfolded the function of the infinitival preposition, German *zu*, English *to* as a necessary, but not a satisfactory factor for modality. See again (11)-(13) as well as (53)-(54) above.

Let us take (54e) as our point of departure, which may be the starting point also for the diachronic emergence of root modality from the original modal verbs, which, as we recall, were full verbs (Lightfoot's 'pre-modal phase'; Lightfoot 1979; see also Plank 1984) with perfect(ive) meanings inceptively implying nothing but futurity.

Emergent root modality – step 1:

(54) f Das Auto fährt 210km/h
the car rides 210km/hour

indicating possibility on the basis of conventional implicature

An assertion always points at possibility by conventional implicature. In terms of accessible worlds: The set of worlds of things happening includes the set of worlds of possible happenings. If this were not so reality would not be among the possibilities.

(55) The occurrence of the infinitival-directional preposition rejects the epistemic reading, since English *to*, German *zu*, Romance *à,* Scandinavian *å* and the perfective affix, *ga*-V, respectively, exclude s=e – i.e., the precondition of epistemicity, speaker time collapsing with event time, s=e, is excluded. The infinitival-directional preposition elicits futurality, s<e. Recall that all observed instances of covert modal readings excluded epistemic interpretations; see (62) above.

From step 1 above we gain step 2 by universal quantification over the entirety of accessible worlds in which step 1 holds. Thus, from

(56) a *BE-TO*-V(y) entailing λPOSSλV∃y: *POSS/*◊(V(y))
it follows that
b λPOSSλV∀y: *MUST/*□(V(y)).

This, on the basis of Benveniste's generalization about the structural link between *HAVE* and *BE,*

(55) c *HAVE*(x,y) ≡ *BE*(y, with(y, x)),

yields step 3 in allowing for the generalization ("□" for "it is necessary that")

(55) d □(V[+agentive]) – in other words, the external argument of V in *BE-TO*-V must be an agent.

Let us put this derivation down in a short compact survey.

(57) Meaning composition of *MUST*-V: ambiguous between (58a) and (58b) below:
- a x-will [y-V] ⊕ (s<e) ... control = root-modal reading: *will*-at-s, V-at-e; x≠y, i.e., external-source subject
- b x-will [x-V] ⊕ (s=e) ... raising = epistemic reading: *will*-at-s/e, V-at-e/s; internal-source subject x

(58) Derivative link between *HAVE-TO* and *BE-TO*:
- a *HAVE*(x,V)-to-V(x(,y)): on the basis of *BE*(x/y)-*TO*-V we have the two readings:
- a1 *POSS*/◊(V(y)) there is at least one possible world in which V(y) is accessible
- a2 *NECESS*/□(V(y)) V(y) is accessible for all possible worlds
- b from a2 follows typically, though not necessarily: the event denoted by V is agentive, i.e., V has an Agent subject.

The general conclusion is that the ingredients of root modality turn out to be

- accessible possible worlds
  as well as
- the quantification differential with respect to those worlds in which the events hold denoted by the subordinated V.

Recall that epistemicity is derived synchronically – hardly diachronically – by simply the change of interpretation from V(s<e) to V(S=e). This may be achieved grammatically, but it may just as well be a matter of contextual disambiguation – i.e., external to grammatical decision. We have seen that such contexts include the type of aspectual status that the embedded V possesses in relation to the matrix MV. See (41)-(42) above.

9. Does a theory of grammaticalization need the concepts of (inter)subjectification?

Does a theory of grammaticalization need the concepts of (inter)subjectification? We considered the notion of subjectification to be an epiphenomenon that may cover essential parts of what we discussed under the far less presumptuous notion of FCA. But what about covert modality, where the most crucial component of (I)S, i.e. epistemic modality, does not emerge at all in the first place? Consider the emergence of *ought to* from its original possessive meaning (like German *haben*).

It seems that the very notion of (I)S hinges on the assumption that there exists a grammaticalizing path from root MV to epistemic MV. See Table 7-1 and Table 8-1 above. Now consider again the feature-oriented descriptions of modal categories as in (33)-(35) above. There is nothing that characterizes root modals as more subjective than the full verb functions of the MVs in German and Dutch. Given the solidly established distinction of subjective versus objective uses of epistemic *must* (Lyons 1977, Portner 2009: 149) – viz. *The earth must be round*, where the modal has to be derived from the less subjective root meaning of *must* – the general explanative status of (I)S appears to be lost.

Given what the discussion so far has yielded we may want to ask:

(59) Is (I)S a shortcut concept to what includes the components exemplified so far?

(60) Does (I)S contain all features that we think are required for an empirically exhaustive theory of language change and grammaticalization?

(61) Does (I)S apply to diachronic as well as synchronic processes of change (L1 and ToM/FCA questions, metaphorization and metonymization, impaired speech scenarios/neuro-linguistics)?

We shall not be able to answer (59), nor probably any of the other two, unless one appeals to means applied within Foreign Consciousness Alignment theory/FCA (or The Other's Mind Alignment Theory). On the basis of the latter, the answer is "maybe" to (61), but no doubt "no" to (60) and "not tried out yet" to (59). FCA, by contrast, is totally independent from questions like (59)-(61).

Reference to speech impairment with agrammatism of aphasics provides some clues. Agrammatism patients lose disposability of the grammatical functions of auxiliaries and of inflection. This seems the reverse of the diachronic grammaticalizing path that, for example, *HAVE* takes. German agrammatics retain *haben* "have" in its lexical possessive use, but lose the grammatical usage in the periphrastic past: *Er das gesehen* "he-this-seen" – instead of what is normal *Er **hat** das gesehen* "he-has-this-seen" – is an example typical of this specific speech erosion of aphasic agrammarians. What does this have to do with 'subjectification' in the first place? Since we do know that epistemicity is elicitable only for predicative finiteness, the functional loss of the auxiliary *haben* in the case of aphasiacs would seem to be a case of de-epistemization. But would we want to say that this type of loss of grammaticity is a case of 'de-subjectification'? Certainly nothing indicates such a restriction with agrammatics. There is a clash between the phenomenal de-subjectification and the more cognitive notion of subjectification which cannot be lost in the case of agrammatism and aphasiacs.

FCA refers to a collection of techniques (*common ground*, truth hedging, truth negotiation between Sp and Addr, scalarly differentiated accessible worlds, features with *origo*-status) are used for the description and explanation of all sorts of communicative acts and their lexical and grammatical components. We have shown how subparts of this inventory work on expressions of modality and mood, how phenomena of diachronic change are equally captured, and how phenomena far beyond the emergence of epistemic modals may come into the picture that constitutive components of FCA may be able to address (consider aphasic agrammatism). Given that FCA is able to provide accounts for more diverse phenomena than subjectification/(I)S, FCA is methodologically superior.

We considered the notion of subjectification to be an epiphenomenon that covers essential parts of what we discussed under the far less presumptuous notion of FCA. But what about covert modality, where the most crucial component of (I)S, i.e. epistemic modality, does not emerge at all in the first place? It seems that the very notion of (I)S hinges on the existence of the grammaticalizing path from root MV to epistemic MV. Now consider again the feature-oriented descriptions of modal categories in (30)-(35) above. There is nothing that characterizes root modals as more subjective than the full verb functions of the MVs in German and Dutch. Given the calibrated distinction of subjective versus objective uses of epistemic *must* (Lyons 1977, Portner 2009: 149), for example, where both need to be derived from the less subjective root meaning of *must*, the general status of (I)S appears to be totally lost.

It seems that, while (I)S may serve as an epiphenomenon for a small part of these areas and phenomena, its status as a necessary, let alone satisfying, notion for a theory of grammaticalization is largely overdrawn. Given the lack of indispensable explanatory criteria, even its status as an abbreviation for some of the areas covered by FCA is doubtful. Its invention and widely spread and acclaimed use for the purpose of explaining the emerging epistemicity of modals rests on the failure to attain sufficient empirical ground and draw the necessary conclusion from it – under exclusion of superficial inferences (Ockham's Razor).

References

Abraham, Werner 1986. Die Bedeutungsgenese von Modalpartikeln. *Groninger Arbeiten zur germanistischen Linguistik (GAGL)* 27, 1-44.

—. 1989 Vorbemerkungen zur Modalpartikelsyntax. *Linguistische Berichte* 118: 443–465.

—. 1990a Die Grammatikalisierung von Auxiliar- und Modalverben. *Beiträge zur Geschichte der deutschen Sprache und Literatur* 112: 200–208.

—. 1990b. Modalverben in der Germania. In: Marga Reis (ed.), *Akten des VIII: Internationalen Germanistenkongresses. Sektion Kontrastive Syntax*, 79–98. München: Iudicium.

—. 1991a Modalverben in der Germania. In: Eijiro Iwasaki (ed.), *Begegnung mit dem „Fremden": Grenzen – Traditionen – Vergleiche. Akten des VIII. Internationalen Germanisten-Kongresses in Tokio 1990*, Vol. 4, 109–118. München: Iudicium.

—. 1991b Discourse particles in German: How does their illocutive force come about? Between a maximalistic and minimalistic position. In: Werner Abraham (ed.), *Discourse particles. Descriptive and theoretical investigations on the logical, syntactic and pragmatic properties of discourse particles in German and English*, 220–272. [Pragmatics & Beyond, New Series 12]. Amsterdam: John Benjamins.

—. 1991c The grammaticalization of the German modal particles. In: Elizabeth Closs Traugott & Bernd Heine (eds.), *Approaches to grammaticalization*, Volume 2, 331–380. Amsterdam: John Benjamins.

—. 1995. Wieso stehen nicht alle Modalpartikel in allen Satzformen? *Zeitschrift für deutsche Sprache* 23 (2): 124–146.

—. 2002. Modal verbs: epistemics in German and English. In: Sjef Barbiers, Frits Beukema & Wim van der Wurff (eds.) *Modality and its interaction with the verbal system*, 19-50. Amsterdam: Benjamins [Linguistik Aktuell / Linguistics Today 47].

—. 2003. Autonomous and non-autonomous components of 'grammatic(al)ization': Economy criteria in the emergence of German negation. *Sprachtypologie und Universalienforschung (STUF)* 56/4: 325-365.

—. 2005. Event arguments and modal verbs. In: Claudia Maienborn & Angelika Wöllstein (eds.) *Event arguments: Foundations and applications*, 243-276. Tübingen: Niemeyer [Linguistische Arbeiten 501].

—. 2009. Die Urmasse von Modalität und ihre Ausgliederung. Modalität anhand von Modalverben, Modalpartikel und Modus. Was ist das

Gemeinsame, was das Trennende, und was steckt dahinter? In: W. Abraham & E. Leiss (hg.) *Modalität. Epistemik und Evidentialität bei Modalverb, Adverb, Modalpartikel und Modus*, 251-302. [Studien zur deutschen Grammatik 77]. Tübingen: Stauffenburg Verlag.

—. 2010. Illocutive force is speaker concern about the source of information and information sharing. Anchoring multiple speaker-addressee deixis in syntax. Paper and handout for the MIC Conference Paris Nov. 18–19, 2010.

—. 2012. Illocutive force is speaker and information source concern. What type of syntax does the representation of speaker pragmatics require: "constructions" or deep structural analysis? In: Werner Abraham & Elisabeth Leiss (eds.) *Modality and Theory of Mind elements across languages,* 67-108. [Trends in Linguistics. Studies and Monographs 243]. Berlin: de Gruyter.

Abraham, Werner & Elisabeth Leiss (eds.) 2008. *Modality-aspect interfaces: Implications and typological solutions*. (Typological Studies in Language 79.) Amsterdam: John Benjamins.

Abraham, Werner & Elisabeth Leiss (eds.) 2009. *Modalität.* (Studien zur deutschen Grammatik 71). Tübingen: Stauffenburg.

Abraham, Werner & Elisabeth Leiss (eds.) 2012. *Modality and Theory of Mind elements across languages.* [Trends in Linguistics. Studies and Monographs 243]. Berlin: de Gruyter.

Aijmer, Karin 1978. Epistemic modal auxiliaries in English. In: Kirstin Gregersen, Hans Basbøll, & Jacob Mey (eds.) *Papers from the fourth Scandinavian Conference of Linguistics*, 161–168. Odense: Odense University Press.

Bech, Gunnar 1955/1957. *Studien über das deutsche verbum infinitum.* Band 1: 1955, Band 2: 1957. København: Munksgaard in Komm [Historisk-filologiske meddelelser]. Reprint 1983. *Studien über das deutsche Verbum infinitum.* Tübingen: Niemeyer [Linguistische Arbeiten 139].

Benveniste, Émile 1966. *Problèmes de linguistique générale.* [Bibliothèque des sciences humaines]. Paris: Gallimard

Bhatt, Rajesh 2006. *Covert modality in non-finite contexts.* Berlin: de Gruyter [Interface Explorations 8].

Bühler, Karl 1936/2011.*Theory of language.The representational function of language.*Transl. D.F. Goodwin. Amsterdam: John Benjamins. Second revised edition 2011.

Brandtler, Johan 2011. *The Syntax, Semantics and Pragmatics of Polarity Item Licensing.* Amsterdam: Benjamins [Linguistik Aktuell / Linguistics Today].

Coniglio, Marco 2011. *Syntax der deutschen Modalpartikeln. Ihre Distribution und Lizensierung in Haupt- und Nebensätzen*. Berlin: Akademie [studia grammatica 73].

Dekeyser 1998. The modal auxiliary *ought*. From 'possession' to 'obligation'. In: Johan Van der Auwera, Frank Durieux, & Ludo Dejeune (eds.) *English as a human language. To honor Louis Goossens*, 109-119. München: Lincolm Europa.

Depuydt, Leo 1993. *Conjunction, Contiguity, Contingency: On Relationships between Events in the Egyptian and Coptic Verbal Systems*. New York: Oxford University Press.

De Smet, Hendrik & Jean-Christophe Verstraete 2006. Coming to terms with subjectivity. *Cognitive Linguistics* 17: 365–392.

Diewald, Gabriele 1999. *Die Modalverben im Deutschen: Grammatikalisierung und Polyfunktionalität*. Tübingen: Niemeyer [Reihe Germanistische Linguistik 208].

Erb, Marie Christine 2001. Finite Auxiliaries in German. Ph.D.thesis, Katholieke Universiteit Brabant.

François, Alexandre 2003. *La sémantique du rédicat en Mwotlap (Vanuatu)*. Paris-Louvain: Peeters [Collection Linguistique de la Societe de Linguistique de Paris 84].

Fritz, Gerd 1997. Historische Semantik der Modalverben. Problemskizze – exemplarische Analysen – Forschungsüberblick. In: Gerd Fritz & Thomas Gloning (eds.) *Untersuchungen zur semantischen Entwicklungsgeschichte der Modalverben im Deutschen*, 1–157. Tübingen: Niemeyer.

Galand, Lionel 2003. L'aoriste berbere, l'aspect et les valeurs modales. In: Jérôme Lentin & Antoine Lonnet (eds.) *Mélanges David Cohen*, 235-246. Paris: Maisonneuve & Larose.

Gelderen, Elly van 2004. *Grammaticalization as economy*. Amsterdam: Benjamins.

—. 2009. Renewal in the left periphery: Economy and the complementizer layer. *Transactions of the Philological Society* 107/2: 131-195.

—. 2011. *The linguistic cycle. Language change and the language faculty*. Cambridge: Cambridge University Press.

Goossens, Louis 2000. Patterns of meaning extension, "parallel chaining", subjectification, and modal shifts. In: Antonio Barcelona (ed.), *Metaphor and Metonymy at the Crossroads: A Cognitive Perspective*, 149–169. Berlin: de Gruyter.

Haegeman, Liliane 2006 Conditionals, factives, and the left periphery. *Lingua* 116: 1651–1669.

Heine, Bernd & Kuteva, Tania. 2002. *World Lexicon of Grammaticalization.* Cambridge: Cambridge University Press.

Holl, Daniel 2010. *Modale Infinitive und dispositionelle Modalität im Deutschen.* Berlin: Akademie [Studia Grammatica 71].

Hopper, Paul and Elizabeth Traugott 1993/2003. *Grammaticalization.* Cambridge Cambridge Univ. Press.

Jakobson, Roman 1957/1971. Shifters, verbal categories, and the Russian verb. In: Jakobson, Roman: *Selected writings* 2, 130-147. The Hague: Mouton.

Kayne, Richard S. 1999. Prepositional complementizers as attractors. *Probus* 11: 39-73.

Kluge, Friedrich and Elmar Seebold 1989. *Etymologisches Wörterbuch der deutschen Sprache.* Berlin: W. de Gruyter.

Kotin, Michail L. 2008. *Zu den Affinitäten zwischen Modalität und Aspekt. Eine germanisch-slavische Fallstudie.* In: *Die Welt der Slaven.* Internationale Halbjahresschrift für Slavistik LIII, 1, 116-140.

—. 2012. *Gotisch – typologisch und im germanischen Sprachvergleich.* Winter: Heidelberg.

Kratzer, Angelika 1981. In: Hans-Jürgen Eikmeyer & Hannes Kieser (eds.) *Words, worlds, and contexts*, 38-74. Berlin: de Gruyter.

—. 1981 The notional category of modality. In: Hans-Jürgen Eikmeyer and Hannes Rieser (eds.), *Words, worlds, and contexts*, 38–74. Berlin: de Gruyter.

—. 1991 Modality. In: Arnim von Stechow & Dieter Wunderlich (eds.) *Semantik: Ein internationales Handbuch zeitgeno¨ssischer Forschung,* 639–650. Berlin/New York: de Gruyter.

Krug, Manfred G. 2000. *Emerging English modals. A corpus-based study of grammaticalization.* Berlin: de Gruyter.

Langacker, Ronald W. 1990. Subjectification. *Cognitive Linguistics* 1: 5-38.

—. 1998. On subjectification and grammaticalization. In: Jean-Pierre Koenig (ed.) *Discourse and Cognition: Bridging the Gap*, 71–89. Stanford: CSLI.

—. 1999. Losing control: grammaticization, subjectification, and transparency. In: Andreas Blank & Peter Koch (eds.), *Historical Semantics and Cognition*, 147–175. Berlin: de Gruyter.

Leiss, Elisabeth (1985): Zur Entstehung des neuhochdeutschen analytischen Futurs. *Sprachwissenschaft* 10: 250-273.

—. 2000. *Artikel und Aspekt. Die grammatischen Muster von Definitheit.* Berlin: de Gruyter [Studia Linguistica Germanica 55].

—. 2002. Explizite und implizite Kodierung von Deontizität und Epistemizität: Über die grammatische Musterbildung vor der Entstehung von Modalverben. *Jezikoslovlje* 3.1-2: 69-98.

—. 2008. The silent and aspect-driven patterns of deonticity and epistemicity. A chapter in diachronic typology. In: Werner Abraham & Elisabeth Leiss (eds.) *Modality-aspect interfaces – implications and typological solutions*, 15-41. [Typological Studies in Language 79]. Amsterdam: Benjamins

—. 2008 The silent and aspect-driven patterns of deonticity and epistemicity. A chapter in diachronic typology. In: Werner Abraham and Elisabeth Leiss (eds.), *Modality-aspect interfaces: Implications and typological solutions*, 15–42. (Typological Studies in Language 79.) Amsterdam: John Benjamins.

—. 2009 Drei Spielarten der Epistemizita¨ t, drei Spielarten der Evidentialität und drei Spielarten des Wissens. In: Werner Abraham and Elisabeth Leiss (eds.) *Modalität*, 3–24.

Lightfoot, David 1979. *Principles of diachronic syntax.* Cambridge: Cambridge University Press.

Lyons, John 1977. *Semantics*. Cambridge: Cambridge University Press.

—. 1982. Deixis and subjectivity. In: R. Jarvella & W. Klein (eds.). *Speech, Place and Action.* New York: Wiley, 101-124.

Narrog, Heiko. 2010. (Inter)subjectification in the domain of modality and mood. In: Kristin Davidse, Lieven Vandelanotte & Hubert Cuyckens (eds.). *Subjectification, Intersubjectification and Grammaticalization,* 385-429 Berlin: De Gruyter.

Maché, Jakob 2011. How modifiers become epistemic. Ms. Freie Universität Berlin.

Narrog, Heiko 1997. *-mas.u*: Die Grammatikalisierung von Höflichkeit. In: Ulrich Apel et al. (eds.) *Referate des 10. Deutschsprachigen Japanologentages vom 9. bis 12. Oktober 1996 in München*, 688–696. München: iudicium.

—. 2005. Modality, mood, and change of modal meanings – a new perspective. *Cognitive Linguistics* 16: 677–731.

—. 2007. Modality and grammaticalization in Japanese. *Journal of Historical Pragmatics* 8: 269–294.

—. 2010. (Inter)subjectification in the domain of modality and mood – Concepts and cross-linguistic realities. In: Kristin Davidse, Hubert Cuyckens, & Lieven Vandelanotte (eds.) *Grammaticalization, Subjectification, and* Intersubjectification, 385-430. Berlin: de Gruyter [Topics in English Linguistics 66].

Nordlinger, Rachel & Elizabeth Traugott. 1997. Scope and the development of epistemic modality: evidence from *ought to*. *English Language and Linguistics* 2: 295-317.Nübling, Damaris 2010. *Historische Sprachwissenschaft des Deutschen.* Tübingen: Narr.

Nuyts, Jan 2011. Talk on 'Subjectivization' held at the SLE Annual Meeting in Logroño, Spain. Sept. 2011.

—. 2012. Notions of (inter)subjectivity. *English Text Construction*, special issue on 'Intersubjectivity'.

Peirce, Charles S. 1871/1984. The Berkeley review: *Fraser*'s The work of George Berkeley. In: Peirce 1982-2000: Vol. 2 (1984), 461-487.

—. 1982-2000. *Writings of Charles S. Peirce. A chronological edition.* Vol. 1-6. Bloomington: Indiana University Press.

Plank, Frans 1984. The modals story retold. *Studies in Language* 8: 305–364.

Portner, Paul 2009. *Modality*. Oxford: Oxford University Press.

Prokosch, Eduard 1939. *A comparative Germanic grammar*. Philadelphia, Pa.: Linguistic Soc. of America.

Reintges, Chris 2010. Coordination, converbs and clause chaining in Coptic Egyptian typology and structural analysis. In: Isabelle Bril (ed.) *Clause Linking and Clause Hierarchy: Syntax and Pragmatics*, 203-266. Amsterdam: Benjamins [Studies in Language Companion Series 121].

Robert, Stéphane 1991. *Approche enonciative du système verbal: Le cas du Wolof.* Paris: CNRS [Sciences du Langage].

—. 1995. Aoristique et mode subordinatif: liens entre aspect et prédication. In: Janine Bouscaren, Jean-Jacques Franckel, & Stéphane Robert (eds.) *Langues et langage. Problèmes et raisonnément en linguistique (Mélanges offerts a Antoine Culioli)*, 373-389. Paris: Presses Universitaires de France [Linguistique Nouvelle].

—. 2010. Clause chaining and conjugations in Wolof. In: Isabelle Bril (ed.) *Clause Linking and Clause Hierarchy: Syntax and Pragmatics*, 469-498. Amsterdam: Benjamins [Studies in Language Companion Series 121].

Rothstein, Björn & Rolf Thieroff (eds.) 2010. *Mood in the languages of Europe.* Amsterdam: Benjamins [Studies in Language Companion Series 120].

Rumsey, Alan 2003. Language, desire and the ontogenesis of intersubjectivity. *Language and Communication* 23: 169–187.

Simon, Horst J. 2003a. *Für eine grammatische Kategorie „Respekt" im Deutschen. Synchronie, Diachronie und Typologie der deutschen Anredepronomina.* Tübingen: Niemeyer.

—. 2003b. From pragmatics to grammar. Tracing the development of respect in the history of the German pronouns of address. In: Irma Taavitsainen & Andreas H. Junker (eds.) *Diachronic perspectives on address term systems*, 85-123. Amsterdam: Benjamins.

Streitberg, Wilhelm 1910. *Gotisches Elementarbuch*. Heidelberg: Winter.

—. 2000. *Die gotische Bibel.* Band 2: *Gotisch-Griechisch-Deutsches Wörterbuch.* Heidelberg: Winter.

Sweetser, Eve 1982. Root and epistemic modals: causality in two worlds. In: Monica Macaulay, Orin D. Gensler, et al. (eds.) *Proceedings of the eighth Annual Meeting of the Berkeley Linguistics Society*, 484–507. Berkeley, CA: Berkeley Linguistics Society.

—. 1990. *From Etymology to Pragmatics: Metaphorical and Cultural Aspects of Semantic Structure*. Cambridge: Cambridge University Press.

Taine-Cheikh, Catherine 2010. The role of the Berber deictic and TAM markers in dependent clauses in Zenaga. In: Isabelle Bril (ed.) *Clause Linking and Clause Hierarchy: Syntax and Pragmatics,* 355-398. Amsterdam: Benjamins [Studies in Language Companion Series 121].

Talmy, Leonard 1988. Force dynamics in language and cognition. *Cognitive Science* 12: 49–100.

Tanaka, Shin 2011. *Deixis und Anaphorik. Referenzstrategien in Text, Satz und Wort.* Berlin: de Gruyter [Linguistik - Impulse – Tendenzen 42].

Traugott, Elizabeth Closs 1989. On the rise of epistemic meanings in English: an example of subjectification in semantic change. *Language* 65: 31–55.

—. 1995. Subjectification in grammaticalization. In: Dieter Stein & Susan Wright (eds.) *Subjectivity and Subjectivisation: Linguistic Perspectives,* 31–54. Cambridge: Cambridge University Press.

—. 2003. From subjectification to intersubjectification. In: Raymond Hickey (ed.) *Motives for Language Change*, 124–139. Cambridge: Cambridge University Press.

—. 2010. (Inter)subjectivity and (inter)subjectification: A reassessment. In: Kristin Davidse, Hubert Cuyckens, & Lieven Vandelanotte (eds.) *Grammaticalization, Subjectification and Intersubjectification,* 29-71. Berlin: de Gruyter [Topics in English Linguistics 66].

—. 2010. In: Kristin Davidse, Hubert Cuyckens & Lieven Vandelanotte (eds.) *Grammaticalization, Subjectification and Intersubjectification,* 29-71. [Topics in English Linguistics]. Berlin: Mouton de Gruyter.

Traugott, Elizabeth Closs & Richard Dasher 2002. *Regularity in Semantic Change*. Cambridge: Cambridge University Press.

Wright, G. Henrik von 1974. *Erklären und Verstehen*. Frankfurt/M.: Athenäum.

Ziegeler, Debra 2010. Semantic determinism and the grammaticalization of *have to* in English. A reassessment. *Journal of Historical Pragmatics* 11/1: 32-66.

NOTES ON OVERT AND COVERT MODALITY IN ITALIAN AND ROMANIAN

MARCO CONIGLIO AND IULIA ZEGREAN
HUMBOLDT-UNIVERSITÄT ZU BERLIN
AND UNIVERSITY OF VENICE

Abstract: In this paper, we discuss two patterns of modality in Italian and Romanian. Firstly, we will concentrate on one case of overt modality, namely discourse particles. It is a well-known fact that discourse particles can occur in main clauses, but also in certain subtypes of subordinate clauses, namely in embedded contexts which may have independent illocutionary force. The possibility of licensing discourse particles will be taken as a test for distinguishing root-like from true embedded structures. Secondly, we will discuss some cases of covert modality in the two languages. Modality can be interpreted even in the absence of overt lexical material (cf. Bhatt 1999, Abraham (this volume)). Focusing on data from Italian and Romanian, we will show that the two patterns of modality are incompatible with each other. This will be taken as evidence that the types of clauses that display covert modality do not have independent illocutionary force.

1. Introduction

Cross-linguistically, we observe two distinct patterns of modality, namely overt and covert. The most studied one is clearly the former, where modality is made explicit by means of lexical material, such as modal verbs (1), modal/discourse particles (see (3) below), etc.

(1) The book that *must* be read is on the table.

More generally, each language has an inventory of lexical elements expressing modality. Needless to say that there is a vast amount of literature on this topic (cf. Abraham & Leiss 2009 for an overview).

In contrast, the pattern of covert modality has been object of particular attention only in recent years. In his pioneering work, Bhatt (1999) shows that modality can be retrieved and interpreted even in the absence of overt lexical material. For instance, this is the case of infinitival relatives, infinitival questions, and so on (cf. Bhatt 1999:1f). The following example from English illustrates that a modal interpretation, which –in (1)– was due to the modal verb, can be obtained without any modal word being present (cf. Abraham & Leiss, this volume):

(2) The book *to read* is on the table. (= The book that *must* be read is on the table.)

Infinitives are often associated with modal interpretation, not only in English but also in other languages (cf. Jedrzejowski, this volume, for Polish in diachrony, Simik 2011 for Czech).

In this paper, we will provide some patterns of overt and covert modality in two Romance languages, namely Italian and Romanian, and discuss some related syntactic aspects.[1] In particular, we will address two main issues. We will first consider an example of overt modality in the two languages, namely the case of discourse particles (DiscPrts, henceforth).[2] As was shown for other languages as well (German, for instance; cf. Coniglio 2011), we will claim that Italian and Romanian DiscPrts are to be considered modifiers of illocutionary force and can only occur in syntactic contexts which are endowed with such force.

We will then address a second point, namely the issue of covert modality in a cartographic framework. We will discuss some consequences of Bhatt's (1999) approach, who sometimes seems to suggest that some types of the clauses he considers as encoding modality covertly have a full-fledged left periphery. It will be argued that the impossibility for DiscPrts to occur in Bhatt's contexts is a piece of evidence that such clauses never have illocutionary force and are to be taken as syntactically deficient.

---

[1] However, we will sometimes make use of examples from German and English, respectively, given the vast amount of literature on this topic in the two languages.

[2] Notice that, in our view, discourse/modal particles pertain to modality, since the latter can be instantiated – among others – by means of "Ausdrücke der Sprechereinstellung" ('expressions of the speaker's attitude'), as proposed by Meibauer (1994:11f), based on Kiefer (1987), Bierwisch (1980) and Kratzer (1981).

In this paper, we will use the term 'discourse particles' (DiscPrts) to refer in general to both (clause-integrated) CP- and IP-particles. Following the tradition of studies on German, the term 'modal particles' (MPs) will be used only for particles occurring in the IP.

2. Discourse particles as evidence for illocutionary force

Let us consider the first issue, namely the link between the presence of DiscPrts in a clause and its the illocutionary potential. It is a well established fact that DiscPrts are used to express the speaker's attitude or opinion with respect to a proposition (see, for instance, Thurmair 1989, Abraham 2009; see also Haumann & Letnes, this volume, and Modicom, this volume). Consider the following example for German:

(3) Er kann *ja* schon sprechen.
he can PRT already speak
'He can already speak (it is evident / as you know).'

In (3), the speaker uses the particle *ja* to emphasize that the propositional content of the utterance is evident and potentially known to the addressee (cf. Thurmair 1989:200). On the one hand, she utters a proposition ('he can already speak'), on the other hand she adds her attitude or opinion with respect to this proposition and her estimate of the hearer's state of knowledge ('you should know that, since it is evident or straightforward').

From a cognitive point of view, DiscPrts convey (at least) threefold information,[3] namely about:

1) the source of the information;
2) the speaker's assessment of this information;
3) the speaker's estimate of the hearer's state of knowledge.

Therefore, DiscPrts must have access to the illocutionary force of the clause, i.e. to the speaker's intention when uttering a sentence (cf. Austin 1962, Searle 1975).[4] They must be anchored to the speaker as the "author" of a certain speech act and thus they interact with the illocution. In particular, it has been observed that the function of these words is that of modifying the illocutionary force of the clause (Jacobs 1986, 1991, Doherty 1987, Thurmair 1989, Abraham 1991, Zimmermann 2004a,b, etc.).

[3] This idea is taken from Abraham (2009) and Leiss (2009). Based on Diewald's (1999) concept of *double deixis*, they analyze MPs as modal words displaying a *triple deixis*.

[4] For instance, Searle (1975) distinguishes the following main categories of speech acts: assertives, directives, commissives, expressives, and declarations.

In order to understand how this takes place, let us consider the following example from German (taken from Coniglio & Zegrean 2010:12):

(4) Ruf die Polizei!
'Call the police!'
a. Ruf *halt* die Polizei!
b. Ruf *mal* die Polizei!
c. Ruf *doch* die Polizei!
d. Ruf *JA* die Polizei!
bloß, *nur*, etc.

↓ cogent order

The (basic) sentence in (4) German is an imperative clause and has the typical illocutionary force of an order. In German, there are a number of particles which are compatible with the imperative clause type, such as *halt*, *mal*, *doch*, etc. If we insert a MP in (4), we obtain different nuances of the same order. In the examples, we assumed that the order becomes more cogent according to the particle used (*halt*, *mal*, *doch*, *JA*, etc.). This description of the facts may be somehow simplistic, but nonetheless we observe that the illocutionary force is slightly different in each case. So, for instance, we interpret (4b) as a suggestion, and (4d) as a strong order.

The great number of MPs in German allows for a fine-grained nuancing of illocutionary force. As was observed by Jacobs (1986, 1991), we could argue that the functions of particles is that of taking on the illocutionary force of a given clause (X) and of turning it into a different, more precisely specified illocutionary force (X'). This could be represented as follows (cf. Coniglio & Zegrean 2010:13):

(5) X + PRT = X' (where X stands for illocutionary force)

Since DiscPrts modify illocutionary force, it is logical to conclude that they only appear in clauses endowed with such force (cf. Jacobs 1986, 1991, Doherty 1987, Thurmair 1989, Coniglio 2008, 2011, Abraham 1991, 2009, 2012). This can be shown not only from a pragmatic but also from a syntactic point of view.

In the following part, we will briefly consider some syntactic arguments coming from the distribution of DiscPrts in main and embedded clauses, i.e. we will show that DiscPrts are main clause phenomena (in the sense of Emonds 1970) and that they can only occur in clauses that can be proven to have illocutionary force on independent grounds (cf. Coniglio 2007c, 2009, 2011, Abraham 2009, 2012, Coniglio & Zegrean 2010).

2.1 Discourse particles in the cartography of the clause

2.1.1 Discourse particles in main clauses

We will first consider the distribution of DiscPrts in main clauses. Since these types of clauses are endowed with illocutionary force by definition, we expect that they can license DiscPrts. And this is indeed what we observe both in Italian and Romanian. CP and IP particles are probably attested in both languages although there is no systematic literature on this topic as there is for German, for instance.[5] Let us consider each language separately.

As for Italian, it has been pointed out that this language has IP particles of the type we find in German. Among others, the existence of MPs in Italian has been claimed by Burkhardt (1985), Radtke (1985), Held (1985), Coniglio (2008, 2011), and Cardinaletti (2011). Some examples of this kind of particles are *mai*, *poi*, *pure*, etc. (when used in their particle function).[6] Consider the following example, where *pure* occurs in the IP of the clause:

(6) Chiama *pure* la polizia!
call PRT the police
'Call the police! (if you feel like it)'

Furthermore, there is evidence that Italian also displays a small inventory of CP particles, such as certain uses of *almeno*, *magari*, *proprio*, etc. (also cf. Bazzanella 1995, Bonvino, Frascarelli & Pietrandrea 2008, Coniglio & Zegrean 2010). But there is no systematic work dedicated to the syntactic properties of these types of discourse elements.

---

[5] Cross-linguistically, DiscPrts appear (also cf. Del Gobbo & Poletto 2008):

1. in the IP, such as in Italian (Burkhardt 1985, Radtke 1985, Held 1985, Coniglio 2008, Cardinaletti 2009), German (Coniglio 2005, 2007a,b), Romanian (Coniglio & Zegrean 2010), etc.
2. in the CP, such as in Italian (Burkhardt 1985, Radtke 1985, Held 1985, Coniglio & Zegrean 2010), Romanian (Coniglio & Zegrean 2010), Cantonese (Law 2002), Veneto dialects (Munaro & Poletto 2004), etc.

[6] Notice that DiscPrts are usually polyfunctional words. For instance, all the elements mentioned for Italian also have other adverbial uses. Therefore, our observations do not refer to all occurrences of these words, but only to their particle uses.

With regard to Romanian, there is hardly any syntactic literature on this topic.[7] Coniglio & Zegrean (2010) show that Romanian displays both CP and IP particles. Some examples of particles which occur in both the CP and in the IP are *doar*, *chiar*, *numai*, *măcar*, *barem*, *tocmai*:

(7) De mâine cineva va veni *doar* cu o soluţie
from tomorrow somebody will.3SG come.up PRT with a solution
'From tomorrow on somebody will (evidently) come up with a solution.'

As mentioned earlier for Italian, Romanian too has particles which can only occur in the CP, such as *oare*, and possibly *or*, *păi*, and *apoi* (Coniglio & Zegrean 2010):

(8) *Oare* şi maşina şi -a vândut -o Ion până la urmă?
PRT also car-ART REFL have.3SG sold -it Ion until at end
'Has Ion sold his car, too, in the end (I wonder)?'

Now, if we consider the distinction between IP and CP particles in the two languages, we can observe that DiscPrts do not occur randomly in the clause. Particles of the I-type have to occur in the highest projections of Cinque's (1999) hierarchy of the functional projections of the clause. CP particles also seem to occur only in between certain projections of Rizzi's (1997, 2001) articulated left periphery (see below).

As was shown in Coniglio (2005, 2008, 2011) and Coniglio & Zegrean (2010), German, Italian, and Romanian MPs occupy the highest projections in Cinque's (1999) functional structure of the IP. Let us consider Cinque's (1999) hierarchy of functional projections:

---

[7] See, however, Thun (1984) for an interesting comparison between German and Romanian DiscPrts, mainly based on their semantic-pragmatic properties. Also see Hill (2002), who analyses *oare* as an "optional complementizer" in Fin°; Manoliu Manea (1985), who considers *chiar* as an 'insinuating particle'; Manoliu Manea (1993) for *doar* as an element negating expectations; and Hill (2007) about the distinction between particles of 'direct' and 'indirect address'.

(9) The universal hierarchy of clausal functional projections (Cinque 1999:106):

[*frankly* Mood$_{\text{speech act}}$ [*fortunately* Mood$_{\text{evaluative}}$
[*allegedly* Mood$_{\text{evidential}}$ [*probably* Mod$_{\text{epistemic}}$ [*once* T(Past)
[*then* T(Future) [*perhaps* Mood$_{\text{irrealis}}$ [*necessarily* Mod$_{\text{necessity}}$
[*possibly* Mod$_{\text{possibility}}$ [*usually* Asp$_{\text{habitual}}$ [*again* Asp$_{\text{repetitive(I)}}$
[*often* Asp$_{\text{frequentative(I)}}$ [*intentionally* Mod$_{\text{volitional}}$ [*quickly* Asp$_{\text{celerative(I)}}$
[*already* T(Anterior) [*no longer* Asp$_{\text{terminative}}$ [*still* Asp$_{\text{continuative}}$
[*always* Asp$_{\text{perfect(?)}}$ [*just* Asp$_{\text{retrospective}}$ [*soon* Asp$_{\text{proximative}}$
[*briefly* Asp$_{\text{durative}}$ [*characteristically(?)* Asp$_{\text{generic/progressive}}$
[*almost* Asp$_{\text{prospective}}$ [*completely* Asp$_{\text{SgCompletive(I)}}$ [*tutto* Asp$_{\text{PlCompletive}}$
[*well* Voice [*fast/early* Asp$_{\text{celerative(II)}}$ [*again* Asp$_{\text{repetitive(II)}}$
[*often* Asp$_{\text{frequentative(II)}}$ [*completely* Asp$_{\text{completive(II)}}$

By testing the positions which MPs can occupy with respect to the adverbial classes considered by Cinque (1999), we can conclude that MPs do not occupy a fixed position in the articulated structure of the IP. In particular, they may occupy one (or more) positions in between the group of Cinque's (1999) 'higher' adverbs, as illustrated in (10) and exemplified in (11) for German and in (12) for the Italian particle *poi*. Crucially, they cannot occur lower than the base position of the higher class of repetitive adverbs (cf. Coniglio 2005, 2007a,b):

(10) Positions accessible to MPs (Coniglio 2008:100)
(√) > Mood$_{\text{speech act}}$ > (√) > Mood$_{\text{evaluative}}$ > (√) > Mood$_{\text{evidential}}$ >
(√) > Mod$_{\text{epistemic}}$ > (√) > T(Past) > (√) > T(Future) >
(√) > Mood$_{\text{irrealis}}$ > (√) > Mod$_{\text{necessity}}$ > (√) > Mod$_{\text{possibility}}$ >
(√) > Asp$_{\text{habitual}}$ > √ > Asp$_{\text{repetitive(I)}}$ > * > Asp$_{\text{frequentative(I)}}$ > * > ...

(11) Der Attentäter ist ... von der Polizei festgehalten worden.
the assassin is by the police detained been

a.	... *<ja>*	glücklicherweise	*<ja>* ...	Mood$_{\text{evaluative}}$	*fortunately*
b.	... *<ja>*	damals	*<ja>* ...	T(Past)	*then*
c.	... *<ja>*	normalerweise	*<ja>* ...	Asp$_{\text{habitual}}$	*usually*
d.	... *<ja>*	nochmals	**<ja>* ...	Asp$_{\text{repetitive(I)}}$	*again*

Coniglio (2008:100)

(12) a. Non era *<poi>* francamente *<poi>* così male.
b. Non era *<poi>* allora *<poi>* così male.
c. Non era *<poi>* di solito *<poi>* così male.

d. Non era <*poi*> di nuovo <**poi*> così male.
e. Non era <*poi*> spesso <**poi*> così male.
not it.was PRT frankly/then/usually/again/often PRT so bad
(Coniglio 2008:114)

With respect to the merging position of CP particles in Italian and Romanian, it must be pointed out that further research is necessary. For instance, it has not yet been determined which positions they can occupy in an articulated structure of the left periphery *à la* Rizzi (1997). Nonetheless, based on Frascarelli & Hinterhölzl's (2007) hypothesis of different positions for topicalized constituents, first spot tests have shown that – though judgments are subtle – Italian and Romanian CP particles appear to obligatorily precede FamiliarTopic (and probably also ContrastiveTopic) (13). However, they cannot occur higher than ShiftingTopic (14). The following contrast illustrates the position in the CP of the Romanian particle *doar*:

(13) *Doar* băiatul cine mi l-a văzut?
PRT boy-ART who to.me him-have.3SG seen
'(I say,) who has seen my boy?'

(14) <**Doar*> Băiatul, <*doar*> nimeni nu l-a văzut.
PRT boy-ART PRT nobody not him.CL-have.3SG seen
'As for the boy, (obviously) nobody has seen him'.

But let us now turn our attention to another important property of DiscPrts, namely their distribution in subordinate clauses, which will be shown to be revealing of the presence of illocutionary force in the sentences where they occur.

2.1.2 Discourse particles as embedded root phenomena: accounting for the distributional facts

Independent syntactic evidence for postulating a link between particles and illocutionary force comes from the distribution of DiscPrts in subordinate clauses. In particular, it has often been claimed that DiscPrts only appear in those subordinate clauses that are endowed with root properties and with illocutionary force (Jacobs 1986, 1991, Doherty 1987, Thurmair 1989, Abraham 1991, 2009, 2012, Coniglio 2008, 2011). Let us consider the contrast in (15) and (16) for Italian:

(15) Se Gianni ha (*pur) detto che non verrà,
if Gianni have.3SG PRT said that NEG come.FUT.3SG

allora non verrà.
then NEG come.FUT.3SG

'If Gianni said that he won't come, then he won't come.'

(16) Se Gianni – come dici – ha *pur* detto che
if Gianni as say.2SG have.3SG PRT said that

non verrà, perché allora ha prenotato l'hotel?
NEG come.FUT.3SG why then have.3SG booked ART-hotel
'If Gianni – as you say – said that he won't come, then why did he book the hotel?' (Coniglio 2008:117f)

The particle *pur* is grammatical in the conditional in (16), but not in (15). As will be argued below, while the first type of adverbial (what Haegeman 2002 calls 'peripheral adverbial') has root properties, the latter type ('central adverbial') does not. Crucially, the distribution of the particle correlates with these specific clausal properties.

Notice that similar observations can be made for Romanian as well (cf. Coniglio & Zegrean 2010:24f):

(17) Cu Ioana am vorbit la telefon mai devreme,
with Ioana have.1SG talked at phone more early

în timp ce *oare* Maria a telefonat azi?
while PRT Maria have.3SG called today?

'I talked to Ioana earlier on the phone, (while) has Mary called today (I wonder)?'

(18) Nu l -am mai vazut de-atunci pe Ion, căruia
not him -have.1SG more seen since Ion_{ACC}, who_{DAT}

doar i -am spus să treacă pe-aici când vrea.
PRT $\text{he}_{\text{CL.DAT}}$ have.1SG told SUBJ pass.by here when wants

'I haven't seen John since then, to whom I DID tell to pass by whenever he wanted.'

(19) Nu l -am mai vazut de-atunci pe băiatul căruia
not him_{CL} -have.1SG more seen since boy-ART_{ACC} who_{DAT}

(*doar*) i -am spus să treacă pe-aici când vrea.
PRT $he_{CL.DAT}$ -have1SG told SUBJ pass.by here when wants

'Since then, I haven't seen the boy to whom I DID tell to pass by whenever he wanted.' (Coniglio & Zegrean 2010:24f)

The interrogative particle *oare* can appear in an (interrogative) contrastive clause such as (17), which is syntactically independent from its matrix clause, as proved by their different illocutionary force. Furthermore, in (18) and in (19), we observe a clear contrast with respect to the distribution of *doar* in appositive and restrictive relatives. Only the appositive relative in (18) has root properties and can thus license the particle.

Now, the question arises as to how the two types of subordinate clauses differ from each other. Based on their different syntactic properties with respect to the matrix clause, Haegeman (2002, 2004a,b, 2006) distinguishes between central adverbials on the one hand, which are embedded in the main clause, and peripheral adverbials on the other, which are to be considered as somehow independent from the matrix clause.

The case of central adverbials is represented in (20). Here, the event described in the central adverbial directly modifies the event in the matrix clause and is syntactically merged inside the IP of the latter:

(20) Central adverbials (Haegeman 2002:131) (event-related)
E.g.: I think that John will buy the book if he finds it.

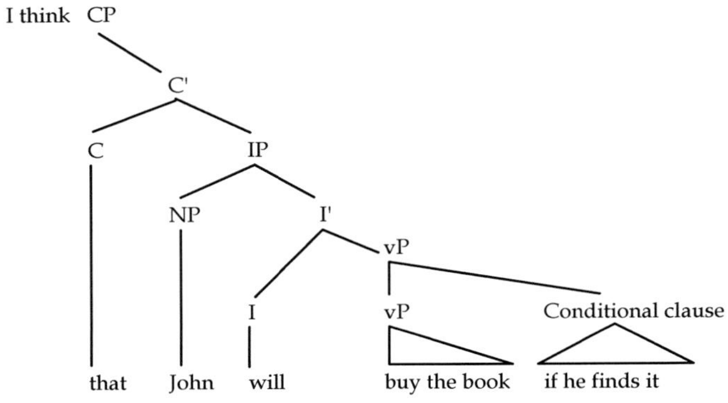

Crucially, peripheral clauses are characterized by their different merging point with respect to that of central adverbials. In (21), we see that the event in the subordinate clause does not directly modify the event in the matrix clause and is not part of it. The subordinate clause is merged to the main clause only after the CP of the latter has been projected. Therefore, there is only a discourse relation between the two clauses:

(21) Peripheral adverbials (Haegeman 2002:132) (discourse-related)
E.g.: If he *probably* won't be in this afternoon, I won't wait for him.
Haegeman (2006:1652)

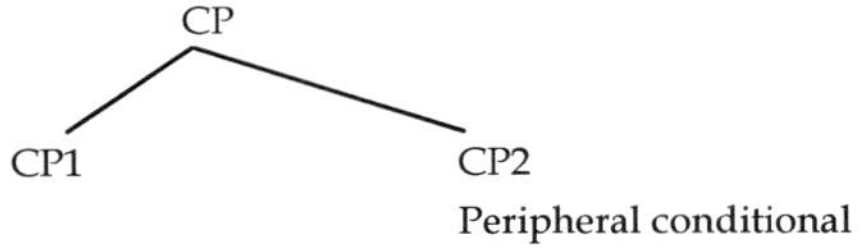

For reasons of space, we cannot consider Haegeman's arguments in detail. Here we must refer to her work for further clarification.

An important aspect of her analysis is that central clauses are more integrated into the matrix clause because their left periphery has a less articulated structure. In contrast, peripheral subordinates are less integrated (or not integrated at all) because they project the whole structure of the CP layer (cf. Rizzi 1997), thus resisting full integration. This is represented in (22). As was shown by Haegeman (2002, 2004a,b, 2006) by means of syntactic tests, peripheral clauses display projections for illocutionary force and for topics and focussed constituents:

(22)	a	Central adverbials:	Sub				Mod*	Fin
	b	Peripheral adverbials:	Sub	**Force**	Top*	Focus	Mod*	Fin
	c	Root clauses:		**Force**	Top*	Focus	Mod*	Fin

Haegeman (2002:159)

The fundamental difference between central and peripheral clauses consists in the presence or absence of the syntactic projection ForceP. According to Haegeman, the head Force encodes information necessary for anchoring the utterance to the speaker (and therefore it also serves to license independent temporal reference, epistemic modality, topicalisation, markers of illocutionary force, etc.) (cf. also Roussou 2000).

If we apply Haegeman's hypothesis of a different internal syntax of subordinate clauses to complement clauses and to relatives, we obtain the following picture:

(23) The left periphery of embedded clauses (taken from Coniglio 2008:105):

Complement clauses	non-factive complements	full
	factive complements	reduced
Adverbial clauses	peripheral adverbials	full
	central adverbials	reduced
Relative clauses	appositive relatives	full
	restrictive relatives	reduced

While subordinate clauses with a reduced structure do not display the full structure of the CP, their full counterparts are assumed to have the whole articulated periphery and in particular a projection for illocutionary force.

Now, we pointed out above that DiscPrts are considered as modifiers of illocutionary force. By considering their distribution with respect to the properties of the left periphery of subordinate clauses, one would expect for them to occur only in those types of clauses that have a fully articulated left periphery. Only full-fledged subordinates are assumed to be endowed with illocutionary force. As was shown for German MPs in Coniglio (2007c, 2011), this expectation is borne out by facts (also cf. Coniglio & Zegrean 2010 on Italian and Romanian DiscPrts in general):[8]

(24) Distribution of German MPs in root and embedded clauses (Coniglio 2007c:27)

Clause types	**MPs**
Embedded clauses with a reduced CP	-
Embedded clauses with a full CP	+
Root clauses	+

Now, if we consider in (23) the types of clauses which are assumed to have a projection ForceP, and if we compare these with the distribution of DiscPrts in (24), we come to the conclusion that the postulated link between DiscPrts and Force is also syntactically justified: DiscPrts only occur in clauses endowed with illocutionary force.

Following a proposal by Abraham (1991), Coniglio (2007c, 2011) explored the syntactic link between MPs and the left periphery of the clause (also cf. Haumann & Letnes, this volume). In particular, by exploiting a similar mechanism of syntactic linking recently proposed by

[8] For instance, this was shown for Italian by means of the contrast between (15) and (16) above.

Bayer (2012) for the German particle *denn*, Coniglio (2011) further extended such an analysis to all German MPs:

(25) Agree relation between MPs and Force°:

a. $\text{Force}^{\circ}_{\langle\text{Speaker}\rangle} \ldots [_{\text{IP}} \ldots \text{MP}_{\langle\text{uSpeaker, illocut. feat.}\rangle} \ldots [_{\text{VP}} \ldots]]$

AGREE ⟶

b. $\text{Force}^{\circ}_{\langle\text{Speaker, illocut. feat.}\rangle} \ldots [_{\text{IP}} \ldots \text{MP}_{\langle\cancel{\text{u}}\text{Speaker, }\cancel{\text{illocut. feat.}}\rangle} \ldots [_{\text{VP}} \ldots]]$

MPs have, according to Coniglio (2010), two kinds of features: one related to the Speaker and one related to their function as modifiers of illocutionary force. When checking their uninterpretable feature [uSpeaker] by means of the interpretable counterpart in Force°, they transfer their feature related to illocutionary force to the left periphery. This syntactic mechanism would explain how MPs may modify illocutionary force. Such an Agree-mechanism could be postulated for all types of DiscPrts (not only for IP-particles). For instance, this was already shown in Coniglio & Zegrean (2010) for Romanian and Italian particles.

We will now turn our attention to considering the possible distribution of DiscPrts in patterns of covert modality in Italian and Romanian. But before moving to covert modality, let us summarize the results so far. In the previous sections, we have argued that:

- Italian and Romanian DiscPrts are embedded root phenomena, i.e. they are characterized by the property of being able to occur only in clauses endowed with illocutionary force (Jacobs 1986, 1991, Doherty 1987, Abraham 1991, 2009, 2012, Coniglio 2008, 2011).

- DiscPrts are therefore undisputable criteria for identifying the presence of illocutionary force in a clause (Coniglio 2011).

- Illocutionary force is represented in the clause structure in ForceP, which is projected in all root-like clauses (main and peripheral subordinates in the sense of Haegeman 2002 and further work).

3. Covert modality

In what follows, we intend to prove that the contexts where modality can be interpreted as covert are not associated with an extended left periphery. We will do this by means of the test we have discussed so far, namely the presence *vs.* absence of DiscPrts. A cartographic view of the functional structure of the clause supports the hypothesis that such contexts are impaired as far as their left periphery is concerned.

Covert modality is modality which is interpreted although it is not associated with any lexical item in the structure. Bhatt (1999) investigates the distribution and interpretation of covert modality in two main contexts in which it appears: infinitival questions and non-subject infinitival relative clauses (see (26)-(27)), correlating this phenomenon with a difference in their structure with respect to subject infinitival relatives, which may or may not encode modality (cf. (28) in contrast with (29), respectively).[9] Other environments which display covert modality are exemplified in (30)-(32) (Bhatt 1999:1f).

(26) Tim knows [how to solve the problem].
(= Tim knows how one / he could / should solve the problem.)
wh-infinitival question complement

(27) Jane found [a book to draw cartoons in] for Sara.
(= Jane found a book for Sara one could/should draw cartoons in.)
non-subject infinitival relative

(28) [The man to fix the sink] is here.
(= The man whose purpose is to fix the sink is here.)
subject infinitival relative

(29) The [first man [to walk on the moon]] visited my school yesterday.
subject infinitival relative (Bhatt 1999:9, 3)

(30) Sue went to Torino [to buy a violin].
(= Sue went to Torino so that she could buy a violin.)
purpose clause

(31) Bill has to reach Philadelphia before noon.
(= Bill must reach Philadelphia before noon.)
have to *construction*

(32) Will is to leave tomorrow.
(= Will is scheduled / supposed to leave tomorrow.)
is to *construction*

[9] A third environment Bhatt (1999) analyses are (covert) ability modals, e.g. *This machine peels fifty oranges in an hour* (Bhatt 1999:8). We will not be concerned with these types of modals in this paper.

The main questions that Bhatt (1999) addresses in his investigation of infinitival relatives and infinitival questions are the following:[10] why are some but not all infinitival relatives modal? Why are all infinitival questions modal? What type of modality is it and what is it source? In this paper, we will not be concerned with these aspects. What we will question though is the implications of what Bhatt considers to be the locus of modality, as briefly described in the next section.

3.1 Bhatt (1999) and some cartographic implications

For Bhatt (1999), subject infinitival relatives (e.g. *the man to fix the sink*) (henceforth SiRs) differ structurally from non-subject infinitival relatives (e.g. *the book to read*) (non-SiRs). Importantly, non-modal readings are only possible with SiRs (cf. also Kjellmer 1975, Geisler 1995).

(33) a. This is [the best book __ to appear until now (on this topic)].
(non-modal, subject gap)
b. This is [the best book to read __]. (modal, object gap)
(Bhatt 1999:40, 62)

Specifically, SiRs are assimilated structurally to reduced relatives. The properties that indicate that SiRs are reduced are given below (Bhatt 1999:9f):

(i) the relativized element is always in subject position,
(ii) the subject position does not receive case,
(iii) the relativization is very local – only the matrix subject can be relativized,
(iv) the clausal structure that functions as a reduced relative can appear as the complement of predicative *be,*
(v) no complementizer is permitted,
(vi) no relative pronoun is permitted.

In Bhatt's analysis, SiRs do not have a CP projection (thus there is no A'-movement to Spec,CP for predicate formation). The left periphery is reduced, hence – according to Haegeman's (2002) analysis – we would expect that these environments have no illocutionary force and that they

[10] The *have to* construction is discussed in Bhatt (1997) and in Abraham (this volume).

do not allow for main clause phenomena, among which DiscPrts (see § 3.3.1 below).[11]

On the other hand, non-SiRs and infinitival questions are assimilated to full relatives: according to Bhatt, they involve a CP projection (and a relative Op undergoes A'-movement to Spec,CP). Of particular relevance to our point is that Bhatt identifies the infinitival [+rel/wh] C° as the locus of modality. This would wrongly lead us to the conclusion that these types of clauses have illocutionary force. However, in the following sections we will show that this intuition is not supported by the distribution of DiscPrts.

3.2 Covert modality in Italian and Romanian

In what follows, we attempt to replicate the patterns of covert modality that Bhatt (1999) identified for English in the two Romance languages we treat in this paper. The examples in (32)-(35) and (36)-(42) illustrate the environments for Italian and for Romanian, respectively.[12]

(34) Gianni sa come risolvere il problema.
Gianni knows how to.solve the problem
'Gianni knows how he can / could / should solve the problem.'
wh-infinitival question complement

(35) Il libro da leggere è sul tavolo.
the book PREP to.read is on-the table.
'The book to read is on the table.'
non-subject infinitival relative

(36) Gianni ha molti amici con cui uscire.
Gianni has many friends with whom to.go.out
'Gianni has many friends with which he can / could go out.'
non-subject wh-infinitival relative

---

[11] Bhatt (1999:4) suggests that "The modality in the subject infinitival relative *The book to be read for class* has the same source as the modality in *The book is to be read for class*. This source is internal to the infinitival clause; it is independent of the appearance of the infinitival clause as part of a (reduced) relative clause." See Ch. 2 of Bhatt (1999).

[12] In Italian, the *have to* is antiquated or regional, while the *is to* construction is not available.

(37) Gianni è andato a Torino per/a comprare un violino.
Gianni is gone to Turin for/to to.buy a violin
'Gianni went to Turin to buy a violin.' *purpose clause*

In Romanian, most of the infinitival constructions with modal interpretation cannot be reproduced, since the use of the infinitive in this language has undergone a drastic reduction, like in other Balkan languages. Thus, a finite mood (subjunctive) is used instead. Importantly, the subjunctive mood is typical for central embedded clauses (thus, in such contexts that do not allow DiscPrts, see § 3.3.1).[13]

(38) Ion ştie cum să rezolve exerciţiul.
Ion knows how SUBJ solve.3SG exercise-the
'Ion knows how he can/could/should solve the exercise.'
wh-infinitival question complement

(39) Ion are mulţi prieteni cu care să iasă.
Ion has many friends with whom SUBJ go.out.3SG
'Ion has many friends with which he can/could go out.'
(non-subject) subjunctive relative[14]

(40) Ion a sunat (ca) să alfe noutăţile.
Ion has called (that) SUBJ find.out.3SG news-the
'Ion called so that he could find out the news.'
subjunctive purpose clause

(41) Ion a sunat pentru a alfa noutăţile.
Ion has called for to find.out news-the
'Ion called so that he could find out the news.'
infinitival purpose clause

---

[13] We disregard here root clauses in which the subjunctive has an imperative value:
i. Să vii aici!
SUBJ come.2SG here
'Come here!'

[14] The impersonal construction with *se* can also appear in these clause types, the interpretation of which would still be modal (non-epistemic, in particular):
i. Ion ştie cum se rezolvă exerciţiul. *wh complement*
Ion knows how SE solve.3SG exercise-the
'Ion knows how one can/could/should solve the exercise.'
ii. Ion deţine multe instrumente cu care se cântă. *relative clause*
Ion owns many instruments with which SE play.3SG
'Ion owns many instruments which one plays.'

(42) Ion are de citit multe cărţi.
Ion has SUP read many books
'Ion must read many books.'

have + supine (non finite)[15]

(43) Ion are de plecat mâine dimineaţă.
Ion has SUP left tomorrow morning
'Ion is scheduled/supposed to leave tomorrow morning.'

have + supine (non finite)

(44) E de lucrat mult la acest aspect.
is SUP worked a.lot at this aspect
'It needs to be worked a lot on this aspect.'

be + supine

The sets of data above show that in Italian, just like in English, the contexts where covert modality can be retrieved are all of the infinitival type, while in Romanian the only infinitival construction is the purpose clause (introduced by *for*). All other clauses that receive a modal interpretation are either non-finite (supine) or finite (subjunctive).

The free translation of the Italian and Romanian clauses confirms Bhatt's observation for English, namely that covert modality is deontic (or bouletic, and possibly also circumstantial), but never epistemic (Bhatt 1999:114, 128, 130). Based on this fact, an important correlation with the cartography of the clause will be drawn in § 3.3.2.

3.3 Some critical aspects

At this point, we want to address two main issues as being critical in Bhatt's (1999) analysis of structures which encode covert patterns of modality.

Firstly, according to Bhatt, non-SiRs and infinitival questions project a left periphery, similarly to full relative clauses. It follows that if the CP layer were projected, Force° should encode illocutionary force. However, as we will show below, such infinitival clauses do not allow DiscPrts; they are "central" in the sense of Haegeman (2002 and following work).

Secondly, for Bhatt (1999), modality in such infinitival clauses is encoded in C°. Cartographic work by Cinque (1999, 2001) establishes a

---

[15] The Romanian *supine* can be adjectival, nominal or verbal, depending on the syntactic categories that select it. Cf. Soare (2007) for an analysis against the 'mixed category' behavior of the *supine.*

hierarchy of functional projections, showing that modality is encoded in the IP layer, and not as high as the CP.

The absence of DiscPrts, of certain types of adverbs, of epistemic modality, of topicalized and focussed constituents in these kinds of constructions can be explained straightforwardly if we assume that the syntactic structure of these clauses is reduced in the sense of Haegeman (2002 and following work) (also cf. Hooper & Thompson 1973:484f), or at least not as extended as hinted in Bhatt (1999).

3.3.1 Force in non-finite contexts?

Let us now look at the first issue, namely that for Bhatt (1999) non-SiRs involve a CP projection. Although he does not refer to cartographic decomposition of the CP layer, we may translate the presence of the CP into the projections of (at least a part) of Rizzi's (1997, 2001) left periphery:

(45) Force (Top*) Int (Top*) Foc (Top*) Fin IP (Rizzi 2001)

If ForceP were projected in these contexts, it should also encode the illocutionary force of the clause (leaving aside the issue that such clauses should also license topicalized and focussed constituents). Thus, such clauses should allow for DiscPrts to appear, contrary to fact:

(46) Il libro da non leggere (**mica*) è sul tavolo.
the book PREP not to read PRT is on-the table
'The book that must not be read is on the table.'
(cf. 35) *Italian*

(47) Ion are mulţi prieteni cu care (**doar*) să iasă.
Ion has many friends with who PRT SUBJ go.out.3SG
'Ion has many friends with which he can / could go out.'
(cf. 39) *Romanian*

Given the cartographic representation of the left periphery, we suggest that only a part of the CP layer is projected in Bhatt's non-SiRs and infinitival questions (if it is projected at all), in line with recent theories on the left periphery of subordinate clauses. As we will see in the next section, a truncation hypothesis would probably involve also lower clausal projections, namely those in the IP.

3.3.2 The projections related to modality in a cartographic approach

Turning to the second issue mentioned above, Bhatt (1999:16) puts forward the idea that non-SiRs (and infinitival questions) involve a CP projection. One of his arguments is that C° is identified as the locus where modality is encoded (possible relative and interrogative pronouns are to be posited in CP as well).

A theory-internal argument against Bhatt's claim that certain infinitival clauses project a (full) CP is given below. We will refer to Cinque's (1999, 2001) hypotheses on the cartography of the clause, since he makes the first articulated proposal as to the positioning of the syntactic projections related to modality.

Based on (free and bound) verbal morphology and on the relative order of adverbs in different languages, Cinque (1999) defines the exact positioning of the syntactic projections related to epistemic (and alethic) modality (cf. (48), where the relevant projections are indicated in bold). However, he does not say much about the position of the projections related to root modality with respect to the other clausal projections. Nonetheless, he proposes the hierarchy in (49), which indicates the relative order of the projections for root modality.

(48) The universal hierarchy of clausal functional projections (Cinque 1999:106):

[*frankly* Mood$_{\text{speech act}}$ [*fortunately* Mood$_{\text{evaluative}}$
[***allegedly*** **Mood$_{\text{evidential}}$** [***probably*** **Mod$_{\text{epistemic}}$** [*once* T(Past)
[*then* T(Future) [*perhaps* Mood$_{\text{irrealis}}$ [***necessarily*** **Mod$_{\text{necessity}}$**
[***possibly*** **Mod$_{\text{possibility}}$** [*usually* Asp$_{\text{habitual}}$ [*again* Asp$_{\text{repetitive(I)}}$
[*often* Asp$_{\text{frequentative(I)}}$ [***intentionally*** **Mod$_{\text{volitional}}$**
[*quickly* Asp$_{\text{celerative(I)}}$ [*already* T(Anterior) [*no longer* Asp$_{\text{terminative}}$
[*still* Asp$_{\text{continuative}}$ [*always* Asp$_{\text{perfect(?)}}$ [*just* Asp$_{\text{retrospective}}$
[*soon* Asp$_{\text{proximative}}$ [*briefly* Asp$_{\text{durative}}$
[*characteristically(?)* Asp$_{\text{generic/progressive}}$ [*almost* Asp$_{\text{prospective}}$
[*completely* Asp$_{\text{SgCompletive(I)}}$ [*tutto* Asp$_{\text{PlCompletive}}$ [*well* Voice
[*fast/early* Asp$_{\text{celerative(II)}}$ [*again* Asp$_{\text{repetitive(II)}}$ [*often* Asp$_{\text{frequentative(II)}}$
[*completely* Asp$_{\text{completive(II)}}$

(49) Mod$_{\text{epistemic}}$ ... > Mod$_{\text{necessity}}$ > Mod$_{\text{possibility}}$ > Mod$_{\text{volition}}$ > Mod$_{\text{obligation}}$ > Mod$_{\text{ability/permission}}$ (Cinque 1999:81)

By checking reciprocal positions of restructuring verbs in Romance languages,[16] in a later work Cinque (2001) shows that the projections related to root modality are to be posited among the (low) aspectual projections.

(50) Revised hierarchy of clausal functional projections from $\text{Asp}_{\text{habitual}}$ (Cinque 2001:153):

… $\text{Asp}_{\text{habitual}}$ > $\text{Asp}_{\text{delayed/finally}}$ > $\text{Asp}_{\text{predispositional}}$ > $\text{Asp}_{\text{repetitive(I)}}$ > $\text{Asp}_{\text{frequentative(I)}}$ > $\textbf{Mod}_{\textbf{volition}}$ > $\text{Asp}_{\text{celerative(I)}}$ > $\text{Asp}_{\text{terminative}}$ > $\text{Asp}_{\text{continuative}}$ > $\text{Asp}_{\text{perfect}}$ > $\text{Asp}_{\text{retrospective}}$ > $\text{Asp}_{\text{proximative}}$ > $\text{Asp}_{\text{durative}}$ > $\text{Asp}_{\text{progressive}}$ > $\text{Asp}_{\text{prospective}}$ > $\text{Asp}_{\text{inceptive}}$ > $\textbf{Mod}_{\textbf{obligation}}$ > $\textbf{Mod}_{\textbf{ability}}$ > $\text{Asp}_{\text{frustrative/success}}$ > $\textbf{Mod}_{\textbf{permission}}$ > $\text{Asp}_{\text{conative}}$ > $\text{Asp}_{\text{completive(I)}}$ > Voice > $\text{Asp}_{\text{celerative(II)}}$ > $\text{Asp}_{\text{inceptive(II)}}$ > $\text{Asp}_{\text{completive(II)}}$ > $\text{Asp}_{\text{repetitive(II)}}$ > $\text{Asp}_{\text{frequentative(II)}}$ …

As shown above, according to Cinque (1999, 2001), modality is encoded in the IP and not in the CP. From a cartographic perspective, we should assume that covert modality is interpreted in the same projections where overt modality is encoded, namely in the IP, and not in the CP (layer). Moreover, the cases of (covert) modality considered in Bhatt are never epistemic (Bhatt 1999:114). Covert modality can only be deontic/bouletic (and possibly circumstantial).

Summing up, theory-internal arguments lead us to assume that Bhatt's cases of covert modality are encoded in the lower projections of the IP. The interpretability of modality in such cases constitutes no evidence for the presence of a (complete) CP.

Furthermore, if modality were encoded in the infinitival [+rel/wh] C° and thus the whole structure were projected, we would expect for all adverbs in Cinque's (1999) hierarchy, too, to be able to appear in these

---

[16] For instance, in order to demonstrate that the underlying sequence is $\text{Asp}_{\text{terminative}}$ > $\text{Asp}_{\text{continuative}}$, Cinque makes use of examples such as the following one (where clitic climbing is a piece of evidence for monoclausality):

i. Lo finì di continuare a ripetere.
it she.finished to continue to repeat
'She stopped keeping on repeating it.'

ii. * Lo continuò a finire di ripetere.
it she.continued to finish to repeat
'She kept on finishing to repeat it.'

contexts; facts do not bear out this prediction. The higher part of the IP seems to be impaired or not available as well:[17]

(51)	Il	libro	(*forse)	da	leggere	è	sul	tavolo.	*Italian*
	the	book	maybe	PREP	to.read	is	on-the	table.	

It might well be the case that – as argued by Bhatt (1999) – some types of infinitival clauses display a more articulated structure than others. However, from a cartographic perspective, it is necessary to establish which projections are really involved, since part of the IP and all (or part of) the CP seem to be impaired or not available also in the more extended cases.

4. Conclusions

The aim of this paper was twofold. Firstly, it was shown that Italian and Romanian discourse particles are to be considered as crucial criteria for the presence of illocutionary force (also cf. Coniglio & Zegrean 2010, Coniglio 2011). DiscPrts (or modal particles, according to the German tradition) are overt elements generated in specific positions in the modal area of the IP or higher, in the CP layer (cf. Coniglio 2008, 2011, Cardinaletti 2011, among others). Importantly, they are correlated with the highest CP projections (which interact with the discourse level). On the basis of their distribution in different clause types, we concluded that the presence of such particles is a clear indication of the illocutionary independence of a clause. Secondly, we presented data for patterns of covert modality in Italian and Romanian in environments which are typologically equivalent to Bhatt's (1999) data for English. It was shown that – due to the impossibility of licensing discourse particles (and in general epistemic modality) and to other theory-internal considerations – these constructions probably have to be considered as illocutionarily dependent clauses displaying a syntactically reduced structure.

---

[17] Notice that the IP of these constructions is probably not thoroughly impaired. Thus, for instance, restructuring verbs are sometimes available. E.g.:

i.	il	libro	da ricominciare	a leggere	...
	the	book	to restart	to read	

'The book that we should / could restart reading ...'

It would be interesting to carry further research on the exact projections of the IP (and of the CP) that are impaired (or available) in these constructions.

Acknowledgments

We would like to thank Werner Abraham and Elisabeth Leiss, who organized the Workshop on Covert Patterns of Modality (held at 44th Annual Meeting of the Societas Linguistica Europaea, Universidad de La Rioja, Logroño, Spain, 8-11 September 2011), the participants to the workshop, and the audience for comments and discussion on the paper presented there.

References

Abraham, W. (1991), Discourse particles in German: How does their illocutive force come about? In W. Abraham (ed.), *Discourse Particles.* Amsterdam: Benjamins, 203-252.

—. (2009), Die Urmasse von Modalität und ihre Ausgliederung. Modalität anhand von Modalverben, Modalpartikel und Modus – was ist das Gemeinsame, was das Trennende, und was steckt dahinter? In W. Abraham & E. Leiss (2009), 251-302.

—. (2012), Illocutive force is speaker and information source concern. What type of syntax does the representation of speaker deixis require? Templates vs. derivational structure? In W. Abraham & E. Leiss (eds.), *Modality and the theory of mind elements across languages.* [Trends in Linguistics 243]. Berlin: de Gruyter Mouton, 67-108.

—. (this volume), Covert patterns of modality in typological comparison.

Abraham, W. & E. Leiss (eds.) (2009), *Modalität. Epistemik und Evidentialität bei Modalverb, Adverb, Modalpartikel und Modus.* Tübingen: Stauffenburg [= Studien zur deutschen Grammatik 77].

Abraham, W. & E. Leiss (this volume): Introduction.

Austin, J. L. (1962), *How to do Things with Words: The William James Lectures delivered at Harvard University in 1955.* Oxford: Clarendon.

Bayer, J. (2012), From modal particle to interrogative marker: a study of German *denn.* In L. Bruge, A. Cardinaletti, G. Giusti, N. Munaro & C. Poletto (eds.), *Functional heads. The cartography of syntactic structures,* volume 7, 13-28. [Oxford Studies in Comparative Syntax]. Oxford: OUP.

Bazzanella, C. (1995), I segnali discorsivi. In L. Renzi, G. Salvi & A. Cardinaletti (eds.), *Grande grammatica italiana di consultazione. Tipi di frase, deissi, formazione delle parole*, vol. 3. Bologna: Il Mulino, 225-257.

Bhatt, R. (1999), Covert modality in non-finite contexts. PhD dissertation, University of Pennsylvania.

Bierwisch, M. (1980), Semantic structure and illocutionary force. In J. R. Searle, F. Kiefer & M. Bierwisch (eds), *Speech Act Theory and Pragmatics*. Dordrecht: Reidel, 1-35.

Bonvino, E., M. Frascarelli & P. Pietrandrea (2008), Semantica, sintassi e prosodia di alcune espressioni avverbiali nel parlato spontaneo. In M. Pettorino, A. G., M. Vallone & R. Savy (eds), *La comunicazione parlata. Atti del congresso internazionale Napoli 23-25 febbraio 2006*. Naples: Liguori Editore, 565-607.

Burkhardt, A. (1985), Der Gebrauch der Partikeln im gesprochenen Deutsch und im gesprochenen Italienisch. In G. Holtus & E. Radtke (eds), *Gesprochenes Italienisch in Geschichte und Gegenwart*. Tübingen: Narr, 236-275.

Cardinaletti, Anna (2011), German and Italian modal particles and clause structure. In T. Biberauer & M. Sheehan (eds.), *Particles through a modern syntactic lens*. Berlin: de Gruyter [special guest-edited issue: *The Linguistic Review* 28/4], 493–531.

Cinque, G. (1999), *Adverbs and Functional Heads: A Cross-Linguistic Perspective*. Oxford: Oxford University Press.

—. (2001), 'Restructuring' and the order of aspectual and root modal heads. In G. Cinque & G. Salvi (eds.), *Current Studies in Italian Syntax. Essays Offered to Lorenzo Renzi*. Amsterdam: Elsevier, 137-155.

Coniglio, M. (2005), Deutsche Modalpartikeln: eine syntaktische Analyse. MA thesis, Ca' Foscari University of Venice.

—. (2007a), Deutsche Modalpartikeln: ein Vorschlag zu ihrer syntaktischen Analyse. In E.-M. Thüne & F. Ortu (eds), *Gesprochene Sprache – Partikeln*. Frankfurt am Main: Lang, 103-113.

—. (2007b), German modal particles in the IP-domain. *Rivista di grammatica generativa* 32, 3-37.

—. (2007c), German Modal Particles in Root and Embedded Clauses. *University of Venice Working Papers in Linguistics* 17, 109-141.

—. (2008), Modal particles in Italian, *University of Venice Working Papers in Linguistics* 18, 91-129.

—. (2009), Deutsche Modalpartikeln in Haupt- und Nebensätzen. In W. Abraham & E. Leiss (2009), 191-221.

—. (2011), *Die Syntax der deutschen Modalpartikeln: ihre Distribution und Lizenzierung in Haupt- und Nebensätzen*. Berlin: Akademie.

Coniglio, M. & I. Zegrean (2010), Splitting up Force. Evidence from discourse particles. *University of Venice Working Papers in Linguistics* 20, 7-34.

Del Gobbo, F. & C. Poletto (2008), Tipi di particelle frasali. Handout for the 14th Giornata di Dialettologia, Università di Padova, 20th June 2008.

Diewald, G. (1999), *Die Modalverben im Deutschen. Grammatikalisierung und Polyfunktionalität*. Tübingen: Niemeyer.

Doherty, M. (1987), *Epistemic Meaning*. Berlin: Springer.

Emonds, J. (1970), *Root and Structure-preserving Transformations*. PhD dissertation, MIT.

Frascarelli, M. & R. Hinterhölzl (2007), Types of Topics in German and Italian. In S. Winkler & K. Schwabe (eds), *On Information Structure, Meaning and Form*. Amsterdam: Benjamins, 87-116.

Geisler, C. (1995), Relative Infinitives in English. PhD dissertation. Uppsala: Uppsala University [Studia Anglistica Upsaliensia 91].

Haegeman, L. (2002), Anchoring to speaker, adverbial clauses and the structure of CP. *Georgetown University Working Papers in Theoretical Linguistics* 2, 117-180.

—. (2004a), Topicalization, CLLD and the left periphery. *ZAS Papers in Linguistics* 35(1), 157-192.

—. (2004b), The syntax of adverbial clauses and its consequences for topicalisation. *Antwerp Papers in Linguistics* 107, 61-90.

Haegeman, L. (2006), Conditionals, factives and the left periphery. *Lingua* 116, 1651-1669.

Haumann, D. & Letnes, O. (this volume), German *wohl* – an evidential?

Held, G. (1985), *Ma*, *dico*, sei *proprio* dura, *eh*! – Zu Formen und Funktionen einiger lexikalischer Verstärkungsmittel in Dialogreaktionen. In G. Holtus & E. Radtke (eds), *Gesprochenes Italienisch in Geschichte und Gegenwart*.Tübingen: Narr, 300-328.

Hill, V. (2002), Complementizer Phrases (CP) in Romanian. *Rivista di Linguistica* 14(2), 223-248.

—. (2007), Romanian adverbs and the pragmatic field. *The Linguistic Review* 24, 61-86.

Hooper, J. B. & S. A. Thompson (1973), On the applicability of Root Transformations. *Linguistic Inquiry* 4, 465-97.

Jacobs, J. (1986), Abtönungsmittel als Illokutionstypmodifikatoren. *Groninger Arbeiten zur Germanistischen Linguistik* 27, 100-111.

—. (1991), On the semantics of modal particles. In W. Abraham (ed.), *Discourse particles. Descriptive and theoretical investigations on the logical, syntactical, and pragmatic properties of discourse particles in German*, Amsterdam: Benjamins, 141-162.

Kiefer, F. (1987), On defining modality. *Folia Linguistica* XXI, 67-94.

Kjellmer, G. (1975), Are relative infinitives modal? *Studia Neophilologica* 47, 323-332.

Kratzer, A. (1981), The notional category of modality. In H.-J. Eikmeyer & H. Rieser (eds), *Words, Worlds, and Contexts. New approaches in Word Semantics*. Berlin / New York: de Gruyter, 38-74.

Law, A. (2002), Cantonese sentence-final particles and the CP domain. *UCL Working Papers in Linguistics* 14, 375-398.

Leiss, E. (2009), Epistemicity, evidentiality, and Theory of Mind. Paper read at the Annual Societas Linguistica Europaea Meeting 2009, Lisbon, Workshop on "Theory of Mind or Relevance – linguistic description and communicative explanation".

Manoliu Manea, M. (1985), Conventional Implicature and cross language analysis of 'Insinuating words': Fr. Même - Rom. chiar. *Revista de Filologia Romanica* 3, 153-165.

—. (1993), *Gramatică, pragmasemantică şi discurs*. Bucureşti: Litera.

Meibauer, J. (1994), *Modaler Kontrast und konzeptuelle Verschiebung: Studien zur Syntax und Semantik deutscher Modalpartikeln*. Tübingen: Niemeyer [Linguistische Arbeiten 314].

Modicom, P.-Y. (this volume), Shared knowledge and epistemic reductionism: covert semantics of the German modal particles.

Munaro, N. & C. Poletto (2004), Sentential particles and clausal typing in the Veneto Dialects. *ZAS Papers in Linguistics* 35(2), 375-397.

Radtke, E. (1985), Abtönungsverfahren im gesprochenen Italienisch. Zu *magari, figurati* und Rekurrenzstrategien. In G. Holtus & E. Radtke (eds), *Gesprochenes Italienisch in Geschichte und Gegenwart*. Tübingen: Narr, 280-299.

Rizzi, L. (1997), The Fine Structure of the Left Periphery. In L. Haegeman (ed), *Elements of Grammar*. Dordrecht: Kluwer, 281-337.

—. (2001), On the position "Int(errogative)" in the left periphery of the clause. In G. Cinque and G. P. Salvi (eds.), *Current Studies in Italian Syntax. Essays offered to Lorenzo Renzi.* Amsterdam: Elsevier [North Holland Linguistic Series: Linguistic Variations 59], 287-296.

Roussou, A. (2000), On the left periphery: modal particles and complementisers. *Journal of Greek Linguistics* 1, 65-94.

Šimik, R. (2011), Covert modality in modal existential wh-construction. Handout of the talk presented at the Workshop on *Covert Patterns of Modality*, 44th Annual Meeting of the Societas Linguistica Europaea, University of La Rioja, Logroño, September 8-11.

Soare, E. (2007), Morphosyntactic mismatches revisited: the case of the Romanian supine. *Acta Linguistica Hungarica* 54 (2), 173-192.

Searle, J. R. (1975), A Taxonomy of Illocutionary Acts. *Language, Mind, and Knowledge* 7, 344-369.

Thun, H. (1984), *Dialoggestaltung im Deutschen und Rumänischen. Eine strukturell-kontrastive Studie zu den Existimatoren*. Tübingen: Narr.

Thurmair, M. (1989), *Modalpartikeln und ihre Kombinationen*. Tübingen: Niemeyer [Linguistische Arbeiten 223].

Zimmermann, M. (2004a), Zum Wohl: Diskurspartikeln als Satztypmodifikatoren. *Linguistische Berichte* 199, 1-35.

—. (2004b), Discourse particles in the left periphery. *ZAS Papers in Linguistics* 35(2), 543-566.

COVERT MODALITY AND CONTEXT SHIFT: THE 'PERPLEXIVE' CONSTRUCTION

ASLI GÖKSEL AND BARIŞ KABAK
BOĞAZIÇI UNIVERSITY
AND UNIVERSITY OF WÜRZBURG

Abstract: We investigate the covert emotive and modal properties of a hitherto unanalyzed construction in Turkish, the *perplexive*, which is used to narrate a past event that has left the speaker, among other emotional states, in perplexity. Structurally, the perplexive is string identical to the imperative construction, involves puzzling and counter-intuitive mappings between form and function. While the event is unambiguously embedded in the past, it is expressed by the imperative mood. Furthermore, the second person pronoun and all subsequent agreement marking refer to a third person in the narrative. We propose that the covertness is unraveled by the overt use of the second person pronoun, one of whose functions in an otherwise pro-drop language is the encoding of a context shift. Coupled with the imperative mood and a verb of impulse, the use of this pronoun, the precise shape of which is determined by the level of formality in the utterance time, extends a directive to the addressee to situate himself in the event time to share the speaker's emotions. As such, the components of the perplexive are cumulatively forced to have an interpretation that lies outside their canonical use at the time of utterance.

1. Introduction

In this paper, we examine a hitherto unanalyzed type of construction used in informal registers of Turkish, which we name the 'perplexive'. The perplexive is used when narrating a past event that has left the narrator in perplexity, surprise, disbelief, and sometimes annoyance or irritation. The event is brought about typically but not exclusively by a protagonist who is often not one of the discourse participants, and who is always treated as a narrative third-person. Although Turkish has other means to mark the perfective past, this construction does not have a specialised morpheme expressing this function and is string identical in some of its uses to the imperative construction (1).

(1) *Sen Ayşe-ye sormadan ver eski eşyalar-ı./!!*
you Ayşe-dat without.asking give.away old furniture-acc

(i) 'Give away the old furniture without asking Ayşe.' [Imperative]

(ii) '[Would you believe it?!] S/he gave away the old furniture without asking Ayşe!!' [Perplexive]

In (1ii), although the verb (*ver* 'give') is structurally in the imperative mood, it unambiguously conveys a perfective/past reading in the indicative mood. Furthermore, despite the fact that the subject (*sen* 'you') is marked as the second person singular, it denotes a third person in the narrative discourse. In Turkish, the appearance of overt pronominal and lexical subjects is syntactically optional and determined to a great extent by the discourse–pragmatic context (Erguvanlı, 1984, Enç, 1986, Öztürk 2001). Taking the basic insight in Enç (1986), who claims that one of the functions of an overt pronoun is to encode a shift in the topic or center of topic in Turkish, we extend the function of the subject pronoun to cover a broader type of shift: (i) from second to third person, and (ii) from imperative mood to perfective aspect and past tense, as the reference point of the narrated event lies unambiguously in the past. We thus claim that while the function of the second person pronoun is to indicate a shift in the centre of topic in canonical imperatives (1i), the same pronoun encodes the locus of the context shift associated with the perplexive in (1ii).

Drawing on parallelisms with the conditional and narrative uses of imperatives in other languages (e.g., Fortuin 2000, Fortuin & Boogaart 2009), we show that the imperative, morphosyntactically the least marked construction in Turkish, has a tripartite function as a directive, as an irrealis marker and as a perfective and past tense marker. We argue that the usage of an overt pronoun, together with 'verbs of impulse', encodes an instruction to the hearer to act upon the utterance purely as an attestant, rather than interpret it as referring to himself. As such, the perplexive is an instance of covert modality, the components of which compositionally encode the perplexity of the speaker, thereby forcing the hearer to become an unsuspecting witness in a past event and to empathise with the speaker. We further observe that the perplexive construction concurrently expresses elements linked to event time and to utterance time and discuss the differences between this construction and mirative constructions.

In what follows, we first describe the structural properties and function of the perplexive construction and provide data from various sources. Sections 3-5 look further into the particulars of the components: the second person pronoun, imperative marking and the verbs of impulse, respectively. Based on the discussion of each of these components, we summarise and expand upon our proposal in section 6, where we further discuss the contribution of each of these components in deriving the perplexive construction. We conclude in section 7 with avenues for further research.

2. The perplexive construction: Structural properties and function

2.1 Structure

There are three crucial components of the perplexive construction:

(i) The subject of the sentence is second person (agreeing with the predicate, see (ii) below). All references to this person (e.g. possessive marking) are also obligatorily in the second person. The second person pronouns are *sen* (singular familiar) and *siz* (plural or singular formal). We henceforth refer to this group of pronouns as '*s*-pronoun'.
(ii) The predicate of the perplexive construction is the imperative form of the verb: The imperative verb either has -Ø marking to express the second person *singular familiar* form, or it contains the suffix *-(y)In* to express the second person *plural* form or the second person *formal* form. This is illustrated in Table 2-1.

Table 2-1. The imperative form in Turkish.

verb root	second person sg. familiar	second person pl. / formal
izle- '(to) watch' otur- '(to) sit'	izle-Ø 'watch!' otur- Ø 'sit!'!'	izle-**yin** 'watch!' otur-**un** 'sit!'

(iii) The perplexive construction often contains a serial verb. This verb is selected from a small set of lexical verbs, here devoid of their lexical meaning and simply denoting impulse, overriding their literal sense. We refer to these verbs as verbs of impulse and discuss their contribution to the perplexive construction in section 5. Note that these are also imperative in form, and are inflected in the same way as the main verb in (ii), as illustrated in Table 2-2.

Table 2-2. Verbs of impulse in the imperative mood.

verb root	second person sg. familiar	second person plural / formal
kalk- '(to) rise'	kalk-Ø	kalk-**ın**
tut- '(to) hold'	tut-Ø	tut-**un**
git- '(to) go'	git-Ø	gid-**in**

A verb of impulse is often right-adjacent to the *s*-pronoun, therefore these utterances usually begin with *sen kalk*, *sen tut*, *sen git*, which we indicate as SEN_KALK.IMP, SEN_TUT.IMP, SEN_GİT.IMP (but see 16b for an example where the referent comes between the pronoun and the verb of impulse).

To recapitulate, the covertness in a perplexive construction stems from an intricate interplay of the *s*-pronoun, the verb of impulse, and the imperative verb form, which are devoid of their canonical illocutionary force. More specifically, they neither urge the addressee to carry out a particular command or act in a certain way, nor do they imply the other functions of the imperative such as signalling permission, prohibition, or exhortation of any kind. Crucially, the perplexive is a declarative construction, where the *s*-pronoun picks up its referent from outside the clause, either from the discourse environment or the previous sentence. These points are illustrated in (2) where the referent is a third party outside the discourse context, and in (3) where the referent is supplied in the beginning (*salak bir devlet* 'a ridiculous state').[1]

(2) *Sen kalk tüm film-i izle sonra son-un-u kaçır. (İşte olay orada koptu.)*
SEN_KALK.IMP whole film-ACC watch.IMP then end-3POSS.SG-ACC miss.IMP (That's where all hell broke loose.)

[1] The abbreviations used here are: ABL: ablative, ACC: accusative, AUX: auxiliary, COMP: complementiser, DAT: dative, EV: evidential, FAM: familiar, FRM: formal, IMP: imperative, IMPF: imperfective, INT: interrogative, P: past, PRIV: privative, PL: plural, POSS: possessive PROG: progressive, s-pronoun: the second person subject of perplexives, SG: singular. All the examples are written as they appear in the original source, thus may have orthographial and punctuation errors. In the text, we refer to the speaker by using feminine pronouns, and to the addressee by using masculine pronouns for reasons of simplicity.

'[Would you believe it?!] S/he watched the whole film and then missed the ending! (That's where all hell broke loose).'
(Status statement at Twitter:
http://twitter.com/hyaman/status/19973439707)

(3) *salak bir devlet ya bir kürtce okullarda egitilsin ozaman devlet bölünürmü. ama sen kalk kürtleri türklestirmeye calis kürtlere zorla türkce egitim ver anadili yasakla sonra kürt halkı ayaklansın sonrada da terörist de ooo ne güzel*
[This is] a ridiculous state man, first Kurdish should be taught in schools, then [see if] the country splits up. But SEN_KALK.IMP try.IMP to Turkify the Kurds, teach.IMP Kurds Turkish by force, ban.IMP the mother tongue, then the Kurds revolt-OPT, then call.IMP them terrorists... cheeky, man.
'[Would you believe it?!] They tried to Turkify the Kurds…)
(Comment to a youtube video:
http://www.youtube.com/watch?v=kWcSS7U30vw)

In (2), the speaker is voicing her irritation about someone missing the end of a film. In (3) the referent is *the ridiculous state*, situated in the sentence before the perplexive construction.

It should be noted that the referent of an *s*-pronoun can also be supplied later in the discourse, as (4) below illustrates, where the perplexive construction is followed by a sentence which identifies the referent as Atatürk:

(4) *Sen kalk, dört kadınla evlenebileceğin bir dönemde dünyaya gel, sonra değerini bilmeyip tek kadınla evlilik sistemini getir. Aaaah ah. Çılgın diskolara gitmek, sabahlara kadar içip, içip rock yapmak, babasının mersedesini alıp söyle bir Emirgan turu çekmek dururken. Bunları yapmadı Atatürk. Keyif çatmadı. Tüm hayatını ülkesinin kurtuluşuna ve uygarlaşmasına harcadı.*
SEN_KALK.IMP come.IMP to this world at a time when you can marry-POSS.2SG four women, then dismiss.IMP the benefits of this and introduce.IMP monogamy. But no… Instead of going to raving discos, to drink all night and to rock, to take his father's Mercedes and go to Emirgan. Atatürk didn't do any of these. He didn't take time out. He spent all his life for the independence and modernisation of his country.
'[Would you believe it?!] He came to this world…)
(http://wolkanca.com/ataturke-aciyorum/)

The referent of the s-pronoun can be the same as the (absent) addressee, as (5) demonstrates. More specifically, after using an *s*-pronoun, the speaker changes her viewpoint and continues by addressing the persons (here the government) who are absent from the environment of the discourse:

(5) *Sen kalk av tüfeği kullanma yaşını 18 e çek, silah kullanma yaşını 20 ye çek ondan sonrada ateşli silah kullanana 2 yıldan 5 yıla kadar hapis cezası ver, yahu ne yaptığınızı siz de bilmiyosunuz ya bakalım ne olacak.*
SEN_KALK.IMP bring.down.IMP the age of possession of hunting rifles to 18, reduce.IMP the age of arms usage to 20, then impose.IMP a 2-to-5 year prison sentence to arms users, man, even you don't know what you're doing, so let's wait and see.[2]
('[Would you believe it?!]. They brought down…)
(Comment to news at
http://www.malatyaguncel.com/news_detail.php?id=46287)

When there is any other reference to the person denoted by the *s*-pronoun such as a possessive pronoun or agreement marker, these also have to be in the second person (6).

(6) ***Sen** git hasta ol-duğ-**un**-u karı-**n**-a söyle-me!!*
SEN_GİT.IMP ill AUX-COMP-**2POSS.SG** wife-**2POSS.SG**.-DAT say-NEG.IMP
'[Would you believe it?!] He hasn't told his wife about his illness!'

A final remark about the structural properties of the perplexive construction is that the referent itself can be included in the perplexive construction. In (7) below, the referent is *Ali*, and the pronoun that follows is still the second person singular.

(7) *Ali sen tut ev-i sat-tığ-ın-ı hepimizden gizle!!*
Ali SEN_TUT.IMP house-ACC sell-comp-2POSS.SG-ACC keep.secret.IMP
'[Would you believe it?!] Ali kept it secret from all of us that he sold the house!!'

---

[2] This is an example that also illustrates the various deictic functions of the second person pronoun, to be elaborated in section 3.1.1.

Table 2-3 below illustrates the essential components of the perplexive. The table also reflects the order in which the overt referent, the subject, the verb of impulse and the main verb are most likely to appear in a sentence. We will revise this table in section 6.

Table 2-3. Components of the perplexive.

1 Overt referent (optional)	2 Subject	3 Verb of impulse	4 Possessive markers (where required)	5 Marking on main verb
a third party (e.g. *Ali*)	second person pronoun: *sen*/*siz*	*tut* *kalk* *git*	second person markers: *-Ø/-(I)n*	second person imperative: *-Ø/-(y)In*

2.2 Function

The function of the perplexive construction is to express a mixture of speaker attitudes towards an event that has already taken place. Their expressed common denominator is the expression of the following emotional states:

(i) perplexity or incomprehension towards a past event that was not expected, and
(ii) disapproval / disappointment and / or irritation / fury towards the perpetrator of the event or towards the resulting state-of-affairs

To illustrate, in (3), the speaker is critical about the agent of the action, the state of Turkey. In (4), the enforcement of monogamy by Atatürk (the founder of the Republic of Turkey) is seen as disappointing (possibly sarcastically), although the speaker holds Atatürk in high regard as is apparent in the sentence to follow.

Due to the element of surprise inherent in perplexive constructions, one might at first be inclined to equate them with mirative constructions. First, both the mirative and the perplexive have perfective aspect. Second, the mirative indicates new information which has come to the attention of the speaker or which is brought into the discourse (see DeLancey 1997, 2001, Lazard 1999, Malchukov 2004 and the references therein). The perplexive construction also has this flavour. As a result, both the mirative and the perplexive embody an element of surprise. However, there are several reasons to separate the two and regard them as distinct grammatical categories. While the perplexive construction also brings forth a piece of unexpected information, the event in question can have been witnessed directly by the speaker and is crucially set in the remote past. This is unlike the mirative which can refer to the recent/immediate past when referring to an unexpected event. This latter type of modality is in fact encoded by a separate marker in Turkish, the evidential marker *-miş*. Among its many functions, the Turkish evidential encodes the mirative (DeLancey 1997, based on Slobin & Aksu-Koç 1982) as a modality embodying surprise, but, crucially, to describe an event that the speaker has just become aware of. Thus the perplexive construction cannot be seen on a par with the mirative, nor can it be described as part of evidential modality which is argued to cover the mirative (DeLancey 2001). Most importantly, however, what sets the two apart is (i) the fact that the perplexive construction necessarily indicates disapproval or disappointment, and (ii) it necessarily expresses an outburst as a result of this disapproval/ disappointment, signalled by verbs of impulse.

3. Analysis: Deriving covert modality through cumulative exponence

One of the intriguing aspects of the perplexive construction is that it uses the marker of the imperative mood to mark the past tense indicative. Below, we will argue that this shift in modality specification is mediated through cumulative exponence of the properties of two grammatical features: the pronouns of Turkish (and the role their overt expression plays in the interpretation of an utterance), and the imperative whose function is not restricted to that of a command. Below we take each one in turn.

3.1 Antecedents and interpretation of pronouns in Turkish discourse

As mentioned above, the second person pronoun refers to someone other than the addressee in the utterance time and this other person is a third party external to the deictic center of the speaker.[3] Below, we discuss these issues in the context of pronominal reference in Turkish and come to the

---

[3] This does not preclude the possibility that the *s*-pronoun might refer to the addressee, or even to the speaker herself (see fn. 11). But this reference is crucially situated within the event time and not in the utterance time.

conclusion that (i) the usage of second person to indicate the third person (or 'person shift' in general) is not eccentric, given the properties of the reference of pronouns in Turkish discourse, and (ii) the usage of an overt subject in the form of a pronoun indicates a shift in context, which we propose is an extension of the more specific 'shifter' function of pronouns suggested by Enç (1986).

Although the role of the second person pronouns of Turkish has been discussed in the literature with respect to the selection of the informal *sen* and the formal *siz* (see e.g., Hatipoğlu 2008 and references therein), to our knowledge, the discourse antecedents of these pronouns have not been addressed in detail. The assumption has been that a pronoun is lexically specified to refer to a particular person. These pronouns can refer to individuals (i.e. singular; *ben* 'I', *sen* 'you' (familiar), *siz* 'you' (formal), *o* 'he/she/it'), to groups (i.e. plural; *biz* 'we', *siz* 'you all', *onlar* 'they'), to individual members within groups (*bizler* 'we each member of our group', *sizler* 'you, each member of your group', see e.g., Göksel & Kerslake 2005). The general understanding has been that the grammatical first, second and third persons have direct reference to the speaker, the addressee and to the party/parties external to the discourse, respectively. However, below, we shall see that this is not the case.

3.1.1 Role switching

There are various cases where a pronoun refers to a person other than the one it is lexically specified for, such as the impersonal *you* attested in many languages (Hyman 1994). Further, the reference of pronouns is tightly linked with the position they occur in or whether they encode cross-reference or switch reference (Frajzyngier 1997 and references therein).[4] The properties of reference that we discuss in this paper are different from such usages. It should be noted that the mismatch between grammatical person and the referent is in fact not restricted to the second person-to-third person shift in Turkish. For example, a speaker can use the third person pronoun to convey exasperation towards the addressee:

(8) **Addressee (second person) expressed as third person (2⇨3):**
Ben burda ne anlat-ıyor-um. ***O*** *bana ne söylü-yo.*
I here what explain-PROG-1SG. S/he me.DAT what tell-PROG.3SG

---

[4] It is worth noting here that in such an impersonal construction, Turkish prefers second person agreement marking on the verb to an overt second person pronoun. We assume that the reason for this is the function of overt pronominal usage in Turkish, discussed in 3.2.

'I'm trying to explain something to you but you aren't listening!'
Lit.: 'What am I explaining here. What is s/he telling me.'

The referent of the third person pronoun *o* 'he'/'she' in (8) is the addressee. Similarly, an absent party can be referred to by using a second person pronoun, as illustrated by (9) and (10) below. In (9), the second person pronoun and second person markings refer to the third person, *The Republic of Turkey*. Similarly in (10) the second person refers to the specific indefinite item *kişi* 'person'.

(9) **Absent party (third person) expressed as second person (3⇨2):**
Türkiye Cumhuriyeti her konuda olduğu gibi burada da yukarıdan bir tavır takınıyor. Takınacak tabii: Devlet ***onda,*** *silah* ***onda,*** *çoğunluk* ***onda,*** *medya* ***onda.*** *İyi, bu kadar ''büyük****sen****", karşı****n****daki insanı anlayışla karşılamak da* ***senin*** *o "büyüklüğ****ün****ün" zorunlu parçasıdır.*
'The Republic of Turkey, as always, takes a patronising stance in this case as well. And this is not surprising: **It** possesses the state, **it** possesses the arms, **it** has the majority, **it** has the media. Good then, if **you** are so 'great', it is the mandatory condition of that 'greatness of **yours**' to understand the person who **you** are dealing with.'
(Murat Belge, 27 October 2009, *Taraf* (newspaper))

(10) **Absent party (third person) expressed as second person (3⇨2):**
*Herhangi bir sorunu çözme konumunda olan kişi, bu çözümün yöntemi olarak şiddeti, şiddet içeren herhangi bir tedbiri seçiyorsa, ciddi bir risk alıyor demektir. Ya uyguladığ****ın*** *şiddet sorunu umduğ****un*** *şekilde çözmeyip azdırırsa? Şiddetin şiddeti üreteceği bilinmeyen bir şey değil.* ***Senin*** *tedbir****in*** *böyle sürekli kendini yeniden- üreten bir karşılıklı şiddet furyasına yol açarsa, durmadan insanlar ölür, durmadan kaynaklar şiddete harcanırsa, ne yapar****sın*** *bunu nasıl durdurur****sun****?*
'If a person in a position qualified to solve a problem chooses to use force or a measure involving force, this means that s/he is taking a big risk. What if the force **you** use does not solve the problem as **you** wish but rather reinforces it? It is not an unknown fact that force breeds force. If **your** measure breeds an environment of mutual usage of force, if people continually get killed, if resources are used to feed force, what will **you** do, how will **you** stop this?'
(Murat Belge, 16 August 2010, *Taraf* (newspaper))

The following example illustrates cross-usages of several pronouns within a single text produced by a single speaker. We provide the first part of the text to give an indication of the context and then provide only the relevant utterances in the remainder of the text.

(11) **Cross-usages of pronouns within a single discourse:**
*Son günlerde bazı kesimlerce gündeme getirilmeye çalışılan konulardan biri de 2011 seçimlerinde seçim ekonomisi uygulayacak diyorlar. Bu halk oylamasında dediler ya devletin tüm imkanlarını seferber ettiler. Doğru hazine yardım yaptı. Onu kullanıyor**uz**$_i$. Ama **ana muhalefete**$_j$ de yaptı. Grubu olan partiler yardımını alıyor...*
'Recently one of the issues brought about by some people has to do with the 2011 elections, they say he will implement election economy. Recall that they said in the referendum they used all the resources of the country. True, the treasury helped. **We**$_i$ are using it. But they did it to the **main opposition**$_j$ too. Parties with a group benefit from this.'

i. *Devletin araç gereçleri ile geziyor*$_i$ (3sg.)
ii. *Kardeşim sen*$_j$ (2sg.fam.) *başbakan veya başbakan yardımcısı olduğun*$_j$ (2sg.fam.) *zaman oluyor da ben*$_i$ (1sg.) *gezdiğim*$_i$ *zaman niye rahatsız oluyorsun*$_j$ (2sg.fam.)
iii. *Bu yasa*$_k$*larla sana*$_i$ (2sg.fam.) *verilmiş hak.*
iv. *Diyor*$_k$ (3sg.) *ki 'Ülkenin başbakanı şu tarihe kadar kullanır' diyor*$_k$ (3sg.).
v. *Bu size*$_i$ (2sg.frm) *verilmiş hak.*
vi. *Makama tahsisli araçlar vardır. Hizmete tahsisli araçlar vardır. Hizmete tahsisli aracı memurlar kullanır.*
vii. *Biz*$_i$ (1pl.) *makam sahibiyiz*$_i$ (1pl.)
viii. *Makam sahibi makama tahsisli olanı kullanır. Bu onun en doğal hakkıdır* [....]. *Bunlar tutmuyor.*
ix. *Tutmadığını milletim*$_i$ (1sg.) *Pazar günü ortaya koydu.*
x. *Yok hanımın*$_i$a (3sg.) *alıyor, kızın*$_i$a (3sg.) *alıyor çocuğun*$_i$a (3sg.) *alıyor* (3sg.).
xi. *Yasa diyor*$_k$ (3sg.) *ya. Herhalde hanımsız dolaşacak halim*$_i$ (1pl.) *yok.*

i. He$_i$ goes around in official cars.
ii. My good man, when you$_j$ were prime minister or secretary of state, [all this] was fine, but when I$_i$ use [them] why are you$_j$ upset?

iii. This is a right given to you_i by law_k.
iv. It_k says 'the prime minister can use [it] up to this or that date' it_k says.
v. This is a right given to you_i.
vi. There are cars allocated to a position. There are cars allocated to a public service. Civil servants use cars allocated to a public service.
vii. We_i hold a position.
viii. The bearer of a position uses cars allocated to that position. This is his most natural right [...]. These are not rational.
ix. My country proved this on Sunday.
x. And then he_i buys for his_i wife, he_i buys for his_i daughter, he_i buys for his_i child.
xi. The law says so. I_i am not expected to go around without (my) wife, am I_i?

(Tayyip Erdoğan (Prime Minister of Turkey) 16 September 2010 *Radikal* (newspaper))

In (11) the speaker refers to himself (directly or indirectly) by using five different pronouns: the 1st person singular (ii) and plural (vii), the second person singular informal (iii) and formal (v), and thidrrd person singular (x). (Note that there is only one instance of marking of reported speech, (iv)) Furthermore, the same pronoun sometimes has multiple references: *Sen* 'you' is used for the speaker himself (iii) and the addressee (ii). third person marking is used for an external party (the law, iv) as well as the speaker (x).

Reference to an external party may also be achieved by the usage of the first person pronoun and the 1st person marking, as can be seen in (12). In this example, the speaker, a taxi driver, uses first person marking throughout, to talk about another person:

(12) **Absent party (third person) expressed as first person (3⇨1):**
Ben karı-m-ı köyden getir-miş-im, bir de ev-ler-e temizliğ-e gönder-iyor-um.
I wife-1POSS-ACC village-ABL bring-P-1SG and home-PL-DAT cleaning-DAT send-PROG-1SG
(*Köyden neden geleyim ki o zaman?*)
('Why would I come here from the village in the first place then?')
'He brought his wife from the village and still sends her to work as a cleaning woman, so why did he come from the village in the first place.'

Lit: 'I brought my wife from the village, and now I send her to homes as a cleaning woman.'
'So, why come here in the first place then?'
(Words of a taxi driver, Arnavutköy, Istanbul, May 2011)

In this subsection, we showed that pronouns and person markers can be used for referring to persons other than those specified in their literal lexical usage.[5] In section 6 we will expand on the connection of this to a shift of context.

We next look at the function of the class of pronouns as topic shifters in Turkish, which provides insight into the context shifting property of pronouns in the perplexive construction.

3.2 Pronouns as topic shifters

It is well established by now that in Turkish, where person marking is obligatory on the verb and pronominal subjects can be omitted, the overt expression of a subject pronoun indicates a topic shift (Enç 1986, Öztürk 2001). Thus, in a text such as the one below the pronouns cannot be dropped:

(13) *Ben* *sinema* *sev-er-im,* *sen* *sev-mez-sin.*
I cinema like-AOR-1SG You like-NEG.AOR-2SG
'I like cinema, you don't.'

This contrasts with the unacceptability of the overt realization of pronoun that is identical to the previous topic (unless the pronouns are focused):

(14) *(?Ben)* *sinema-ya* *git-ti-m* *(*ben)* *film* *seyret-ti-m.*
I cinema-DAT go-P-1SG I film watch-P-1SG
'I went to the cinema and watched a film.'

Enç (1986) investigates the status of such pronouns as those in (13) and proposes that they are not used exclusively as topic shifters, but they also play a role in shifting the center of topic. A pronoun is used for changing

---

[5] Such cross-usage of pronouns is attested in other languages. In Dutch, the second person pronoun can be used for expressing the speaker (Zeijlstra 2011). Interestingly, in this usage as well, the pronoun comes with additional implicatures and brings with itself the indication of an expected empathy from the hearer, a point which we will expand in section 4.

the topic of the discourse even though that particular pronoun may be referring to a previously set topic:

(15) *Ali Amerika-dan dön-müş. O uzaklar-ı hiç sev-mez.*
Ali America-ABL return-EV.3SG he distant.lands-ACC at.all like-NEG.AOR.3SG
'Ali has returned from America. He doesn't like to be in far away places at all.'

In the first sentence in (15), the topic is *Ali*. In the second sentence, a pronoun coreferential with *Ali* is again obligatory, as the center of the topic of conversation has changed from 'Ali' to 'Ali's dislike of far away places'. Such examples show that the usage of pronouns fulfils the discourse function of shifting the center of topic in the flow of discourse, and that pronouns are not merely used for changing the grammatical topic of the sentence. Our proposal is that the function of pronouns, more specifically *s*-pronouns, is not just restricted to topic shifting. They can also shift the context, and consequently the *perspective* of the discourse participants by mentally transpositioning them in a previously occurring setting. We return to this and elaborate on the interaction of *s*-pronouns with other components of the perplexive construction in section 6. Below we make a slight diversion and investigate the structural conditions of the referent of the *s*-pronoun in perplexive constructions.

3.3 Further observations on the reference and properties of the pronoun

In this section we expand our investigation to elucidate other properties of the *s*-pronoun and its referent. In particular, we expand on the following:

(i) the occurrence of the referent of the *s*-pronoun within the perplexive construction
(ii) the [+/- animacy] of the referent
(iii) the form of the *s*-pronoun: whether it is second person familiar or the second person formal, and the conditions for this choice

3.3.1 Inclusion of the referent in the perplexive

The perplexive construction sometimes contains the referent of the subject pronoun:

(16) a. *Ahmet*$_i$ *sen*$_i$ *tut*$_i$ *kedi-ye incir yedir*$_i$.
Ahmet SEN_TUT.IMP cat-DAT fig feed.IMP
'[Would you believe it?!] Ahmet fed the cat figs!'
b. *Sen*$_i$ *Ahmet*$_i$ *tut*$_i$ *kedi-ye incir ye-dir*$_i$.
SEN Ahmet TUT cat-DAT fig feed.IMP
'[Would you believe it?!] Ahmet, fed the cat figs!'

As can be seen, the referent of *sen* 'you' can optionally be included in the sentence overtly, either before the *s*-pronoun as in (16a), or after it as in (16b). In a situation where the third party has not been introduced into the discourse, the introduction of this person may be encoded in the sentence, as in the exchange below:

(17) A. *Çok sıkıntılı görün-üyor-sun. Ne oldu?*
very worried seem-PROG-2SG What be-P?
'You seem very worried. What happened?'

B. *(Sorma...) Ali sen tut bizim antika halı-yı mezat-a ver!*
(ask-NEG.)Ali SEN_TUT.IMP our antique rug-ACC auction-DAT give.IMP
'(Oh, man...) Ali put our antique rug in an auction!'

If the person in question (third party) is not too familiar to the addressee, s/he can alternatively be introduced by means of the topic marker *var ya* (lit.) 'there is':

(18) B. *(Sorma.)Ali*$_i$ *var ya...Sen*$_i$ *tut bizim antika halı-yı mezat-a ver!*
(ask-NEG.)Ali there.is...SEN_TUT.IMP our antique rug-ACC auction-DAT give.IMP
'(Oh, man...) You know Ali...?! He put our antique rug in an auction!'

3.3.2 The [+/-animacy] of the referent of the *s*-pronoun

In all the examples above, the referent of the *s*-pronoun is [+human]. But the *s*-pronoun can also be [–human] or [–animate], with effects of personification:

(19) *Sen tut Ali-nin sevgili kedisi ol!*
SEN-TUT Ali-GEN dear cat-3POSS.SG be.IMP
'[Would you believe it?!] S/he became Ali's dearest cat.'

(20) *Bizim şu porselen vazo var ya... On-u yıka-dık-tan sonra yan yatır-mış-lar...*
our this porcelain vase there.is... it-ACC wash-COMP-ABL after sideways lay-EV-3PL
Sen tut masa-nın kenar-ın-dan kay düş kır-ıl.
SEN.TUT table-GEN side-3POSS.SG-ABL slide.IMP fall.IMP break-PASS.IMP
'You know this porcelain vase of ours...Someone placed it sideways on the table after washing it and [would you believe it?!] it slid and fell and broke.'

In (19) the *s*-pronoun refers to a cat, and in (20) it refers to a vase. These examples further indicate the extent of the mismatch between the strict lexical specification of a pronoun and its referent.

3.3.3 Encoding the social distance between the addressee and the speaker

We mentioned above in section 2 that the pronoun of the perplexive constructions can either be the familiar (*sen*), or, when the referent denotes a group, the second person plural form (*siz*). The second person plural is homonymous with the second person formal in Turkish. Interestingly, the choice between the familiar and formal form of the pronoun sometimes depends on the social relation between the speaker and the addressee.[6]

[6] In addition to the usage described here, the second person pronoun can be used in other constructions, some of which are idiomatic:
(i) *Sen mi-sin polis-le top oyna-yan*
sen INT-2SG police-COM ball play-COMP
'S/he made the bad decision of playing football with the police.'
http://www.radikal.com.tr/Radikal.aspx?aType=RadikalDetayV3&ArticleID=1047639&Date=28.04.2011&CategoryID=77

Compare (21) and (22) below. Although the referent is the same third person in both cases, the second person formal form is used in (22) due to the assumed or actual level of formality that imposes a T-V distinction as a marker of social distance between the speaker and the addressee.

(21) ***Sen** tut Ali-yi hırsızlık-la suçla!*
SEN_TUT.IMP.2FAM Ali-ACC theft-PRIV accuse.IMP.2FAM
'[Would you believe it?!] S/he accused Ali of theft!'

(22) ***Siz** tut-un Ali-yi sahtekarlık-la suçla-yın!*
SİZ_TUT.IMP-2FRM Ali-ACC theft-PRIV accuse.IMP-2FRM
'[Would you believe it?!] S/he accused Ali of theft!'

We shall return to the dual role of the second person in section 6.

4. Imperative marking

A burgeoning question that remains unanswered so far is why the perplexive uses the kind of structure that precisely corresponds to the imperative mood.[7] We suggest that two aspects of the imperative marker contribute to the perplexive construction. These are the directive function of the imperative and its irrealis modality. Below we suggest how these

---

The reader is also referred to Fortuin (2010) and Biq (1991) for the various other functions of the second person pronoun attested in other languages.

[7] One might question the imperative status of the marking in perplexive constructions, as in some verb forms the imperative is identical to the optative as illustrated in (i) and (ii):

(i) *Sen oku diye çalış-tı-m*
you study.OPT COMP work-P-1SG
'I worked so that you could study.'

(ii) *Şu kitabı oku hemen!*
this book-ACC read.IMP immediately
'Read this book immediately.'

Using the overt optative marker *–(y)A* resolves this issue. The optativity of the verb form in (i) is evident because it can be paraphrased by another optative form (iii), whereas (ii) cannot be paraphrased by the same marker in standard Turkish as illustrated in (iv), and perplexives are ungrammatical with this marker (v):

(iii) *Sen oku-ya-sın diye çalıştım.*
study-OPT-2SG

(iv) **?Şu kitabı oku-ya-sın hemen!*

(v) **Sen tut-a-sın...*

two go hand-in-hand in covertly making way to the perfective aspect and the factive mood (indicative past).

While the imperative has functions other than encoding commands (see, for example, Fortuin & Boogaart 2009), its occurrence in the perplexive construction is peculiar at first glance.[8] Given that the event expressed in the perplexive construction is without any doubt factual (realis), set in the past and perfective, the construction would be expected to bear one of the past tense or perfective markers already available in the language. While in narrative usages an imperfective marker can be used to denote a past event,[9] the conditions are different here: In the perplexive construction an irrealis modality marker is used to indicate the realis. We take this to constitute an instance of covert modality. However, these seemingly counterintuitive aspects of the construction find an explanation

---

[8] It is worth mentioning that the imperative is used in several other types of constructions, some idiomatic, and that it marks different moods and aspects:

(i) *Gid-er-se-n git.*
go-AOR-COND.COP-2SG go.IMP
'I don't care if you go.' (dismissive)

(ii) *Sen orda gül gül bak sen-i ne yap-ıca-m.*
you there laugh.IMP laugh.IMP see.IMP you-ACC what do-FUT-1SG
'You go on laughing there and see what I'll do with you!'
(imperfective, bullying)

(iii) *Siz yi-yin o hamburger-ler-i, sonra kilo-lar-ı ben ver-e-yim.*
you eat-IMP.2PL those hamburger-PL-ACC, then kilo-PL-ACC I give-OPT-1SG
'How will you give all those kilos when you eat those hamburgers?'
(sarcastic, critical)

(iv) *Abart!*
exaggerate.IMP
'You are exaggerating.' (imperfective, cynical)

(v) *Gel de inan.*
come.IMP CONJ believe.IMP
'I don't believe him/her.' (cynical)

(vi) *Sen alışveriş yap ben de o zaman yemek yaparım.*
you shopping do.IMP I CONJ then meal cook-AOR-1SG
'If you do the shopping I will cook.' (conditional)

It may be possible to subsume all these usages of the imperative under a single heading, but this topic is beyond the scope of this paper.

[9] For example, the progressive (imperfective) marker can be used to express a past event, similar to the usage of the present tense marker in English:

(i) *Şimdi bu gid-iyo. Zili çal-ıyo….*
now he go-IMPF. bell-ACC ring-IMPF
'Then he goes there, rings the bell…'

if we take the usage of irrealis modality to express a directive to the addressee to imagine himself in a situation that has occurred in the past. This is especially evident since the speaker is required to mark the social distance between herself and the addressee, as discussed in 3.3.3 above, while referring to a third party outside the utterance time. That is, the mapping between the *s*-pronoun and the protagonist in the narrative is not direct, but rather mediated through the mind of the addressee. More specifically, we suggest that the imperative achieves the illocutionary force of virtually calling upon the addressee to share with the speaker how odd the to-be-narrated event is by putting himself into the protagonist's shoes, and share the experience. This is in agreement with the use of irrealis as portraying 'situations as purely within the realm of thought, knowable only through imagination' (Mithun 1999: 173). Thus, the directive function of the imperative is fulfilled, as is the irrealis component of the perplexive.

Having established the contribution of the imperative in terms of its directivity and irrealis modality, we are faced with the following question: What part of the perplexive encodes a past event? We suggest that this element must also be covertly expressed by the imperative, as (a) there are no other contenders that can act as aspectual markers, and (b) that for the listener, intuitively the perfectivity of this construction seems to be interpreted directly through the presence of the verb, e.g. when the imperative marked verb of impulse is uttered (see below). We propose that the past and perfective reading is a by-product of the context shift induced by the *s*-pronoun. When the intended perlocutionary effect is achieved, i.e., when the addressee changes his perspective and transforms himself into a different context where he puts himself into the shoes of the protagonist, there is no other option for him to interpret the proposition other than by transforming its modality from irrealis to realis, and consequently reconstruct it as a narrative which left the speaker in perplexity. We thus propose a tripartite value for the imperative:

(i) a directive which calls upon the addressee to share the emotions of the speaker
(ii) irrealis modality which places the addressee in an imaginary world (for him)
(iii) the perfectivity of an event marked through a context shift

Below we turn to the final component of the perplexive construction, the verbs of impulse.

5. Verbs of impulse and the marking of emotions

We mentioned above that there is a small group of words that optionally follows the *s*-pronoun in perplexive constructions. These verbs, the most common ones being *kalk* (lit.) 'rise', *tut* (lit.) 'hold', *git* '(lit.) 'go' and a few others, are not used in their literal sense, but rather as aspectual markers of suddenness and non-expectancy. These verbs are found in other constructions where they have previously been analysed as serial verbs (see Csató 2003):

(23) a. *Tut-tu elbise-m-i çöp-e at-tı.*
TUT-P dress-1POSS.SG-ACC rubbish-DAT throw-P
'Fancy that! S/he threw away my dress!'
b. *Kalk-tı bana bağır-dı.*
KALK-P I.DAT scream-P
'Fancy that! S/he screamed at me!'

Here we would like to draw attention to the semantic similarity of these constructions and perplexives. The function of the verbs of impulse is to encode not only the surprise of the speaker through the suddenness of the event, but also disapproval, disappointment, irritation, and anger, which seem to be prevalent in all their usages.

The impulsive aspect (by which we mean an impulsive reaction to a sudden event) encoded in these verbs is further supported by the fact that they are incompatible with individual-level readings of predicates. If for example, the speaker suddenly realizes that a particular cat belongs to Ali and moreover approaches this situation with disapproval, this cannot be expressed in the following way:

(24) **Sen tut Ali-nin bir kedi-si ol.*
SEN_TUT.IMP ALİ-GEN a cat-3POSS:SG be
(Intended reading '[Would you believe it?!] She is Ali's cat!')

However, a stage-level reading is available for a similar construction:

(25) *Sen tut Ali-nin en sevgili kedi-si ol.*
SEN_TUT.IMP ALİ-GEN most dear cat-3POSS:SG become
'[Would you believe it?!] She became Ali's dearest cat.'

6. Summary and discussion

Our proposal builds on the above mentioned properties of pronouns as shifters of topic. In section 3.2, we mentioned that the presence of a pronoun has been analyzed as signaling a shift in the sentence topic or a shift in the center of discourse. It has already been proposed in the literature that pronouns are shifters, which change the flow of discourse by altering the topic of a sentence, or the topic of the discourse. We claim that the perplexive takes the shift function of pronouns beyond topichood and extends it to context by situating the participants in the time of the event. The indications for the shift in context are the following:

(i) The marker of second person used for referring to a party who is absent in the time of utterance situates the speaker in the time of the event. It renders the flavor that the speaker is addressing the person she is talking about in the time of the event, i.e. no second person is implied at the time of utterance, and therefore the *s*-pronoun can only refer to the time of the event.

(ii) Along the same lines, the imperative marking, the marker of irrealis mood, also gets its share from this context shift, hence covertly marks past tense and perfective aspect.

However, these are not the sole signals of the *s*-pronoun and the imperative. The *s*-pronoun, through the choice of form between the formal and the familiar, is linked to the time of utterance since the decision of the particular form of the *s*-pronoun depends on the level of formality of the relation between the speaker and the addressee, as we have seen in Section 3.3.3 above. The imperative is also linked to the utterance time through its function as a directive towards the addressee to situate himself at the time of the event to share the emotions of the speaker. The usage of a verb of impulse bolsters this transition: The adverbial interpretation of suddenness imparted by a verb of impulse is relevant in the past time, hence is linked to the time of event. It indicates the sudden realization of the event which is the source of surprise at the time the event takes place. The element of disapproval or disappointment on the other hand is linked possibly to the event time, but undeniably also to the time of utterance.

Thus, a context shift takes place through the usage of the *s*-pronoun, by which we mean the speaker situates herself in an environment of the past and chooses the pronouns, modality marking, and adverbial modification commensurate with that environment. Both the pronoun and the modality marker are forced to have an interpretation that is not part of their lexical specification at the time of utterance. There are, however, signals that are related to the time of utterance as described above. Hence, we simultaneously see the extended exponence of particular morphosyntactic features and the cumulative exponence of particular functions. We summarize the function-form mapping in Table 6-1 and link these items to event time and utterance time in Table 6-2.

Table 6-1. Function-form correspondences in the perplexive construction.

FUNCTION	FORM
Context shift	*s*-pronoun
Familiarity level between speaker and addressee	
Directive mood	Imperative form of verb
Irrealis mood	
Perfective aspect / past tense	
	Person marking on verb
Suddenness	Verb of impulse
	Exclamative prosody
Disapproval / disappointment/irritation/anger	

Table 6-2. Functions marked by each item with respect to Event Time and Utterance Time.

	Pronoun	Serial verb of impulse: Stem	Serial verb of impulse: Modality / aspect	Main verb modality	Person marking	Prosody
UTTERANCE TIME	Context shift ; Directive		Past / Perfective; Directive for irrealis;	Past / Perfective; Directive for irrealis;		
	Level of familiarity between speaker and addressee				Level of familiarity between speaker and addressee	
		Disappointment / Disapproval				Disappointment/ Disapproval
EVENT TIME	Surprise	Surprise / Suddenness / Impulsiveness	Imperfective	Imperfective		

It should be noted that the prosodic contour of these constructions may add to the above surveyed components of the construction.[10] Perplexives seem to be uttered in high pitch throughout, similar to other members of the family of exclamatives of which they are a part. The highest peak falls on the immediately preverbal position. Interestingly, preverbal stress and pitch is one of the properties of presentational focus sentences in Turkish. The fact that perplexives overwhelmingly have the SOV order, the order of presentational focus sentences, places them among those constructions that present all new information (see Göksel & Özsoy 2000, 2003) for the expression of presentational focus in Turkish). This is not surprising, as perplexive constructions highlight events that are new to the addressee.

7. Conclusion

Our primary aim in this paper has been to bring to attention a hitherto unanalyzed construction in Turkish, a construction we name *perplexive* in an attempt to capture its covert emotive and modal properties. We have teased apart various grammatical functions in this construction and traced them to particular forms. The pattern of covert modality subsumed under the perplexive construction builds upon an intricate interaction of various elements in the clause. The insight it brings to the discussion of covert modality is that the signal for perplexive modality does not arise from a particular modal particle with an additional and hitherto undiscovered function, but rather a complex network of form to function and function to form correspondences in a cumulative fashion. Needless to say, much work has to be done on each one of these forms to understand their particular place in the context of Turkish grammar as well as cross-linguistically.

One of our most important findings is the concurrent expression of items relevant to event time and those relevant to utterance time. The most telling of these is in the marking of the subject of the construction, the *s*-pronoun. This pronoun seems to address the agent of an event in the past, yet at the same time uses the form appropriate for the addressee in the utterance time. The *s*-pronoun, moreover, is the encoder of a context shift, showing that the function of pronouns in Turkish covers more than what has been attributed to them as topic shifters. In other words, the functions

[10] Many languages use prosody to mark surprise (e.g., Ladd 2008). Interestingly, some languages have morphemes to indicate this function. In East Dangla "marking the subject by means of a preverbal clitic indicates that the clause, or some component of the clause, [is] unexpected" (Shay 2008: 90).

of *s*-pronouns surpass the types of shift associated with them in the current literature.[11]

Yet another instructive finding is that the perplexive construction forces the speaker to block the primary lexical features of the pronoun, as well as one of the primary features of the imperative to achieve another effect: the hypothetical situation in which the addressee is part of the past event. Such a violation seems to support the idea that speakers presuppose as much as possible in their contribution to conversation and hearers try to make the most sense of what they are presented with (Principle of Relevance, Sperber & Wilson 1986). In perplexives, the speaker violates the quality/economy of communication by consistently calling the hearer to override the primary function of particular lexical items. This may be conceived as a strategy to invite the hearer to assess the propositional content of the sentence uttered by the speaker, and her emotions and attitude. Constructions as such can be subsumed under the wider-realm of addressee-involving conversational increments (see e.g., Göksel, Kabak & Revithiadou in press for non-local doubling in Greek and Turkish, which conveys a similar illocutionary act).

Here we merely scratched the surface by investigating the conversational implicatures of the perplexive construction. It would be interesting to evaluate them within theories of pragmatics and in contrast to similar constructions in different languages. The communicative aspects of such addressee-involving constructions in the wider realm of the pragmatics of linguistic interaction also constitute a fruitful area for future research.

Acknowledgements

We would like to thank the audiences at the Workshop on Covert Patterns of Modality at the 44th Annual Meeting of the Societas Linguistica Europaea, 8-11 September 2011, Universidad de la Rioja, Logroño, Spain for their comments. We are grateful to Werner Abraham, Elisabeth Leiss and an anonymous reviewer for their feedback and editorial help. Needless to

[11] It should be noted that the *s*-pronoun can also refer to the speaker if the speaker herself views the past event from outside. Example (2) in section 2 is illustrative in this respect. There, the referent of the *s*-pronoun may also be the speaker herself, as viewed from the outside. This would mean that, in hindsight, the speaker finds her own action perplexing and disappointing. Hence, once a context shift is set, the referent of the pronoun can be the speaker herself. This is a further instantiation of a context shift, which can readily be accommodated within our proposal without an appeal to any further mechanisms.

say, all errors are our own. The contribution of Aslı Göksel was supported by Boğaziçi University Research Fund (BAP 5842).

References

Biq, Y.-O. (1991). The multiple uses of the second person singular pronoun in conversational Mandarin. *Journal of Pragmatics* 16, 307-321.

Csató, É. Á. (2003). A typology of Turkish double-verb constructions. In A. Sumru Özsoy *et al.* (eds.) *Studies in Turkish Linguistics*. Istanbul: Boğaziçi University Press. 105-110.

DeLancey, S. (1997). Mirativity. The grammatical marking of unexpected information. *Linguistic Typology* 1, 33-52.

—. (2001). The mirative and evidentiality. *Journal of Pragmatics*, 33(3), 369-382.

Enç, M. (1986). Topic switching and pronominal subjects in Turkish. In D. I. Slobin and K. Zimmer (eds.) *Studies in Turkish Linguistics*. Amsterdam / Philadelphia: Benjamins.

Erguvanlı, E. (1984). *The function of word order in Turkish grammar*. Berkeley, CA: University of California Press.

Fortuin, E. (2000). *Polysemy or monosemy: Interpretation of the imperative and dative-infinitive construction in Russian*. Doctoral Dissertation, ILLC, Amsterdam University. Amsterdam: ILLC Dissertation Series.

—. (2010). Explicit second person subjects in Russian imperatives: Semantics, word order and a comparison with English. *Linguistics* 48(2), 431-486.

Fortuin, E. & R. Boogaart (2009). Imperatives as conditional: From constructional to compositional semantics. *Cognitive Linguistics* 20(4), 641-673.

Frajzyngier, Z. (1997). Pronouns and agreement: Systems interaction in the coding of reference. In H. Bennis, P. Pica & J. Rooryck (eds.) *Atomism and binding*. Dordrecht: Foris. 115-140.

Göksel, A and C. Kerslake (2005). *Turkish. A Comprehensive Grammar*. London: Routledge.

Göksel, A. & A. S. Özsoy (2000). Is there a focus position in Turkish? In A. Göksel & C. Kerslake (eds.) *Studies on Turkish and Turkic Languages*. Wiesbaden: Harrassowitz. 219-228.

Göksel, A. & A.S. Özsoy (2003). dA, a focus/topic associated clitic in Turkish. *Lingua* 113. 1143-1167.

Hatipoğlu, Ç. (2008). Analysis of the social meanings of the second person pronoun Sen in Turkish. *Dilbilim Araştırmaları*, 15-29.
Göksel, A., B. Kabak, & A. Revithiadou. In press. Prosodically constrained non-local doubling. *The Linguistic Review*.
Ladd, D. R. (2008). *Intonational phonology*. Cambridge: Cambridge University Press.
Lazard, G. (1999). Mirativity, evidentiality, mediativity, or other? *Linguistic Typology* 3, 91-109.
Malchukov, A. L. (2004). Towards a semantic typology of adversative and contrast marking. *Journal of Semantics* 21(2), 177-198.
Mithun, M. (1999). *The Languages of Native North America*. Cambridge: Cambridge University Press.
Öztürk, B. (2001). Turkish as a non-pro-drop language. In E. Taylan (ed.) *The verb in Turkish*. Amsterdam / Philadelphia: Benjamins. 239-259.
Shay, Erin (2008). Coding the unexpected. In Z. Frajzyngier and E. Shay (eds.) *Interaction of morphology and syntax, Case studies in Afroasiatic*. Amsterdam / Philadelphia: Benjamins. 85-105.
Slobin, D. I. & A. Aksu-Koç (1982). Tense, aspect and modality in the use of the Turkish evidential. In P. J. Hopper (ed.) *Tense, aspect: Between semantics and pragmatics*. Amsterdam / Philadelphia: Benjamins. 185-200.
Sperber, D. & D. Wilson (1986). *Relevance: Communication and cognition*. Oxford: Blackwell.
Zeijlstra, H. (2011). Let's talk about you and me. http://ling.auf.net/lingBuzz/001233.

INDICATIVE VERB FORMS AS MEANS OF EXPRESSING MODALITY IN ROMANCE LANGUAGES

GERDA HAßLER
UNIVERSITY OF POTSDAM

Abstract: In the Romance languages, verbal mood, modal verbs, modal particles and modal adverbs along with some coordinators and subordinators are available as central categories to express modality. In addition to this richness of means to encode modality, indicative verb forms also often assume the function of anchoring propositions in virtuality or signaling the speaker's insecurity. This paper will explore the modal uses of the imperfect verb forms by focusing not on their indicative meaning as mood, but rather on how the imperfect verb forms modalize the utterance and become a means of expressing epistemic modality. These uses can be explained by a general affinity between aspect and modality with respect to their 'openness', which is manifested in the case of the imperfect as a metonymic bridge from imperfectivity to epistemic modality. Imperfect verb forms can indicate double deixis, allowing the speaker to refer to a source of the communicated information without, however, naming this source. These forms (fr. *imparfait*, it. *imperfetto*, port. *imperfeito*, sp. *imperfecto*) can thus be classified as a means of coding covert modality.

1. Introduction

In addition to the verbal moods, the Romance languages have central parts of speech such as modal verbs (it. *dovere* 'to have to'), modal particles (sp. *bueno* 'well'), modal adverbs (fr. *probablement* 'maybe') as well as coordinators (sp. *según*) and subordinators (it. *comunque*) that are used to express modality. Nevertheless, there are also hidden forms of modality, i.e. linguistic means which are not specialized to express this concept, i.e. in which modality is not overtly represented morphologically (cf. Abraham 2009: 251). Previously, *covert modality* was mainly studied in English in infinitival contexts (Bhatt 2006). This paper will investigate the Romance *imperfect* as a possible expression of covert modality. The term *imperfect* is used here for verb forms such as the French *imparfait*, the Italian *imperfetto*, the Portuguese *imperfeito* and the Spanish *imperfect*. In their prototypical temporal meaning – apart from the whole array of other possible meanings – these verb forms are used to express an action or occurrence in the past, thereby marking duration, iteration or the overlapping of actions. The paper will discuss indicative verb forms that due to their mood would not appear suitable for expressing potential or irreal modality. However, can the imperfect – by itself and without contextual support – express modality in the first place? Or does it depend on the interaction with other means (e.g. syntactic constructions, adverbs, discourse markers)? How is the marking of modality distributed in the individual Romance languages in terms of verbal forms and other linguistic means? Are there characteristic changes in the use of specific verbal forms, which additionally indicate the speaker's perspective?

To elucidate some of these questions regarding the imperfect, I will first present the modal use of the imperfect and propose explanations for it. Then I will discuss the textual features of modally used imperfect verb forms.

2. Modal Use of the Imperfect in Romance Languages

Like Fernández Ramírez (1986) before him, García Fernandez (2004: 90ff.) uses the term *imperfectos modalizados* ('modalized imperfects'), by which he means "una serie de usos del imperfecto etiquetados de diferentes maneras cuyo denominador común es el de la modalización" ('a series of different uses of the imperfect that are labeled differently and the common denominator of which is the modalization', García Fernández 2004: 90). In fact, in its "non-typical" use, the imperfect can convey nonfactuality and counterfactuality. Non-factual utterances are those in which the speaker makes no statement about the veracity of the utterance; in counter-factual utterances the narrator negates this veracity. In the following example the business deal is by no means concluded. On the contrary, closure of the deal is declared to be impossible because a condition is lacking.

(1) Si yo pudiera, mocito, este trato se **cerraba**
if I could, fellow, this deal REFL **close.3.S.IPFV**
'If I could, fellow, this deal would be closed.'
(García Lorca, Poesía Española, Antología por Gerardo Diego, 313)

The function of the English modal verb *would* is assumed in the Spanish sentence by the imperfect. In examples like (1) the conditional construction provides a context for the interpretation of the imperfect as irrealis. However, the use of the imperfect is different in the following sentence from language used in the press:[1]

(2) Peres **reconocía** ayer que el presidente sirio, Hafez El Assad, será el gran ausente de la cumbre, si bien ha sido informado por Mubarak de todos los detalles.
'Peres **acknowledged (IPFV)** yesterday that the Syrian president, Hafez El Assad, would be the "great absentee" at the summit, although he was informed by Mubarak about all the details.'
(La Vanguardia, 02/02/1995, Política)

In this case, the use of the imperfect appears to contradict all prototypical characteristics: What is reported here is a singular, temporally localized and completed utterance by Peres. This would seem to call for the use of the simple perfect, like in the following example (3):

(3) Juppé **reconoció** ayer que los ingresos fiscales "están en una auténtica situación de siniestro", al no haberse cumplido las previsiones de crecimiento.
'Juppé **acknowledged.PRF** yesterday that tax revenues are "in a really disastrous situation", since the growth forecasts were not fulfilled.'
(La Vanguardia, 30/09/1995, Economía y Hacienda)

Why doesn't the example in (2) meet our expectations in terms of the "prototypical" use of the verb? Later on we will see that the use of the imperfect in journalistic texts has to do with the reduction of the recourse obligation of the journalist, i.e. the extent to which he or she takes responsibility for the written content. The use of the imperfect arises here from the modality as means of bringing forth the opinion of the speaker on the validity of the facts expressed by the utterance. In this case contextual elements are not available for the expression of modality. Here modality is *hidden* in the truest sense.

If the imperfect can modalize independently, it seems reasonable to cast doubt on the so-called prototypical properties of the imperfect. The temporal characteristics of the imperfect in the Romance languages can

---

[1] In the examples in which all that matters is the imperfect form, the interlinear translation is dispensed with and the imperfect form – deviating from the original – is **highlighted**.

only be assumed in a very general way, as Bertinetto (1986: 353ff.) already pointed out. The examples (4) to (6) illustrate the weak temporal markedness of the imperfect:

(4) Il **partait** lorsque le téléphone sonna.
he **leave.3.IND.IPFV** when the phone rang.PRF.
'He was just leaving when the phone rang.' (→ Past)

(5) Si tu **étais** ici, quel bonheur.
if you **be.3.IND. IPFV** here what bliss
'If you were here, what bliss.' (→ Present)

(6) Il serait heureux s'il **réussissait** à son examen.
he would be happy if he **pass.3.IND. IPFV** to his exams
'He would be happy if he passed his exams.' (→ Future)

In older texts the Italian *imperfetto* form has an aspectual function in the majority of cases, i.e. it expresses the temporal indeterminacy and the incompleteness of real actions and processes. Bertinetto describes the temporal-aspectual function of the imperfect as "maniera assolutamente indeterminata attraverso cui il processo viene esibito" ('an absolutely undetermined manner by means of which process is expressed', Bertinetto 1986: 346). This semantic indeterminacy opens up the possibility to view the presented process with respect to its validity as undetermined and open. In connection with its open temporal extensiveness it becomes the background of the text. In the following example used by Bertinetto (1986: 346, cf. also Dessì Schmid 2010: 43) the simple perfect is used to introduce a new characteristic and to mark the temporal distance to the speech moment, while the imperfect is used in a purely aspectual way to mark durability and simultaneity:

(7) Agamemnon **era** bello huomo e di bello tempo, molto fiero e molto savio, e *fue* il più riccho e poderoso d'avere e d'amici che fosse in tutta la Grecia.
'Agamemnon **was.IPFV** a handsome man, in his prime, very proud and very wise, and he *was*.PRF the richest and most powerful in wealth and friends in all of Greece.'
(*Istorietta troiana*. Bertinetto 1986: 346)

The *imperfecto* is similarly used in Spanish, where it also occurs in aspectual opposition, but on the other hand is used as absolute narrative tense (*tiempo narrativo absoluto*, Cano Aguilar 1988: 160). In Old Spanish, along with its use as absolute narrative tense, the imperfect could also be used to describe definite and completed actions, alternating with the simple perfect in that capacity. However, in such uses it always described actions or conditions that constitute the background for those that were expressed in simple perfect. Analogous to the Italian example (7), in the following sentence a new characteristic is introduced with the simple perfect, while the subsequently mentioned markings in the background are associated with the imperfect (cf. Dessì Schmid 2010: 44):

(8) E sabet que *fue* Gayo omne muy grand de cuerpo, et de color amariello; pero el cuerpo **era** feo e **auie** la ceruiz et las piernas muy delgadas [...]
'You have to know that Gayo *was*.PRF a man of tall size and of yellow color, but his body **was.IPFV** ugly and **had.IPFV** a slender neck and very slim legs [...]'
(Prom. Crón. Gral. Menéndez Pidal 1977: 116/a/6-9)

The possibility of combining different aspectual values in the same text, whereby the choice of the imperfect depended on a subjective interpretation as background, was reduced in the course of generalizing the absolute imperfective meaning, which also led to a general increase in imperfect forms (Dessì Schmid 2010: 45; cf. Weinrich 2001: 159). The subjective variation of perfect and imperfect verb forms according to the straightforwardness or subtlety of the communicated information – as in the Old Italian (7) and Old Spanish (8) example – would no longer be possible today.

The imperfect in Romance languages has thus evolved into a verb form that can be described as undetermined, incomplete, and regularly characterizing the textual background. There are different explanatory approaches for its modal use. I would like to present two of these and then develop a third one.

3. Explanations of the Modal Use of the Imperfect

3.1 Aspectual coding of modality

The repeated observation in linguistic research regarding the propensity of the past tense to be used modally (e.g. Coseriu 1976, Fleischmann 1982, Reyes 1990, Detges 2001, Comrie 1976, Dessì Schmid 2010) is aptly rendered by James: "There is clearly a universal semantic link between the notion of past tense and the notion of remoteness from reality" (James 1982: 396). However, it has not yet been plausibly demonstrated what this link between past and modality should exactly look like. Moreover, we had already established for the imperfect, to which we intend to restrict our study, that it is not really specialized in expressing the past. It thus seems more appropriate to investigate a relationship between aspectuality and modality.

Abraham (2009: 251f.) assumes an aspectual coding of modality in languages without sufficient modal verbs and states (cf. also Abraham 2008):

> "Typologisch ist interessant, dass sich wohl in einer Reihe von Sprachen Modalität in Abhängigkeit vom Aspekt des eingebetteten Infinitivs ausgelöst findet, in anderen Sprachen hingegen versteckt bleibt [...], jedoch trotzdem klar, nämlich aspektuell kodiert ist." (Abraham 2009: 251f.)
>
> ('Typologically, it is interesting that in a number of languages modality is triggered depending on the aspect of the embedded infinitive. In other languages modality remains hidden [...], but it is nevertheless clear that it is aspectually coded.')

From this Abraham and Leiss developed several hypotheses, which altogether suggest that in languages that lose the category of the verbal aspect, clear traces of a 'functional' aspect remain preserved, which are expressed in an aspectual or aspect-like markedness (e.g. in Abraham 1991, 1998, Abraham/Leiss 2008: XII-XIII, Leiss 2008, 2009). Central to this is the thesis of the validity of the universal-protototypical function of the aspect category at all and its lasting effect on grammatical change in particular (Kotin 2008: 116).

Kotin (2008) also showed the general logical relationships between modality and aspectuality using the Slavic-Germanic contrasting corpus *Buch der Psalmen*. The fact that the number of modal verbs in the German corpus is not comparable to any Slavic language is evidence that the categorical-grammatical functions encoded by the modal verb constructions in German are encoded by other means in the Slavic languages. Based on his research, Kotin finds confirmation for the following hypotheses:

- The postulate of an association between perfect aspect and "root modality" and imperfect aspect and epistemic modality of modal verbs (see already Abraham 1991).
- The hypothesis that the erosion of the aspect category in the Germanic languages led to the expansion of the system of modal verbs, which in

their deontic meaning assume the coding of the perfect aspect function, while epistemic meanings generally indicate imperfectivity.

- The weak representation of modal verbs in the "aspect" languages like the Slavic ones and their rapid development in "aspectless" languages (Germanic languages).[2]

Abraham and Leiss justify the plausibility of their typological thesis "In the absence of modal verbs, aspect fills the expressive gap" (Abraham/ Leiss 2008: XIV) with the fact that modal verbs were originally perfect forms with a present meaning. In their opinion, modal verbs represent something specific about the Germanic languages "despite the fact that there are solitary modal verbs in Romance and non-IE languages" (Abraham/Leiss 2008: XIII). They only give a brief assessment regarding the Romance languages: "Notice that the aspectual Romance languages (*passé simple* vs. *imparfait* as in French) have at most two modal verbs none of which shares the accompanying systematic properties (systematic root plus epistemic readings; origo shifting properties in the Peircian and Jakobsonian sense; true evidentiality quite outside of modal epistemicity) of the German(ic) ones." (Abraham/Leiss 2008: XVI)

Can the Romance languages really be viewed as aspectual languages in which modal verbs are only weakly developed? First, it must be established that there are indeed polysemous modal verbs, which, for example, have a deontic and an epistemic reading:

(9a) fr.	Il	doit	rentrer	à la maison.
	he	must[obligation/supposition]	return	to the house
(9b) sp.	Debe		ir	a casa.
	[he]must [obligation/supposition]		go	to home

'He must go home [because he is expected there.]'
'He must have gone home [, because I don't see him any more at the office and he can't be anywhere else.]'

[2] Deontic modal verbs used in conjunction with the infinitive of the root verb encode the perfect aspectuality in the absolute majority of the cases. In the Slavic versions of the Psalter they correspond to the root verb in the perfective aspect, whereby the modal verb is almost always lacking. If in the Slavic language the corresponding root verb is in the imperfect aspect, in most cases it is a matter of marked use, possibly resulting from an additional imperfectivization. In the cases in which the German text contains modal verbs in conjunction with infinitives of verbs of imperfective action (duratives, iteratives) they are usually rendered in the Slavic versions by verbs in the perspective aspect, often even in cases when perfectivization is usually relatively rare in the Slavic language (cf. Kotin 2008).

While the sentences under (9) – depending on the linguistic and situational context – can express both that the person named as subject is obliged to do something (deontic modality) as well as, in certain contextual conditions, a conclusion of the speaker (epistemic modality, inferential evidentiality[3]), the use of a perfect verb form, in this case the *passé composé*, – similar to what Abraham determined for German – usually triggers an epistemic reading:

(9) fr. Il doit être rentré à la maison.
He must be returned to ART house
'He must have gone home.'

Furthermore, it seems problematic to designate the Romance languages as real aspectual languages. These languages do indeed have verb forms which show aspectual features; however, a sentence in which both partners of an aspect correlation would be used meaningfully is not possible in the Romance languages. While the correlatively bound aspect pair *сдавать* (imperfective) / *сдать* (perfective) in Russian is alone sufficient to convey the opposition of 'attempt' and 'result' due to the aspect correlation, the use of an imperfect and a perfect verb form is not sufficient to express this opposition in French. The purposefulness in the lexical meaning of *passer* would overlay the aspectual meaning here; a meaningful sentence could not be formulated:

(11) Он сдавал экзамен, но не сдал
he pass.3.S.IPFV examination but not pass.3.S.PFV
'He tried to pass the examination, but he did not succeed.'
(12) *Il passait l'examen, mais il ne l'a pas passé.
he pass.3.S.IPFV the examination but he not it has NEG. pass.3.S.PFV

In sum, it does not seem unrestrictedly possible to explain the modal behavior of the Romance imperfect with the typological criterion of an aspect language and the absence of modal verbs which cause double displacement. However, since the connection between aspectuality and

[3] For the evidential meaning of the French *devoir* cf. Dendale 1994. Kronning (2004 : 49) explains the epistemic meaning of *devoir* in the following way: "Ce verbe dénote, selon notre analyse, une modalité complexe – l'«universalité mondaine» (le NECESSAIREMENT VRAI) – qui, montrée, produit l'effet de sens quantificationnel du PROBABLEMENT VRAI, modalisation complexe qui résulte d'une médiation inférentielle."

modality appears to us to be decisive, we introduce a further argument for this in the section below.

3.2 Aspect as a metonymic bridge

With reference to Detges (2001), Dessì Schmid (Dessì Schmid 2010: 58-61) explains the use of modalized imperfect forms as a metonymic process starting from its aspectual meaning. The indeterminacy, the uncompleted character of the represented process, and its textual background function – features of the expression of imperfect aspectuality – form the bridge to irrealis modality.

By using the imperfect, the speaker makes a very economical decision. The encyclopedic knowledge of the speaker about the fact that something has a lower level of assertiveness in terms of beginning and end or is true only under certain conditions enables the transmission to the facts that are to be modalized. Thus, in the following sentence the imperfect (*podías*) is used in the irrealis construction for the conditional.

(13) Si hubiese otra taberna abierta a estas horas, te **podías** despedir de mi como cliente.
'If there was another open tavern at this late hour, you could bid farewell to me as a client.' (cf. Fernández Ramírez 1986:276)
(I. Aldecoa, En el kilómetro 400, en Libro de Lecturas, 37)

The reason why the bridge from aspectuality to modality is termed metonymic is due to the contiguity of the two functions: imperfective aspectuality leads to modality due to its indeterminacy.

Just as in an utterance like (14) in which the action of going out is understood as only attempted and not really completed, the imperfect aspectuality enables the open-endedness. An action that is presented during its course can be conceived in such a way that its result, and ultimately the action itself, appear as open.

(14)	Ana	salía	cuando	sonó	el teléfono.
	Ana	leave.3.IPFV	when	ring.3.PFV	ART telephone

'Ana was leaving when the telephone rang.'

The explanation of the modal meaning of the imperfect using the metonymic bridge does not seem to us to contradict the typological explanation. Rather, it seems to meaningfully supplement this explanation due to the aspect-modality complementarity that cannot be substantiated for the Romance languages.

3.3 Doubling of perspective and deixis

In certain uses the imperfect also refers to an information source which can manifest itself as a remembered utterance of another person, hearsay or cognitive processes occurring in the speaker himself or herself.

The utterance (15) with an overt specification of the source could be reformulated using the reference function of the *imperfecto* as (16):

(15)	Juan	viene	mañana,	según	me	anunciaron.
	Juan	come.3.S.PRS.	tomorrow	as	me	announce.3.PL.PFV.

'Juan is coming tomorrow, as I was told.'

(16)	Juan	**venía**	mañana.
	Juan	come.3.S.IPFV	tomorrow

'Juan is supposed to come tomorrow.'

The verb form *venía* would not be understood here as a reference to an already past coming, which is clear through the use of the temporal adverb *mañana*. Rather, *venía* refers to a previous utterance in which Juan's coming was announced. The *imperfecto* presupposes this utterance and refers to it. Besides its "prototypical" reference in the temporal respect, it has also partially lost its aspectual function and taken on an epistemic-evidential meaning.

Thanks to the studies by Reyes[4] on the evidential value of the *imperfecto* in Spanish, it has been shown that in sentences such as (17) the reference to the origin of the speaker's knowledge from an external, uncertain source is possible solely via the verb form.

(17)	El tren	**llegaba**	a las ocho.
	The train	arrive.3.S.IPFV	at ART eight

'The train is supposed to arrive at eight.'

[4] Reyes (1994) chose the term *valor citativo* for the intertextual reference function of the Spanish *imperfecto*. It is, however, more appropriate to speak of the evidential value of the imperfect because it is not clear whether a statement is really quoted or whether the rendered knowledge of the speaker simply originates from an uncertain or insufficiently remembered source.

Utterances such as (18) and (19) are understood as statements about past or future facts that the speaker knows about due to the testimony of others or from his/her own reflections:

(18) No voy a buscar al niño a la escuela porque
not go.1.S.PRS to look for ART boy to the school because

hoy iba su padre a buscar=lo.
today go.3.S.IPFV his father to look for=him

'Today I'm not going to pick up the boy at school because I think his father is going to pick him up.'

(19) ¿Viste al novio? Venía ayer a ver Lolita.
see ART.ACC bridegroom come.3.S.IPFV yesterday to see Lolita
'Have you seen the bridegroom? I heard he came yesterday to see Lolita.'

With explicit lexical and syntactic marking of evidentiality as a reference to the source or as protection of information, these statements could appear as follows:

(18') No voy a buscar al niño porque hoy su padre, *según está programado*, **iba** a buscarlo. (Or: Su padre dijo que lo iba a buscar hoy.)
'I'm not going to get the child, because *according to the schedule* his father will pick (**3.S.IPFV**) him up today.' (Or: 'His father said he was going to pick (**3.S.IPFV**) him up today.')

(19') ¿Viste al novio? *Me dijeron que* **venía** ayer … a ver a Lolita.
'Have you seen the bridegroom? I heard he came **(3.S.IPFV)** yesterday to see Lolita.'

The relationship of these statements, (18) and (19), to their variants with explicit lexical and syntactic marking as reported speech or as an opinion as in (18') and (19') can be viewed as transfer of the referring function of the omitted elements to the verb form which regularly occurs in their context. The double deixis existing in the sentence (20), where the second deictic center is explicitly named ('his father'), is also clear in the simple sentence (21), simply due to the imperfect, without embedding the expressed statement or without explicitly naming the producer.

(20) **Su padre** dijo **que** lo *iba* a buscar hoy.
his father said that him [he] was going to (IPFV.) pick up today.
'His father said that he would pick him up today.'

(21) Hoy *iba* su padre a buscarlo
Today was going (IPFV.) his father to pick up= him
'Today his father wants to pick him up.'

While in some contexts the opening of a second deixis can be shown and reconstructed through the imperfect, it is nevertheless problematic to generally designate such uses of the imperfect as evidential. Often the imperfect simply expresses an insecurity of the speaker about the reported facts and could be followed by a question tag. The reference to an actual source of knowledge can fade into the background:

(22) El tren llegaba a las ocho, ¿verdad?
The train arrive.3.S.IPFV at ART eight truth
'The train is supposed to arrive at eight, isn't it?'

While the modal function of the Spanish *imperfecto* has already been studied for some time (e.g. Reyes 1990, 1994, Haßler 1997, 2001, Volkmann 2005), in the last part of my paper I would like to discuss the occurrence of the imperfect in other Romance languages, which is especially manifested in certain types of texts.

4. Fixation of the Modal Uses of the Imperfect in Certain Types of Texts

In some types of texts the reference of recourse obligation for the content of the utterance to another center outside of the speaker deixis is especially important for the content of the utterance. Already in 1983, based on the over-dimensional use of the French *conditionnel* in journalistic language, Raible showed that the speaker can reject recourse obligation and thus avoid legal consequences (Raible 1983: 276). However, that does not lead to the conclusion that the use of the *conditionnel* to indicate a source of information must always represent a refinement in the delineation of individual evidential meanings. The frequent use, particularly in press texts, is manifested as a simplification of two constructions which as such are no longer distinguishable in the simplified form. In the following examples it remains open whether the use of the *conditionnel* expresses a conclusion of the journalist or renders the speech of another person, whether inferential or quotative evidentiality is present. See (23) and (24) :

(23) Les jeunes **préféreraient** que l'employeur se sente
ART young prefer.3.PL.COND that ART employer REFL feel.S.SBJV

responsable de l'avenir qu'il leur prépare
responsible of ART future which he them prepares

'Young people would prefer that the employer would feel responsible for their future.'
(2000-12-02)

(24) Pour l'UCI le contrôle anti-dopage du Tour de France 2000 est
for the ICU the control anti-doping of=ART Tour de France 2000 is

terminé. Les Jeux de 2008 à Paris **coûteraient** 7 milliards
over. The Games of 2008 in Paris cost.3.PL.COND 7 billion

de francs aux collectivités.
of francs in ART funds public

'For the ICU, the anti-doping control of the Tour de France is over. The 2008 Games in Paris would cost 7 billion franc in public funds.'
(2000-12-02)

Today the imperfect form already appears in a similar function in the Romance languages.[5] As we have already seen, the imperfect enables the opening of another speaker deixis, without requiring the naming of the other deictic center. Such uses are particularly conspicuous in the language of the press. The imperfect forms in (25) to (27) are used to portray singular, completed and temporally determined actions. Although perfective verb forms could indeed be expected here, the journalists use the imperfect, which allows them to evade responsibility for the content and to indicate that they have gained the information from observation, from another person, or from their own reflection, without specifying an exact source.

[5] Cf. also Labeau & Larrivée (2005).

(25)

Diego Mateo del Peral,	**recibía**	un oficio	del
Diego Mateo del Peral,	**receive.3.S.IPFV**	an official letter	of=ART

rector de la Universidad.
rector of the university

'Diego Mateo del Peral is said to have received an official letter from the rector of the university.'

Al día siguiente de aparecer en las páginas de este diario un artículo suyo sobre la situación de la Universidad, el director del Colegio Mayor Diego de Covarrubias, *Diego Mateo del Peral,* ***recibía*** *un oficio del rector de la Universidad* Complutense de Madrid en el cual le comunicaba que había propuesto su cese inmediato a la junta de gobierno de la referida universidad.
(El País, Educación, 04/08/1997)

(26)

Un soldado croata	**disparaba**	ayer	con antiaéreos
A soldier Croatian	**fire 3.S.IPFV**	yesterday	with anti-aircraft missiles

'A Croatian soldier is said to have fired anti-aircraft missiles yesterday.'

Un soldado croata ***disparaba*** *ayer con antiaéreos* contra posiciones terrestres serbias situadas a 200 metros. NIKOLA SOLIC. AP
(La Vanguardia, Ciencia Militar, 02/05/1995)

(27)

Ese mismo día	**moría**	el genio	del	idioma
this same day	**die**.3.S.IPFV	the genius	of the=ART	language

castellano	con Miguel de Cervantes Saavedra.
Castilian	with Miguel de Cervantes Saavedra

'On the same day the genius of the Castilian language is said to have died with Miguel de Cervantes Saavedra.'

Hace algunos algunos días, con el título Cervantes y Shakespeare, salió publicada en su leído diario una erudita relación de la fecunda producción del famoso poeta inglés. Al final se afirma lo siguiente: "La más alta cumbre de las letras inglesas murió el 23 de abril de 1616. *Ese mismo día* ***moría*** *el genio del idioma castellano con Miguel de Cervantes Saavedra*". (El Tiempo, Literatura, 01/06/1990)

Similarly, in other Romance languages, uses of the imperfect can be found which do not indicate a course of a process without determination and limitation, but which focus on a temporally limited and completed process. Here too, the imperfect reduces the responsibility of the speaker, in this case the journalist, and refers to an undetermined source, as in (28) and (29):

(28)	On	y	**disait**	que le directeur du	corps de ballet	ne
	one	there	**say**.3.S.IPFV	that the director of=ART	troop of ballet	not

lui	avait	vraiment	pas laissé	de passe-droit
her	had	really	NEG.allowed	PREP preferential

'According to sources there, the ballet director would truly never have given her preferential treatment.'

On y disait que le directeur du corps de ballet ne lui avait vraiment pas laissé de passe-droit, la considérant comme un membre à part entière de sa troupe plutôt que comme une actrice.
(source: http://www.voir.ca/cinema/fichefilm.aspx?iIDFilm=5045)

(29)	Há já	algum	tempo	alguém	**evidenciava**	num
	ago already	some	time	someone	show.3.S.IPFV	in=ART

artigo	do Jornal Terras da Beira,	as qualidades da equipa.
article	Jornal Terras da Beira	the qualities of=ARTteam

'Already some time ago someone is said to have showed the qualities of the team in a newspaper article in Terras da Beira.'

Há já algum tempo alguém evidenciava num artigo do Jornal Terras da Beira, as qualidades da equipa candidata à Câmara Municipal da Guarda liderada por Carlos Andrade apelidando-a de "Dream Team" (CDP, 18 Set 97, A voz que vai morrer em directo)

Particularly striking is the systematic use of the imperfect in stock market reports. Although these depict concrete figures and processes, the author does not wish to vouch for these and refers to an external source without naming it:

(30) La Bourse de New York **prenait** pour sa
The Stock Exchange of New York **take.3.S.IPFV** for POSS

part 3,78% peu après son ouverture.
part 3.78 % shortly after POSS opening.

'According to sources, shortly after its opening, the New York Stock exchange rose 3.78 %.'
(source: http://www.laliberte.ch/?depeche=27112)

(31) L'action d'Isacsoft **perdait** 1,5 cent
ART stocks of Isacsoft **lose.3.S.IPFV** 1.5 cent

'According to sources According to sources Isacsoft stocks fell 1.5 cents to 35.50 cents Tuesday afternoon on the TSX Venture Exchange.

L'action d'Isacsoft perdait_1,5 cent à 35,50 cents mardi après-midi à la Bourse de croissance TSX.
(source: http://www.lapresseaffaires.com/article/ 20070327/ LAINFORMER /70327146/5891/LAINFORMER01)

(32) Repsol, que ayer **pagaba** dividendo movió 23.984 millones de pesetas
Repsol which yesterday **pay.3.S.IPFV** dividend moved 23,984 million of pesetas
'Repsol which yesterday paid dividends, moved 23,984 million pesetas.'
Repsol, que ayer **pagaba** dividendo movió 23.984 millones de pesetas, y Fecsa, que lo paga hoy 6.310 millones de pesetas.
(El Mundo, 09/01/1996, Negocios)

(33) El presupuesto de estas obras complementarias
The budget of DET work.PL additional PL

ascendía a 35 millones de pesetas.
amount.3.S.IPFV to 35 millions of pesetas

'The supplementary budget for this additional work is said to amount to 35 million pesetas.'
(La Vanguardia, 02/07/1995, Política)

Hence, also in such texts, the imperfect opens up a double deixis – that of the author and that of the source. In a similar function, the imperfect has long been known as the typical verb form in free indirect speech in literary texts (cf. Bres 2005, Haßler/Volkmann 2009, Volkmann 2009)[6]:

(34) Le professeur se mit alors en colère. *Il ne* ***supportait*** *plus la paresse de son élève. Il finirait par ne plus s'en occuper si celui-ci* ***trouvait*** *sans arrêt des excuses pour ne pas faire ses devoirs…*

Il	ne	**supportait**	plus la	paresse	
he	no	**put up.S.IPFV**	longer	the	laziness

si celui-ci	**trouvait**	sans arrêt	des	excuses
if he	find **3.S.IPFV**	constant	ART	excuses

'The teacher began to lose his temper. He would no longer put up with his student's laziness. He would no longer listen if this student constantly found excuses for not doing his homework.'

5. Summary

As we have seen, the use of the imperfect is well established in the Romance languages for unique and self-contained actions that are not considered durative. In marked uses of this kind modal and evidential factors come into play. This demonstrated usage, on the one hand, confirms the affinity of imperfectivity to epistemic modality and can be explained by means of a metonymic bridge between aspect and modality. The use of the imperfect allows for the establishment of a double modal deixis in the text, enabling the producer of the text to refer to a source of the communicated information without, however, naming this source.

References

Abraham, Werner. 1991. Modalverben in der Germania. In: Eijirô Iwasaki (ed.), *Begegnung mit dem „Fremden". Akten des VIII. Internationalen Germanisten-Kongresses in Tokio 1990*. Vol. 4, 109–118. München: Iudicium.

---

[6] For similar considerations with regard to the temporal quality of the past tense cf. Hamburger 1957 and for its deictic function cf. Rauh 1982-1983.

—. 1998. The aspectual source of the epistemic-root distinction of modal verbs in German. In: Winfried Boeder, Christoph Schroeder, Karl Heinz Wagner & Wolfgang Wildgen (eds.), *Sprache in Raum und Zeit. In memoriam Johannes Bechert.* Band 2: *Beiträge zur empirischen Sprachwissenschaft*, 231- 249. Tübingen: Narr.

—. 2008. On the logic of generalizations about cross-linguistic aspect-modality links. In: Abraham & Leiss 2008 (eds.), 3-13.

—. 2009. Die Urmasse von Modalität und ihre Ausgliederung. Modalität anhand von Modalverben, Modalpartikel und Modus. Was ist das Gemeinsame, was das Trennende, und was steckt dahinter? In: Abraham & Leiss 2009 (eds.), 251-302.

Abraham, Werner & Elisabeth Leiss (eds.). 2008. *Modality-Aspect Interfaces. Implications and typological solutions*. Amsterdam / Philadelphia: Benjamins (Typological Studies in Language, 79).

Abraham, Werner & Elisabeth Leiss (eds.). 2009. *Modalität. Epistemik und Evidentialität beim Modalverb, Adverb, Modalpartikel und Modus*. Tübingen: Stauffenburg (Studien zur deutschen Grammatik, 77).

Bertinetto, Pier Marco. 1986. *Tempo, Aspetto e Azione nel Verbo Italiano. Il sistema dell'indicativo*. Florencia: Accademia della Crusca.

Bhatt, Rajesh. 2006. *Covert Modality in Non-finite Contexts*. Berlin / New York: de Gruyter.

Bres, Jacques. 2005. *L'imparfait dit narratif.* Paris: CNRS éditions.

Cano Aguilar, Rafael. 1988. *El español a través de los tiempos*. Madrid: Arco Libros.

Comrie, Bernard. 1976. *Aspect*. Cambridge: Cambridge University Press.

Coseriu, Eugenio. 1976. *Das romanische Verbalsystem*. Ed. Hansbert Bertsch. Tübingen: Narr.

Dendale, Patrick. 1994. Devoir épistémique, marqueur modal ou évidentiel? *Langue Française* 102: 24-40.

Dessì Schmid, Sarah. 2010. 'Modal uses' of the Italian *imperfetto* and the Spanish *imperfecto*: a comparison. In: Martin G. Becker and Eva-Maria Remberger (ed.), *Modality and Mood in Romance. Modal interpretation, mood section, and mood alternation*, 39-66. Berlin / New York: de Gruyter.

Detges, Ulrich. 2001. Grammatikalisierung. Eine kognitiv-pragmatische Theorie dargestellt am Beispiel romanischer und anderer Sprachen. Habilitationsschrift. Universität Tübingen.

Fernández Ramírez, Salvador. 1986. *Gramática española*. Vol. 4: *El verbo y la oración*. Madrid: Arco Libros.

Fleischman, Suzanne. 1982. *The future in thought and language: diachronic evidence from Romance*. Cambridge: Cambridge University Press.

García Fernández, Luis. 2004. El pretérito imperfecto: repaso histórico y bibliográfico. In: Luis García Fernández & Bruno Camus Bergareche (eds.), *El pretérito imperfecto*, 13-5. Madrid: Gredos.

Hamburger, Käte. 1957. *Die Logik der Dichtung*. Stuttgart: Klett.

Haßler, Gerda. 1997. Texte im Text. Überlegungen zu einem textlinguistischen Problem. In: Gerda Haßler (ed.), *Texte im Text. Untersuchungen zur Intertextualität und ihren sprachlichen Formen*, 11-58. Münster: Nodus Publikationen.

—. 2001. Kontrastive und typologische Überlegungen zur epistemischen Modalität in den romanischen Sprachen und im Deutschen. In: Gerd Wotjak (ed.), *Studien zum romanisch-deutschen und innerromanischen Sprachvergleich. Akten der IV. Internationalen Tagung zum romanisch-deutschen und innerromanischen Sprachvergleich (Leipzig, 7.10.-9.10.1999)*, 169-184. Bern et al.: Peter Lang.

Haßler, Gerda & Gesina Volkmann (eds.). 2009. *Deixis y modalidad en textos narrativos*. Münster: Nodus Publikationen.

James, Deborah. 1982. Past Tense and the Hypothetical: A Cross-Linguistic Study. *Studies in Language* 6 (3): 375-403.

Kotin, Michail L. 2008. Zu den Affinitäten zwischen Modalität und Aspekt. Eine germanisch-slavische Fallstudie. *Die Welt der Slaven* 53: 116-140.

Kronning, Hans. 2004. Modalité et médiation épistémiques. In: Régine Delamotte-Legrand, (ed.), *Les médiations langagières*. Volume I. *Des faits de langue aux discours*, 35-65. Rouen: Publications de l'Université de Rouen.

Labeau, Émmanuelle & Pierre Larrivée (eds.). 2005. *Nouveaux développements de l'imparfait*. Amsterdam / New York: Rodopi.

Leiss, Elisabeth. 2008. The silent and aspect-driven patterns of deonticity an epistemicity. A chapter in diachronic typology. In: Abraham & Leiss 2008 (eds.), 15-41.

—. 2009. Drei Spielarten der Epistemizität, drei Spielarten der Evidentialität und drei Spielarten des Wissens. In: Abraham & Leiss 2009 (eds.), 3-24.

Raible, Wolfgang. 1983. Knowing and Believing – and Syntax. In: Herman Parret (ed.), *On Believing. Epistemological and Semiotic Approaches – De la croyance. Approches épistémologiques et sémiotiques*, 275-291. Berlin / New York: de Gruyter.

Rauh, Gisa. 1982-1983. Über die deiktische Funktion des epischen Präteritum: Die Reintegration einer scheinbaren Sonderform in ihren theoretischen Kontext. *Indogermanische Forschungen* 87-88: 22-55, 33-53.

Reyes, Graciela. 1990. Tiempo, modo, aspecto e intertextualidad. *Revista Española de Lingüística* 20: 17-53.

—. 1994. *Los procedimientos de cita: citas encubiertas y ecos*. Madrid: Arco/Libros.

Volkmann, Gesina. 2005. *Weltsicht und Sprache. Epistemische Relativierung am Beispiel des Spanischen*. Tübingen: Narr (Tübinger Beiträge zur Linguistik. 481).

—. 2009. La doble deixis como recurso de relativización epistémica en *Cinco horas con Mario* de Miguel Delibes. In: Haßler & Volkmann 2009 (eds.), 115-131.

Weinrich, Harald. [6]2001. *Tempus. Beschriebene und erzählte Welt*. München: Beck.

Impersonal Dative Constructions as Covert Root-Modality Patterns

Michail L. Kotin
University of Zielona Góra

Abstract: In the Slavonic languages as well as in older Germanic, impersonal constructions with datives occur together with reflexive verbs or infinitives as a means of encoding modal meanings such as possibility or obligation/necessity. This type of (deontic) root modality occurs independently of overt modal signals such as finite modal verbs, modal predicatives, modal adverbs or modal particles. In this way we can speak of a prototypical pattern of covert modality. Some of these sentences are even incompatible with additional modal signals. However, there remains another means of encoding modality, i.e. the impersonal dative construction. Each of these construals has a synonymous counterpart in the form of a personal-categorial sentence displaying an obligatory overt modal. In the latter constructions, nominatives convey the same semantic function as datives in impersonal sentences. However, the lack of overt modality in impersonal dative constructions is characteristically linked to strong restrictions on the selection of verbal aspect. Most impersonal dative constructions select the imperfective aspect of the main verb or a non-lexical equivalent.[1]

1. Introduction: Covert modality emerging from dative constructions

In modern Germanic languages oppositions in diathesis like those illustrated in (1b) are peripheral,

(1a)	Ich friere. I freeze 'I am freezing.'	(1b)	Mir ist (es) kalt. me is (it) cold 'I am cold.'

[1] Thanks are due to three anonymous reviewers.

(2a)	Er weiß das. he knows that	(2b)	Ihm ist das bekannt. him is that well-known
(3a)	Ich erwäge Folgendes I consider (the) following	(3b)	Mir schwebt Folgendes vor… me thinks (the) following [post verbal particle] 'I'm toying with the following idea.'

Depending on the semantics of the predicate and on its event structure, the semantic function of dative arguments in impersonal sentences[2] like those in (1b), (2b) and (3b) can be broadly described as one of an experiencer (cf. Abraham 2006, 23 f.), or as the subject of a state.

In the Slavonic languages such impersonal dative constructions are very frequent and no doubt belong to the nucleus of their syntactic paradigms (cf., among others, Bulygina 1982, Pupynin 1992, Gradinarova 2010), as for example in Russian (4a,b)-(6a,b). (See note 3 for abbreviations of grammatical categories.[3])

---

[2] The terminology of impersonality is not uniform, and it has demonstrated significant differences in the definition of personal as opposed to impersonal constructions. Traditionally, clauses are regarded as impersonal in nominative-accusative languages if they have no subject or convey a so-called formal subject. Thus, the term *impersonal passive* is used to denote German passive clauses which lack a subject (*Im Raum wurde laut gesprochen* 'in the room (there) was loud speaking'). In this traditional terminology clauses with 'weather' verbs such as *Es regnet* are also considered to be impersonal, as are sentences of the type *Mich friert*, etc. (cf. Malchukov/Siewierska 2011, 1ff.). A typologically based definition also includes sentences which are 'semantically' impersonal, like *all* passive clauses, since they force semantically 'impersonal' readings of originally 'personal' sentences (i.e. those which contain an agentive subject), e. g. *Pete was opening the window* vs. *The window was being opened* (in traditional terminology sentences of the latter type have to be regarded to as *personal* passive clauses). Although this latter definition of impersonality appears to be more comprehensive (cf. Malchukov/Ogawa 2011, 19ff.), it is not relevant for this paper, as the sentences discussed here are impersonal from both points mentioned above.

[3] N = noun or pronoun in nominative, D = noun or pronoun in dative, G = noun or pronoun in genitive, PS = the Russian subjunctive particle *бы (by)* encoding volition, MP = the Russian modal predicative *нужно (nuzhno)*, *требуется (trebuyetsya)*, *предстоит (predstoit)* encoding necessity or an unavoidable act or a process in the future perspective, KV = verbal copula in the past form, VP = finite verb in the perfective aspect, VI = finite verb in the imperfective aspect, IVP = perfective infinitive, IVI = imperfective infinitive.

(4a) Я мёрзну.
Ya myorznu.
'I freeze.'

(4b) Мне холодно.
Mne kholodno.
me-D cold
'I am cold.'

(5a) Я это знаю.
Ya eto znayu.
I this know
'I know this.'

(5b) Мне это известно.
Mne eto izvestno.
me-D this known
'This is known to me.'

(6a) Я вижу / [представляю себе] это так…
Ya vizhu / [predstavlyayu sebe] eto tak…
I see / [conceive me] it so…
'I see / conceive it so…'

(6b) Мне это видится / представляется так…
Mne eto viditsya / predstavlyayetsya tak…
me-D it sees / conceives.REFL so…
'My vision of it is as follows…'

In this paper we shall be dealing with two main types of impersonal constructions with dative arguments: (i) constructions with a dative argument and a reflexive verb (discussed in section 2), and (ii) constructions with a dative argument and an infinitive (discussed in section 3).

Type (i) can be divided in two subgroups. The first, (i'), does not possess any additional signals of modality, as with the German examples (1b)-(3b) or the Russian example (6b) above. The vast majority of these sentences have synonymous counterparts with an argument in the nominative case, as in the examples (1a)-(3a) and (6a) above. This subgroup will not be dealt with in this paper, for it is not connected with its subject. The second subtype, (i"), discussed in the sections 2.1.–2.3., can be interpreted as exhibiting covert modality, namely the modality of *possibility*. Cf. Russian (7).

(7) Ему не спится.
Yemu ne spitsya.
him-D not sleep.REFL
'He cannot sleep.'

(translation in Abraham (2006: 24), originally due to
Genuišienė's (1987:125f. and 288f.
'He does not feel like sleeping.').

(8)	Мне	сегодня	особенно	хорошо	работается.
	Mne	segodnya	osobenno	khorosho	rabotayetsya.
	me-D	today	especially	well	work.REFL
	'Today I can work especially well.'				

Unlike the constructions of type (i'), the sentences of this latter type (i") as in (7)-(8) do not have a synonymous personal counterpart with a nominative (subject) argument, since the personal sentences with nominatives do not convey additional modal signals. Cf. Russian (7a) and (8a).

(7a)	Он	не	спит.
	On	ne	spit.
	he	not	sleeps
	'He is not sleeping.'		

(8a)	Я	сегодня	особенно	хорошо	работаю.
	Ya	segodnya	osobenno	khorosho	rabotayu.
	I	today	especially	well	work
	'Today I am working especially well.'				

Type (ii) sentences do not occur in the modern West Germanic languages.

However, as will be shown below, in older Germanic dialects (notably Gothic), impersonal dative sentences may be found with readings comparable to those in Russian. Sentences of this type are also at best very rare in the West Slavonic languages, although they are very frequent in East Slavonic, cf. Russian (9).

(9)	Мне	завтра	нужно	ехать / поехать	в город.
	Mne	zavtra	nuzhno	yechat´ / poyechat´	v gorod.
	me-D	tomorrow	necessary	go-IVI / IVP	to city
	'I have to go to the city tomorrow.'				

The overt modal signal (in this case the adverbial *нужно (nuzhno)*) can be dropped without any effect on the modal reading of the phrase as a whole, as long as the embedded infinitive is imperfective. However, with a perfective infinitive, an overt signal of modality is required for the construction to be acceptable, as in the following example.

(9')	Мне	завтра	ехать / *поехать	в	город.
	Mne	zavtra	yechat′ / *poyechat′	v	gorod.
	me-D	tomorrow	go-IVI / *IVP	to	city

If the 'personal' counterpart of such a sentence contains an overt modal signal, the reading of it is prospective rather than modal, irrespective of the aspect of the verb, cf.:

(9a)	Я	завтра	должен	ехать / поехать	в город.
	Ya	zavtra	dolzhen	yechat′ / poyechat′	v gorod.
	I	tomorrow	must	go-IVI / IVP	to city

(9b)	Я	завтра	еду / поеду	в	город.
	Ya	zavtra	yedu / poyedu	v	gorod.
	I	tomorrow	go-IVI / IVP	to	city

'I will go to the city tomorrow.'

The modality of impersonal dative constructions under (9a) and (9b) is one of *obligation* or *necessity*.

As mentioned above, in this paper we shall be looking at both types of impersonal dative constructions, but we shall also be aiming to demonstrate the affinities between the categories of impersonality, the root modality of possibility or obligation/necessity, and the function of the dative case as a potential means of expressing covert modality. The next section will consider Russian impersonal dative constructions with reflexives. Impersonal dative constructions with infinitives in Russian and in Gothic will be treated in Section 3, and a concluding summary of our findings will be presented in Section 4.

2. Impersonal dative constructions with reflexives expressing covert possibility

2.1 Impersonal dative-reflexive-clauses with negation or adverbials

Let us consider the following Russian examples.

(10) Ему сегодня не спалось.
Yemu segodnya ne spalos′.
him-D today not slept-REFL
'He could not sleep today.'

(11) Ему сегодня хорошо спалось.
Yemu segodnya khorosho spalos′.
him today well slept-REFL
'He could sleep well today.'

(12) Ему сегодня плохо спалось.
Yemu segodnya plokho spalos′.
him today badly slept-REFL
'Today he could sleep well.'

(13) *Ему сегодня спалось.
*Yemu segodnya spalos′.
him today slept-REFL

Comparing (10)-(12) and (13) reveals that sentences containing the impersonal construction in question are only acceptable if they convey additional signals such as negation or an adverbial. However, these markers have different functions in the impersonal dative-reflexive sentences, as in examples (10)-(13) from those in their personal nominative-non-reflexive counterparts, as shown in (10a)-(13a).

(10a) Он сегодня не спал.
On segodnya ne spal.
he today not slept
'He didn't sleep today.'

(11a) Он сегодня хорошо спал.
On segodnya khorosho spal.
he today well slept
'Today he slept well.'

(12a) Он сегодня плохо спал.
On segodnya plokho spal.
he today badly slept
'Today he slept badly.'

(13a)	Он	сегодня	спал.
	On	segodnya	spal.
	he	today	slept
	'He slept today.'		

The negation in (10a) negates the state denoted by the verb, in contrast to (10) where the negative particle negates the possibility of the state. Similarly, the adverbs *хорошо (khorosho)* 'well' and *плохо (plokho)* 'badly' modify the verbal predicates in (11a) and (12a) as typical adverbs of quality, whereas in (11) and (12) they additionally convey a modal modification such that the absence of the adverb (or of the negation) makes impersonal sentences of this type impossible.

The difference in the meaning of personal sentences and their impersonal counterparts depends in part on the semantics of the verb. In the case of *sleep* and similar verbs the structural difference is not crucial, since adverbs of quality combined with process or state verbs in principle have very similar readings. The quality of the process usually assumes a corresponding modal reading, such that if somebody **is** sleeping well, it usually implies that **(s)he can/could** sleep well. In other words, if something is factual, we can infer *per se* that it also embraces possibility, cf. the identical claim by Abraham (this volume). In contrast, if these adverbs are used in combination with action verbs, they denote on the one hand either the quality of the action (as in the case of personal sentences), or on the other its modal properties, such as internal or external circumstances which might help or impede its successful realization (as in the case of impersonal dative-reflexive sentences). Example (14) thus contrasts clearly with (14a):

(14)	Сегодня	он	хорошо / плохо	пел.
	Segodnya	on	khorosho / plokho	pel.
	today	he	well / badly	sang
	'He sang well / badly today.'			

(14a)	Сегодня	ему	хорошо / плохо	пелось.
	Segodnya	yemu	khorosho / plokho	pelos´.
	today	him-D	well / badly	sang-REFL
	'While singing he felt well / bad today.'			

In (14a) the adverbs *хорошо (khorosho)* 'well' and *плохо (plokho)* 'bad(ly)' in no way denote the quality of the singing, but refer only to the mood of the singer while singing. That is why in (14) the adverbs can be dropped, while their absence in (14a) would make the sentence ungrammatical. This simple example shows that the modal meaning is not triggered by the reflexive, as Geniušienė (1987, 125) claims, but "is added due to semantic and categorial under-specification" (Abraham 2006, 25) as it is derived from an active clause. As Abraham (2006) shows from the example of Germanic infinitives with the preposition *to* (German *zu*), modal readings arise from the underspecification of the infinitival preposition *to*, which "has desemanticized and grammaticalized in today's syntactic context" (Abraham 2006, 25). A comparable development can be assumed for the dative-reflexive constructions in Slavonic. A derivation from the originally active clause containing the agent (in the nominative case) leads to a construction with the experiencer in the dative, which denotes a quasi 'passive' (or, better, 'inactive') feature, so that the adverbs *хорошо / плохо (khorosho / plokho)* simultaneously change their semantic scope from adverbs of quality characterizing the activity of the subject / agent to semantically 'weak' predicative adverbs denoting the general circumstances of the state of the experiencer. As a result of this development, the construction as a whole takes on an overall modal meaning, and the fact that the adverbs in question are obligatory has no longer a semantic motivation, but rather a syntactic one. If the reflexive pronoun itself conveyed the modal meaning, it would be possible to omit the adverb with this function.

2.2 Impersonal dative-reflexive clauses and (im)perfectivity

Only intransitive verbs occur in this construction ("only originally transitive verbs" in Abraham 2006, 26, is obviously erroneous). Transitive verbs can only appear if they are being used intransitively, that being the reason why verbs of the type 'read' can appear in these constructions, with the direct object omitted, whereas this is not possible for verbs of the type *cut*. The direct object argument (as a semantic function) is disallowed in modal versions, as shown by the contrast between examples (15) and (16):

(15)	Мне	сегодня	что-то	не	читается.
	Mne	segodnya	chto-to	ne	chitayetsya.
	me-D	today	like	not	read-REFL
	'Somehow, I cannot read today.'				

(15a)

*Мне	сегодня	что-то	*хлеб*	не	режется.
*Mne	segodnya	chto-to	*khleb*	ne	rezhetsya.
me-D	today	like	*bread*	not	cut-REFL

'Somehow, I cannot cut bread today.'

The reason for this restriction is that the reflexive suffix *-ся (sya)* is identical with the passive suffix, and in this way, in the case of what appears to be a canonic passive transformation, the preferred reading is always the passive one, as in (16b):

(16a)

Я	режу	хлеб.
Ya	rezhu	khleb.
I	cut	bread

(16b)

Хлеб	режется	легко.
Khleb	rezhetsya	legko.
bread	cut-REFL	easily

'Bread can be cut easily.'

It is quite clear that a dative argument encoding the semantic function of the agent cannot occur in a construction of this type.

2.3 Impersonal dative-reflexive clauses and the semantics of the verb

The reading of sentences with impersonal datives and reflexive verbs can also be quite different in the case of negated phrases, according to whether they contain an action verb or a state/process verb, as shown by example (17) as opposed to (18):

(17)

Ему	сегодня	совсем	не	спалось.
Yemu	segodnya	sovsem	ne	spalos′.
him-D	today	at all	not	slept-REFL

'Today he could not sleep at all.'

(18)

Ему	сегодня	совсем	не	плавалось.
Yemu	segodnya	sovsem	ne	plavalos′.
him-D	today	at all	not	swam-REFL

'Today he could not swim *well* at all.'

In the first case, (17), the experiencer could not sleep, while in the second case, (18), he **was** swimming, but without any pleasure or unwillingly. If we compare (18) with (14a) and (15), we may conclude that in sentences with action verbs the modality of possibility partly coincides with the modality of volition (or the lack of volition), due to the semantics (the event structure) of the verbs in question. On the other hand, impersonal dative-reflexive sentences with state or process verbs – which by definition do not assume volitional readings under any transformation – always have the modal reading of possibility or lack of possibility, as illustrated by examples (7), (10) and (17).

It must be stressed that the class of dative-reflexive constructions contains a verb in the imperfective aspect. That the verb should be imperfective is an absolute rule not only in this particular case, but also with all constructions which contain reflexives in non-reflexive readings, i. e. which encode the inactive diathesis (cf. Khrakovskij 1978, 55f.). Sentences like (19) are without exception ungrammatical.

(19) *Ему не поспалось / плохо поработалось / не спелось.
*Yemu ne pospalos′ / plokho porabotalos′ / ne spelos′.
him-D not slept-$_{\text{PERF.REFL}}$ / badly worked-$_{\text{PERF.REFL}}$ / not sang-$_{\text{PERF.REFL}}$
'He could not sleep / not work well / not sing well.' (perfective)

The non-overt expression of possibility in the constructions of this type is strictly linked to states, processes, or acts being characterized as having duration. If the perfective aspect were used, this would automatically result in an incompatibility between the aspectual and the modal reading.

3. Impersonal dative constructions with infinitives as patterns of (c)overt modality of necessity

3.1 General structural patterns

Let us consider the following structural patterns of Russian:

1. D – MP – IVP/IVI (prospective reading)

(20a) Учителю нужно идти/пойти к директору школы.
Uchitelyu nuzhno idti / poyti k direktoru shkoly.
teacher-D [is] necessary go-IVI/go-IVP to director-D. school-G.
'The teacher has to go to the school director.'

(20b) Учитель должен идти/пойти к директору школы.
Uchitel` dolzhen idti/poyti k direktoru shkoly.
teacher-N [is] obliged go-IVI/go-IVP to director-D school-G
'The teacher has to go to the school director.'

In neither example is a finite verb present, although in the personal sentence (20b) another modal form is used to that in the dative-infinitive impersonal sentence (20a). Nevertheless, both patterns contain overt modal signals of necessity. The grammatical aspect of the infinitive does not influence the modal reading.

2. D – MP – KV – IVP/IVI (retrospective reading)

(21a) Учителю нужно было идти/пойти к директору школы.
Uchitelyu nuzhno bylo idti /poyti k direktoru shkoly.
teacher-D necessary was go-IVI/go-IVP to director-D school-G
'The teacher had to go to the school director.'

(21b) Учитель должен был идти/пойти к директору школы.
Uchitel′ dolzhen byl idti / poyti k direktoru shkoly.
teacher-N. obliged was go-IVI/go-IVP to director-D school-G
'The teacher had to go to the school director.'

The constructions in (21a,b) are similar to the prospective ones under (20), the only difference being the necessity of the copula in the past tense, while no copula is required (or indeed possible) in the present.

3. D – PS – IVP/(IVI) (the temporal reading depends on the context)

(22a) Ему бы сейчас / завтра/ вчера в Берлин поехать / (ехать)!
Yemu by seychas / zavtra / vchera v Berlin poyechat′/ (yechat′)!
him-D PS now/tomorrow/yesterday to Berlin go-IVP / (go-IVI)!
'He should rather go to Berlin now / tomorrow / should have gone to Berlin yesterday.'

(22b) Он бы сейчас / завтра / вчера в Берлин поехал / (ехал)!
On by seychas / zavtra / vchera v Berlin poyechal / (yechal)!
he-N PS now/tomorrow/yesterday to Berlin went-VP / (went-VI)!
'He should rather go to Berlin now / tomorrow / should have gone to Berlin yesterday!'

The personal sentence, (22b), contains a subjunctive form of the finite verb, with the perfective aspect being preferred in such constructions, although the imperfective aspect is not totally disallowed. It modifies the reading of the sentence slightly, but it has no impact on the modal reading, by which volition is being expressed in both cases. Of course, the past tense additionally encodes counterfacticity, as with every subjunctive sentence referring to the past. In the impersonal sentence, (22a), the modality of volition is suppressed through the impersonality of the dative construction. In this case, the source of volition is not the subject of the sentence, but the speaker, who wants the subject to do something. The verb appears in the infinitive rather than the finite form, as is common for constructions of this type.

4. D – IVI (prospective reading)

(23)	Учителю	завтра	идти / *пойти	к	директору	школы.
	Uchitelyu	zavtra	idti / *poyti	k	direktoru	shkoly
	teacher-D	tomorrow	go-IVI/*go-IVP	to	director-D	school-G.

‘The teacher has to go to the school director tomorrow.’

This pattern is especially relevant in the context of this paper. Similar examples are, for instance:

(24)	Ему	завтра	целый	день	работать.
	Yemu	zavtra	celyj	den`	rabotat`.
	him-D	tomorrow	whole	day	work-IVI

‘Tomorrow he must [has (got) to] work all day.’

(25)	Ему	ещё	жить	да	жить!
	Yemu	yeschyo	zhit`	da	zhit`!
	him-D	yet	live-IVI	and	live-IVI

‘May he live a long time!’

In other cases the subjunctive (optative) particle may be used together with an infinitive.

(26)	Мне	бы	жить	и	жить,	сквозь	годы	мчась!
	Mne	by	zhit`	i	zhit`,	skvoz`	gody	mchas`!
	me-D	PS	live-IVI	and	live-IVI,	through	years	running

‘I would like to live long, running through the years!’
(В. В. Маяковский / V. V. Mayakovsky)

3.2 The emergence of covert modality: covert modality, tense, and aspect

Examples (23)-(25) clearly lack any overt indication of modality, but they may (or must) nevertheless have modal readings. These constructions thus genuinely exhibit covert modality, whereas their impersonal counterparts have special overt markers of modality, like the modal predicative in (20b) above.

The modal meaning of the subjunctive marker (the particle *бы (by)*) is volition, as in (26), with the volitional reading being triggered by the additional exponent of modality. If this element were not present, necessity or possibility would be implied, i.e. also any other modal meaning, but not volition.

As shown in (23), the overt exponent of modality can be dropped only in the presence of an imperfective infinitive. Sentences without such a modal adverbial would be ungrammatical. The question then arises how this evidence can be interpreted in the light of the so called ‘Perfectivity-Root Modality Convergence Generalization’, which claims that “there is a close semantic convergence between root modals and perfective aspect.” (Abraham 1986, Abraham/Leiss 2008, XII). At first sight, examples (23)-(25) would appear to disprove this generalization. However, we must recall that modal readings of imperfective forms used in the impersonal dative-infinitive construction, which do not contain an overt exponent of modality, essentially arise from the prospective reading of this construction. This can be easily shown by the ‘past-form-transformation-test’ exemplified in (21c), since constructions of this type are never grammatical (cf. also (21a) and (21b) above):

(21c)	*Учителю	было	идти / пойти	к	директору	школы.
	*Uchitelyu	bylo	idti / poyti	k	direktoru	shkoly.
	teacher-D	was	go-IVI / go-IVP	to	director-D	school-G
	‘The teacher had to go to the school director.’					

This example illustrates two special features of the dative-infinitive construction in the past. The first of these is structural, in that the copula is obligatory in the past-tense, so that the predicate, which is at the same time an overt signal of modality, has to appear as a structural complement of the copula verb (cf. 21a). In the present tense, however, the copula is always omitted, so that the (modal) predicate can be omitted, too.

The second peculiarity is that the imperfective infinitive, which appears only in a ‘present-tense’ clause, cannot have a prospective reading. If we compare impersonal dative-infinitive constructions with imperfective and perfective infinitives with their personal counterparts, we observe that in the case of a perfective infinitive both personal and impersonal clauses have a prospective reading arising directly from the semantics of the perfective aspect (cf. 20a,b as illustrations of the constructions with perfective infinitives). However, if the overt signal of modality of a *personal clause* is dropped and a finite verb is present, the reading will still be prospective (*Я пойду (Ya poydu)* 'I go'-Perf. Pres. 'I will go'). In the case of an *imperfective personal clause* (*Я иду (Ya idu)* 'I go / will go') both present and future readings are possible. *Impersonal clauses*, on the other hand, inevitably have a modal reading (whether overt or covert). Since their characteristic semantic feature is that of root modality, they can only have a prospective reading. Omitting an overt signal of modality has no effect on the prospective reading of the construction as a whole.

This shows that we have to assume a 'temporal' path for the creation of covert root modality in dative constructions with imperfective infinitives. As Leiss (1985; 1992, 191-225) has shown, verbs with imperfective semantics like German *suchen* 'seek' cannot encode prospectivity without additional temporal indicators like the auxiliary *werden* (= 'will / shall')'.

(27) Wir werden den Schlüssel suchen.
we will the key seek
'We will seek the key.'

In contrast, the present tense of verbs with perfective semantics like *finden* 'find' always has a prospective reading, so that combining them with a temporal (prospective) marker like *werden* (= 'will / shall') leads to incompatibility arising from redundancy. As a result the temporal signal is reinterpreted as modal, as shown by the contrast between (28a) and (28b):

(28a) Wir finden den Schlüssel.
we find the key
'We will find the key.'

(28b) Wir werden den Schlüssel finden.
we will the key find
'Probably / Surely we will find the key.'

In Leiss's example, prospective temporality in connection with a perfective verb is reinterpreted as epistemic (non-root) modality. *Mutatis mutandis* the same conclusion can be drawn in the case of root modality which was discussed above using the example of Russian constructions without overt markers of modality. The prospective reading arises directly if a perfective verb is used, so that, for example, (29):

(29)	Ему	нужно	написать	письмо.
	Yemu	nuzhno	napisat`	pis′mo.
	him-D [is] necessary		write-IVP	letter
	'He must / [has to] write a letter.'			

only has a prospective reading. In contrast, (29a),

(29a)	Ему	нужно	писать	письмо.
	Yemu	nuzhno	pisat`	pis′mo.
	him-D [is] necessary		write-IVI	letter
	'He must / [has to] write a letter.'			

is ambiguous. It can imply futurity as in (i) 'tomorrow he has to write a letter', or it may refer to the present as in (ii) 'he is writing a letter, for he must do this now'.

Since imperfective verbs are underspecified from the viewpoint of temporality, and since the present-tense reading of root modals as in (ii) above is extremely marked, if an overt exponent of modality is used in connection with a dative and an imperfective infinitive, it imposes precisely this – marked – present-tense reading. On the other hand, the absence of an overt expression of modality in this construction forces the prospective reading accompanied by covert root modality. This is undoubtedly more compatible with a prospective than with a present-tense reading, as illustrated by (30a) as opposed to (30b):

(30a)	Не	мешай	ему,	ему	*нужно*	писать	письмо!
	Ne	meshay	yemu,	yemu	*nuzhno*	pisat`	pis′mo!
	not	disturb	him,	him-D	necessary [is]	write-IVI	letter
	'Do not disturb him, for he must write a letter [at this moment].'						

(30b)	Ему	сегодня	ещё	писать	письмо.
	Yemu	segodnya	yeschyo	pisat`	pis′mo.
	him-D	today	yet	write-IVI	letter
	'He has to write a letter today [in the future].'				

With clausal negation, however, either a perfective or an imperfective infinitive may occur, as in the following verse by Al. Aronov.

(31) Если у вас нету тёти, / то *вам её не потерять.*
Yesli u vas netu tyoti, / to vam yeyo ne poteryat′.
if with you no aunt, so you-D her not lose-IVP.
И если вы не живёте, / то *вам* и *не умирать.*
I yesli vy ne zhivyote, / to vam i ne umirat`.
And if you not live, so you-D not die-IVI
'If you have no aunt, you will not lose her. And if you do not live, you also will not die.'

This confirms another generalization made by Abraham/Leiss (2008, XIII), i.e. that "Clausal Neg + Perfectivity yields Imperfectivity". If this were not the case, it would not be possible to combine a perfective infinitive and the impersonal dative in the absence of an overt modal signal. Just as a single clause, a single word may also be negated in a sentence with a dative and an infinitive, as for example when the dative argument is negated. However, this type of the dative-infinitive construction is highly marked. It is extremely unusual for a nominal to be negated, if it is only a personal pronoun. In combination with a first person pronoun, negation denotes a lack of necessity, whilst with a second or third person pronoun, it characteristically expresses reluctance on the part of the speaker to be involved with their actions or plans, as shown in (32)-(33).

(32) Не мне тебя учить!
Ne mne tebya uchit′!
not me-D you-Acc teach-IVI
'I do not need to instruct you [for you should manage the situation better than me].'

(33) Не тебе меня учить!
Ne tebe menya uchit`!
not you-D me-Acc teach-IVI
'You have no right to teach me.'

Only the imperfective infinitive can be used in such contexts.

3.3 Dative-infinitive constructions with perfective infinitives in Old Church Slavonic and Gothic

In Old Church Slavonic there was no restriction on the use of the dative-infinitive construction with a perfective infinitive, but it lacked any covert modal reading, as in (34) (Psalm 4).

(34)	Внегда	призвати	ми,	услыша	мя	Бог	правды	моея.
	Vnegda	prizvati	mi,	uslysha	mya	Bog	pravdy	moyeya.
	when	call-IVP	me-D	heard	me-A	God	right-G	my

‘When I called [Him], the God of my righteousness heard me.’

Gothic has a similar construction with the verb *waírþan* ‘become’ and the infinitive of the main verb, e.g.:

(35)	warþ	gaswiltan	þamma	unledin.	Luke 16, 22
	became	die-IVP	the-D	poor-D	

‘The poor man had to die / inevitably died.’

(36)	warþ […]	galeiþan	imma	in	swnagogein.	Luke 6, 1
	became	go-IVP	him-D	in	synagogue	

‘He had / was obliged to go to the synagogue.’

Streitberg ([5/6]1920, §318) considers this construction to be a ‘dativus cum infinitivo’, and he compares it to the Germanic accusative and infinitive (AcI) construction, as in Present German *ich höre die Vögel singen* ‘I hear the birds sing’. The reason for it is not only the similarity between the Germanic AcI and Dativus-cum-Infinitivo/DcI patterns, but also the fact that in the Greek original text *ἐγένετο* (Third Person Aorist Middle of a verb meaning ‘become’) is used, followed by the AcI-construction. Streitberg ([5/6]1920, §318) claims that the construction of this sentence, which can be translated literally as ‘It comes to the death for the poor man’ (compare (35) above), can be ascribed to the desire of the Gothic translator to be maximally precise in rendering the Greek text without violating the rules of Germanic syntax. However, if this construction is compared to the Russian examples discussed, it would not seem unreasonable to assume that an ancient Indo-Germanic pattern was originally inherited and current in Gothic and other older Germanic dialects, although it later died out. The verb *waírþan* ‘become’ is used rather than any overt marker of modality. The whole sentence has an undoubtedly modal reading, encoding covert modality of necessity as in (36) or perhaps ‘unavoidability’, as in (35).

Similar constructions with impersonal (formally reflexive) verbs like *приходиться (prikhodit`sya)* or (archaic) *случаться (sluchat`sya),* both meaning 'happen', also exist in Russian with a dative argument. They have neither temporal nor aspectual restrictions, although *случаться (sluchat`sya)* 'happen' is normally used in the past or future tenses. *приходиться* indicates that the situation is unavoidable, whilst the archaic *случаться (sluchat`sya)* denotes that it is accidental. Only the first of these verbs encodes root modality.

(37) Нам приходится / приходилось / придётся / пришлось
Nam prikhoditsya / prikhodilos′ / pridyotsya / prishlos′
us-D happens-VI / happened-VI / will happen-VP / happened-VP
это делать / сделать.
eto delat / sdelat`.
this do-VI do-VP
'We (will) have / had to do this.'

(38) И случилось Ему в субботу проходить Mark 2, 23
I sluchilos` Yemu v subbotu prokhodit`
And happened-VP Him-D on Sabbath go-through-IVI
засеянными полями.
zaseyannzmi polyami.
grainfields
'One Sabbath He [accidently] went through the grainfields.'

(39) Случилось же ив другую субботу войти Ему
Sluchilos` zhe iv druguyu subbotu voyti Yemu
happened-VP also on other Sabbath go-in-IVP Him-D
в синагогу и учить. Luke 6, 6
v sinagogu i uchit′.
to synagogue and teach-VI
'Another Sabbath He [accidently] went to the synagogue and taught there.'

(40) Случалось ли вам когда-нибудь видеть такое?
Sluchalos′ li vam kogda-nibud′ videt′ takoye?
happened whether you.DAT sometimes see-IVI such
'Have you ever had the opportunity to see something like that?'

Thus, the modal readings of the dative-infinitive construction in Gothic is possible, if clauses in question convey the special lexical marker, i. e. the verb *wairþan* ‚become', which encodes the ‚Aktionsart' of transformativity (cf. (35) and (36)). In connection with dative and infinitive it denotes necessity. Hence, the deontic modality of the construction is connected with perfectivity, for transformational readings always have a genuine categorical link to perfectivity. Similar examples shows the Modern Russian (cf. (39) and (40)). In Old Church Slavonic, the dative-infinitive construction does not have any restrictions concerning the aspect of the verb, but it also does not imply modal readings (cf. (34)).

4. Conclusion

Impersonal dative constructions with reflexive verbs derived from intransitives, most often with clausal negation or a qualitative adverb, do not only convey the overt meaning of a diathesis, but also covert root (i.e. non-epistemic) modality. It can be roughly described as the modality of possibility. By contrast, this modal reading is not found with the corresponding personal constructions which express an active, but non-transitive action or state/process. Since neither the personal nor the impersonal constructions in question have overt signals of modality in the form of modal verbs, modal adverbials, or modal particles, one can postulate a clear pattern of covert modality in the case of impersonal clauses with datives and reflexive verbs with the diathetic suffix *-ся (sya)*. The reading of these clauses may differ depending on the semantics of the verb, which appears in the infinitive. If the impersonal dative-reflexive construction denotes an action, it covertly encodes either the modality of circumstances, which assist or detract from the action, or the mood of the experiencer, reflecting the 'active' role of the same entity occurring as the subject of an active clause. If the construction denotes a state or a process, the covert modal meaning is one of 'passive possibility', reflecting the 'inactive' role of the subject in the personal clause. Hence, while in the first case the difference in the reading of the personal and the impersonal sentence is crucial, it is much less so in the second case. Comparison of both impersonal patterns would confirm the conclusion that covert root modality is not triggered by the reflexive marker. Rather, modality goes back to the semantic and categorial underspecification, which is due to the derivation from active clauses, as claimed by Abraham (2006). Transitive and perfective verbs cannot appear in this construction. Perfectivity is not permitted since these constructions encode the modal characteristics of the process or action in its duration. Transitivity, on the other hand, is not permitted because of the ambiguity of the suffix *-ся (sya)*. If this suffix, when used with a transitive verb, can be interpreted either as a 'strong' passive or as a 'weak' impersonal[4], the first reading will always be preferred, and the second reading will then be blocked.

To sum up, impersonal dative constructions with infinitives always encode root modality, which can occur both overtly and covertly. In the first case, overt modal markers are used both in an impersonal clause and in its personal counterpart, although their actual realization will be rather different. The modality involved can be described as necessity or unavoidability. There are no temporal or aspectual restrictions on this construction. In the second case, the root modality is covert in the impersonal sentence, and no overt modal signals are conveyed. Rather like the reflexive constructions, this type of covert modality is strictly bound to imperfective aspect. The reason for this specific selectional restriction is to be found in the complex relations which obtain between aspectuality, modality, and (prospective) temporality, such as have been observed and described by Abraham repeatedly (ever since his 1986 paper). Because of these relations, dative-infinitive clauses with covert modality can only possibly be interpreted as prospective and imperfective; retrospective and perfective readings are not possible. The combination of a modal adverbial in the present tense with a perfective infinitive forces a prospective reading of the clause. In contrast, using a modal adverbial with an imperfective form is potentially ambiguous. The preferred reading will be prospective because of the aspectual semantics of root modality, but a present tense reading is also possible, albeit marked. If the modal adverbial is dropped, the imperfective infinitive in connection with the dative will also receive a prospective reading. No doubt, an embedded infinitive which is overtly marked for perfectivity usually encodes prospectivity as well, due to its aspectual semantics. Nevertheless, it is disallowed in constructions with covert modality, and a perfective infinitive is only permissible in sentences with clausal negation. However, in line with the generalization formulated by Abraham (in Abraham/Leiss 2008), it is quite possible (and very often the case in practice) for such perfective infinitives to be read with the sense of an imperfective.

In Gothic, dative-infinitive constructions with covert modality which express necessity or unavoidability have the form of the infinitive of

---

[4] According to Khrakovskij (1978, 50ff.), Malchukov/Ogawa (2011, 19ff.) etc., passivity and impersonality are both diatheses. The binary opposition of voice, i.e. active vs. passive, is the central ('strong') part of the categorial field of impersonality. The periphery of 'inactivity' is formed, among others, by reflexive or 'middle' entities. In Russian, Polish, and other Slavonic languages both passives and impersonals in the widest sense can be expressed by the use of the same morpheme (Russian *-sya*, Polish *się*, etc.).

perfective verbs used with a finite form of the transformative-perfective verb *waírþan* 'become' (= Modern German *werden*). As imperfective constructions of this type do not exist in Gothic, one may speak of unmarked patterns of root modality. Nevertheless, these Gothic constructions provide evidence for a common Indo-European pattern of covert root modality through their similarity to patterns of covert modality in Russian, as exemplified by similar constructions with verbs like *случаться (sluchat`sya)* and *приходиться (prikhodit'sya)* 'happen', cf. the examples under (35)-(40).

References

Abraham, Werner (1986): Die Bedeutungsgenese von Modalpartikeln. *Groninger Arbeiten zur germanistischen Linguistik (GAGL)* 27: 1-44.

—. (2006): Introduction. Datives: Structural vs. inherent – abstract vs. morphological – autonomous vs. combinatory – universally vs. language-specifically configurated? In: Hole, Daniel / Mei-nunger, André / Abraham, Werner (eds.): *Datives and Other Cases: Between argument structure and event structure*. Amsterdam: Benjamins [Studies in Language Companion Series 75], 3-46.

Abraham, Werner / Leiss, Elisabeth (2008): Introduction. In: Abraham, Werner / Leiss, Elisabeth (eds.): *Modality – Aspect Interfaces. Implications and typological solutions*. Amsterdam: Benjamins [Typological Studies in Language 79], XI-XXIV.

Bulygina, Tatjana V. (1982): K postrojeniju tipologii predikatov v russkom jazyke [On predicate typology in Russian]. In: Selivjorstova, Olga N. (ed.): *Semantičeskiye tipy predikatov* [Semantical types of predicates]. Moskva: Nauka, 7-85.

Geniušienė, Emma (1987): *The Typology of Reflexives*. Berlin: de Gruyter [Empirical Approaches to Language Typology 2].

Gradinarova, Alla (2010): Bezličnyje konstrukcii s datel'nym subiekta i predikativom na *-o* v russkom i bolgarskom jazykach [Impersonal constructions with dative of the subject in *-o* in Russian and Bulgarian]. *Bolgarskaya rusistika* 3/4: 34-55.

Khrakovskij, Viktor S. (1978): Zalog i refleksiv. In: Maslov, Jurij S. / Bondarko, Aleksandr V. (eds.): *Problemy teorii grammatičeskogo zaloga*. Leningrad: Nauka (LO), 50-61.

Leiss, Elisabeth (1985): Zur Entstehung des neuhochdeutschen analytischen Futurs. *Sprachwissenschaft* 10: 250-273.

Leiss, Elisabeth (1992): *Die Verbalkategorien des Deutschen. Ein Beitrag zur Theorie der sprachlichen Kategorisierung*. Berlin-New York: de Gruyter [Studia Linguistica Germanica 31].

Malchukov, Andrej / Ogawa, Akio (2011): Towards a typology of impersonal constructions. A semantic map approach. In: Malchukov, Andrej / Siewierska, Anna (eds.), 19-56.

Malchukov, Andrej / Siewierska, Anna (eds.) (2011): *Impersonal Constructions. A Cross-linguistic Perspective*. Amsterdam / Philadelphia: Benjamins [Studies in Language Companion Series 124].

Pupynin, Jurij A. (1992): Bezličnyj predykat i subjektno-objektnyje otnošenija v russkom jazyke [Impersonal predicate and subject-object relations in Russian]. *Voprosy yazykoznaniya* 1: 48-63.

Streitberg, Wilhelm (1920): *Elementarbuch des Gotischen*. 5./6. edition. Heidelberg: Winter.

Streitberg, Wilhelm (ed.) (1965): *Die Gotische Bibel*. 4., unaltered edition. Heidelberg: Winter.

Aspectual Patterns of Covert Coding of Modality in Gothic and Old High German

Elisabeth Leiss
University of Munich

Abstract: The aim of this paper is to show that in the "aspect period" of the Germanic languages the modalizing function was extracted from perfective infinitives. In the context of Gothic and Old High German this amounts to the observation that the infinitival preposition *zu* and the perfective aspectual prefix *ga-* can be considered as functional equivalents. Finally, the common denominator of both modalizers will be outlined in order to fully understand covert and semi-covert encodings of modality. The results support Abraham's generalizations on the affinities between deontic readings of modals and perfective aspect, and epistemic readings of modals and imperfective aspect, published in the last 20 years. We claim that the covert encoding of modality is strongly prevalent in aspect languages (see also Abraham/Leiss 2008, Kotin 2008, Leiss 2002), whereas overt encodings explode as a consequence of dissolving systems of verbal aspect.

1. Introduction

The aim of the present paper is to investigate the demarcation line between the covert encoding of root/deontic modality and the first stages in the emergence of overt encoding of root modality with the aim to fully understand what it is that transforms a full verb into a deontic modal. Evidence will be given that covert patterns of modality are aspect-driven. This holds for deontic modality as well as for epistemic modality. A classic example of covertly encoding root/deontic modality is (1).

(1) *Das ist zu machen.* (German)
That is to make
'That is to be done.'

The infinitival construal in (1) is equivalent to (2) and (3):

(2) *Das kann gemacht werden.*
that can done be/become
'That can be done.'

(3) *Das muss gemacht werden*
that must done be/become
'That must be done.'

Holl 2010 suggests that the *zu*-infinitive in German has a modalizing function (see already Abraham 2004). This, of course, also holds for the English *to*-infinitive). Interestingly enough, only root modality can be encoded by embedded infinitives with the help of *zu* (see Abraham, this volume). As soon as modals develop epistemic meaning, the preposition *zu* does not surface any more with the deontic use of the modal verb. It is quite obvious that epistemic meaning conflicts with the infinitival preposition *zu/to*. But how can we explain that deontic modals are incompatible with a prepositional infinitive as soon as they are fully grammaticalized, having developed epistemic reading? Non-grammaticalized, i.e. lexical, semi-modal verbs that are recruited as temporary modals, such as *suchen*, select the *zu*-Infinitive only as in (4):

(4) *Sie sucht zu gefallen.*
she seeks to please
'She wants to please.'

There is a semantic equivalent for (4) that is construed with the regular modal verb *wollen*:

(5) *Sie will gefallen.*
she wants please
'She wants to please.'[1]

As a rule, fully grammaticalized modal verbs in modern Germanic languages are construed without the preposition *zu*. The same holds for epistemic uses of *wollen* such as in (6):

[1] In English the former modal *will* has lost its deontic reading. It grammaticalized into a temporal auxiliary indicating future time reference. In Old High German *wellen* was used as a root modal as well as a temporal auxiliary. The deontic meaning appeared when construed with a perfective infinitive, while the temporal meaning surfaced when construed with an imperfective infinitive. The latter distribution was demonstrated by Scaffidi-Abbate 1981. The insight that modal verbs construed with perfective infinitives trigger deontic meaning is due to Abraham 1989 and 1991.

(6) *Sie will ihm gefallen haben.*
she wants him pleased have
'She pretends to have pleased him [which is quite improbable]'

Going back to earlier stages of German and to Gothic, we notice, however, that deontic modals, as a rule, embed bare infinitives. This holds even for full verbs such as *sokjan* 'seek', one of the verbs that were sporadically recruited to encode deontic meaning:

(7)	*jah*	*soki-da*	*ga-saihvan*	*Jesu,*
	CONJ[2]	seek-PRET.3SG	PF-sehen:INF	Jesus:ACC.SG.M
	'and (he) tried to see Jesus,'[3]			

Of course, Gothic *sokida* is not classified as a modal verb in the grammar books (see Streitberg 1910 and Streitberg 1910/2000). It is a full verb, construed here as a root modal (with a deontic function in the wide sense). Full verbs often take over the function of deontic modal verbs, this without being classified as members of the paradigm of modal verbs. This does not only hold for Gothic, but also for contemporary English and German, for other Germanic languages, and even for languages that are quite devoid of a morphological paradigm of modals such as Finnish. We will return to questions of definition and terminology in the next section. Let us first emphasize, when we take a look at Gothic[4], that spontaneously recruited modals such as *sokjan* were not construed with a preposition equivalent with English *to* or German *zu*. As mentioned above, these lexically recruited modals were construed with bare infinitives only. However, these infinitives were, as a rule, marked with the perfectivizing prefix *ga-*. A closer look at deontic modals shows that this holds for deontic readings in general (see Abraham, this volume, on '(Inter)Subjectification'). The aim of this paper is to show that in the "aspect period" of the Germanic languages the modalizing function was extracted from embedded perfective infinitives. In other words, German *zu* and Gothic *ga-* are functional equivalents[5]. What we have to do is uncover the common

---

[2] List of abbreviations: see at the end of the paper.
[3] Translated in German: 'und wollte Jesus sehen'. The impossibility to translate the meaning by means of the former English modal verb *will* yields a solid impression of the dissolution and transformation of the English modal verb system (for more detail, see Abraham 2002).
[4] Note, that an equivalent of the preposition *zu* (German) or *to* (English) seems to lack almost completely in Gothic (Streitberg 1910).
[5] See also Abraham 2012 who also claims the functional equivalence of the perfective aspectual prefix (*ga-*) in Gothic with the infinitival proposition (*zu*) in German and their counterparts in other languages.

denominator of both modalizers in order to reach a full understanding of covert and semi-covert encodings of modality.

2. Definition of modal verb

When dealing with modal verbs in former stages of a language as well as in other languages without a fully developed system and paradigm of modals, we face the following unsolved problem: We do not know exactly how to select the defining features that qualify a verb as a modal. Another important question in this context also remains unsolved. How many modals make up a modal verb system? Are "one and a half grammaticalized modals" (such as in Finnish) in fact enough to constitute a modal verb system? How many modals does Finnish have: one (*voida*), two (*voida* and *saattaa*), or 45 modals or even more? These are the controversal suggestions discussed in the literature on modals in Finnish (see Kangasniemi 1992:291). If you count only those verbs as modals that display epistemic meaning, then you have one, maybe two modal verbs in Finnish, the second being less grammaticalized (leading to "one and a half modals"). Applying this strict criterion, we are faced with the observation that most of the Romance and Slavic languages do not have more than two modal verbs that are polysemous in the sense that they can trigger also an epistemic meaning beyond their root interpretation. Is this sufficient to constitute a system of modal verbs? Rather not, most of us would agree. On the other hand, when we choose the alternative strategy and qualify each verb that displays a deontic meaning (or root modality) as a real modal verb does, then the number of 45 modal verbs in Finnish may not be exaggerated. Whenever taking this simpler criterion to define modals we are confronted with the fact that the class of modal verbs remains potentially open. The following German examples (and some of the English glosses and translations of it) illustrate this fact:

(8) *Er weiß sich zu benehmen.*
he knows himself to behave
'He knows to behave himself.'

(9) *Sie versteht es zu überzeugen.*
she understands it to convince
'She is able to convince.'

(10) *Sie hat das Potential zu führen.*
she has the potential to lead
'She has the prerequisite abilities to lead.'

(11) *Er ist Manns genug seine Fehler einzusehen.*
he is man-GEN enough his mistakes to admit (ad-to-mit)
'He is tough enough to admit his mistakes.'

(12) *Sie hat die Fähigkeit dir zu helfen.*
she has the ability you:DAT to help
'She has the ability to help you.'

(13) *Wir sind in der Lage den Wettbewerb zu gewinnen.*
we are in the position the competition to win
'We are in a position to win the competition.'

All verbs and predicative constructions chosen in examples (8)-(14) above are replaceable by the German modal verb *können*. The ultimate difference between the alternative formulations above and alternative versions with *können* does not consist in the lexical differences. The central question is whether verbs and constructions in (8)-(14) fulfill the criteria to qualify as modal verbs or as modal predicatives. The verb in (8) is a preterit-present as are most of the modal verbs in the Germanic languages. Nevertheless, *wissen* is not categorized as modal verb in German. It is no more modal than is the English translation by the verb *know*. Why then does *können* in (14) count as a modal verb, while *wissen* does not meet the criteria?

(14) *Er kann sich benehmen.*
he can himself behave
'He can behave himself.'

The only formal difference between (8) and (14) is that (8) is construed with an infinitival preposition, whereas (14) is not. We have seen that the formal characteristics of preterit-presents do not qualify a verb *per se* as a modal. How about the formal criteria of the absence of a prepositional infinitive to qualify as a modal verb? This would discredit *be able *(to)* as a modal verb. The same holds for English *to have *(to)*. But what counts more, it would discredit the Gothic modal *magan* and other modals in Gothic and Old High German as well, as these generally do not take the prepositional infinitive, but the bare infinitive. To make a long story short, we do not have to check all possible formal features to find out what qualifies a modal as a modal. This has already thoroughly been performed by Öhlschläger 1989. The result of his book length investigation is that there is no formal feature that can be singled out as a defining feature for modals in German(ic). None of the investigated features were qualified as a defining feature in the sense that there are no clear exceptions. On the other hand, Öhlschläger found a reliable semantic feature that is characteristic of all clear cases of modals: the presence of a specific kind of functional polysemy. He emphasizes that all verbs classified as modals display epistemic reading in addition to deontic/root meaning. This explains why the preterit-present *wissen* cannot qualify as a modal verb. For the same reason the construction *be able to* in English cannot be classified as a modal verb. The same holds for all recruited modals that display deontic/root meaning only.

Starting from the only reliable defining feature that fully grammaticalized modals display epistemic as well as root meaning, we are faced with the problem, how to research modals in the older stages of Germanic languages. Do languages such as Gothic or Old High German have a paradigm of modal verbs? Almost all diachronic studies on modals are flawed by the methodological approach that takes the point of departure from the system of modals in Modern Standard German projecting this system back to older stages of German. In other words, the modal system of Modern Standard German is presupposed as the fully grammaticalized reference system, and the focus is set on the formal forerunners of this system (see Götz 2001 for this naïve approach). From a methodological point of view, however, this is a completely inappropriate endeavor. Imagine that we live in the year 8000 and that nothing is left of Modern Standard German language, just older texts such as the Gothic bible and OHG texts. How would we be in a position to define which verbs count as modals? We would be in the position of Finnish linguists. Either we count only one modal as a modal (*mugan/magan*) as it is the only modal that displays also an epistemic reading in Gothic and Old High German; or we count every full verb that displays deontic meaning as a modal as soon as it appears with an embedded infinitive. The latter strategy would lead to a potentially open class of modals. The projection back of current modal systems to older stages of a language is methologically flawed for an additional reason. The focus on this system is too narrow as it disregards all encodings of modality that do not have a Modern German counterpart. The results of this constrained view in diachronic studies are, of course, completely unreliable. For this very reason, the modalizing patterns in older stages of Germanic languages and of Gothic still remain largely undisclosed. The very fact that the system of modal verbs explodes in the Germanic languages as a consequence of a dissolving system of verbal aspect has not even been considered as a possible path of investigation. The correlation of a weakening aspectual system and simultaneously expanding modal system remains to be explored thoroughly. Instead of investigations of this kind, however, we are confronted with claims such that there are no grammaticalized means of epistemic encodings in older stages of Germanic languages (Traugott 1989, Diewald 1999, among others). These claims are regularly linked with the suggestion that lexical encodings of epistemicity are functionally equivalent to grammaticalized encodings of modal root meanings. However, this is easy to refute, in the first place, for reasons of the differing complexity of lexical as opposed to grammatical means of encoding (see Leiss 2012a, 2012b).

3. Grammaticalized modals versus lexical modals

Lexical modals are defined as verbs that embed an infinitive and are equivalent in meaning to deontic modal verbs. In contrast to grammaticalized modal verbs, they cannot give rise to an epistemic reading. An additional difference is the lack or presence of the preposition *zu* 'to'. This formal distinction still awaits explanation. The verb in (15) plus the prepositional infinitive seems to be semantically equivalent to the verb in (16) plus bare infinitive:

(15) *Sie wünscht das Examen zu bestehen.* LMV/DMV[6]
she wishes the exam to pass
'She wishes/wants to pass the exam.'

(16) *Sie will die Klausur bestehen.* DMV
she wants[7] the exam pass
'She wants to pass the exam.'

The very difference is that the lexical modal does not unfold an epistemic meaning in syntactic contexts that trigger epistemicity. The insight that perfective infinitives (infinitives of perfective verbs) trigger deontic meaning, whereas imperfective infinitives trigger epistemic meaning goes back to Abraham (1989 and 1991). In terms of mereological features, perfective verbs are inhomogeneous verbs, whereas imperfective verbs are homogeneous[8]. In (17) the analytic construction is bi-phasic (as are all

[6] LMV = lexical modal verb, DMV = deontic (= root) modal verb, EMV = epistemic modal verb.
[7] It is not possible to translate the German preterit-present and modal verb *wollen* by the English equivalent *will* that has grammaticalized into a temporal auxiliary and does not display an epistemic reading. The German preterit-present *will* in (1b) is a fully grammaticalized modal verb in the sense of Öhlschläger (1989), whereas the English counterpart *will* is not.
[8] Homogeneous verbs are defined by the features [+ADDITIVITY] [+DIVISIBILITY], inhomogeneous verbs are defined by the features [–ADDITIVITY] [–DIVISIBILITY]. Homogenous verbs consist of identical parts, whereas inhomogeneous verbs and verb constructions consist of non-identical parts. Consequently, all bounded or

resultative constructions). The first phase is bounded and therefore inhomogeneous, while the second phase consists of homogeneous parts. In (17) the bi-phasic construction *bestanden haben* triggers an epistemic reading, whereas in (18) epistemic reading is blocked:

(17) *Sie will das Examen bestanden haben.* *DMV / EMV
she wants the exam passed have
'She pretends to have passed the exam.'
'It is not very likely that she passed the exam.'

(18) *Sie wünscht das Examen bestanden zu haben.* DMV / *EMV
she wishes to exam passed have
'She wishes/wants to have passed the exam.'

The same behavior shows with so-called lexical equivalents of the modal verbs such as *können* (19-22) and *müssen* (23-26):

(19) *Er kann sich benehmen.* DMV
he can himself behave
'He can behave himself.'

(20) *Er weiß sich zu benehmen.* LMV/DMV
He knows himself to behave
'He knows to behave himself.'

(21) *Er kann sich schlecht benommen haben.* EMV
He can himself well behaved have.'
'He may have behaved himself badly.'

(22) **Er weiß sich schlecht benommen zu haben.*
he knows himself bad behaved to have
'He knows to have behaved badly.'

For English modal *must* equaling the German modal verb *müssen*, see (23-25):

(23)	*She must earn more money.*	DMV
(24)	*She is obliged to earn more money.*	LMV/DMV
(25)	*She must have earned more money.*	EMV
(26)	**She is obliged to have earned more money.*	*

---

perfective verbs are inhomogeneous in quality. From a typological perspective, we observe that perfective verbs are regularly recruited to build up bi-phasic resultative predicatives and constructions.

What we see is that lexical modal verbs encode root/deontic modality only. An epistemic reading is blocked in syntactic contexts that normally trigger epistemicity when construed with grammaticalized modal verbs. What is the explanation of this blocking effect? Is it surfacing because lexical modals embed prepositional infinitives, whereas grammaticalized deontic modals demand the bare infinitive? How about the behavior of auxiliaries such as 'be' and 'have' and their covert modal potential in (27), which can covertly encode the deontic modality of (23), without being able to trigger epistemic readings (see 28)?

(27) She *has to earn more money.* DMV
'She must earn more money.'

(28) **She has to have earned more money.* *

(29) *How is this effect to be explained?* DMV
'How can this effect be explained.'
'How must this effect be explained.'

(30) **She is to have earned more money.* *

The placement of the truth-value on one of two phases in the bi-phasic embedded constructions is the key that makes us understand this blocking effect in lexical modals (DMV) as opposed to grammaticalized modals (DMV). Epistemicity effects can only surface when the embedded verb is homogeneous. Bi-phasic, resultative constructions consist of two phases, the first phase being heterogeneous, the second one being homogeneous. In order to get an epistemic reading the second (homogeneous) phase must be focused. In other words, the truth-value must be attributed to the second phase, not to the first phase. Whenever the first phase is attributed a truth value, deontic reading surfaces (compare (31).

(31) *She must <u>have passed</u> her exams next year to get the position.*

In (31) the first (inhomogeneous) phase of the underlined resultative construction is focused triggering a deontic reading. In (32) the second (homogeneous) phase is focused by preference being the unmarked reading of non-contextualized propositions, whereas (33) licenses epistemic reading only:

(32) *She must <u>have passed</u> her exams.* EMV/(DMV)

(33) *She must <u>have passed</u> her exams to be so relaxed today.* EMV

In order to get an epistemic meaning the second phase (the ongoing result of the event) is focused and truth-evaluated. Lexical modal verbs and covert modality encoded via auxiliaries cannot license epistemic readings, because they do not focus the second phase. They focus the inhomogeneous event part, not, however, the homogeneous result of this event (observation in accordance with Abraham 1989, 1991, 2012). Is it the preposition *zu/to* that blocks epistemic reading in these constructions? According to Abraham (2012) the embedded infinitive has to project the event into the future (in the sense of Ziegler 2008), which is a prerequisite to license a root/deontic reading. In contrast to this, an epistemic reading shows up when future time reference of the event is excluded, such as in (33). The examples (15)-(33) evidence that the preposition *zu/to* invests lexical modals and covert modals with future time reference of the embedded event, which is the indispensible requirement to construe root/deontic meaning. Holl (2010) qualifies these prepositions as modalizers, whereas Abraham (2012) emphasizes the future-projecting function, which he defines as a necessary, albeit not sufficient, condition for the covert coding of root modality. The aim of the next section is to show that the preposition *zu/to* has neither a modalizing nor a temporalizing, but rather an aspectualizing function with temporal and modal side-effects.

4. The encoding of root/deontic modality in Gothic and Old High German

The aim of the next section is to show that the aspect hypothesis proposed above answers the unsolved question why the deontic readings of grammaticalized modal verbs are construed without a *zu*-infinitive. Before turning to this point, a close look at the encoding of deontic meaning in Gothic will support the claim by Abraham (1989, 1990) that modality effects are aspect-driven. In (34) the embedded infinitive of the matrix lexical modal *sokjan* 'to seek', 'to wish' is perfective (prefixed by *ga-*):

(34)	*Jah*	*soki-da*	*ga-saihvan*	*Jesu,*
	CON	*seek*-PRET	PF-see:INF	Jesus:ACC.SG.M.
	and	*seeked*	PF-see	Jesus

'and he wanted/desired to see Jesus,'
[Luk. 19,3]

Compare Modern Standard German: ‚und er suchte Jesus zu sehen'. The difference between the Gothic construction and its Modern Standard German counterpart consists in the Gothic presence/absence of the perfective particle versus the German prepositional infinitive. In other words, the Gothic perfective prefix *ga-* shows up as an equivalent with the Modern Standard German preposition *zu* or Modern Standard English *to.*

The same holds for Old English (see van Gelderen 2004, Ch. 8) and Old High German (see Leiss 2008), where the perfective prefix *ge-/gi-* regularly appears with deontic embeddings, especially with matrix *magan*. It is obvious that a subclass of lexical verbs perform as deontic modals when construed with embedded perfective infinitives. The same holds for the precursors of the Modern Standard German modal verbs, especially *magan*. According to Streitberg (1910/2000: II, 87), *magan* selects the perfective infinitive: "der abhängige Infinitiv ist fast durchweg perfektiv"[9]. What is the reason for this selectional constraint concerning aspect? This constraint is attested for preterit-presents as well as for spontaneously recruited quasi-modals such as *sokjan*. Note also that it is the subordinated infinitive that appears perfectivized, not the matrix lexical modal verb *sokjan* for which a perfective aspect partner *ga-sokjan* is well attested for Gothic, yet not selected to build up deontic modality[10].

To obtain a more complete picture of the effect of the perfectivizing verbal prefix *ga-* we have to take into account the temporal side effects of perfectivity. It is well known since Ultan (1978) that languages show a strong affinitiy between perfectivity and reference to events that are not located in the present. In aspectually prospective languages such as Gothic or Old High German, perfective aspect refers to events in the future, whereas in aspectually retrospective languages, perfective aspect encodes past events. This aspectual feature is exploited in Gothic and other Germanic languages to build up the future projecting feature inherent in all deontic modals (Ziegeler 2008). This interpretation is supported by the following examples of deontic modals in Thai, where deontic modals also do not embed bare verbs, but verbs plus the additional morpheme *ca*, which is the future tense marker in Thai[11]:

(35)	phǒm **ya:k**	**ca**	sanə̌:	khon [...]
	1SG wollen:DMV	FUT	vorschlagen	dass
	'Ich will vorschlagen, dass [...]			

9 "The subordinated infinitive is almost completely perfective".

10 This proves that modal verbs are imperfective or homogeneous in nature. In aspect languages such as Polish, modal verbs are *imperfectiva tantum*, in other words they are imperfective and devoid of a perfective aspect partner (see Piskorz 2012:57). We have to conclude that the bi-phasic preterit-presents are selected as modal verbs because of the homogeneous quality of the second phase, not because of the inhomogeneous quality of the first phase.

11 Examples (35) and (36) are taken from Payawang (2012:203).

The same holds for the modal verbs *khu:ən* and *na:* (both meaning 'shall') in Thai (see Payawang 2012:203). These modals construe with the marker for future tense *ca*, and sometimes an additional perfective marker comes in. In (36) a full sentence containing three deontic modals is cited:

(36)

phǒm	***ya:k***	***ca***	*sanə̌:*	*khon*
1SG	want:DMV	FUT	propose	that

thi:	*ca*	*mi:*	*sid-?ɔ:k-loŋ-khana:nsiə̌əŋ*	*nay*
REL	FUT	have	right to vote	in

ka:nlîəəktaŋ	nan	**khuə:n**	**ca**	da:y	tham
election	in	DMV	FUT	PF	make

khɔ̂:sɔ̀:b	phîə:	wád
exam	to (CONJ:FIN)	measure

khwa:mrú:	khɔ̌:ŋ	tuə?e:ŋ	kɔ̀:n
basic knowledge	POSS	himself	first

'I want to suggest that people who will get the right to vote in elections should first pass an exam in order to test their basic knowledge.'

From this we draw the conclusion that deontic modal constructions contain a functional element that ensures reference to events located in the future. Interestingly enough, this holds for completely unrelated languages such as contemporary Thai and extinct Gothic, which belong to different diachronic strata, to different language families as well as to completely different typological language classes. We also learn from this that full verbs transform into deontic modals when construed with an embedded infinitive or another functional element that has the quality to guarantee future time reference of the modal verb construction. In other words, Thai *ya:k* as well as Gothic *magan* are full verbs in the first place. They transform into modals as soon as the future projecting feature is guaranteed, be it via perfective markers as in Gothic or by the future tense marker as in Thai. In line with this argument, *magan* and *sokjan* have to be classified as full verbs in the first place. They transform into deontic modals under the conditions specified above. The full citation of the fragment in (34) illustrates that *magan* and *sokjan* are construed in a completely parallel way. The second construction with *magan* is elliptic, which underlines the equivalence of both constructions, otherwise ellipsis would not be acceptable:

(37) *jah soki-da ga-saihvan Jesu,*
CONJ seek-PAST.3.SG PFV-see:INF Jesus:ACC.SG.M.
and sought see /perceive Jesus
'and he wanted to see Jesus',

jah ni mah-ta [*ga-saihvan* J.] *faura managein*
CONJ NEG can-past.3.sg. PREP crowd:ACC.SG.F.
and not could [see J.] for the crowd
'and he could not [see Jesus] because of the crowd'

How can we spell out the ellipsis: Is it *saihvan Jesu* or rather *ga-saihvan Jesu*? Considering the arguments unfolded up to now, one is tempted to reconstruct *ga-saihvan Jesu*. But how can we be sure that the reconstruction of the ellipsis is correct? At first sight, the reconstruction seems to be correct for the very reason that the perfective *ga-saihvan* is well attested in Gothic. As most of the Gothic verbs, 'see' materializes in aspectual pairs, just to name the verbs being part of the examples below:

saihvan (IPF) / *ga-saihvan* (PF) 'to see'
sokjan (IPF) /*ga-sokjan* (PF) 'to seek'
waurkjan (IPF) / *ga-waurkjan* (PF) 'to do'
hausjan (IPF) / *ga-hausjan* (PF) 'to hear'
laistjan (IPF) / *ga-laistjan* (PF) 'to follow'
tiuhan (IPF) / *ga-tiuhan* (PF) 'to lead', 'to guide'

There are obviously two possibilities to reconstruct the elliptic infinitive of the *mahta*-construction:

1. either as *ga-saihvan*, thus copying the first construction
2. or as *saihvan*.

Both, the elliptic construction and Streitberg's statement, make *ga-saihvan* the more plausible candidate. A close look at the exceptions noted by Streitberg (1910:197) shows, however, that we have to be careful. There are clear exceptions to the rule that modals embed perfective infinitives. One of these exceptional domains is negation. Negated sentences regularly (but not exceptionlessly) select imperfective embedded infinitives. This distributional behavior is well documented for Modern Russian taught in elementary grammars of Russian (i.e., Tauscher/Birnbaum 1983:252). Deontic verbs regularly select perfective infinitives in affirmative sentences. Imperfective infinitives prevail in negated sentences, but negated sentences with perfective infinitives are documented as well. The latter are very marked and not yet explained in full detail (see Padučeva 2008 and Heindl 2009, for more details). In other words, we are not (yet) in a position to reliably spell out the ellipsis in (37). In the following section, the so-called exceptions will be explained as fully rule-governed constructions. The claim here is that exceptional embedding of imperfective infinitives appears in marked constructions that encode additional grammatical functions. In the following section we will see that the marked selection of imperfective infinitives is to be found in the following domains: negation, future tense, epistemicity, and definiteness.

5. Deontic modals in marked constructions in Gothic and Old High German

5.1. Lexical modals and aspect

There is an intricate and rule governed relationship between root modals, negation and aspect in Gothic and Old High German. We suggested that root modals are originally lexical in nature. They transform into deontic modals as soon as they select and embed a future projecting perfective infinitive. On the other side, they transform into epistemic modals when combined with an embedded imperfective. This holds especially for Gothic *magan*. On the other hand, root modals can transform into analytic constructions of future tense when embedding an imperfective infinitive. This holds especially for the root modals *sculan* 'shall' and *wiljan* 'will'. The future tense reading is less marked than the epistemic one, but more marked than the deontic reading. The common denominator of deontic modals and the respective temporal auxiliaries is that they project into the future. The common denominator of epistemic modals and temporal auxiliaries for future time reference is a formal one: both select the imperfective infinitive. They differ, however, according to the criterion of time reference: root modals with embedded imperfective infinitives and present time reference trigger epistemic reading. The same construction triggers a temporal reading when it refers to events located in the future. We may thus say that root modals are polyfunctional in the sense that they are building blocks for quite a large range of constructions: deontics, epistemics, and future tense. The different outcomes result from different selections of aspect and time reference. Examples for such selectional restrictions and their effects will be given in detail below. Yet, there remains an unsolved question concerning the aspectual restrictions in negated sentences. Deontic modals select the perfective infinitive in affirmative sentences. In contrast to this, they tend to select the imperfective infinitive in negated sentences. The latter situation, however, is far from being without exception. Deontic modals also select the perfective infinitive in negated sentences. This is admittedly less common, but nevertheless requires an explanation. The aim of the next section is to show that all the intricate and seemingly idiosyncratic choices of aspect in the older stages of the Germanic stages can be explained as complex, and mostly covert encodings of grammatical categories by means of aspect. At the end of the present reflections we will return to the unsolved question why deontic modals with negation preferably select the imperfective aspect, and why there are exceptions to this selectional restriction.

5.2. Deontic reading versus future tense reading of modals

According to Streitberg (1910:197) the lexical modals *wiljan* and *sculan* select the perfective infinitive roughly as often as the imperfective infinitive, obviously in sharp contrast to *magan* and its preferred selection of the perfective aspect. We get a more reliable view on this behavior of *wiljan* and *sculan* when we take into account that these verbs are also documented as temporal auxiliaries in analytic constructions of future tense. The same situation still holds for contemporary English and other Germanic languages as it did for Old and Middle High German. Modern Standard German is unique in this respect as it has replaced these auxiliaries by the auxiliary *werden*, due probably to language contact with Slavic languages, where the counterpart auxiliary (*budu* in Russian and equivalent auxiliaries in other Slavic languages) serves to build an imperfective future tense[12]. There are some important parallels between the Slavic languages and Gothic. It holds for both languages that perfective verbs in the formal present tense encode future time reference. Another parallel is that imperfective verbs form the future tense analytically. In Gothic several auxiliaries compete for this function: *duginnan* 'to begin', *haban* 'to have', *wiljan* 'will', and *sculan* 'shall'. Streitberg (1910:200) notes that *duginnan* and *haban* are used as temporal auxiliaries to encode the imperfective future. He also notes that *duginnan* as a rule embeds the imperfective infinitive only (Streitberg 1910:197), in

[12] For more details see Leiss 1985.

sharp contrast to *magan*. These distributions lead to the following working hypothesis:

- *sculan/wiljan* + perfective infinitive yield a root/deontic reading
- *sculan/wiljan* + imperfective infinitive yield an imperfective future

It is well known that in Gothic (Streitberg 1910:200), in Old and Middle High German (Scaffade-Abbidi 1981) only imperfective verbs form an analytic future tense. We also know that the Gothic auxiliaries *sculan* and *wiljan* and their respective forms in Old and Middle High German are used either as deontic modals or as auxiliaries denoting future time reference. How these uses are monosemized is explained nowhere in the reference books nor, to the best of my knowledge, in the research literature. A thorough empirical investigation of this complementary distribution is still to be awaited.

5.3. Deontic reading versus epistemic reading

Not all records of 'modals + imperfective infinitive' classify as analytic imperfective futures. There are constructions with 'modals + imperfective infinitives' that denote present time reference. The effect of this incompatible time reference is reanalysis and reinterpretation, whereby an epistemic modal reading is surfacing. Abraham (1991) evidenced this epistemicity effect convincingly for Modern Standard German.

As epistemic meanings are commonly assumed to grammaticalize later than deontic meanings, no record of epistemicity effects should be found for Gothic. A look at the following example might provide counterevidence to this commonly held wisdom concerning Gothic:

(38) *ibai mag blinds* *blindana* *tiuhan*?
but can blind:NOM.M.SG blind:ACC.M.SG lead:INF
'but can a blind lead a blind' [word by word translation]
[Luk. 6:39]

The word by word translation suggests that the meaning is a root/deontic one. The context, however, does not license a deontic, but an epistemic reading. The speaker questions the possibiltiy that a blind man is in a position to lead another blind man. This translates in terms of paraphrases such as 'but **how** can a blind man lead a blind man?' or 'but can a blind man **really** lead a blind man?'. In Modern German, a modal particle such as *denn* captures the meaning quite well: "Kann *denn* ein Blinder einen Blinden führen?"[13] In other words, the speaker's assessment of the propositional content of the question is involved. Note that for imperfective *tiuhan* the perfective aspect partner *ga-tiuhan* is documented without being selected in the case at hand. It is important to see that the mere fact that *mag* appears in a question does not epistemize the modal verb. Both readings can surface in questions such as (38). Compare the readings in (39) and (40):

(39) 'does a blind man have the ability to lead a blind man.' DMV

(40) 'is it really possible that a blind man leads a blind man.' EMV

It is quite obvious that the root/deontic reading would misinterpret the intended sense, whereas (40) translates the intended meaning. The working hypothesis for further empirical investigations is that the deontic reading is licensed by perfective infinitives, whereas the epistemic reading surfaces with imperfective infinitives.

Most of the instances of Gothic *magan* appear in questions and in negated sentences. In other words, they appear preferably in propositions with wide scope. It is well known that sentence mood and negation scope over mood (realis/irrealis), while epistemic modality scopes over sentence mood, negation, and mood. We conclude that the extremely infrequent instances of *magan* in non-negated declaratives demonstrates that Gothic *magan* is already on its way from mood to modality. In Modern Standard German the root/deontic reading of *magan,* i.e. *mag-mögen,* is extinct, whereas the epistemic one is in use. The root meaning of former *magan* has been replaced by *können* 'can'. In contrast to Modern Standard German *können*, Gothic *kunnan* was not yet used as a root modal, but served as a lexically full verb only.

We learn from this that modal verbs are part of a continuous linguistic cycle where the functions of root modality/deonticity and epistemicity are in constant renewal. It is not the case that there is linear "evolution" from root modality/deonticity to epistemicity (as claimed by Traugott 1989 and others). The very difference between deonticity and epistemicity is captured in terms of markedness oppositions, not in terms of linear diachronic development. From a functional point of view, both functions – the marked one and the unmarked one – are encoded cotemporally. A lot

[13] To be more precise: Modern German modal particles are not only epistemic in meaning, but they transport an additional component: the assessment of the speaker's knowledge and intentions. Apart from this difference, the modal particle *denn* translates the epistemic reading of (38) adequately.

of this parallel encoding is yet undiscovered. The aspectual contexts that licence either root/deontic or epistemic meaning have been neglected for a long time.

We see the same patterns in Old High German, where deontic *magan* selects the perfective infinitive, and epistemic *magan* is the result of the opposite aspect selection (for more detail, see Leiss 2008:28-29), as long as affirmative sentences are involved:

(41) *Uuer* ***mag*** *thaz* ***gi-horen*** DMV
who can that PF-hear
'Who can understand that?' (*Tatian* (Masser-edition) 263, 30)

(42) *Iz* ***mag*** *thoh* ***sin*** *in wani* EMV
It can though be PREP belief
'It may though be imaginable' (*Otfrid* II,7,49)

Krause (1997) documented all instances of modal verb constructions with *magan* in the Old High German Bible Harmony by Otfrid von Weissenburg, which brought to light undisputable epistemic readings. None of these constructions was construed with the perfective infinitive despite the attested frequency of perfective aspect selection. This clear correlation between aspect and modality effects does not show up in negated clauses. These patterns will be explained in the next section.

5.4. Negation and aspect in modal verb constructions

A quite robust finding up to this point has been that deontic modal verb constructions select the perfective infinitive in affirmative clauses. The selection of imperfective infinitives reads either as imperfective future tense or as epistemic constructions. By contrast, modal verb constructions in negated clauses select perfective as well as imperfective infinitives. The selection of the imperfective aspect is far more frequent than the selection of the perfective aspect. The latter is obviously dispreferred and more marked. This selectional behavior is not restricted to Gothic, Old High German, or the Germanic languages. Miestami & Van der Auwera (2011) refer to the results of two unpublished typological studies by Schmid (1980) and Matthews (1990)[14], according to which there is a lot of evidence that perfective aspect is dispreferred in negated clauses in most

[14] Schmid, Maureen Alina (1980): The co-occurrence restrictions in negative, interrogative and conditional clauses: a cross-linguistic study. Ph.D. Dissertation, SUNY Buffalo. / Matthews, Stephen James (1990): A cognitive approach to the typology of verbal aspect. Ph.D.-Dissertation, University of Southern California.

languages. Miestami & Van der Auwera (2011), relying on Miestami (2005), tried to disconfirm these results by choosing a larger sample of languages based on the World Atlas of Linguistic Structures (WALS). They suggest that specific markedness criteria motivate the selection of aspect in negated clauses. Their line of argument is as follows: Negated clauses tend to neutralize the aspectual opposition. Neutralization can be coded by the selection of the unmarked pole of the aspectual distinction. Languages with unmarked imperfective aspect tend to select the imperfective aspect as a default category in negated clauses, whereas the opposite selection surfaces in languages where the perfective aspect is formally unmarked. As Gothic and Old High German mark the perfective aspect, we can predict that negative clauses should select the imperfective infinitive. These affinities between negation and aspect are well documented in the typological literature. Nevertheless, they have not yet been investigated for the older stages of the Germanic languages. The argument held by Miestamo & Van der Auwera (2011) seems to explain the selection of imperfective infinitives in negated modal verb constructions quite well, but we find no explanation for the equally well-documented, but rare cases of perfective verbs in negated modal verb constructions. One explanation might be markedness reversal with negated modal verb constructions, suggested by Leiss (2008). It predicts imperfective aspect with negated deontic modal verb constructions, and perfective aspect with negation of epistemic modal verb constructions, which is supported by the following examples:

(43)	*qimiþ*	*nahts,*	*þanei*	*ni*
	come:3SG.PRES	night:NOM.SG.F	CONJ	NEG
	manna	*mag*	*waurkjan*	
	man:NOM.SG.F	can:3SG.PRES	work:IMPF.INF	

'The night will come where nobody can do/achieve anything' (Joh. 9:4)

In (43) the modal verb embeds an imperfective infinitive instead of the perfective infinitive. The perfective infinitive is preferred in affirmative deontic modal verb constructions, whereas negated clauses prefer the imperfective infinitive. Thus, clausal negation regularly goes together with the imperfective aspect:

(44) *unte ni maguþ hausjan waurd mein* [Joh. 8:43]
selection of *hausjan* (impf) instead of *gahausjan* (pf)
'because you are not able to hear/understand my words'

(45) *i magt mik nu laistjan* [Joh. 13:36]
selection of *laistjan* instead of *ga-laistjan*
'you can not follow me now'

Yet, there are also instances of negated sentences where the modal *magan* selects the perfective infinitive, counter to the expectations for negated clauses. See (46) taken from the Gothic bible (Cor.I, 15:50):

(46)

þei	*leik*	*jah bloþ*	*þiudinassu*
CONJ	flesh:NOM.SG	and blood:NOM.SG	kingdom:ACC.SG

gudis	***ga-niman***	***ni***	***magun***
god:GEN.SG.	PF-take	NEG	can:PRES.3PL

'for flesh and blood cannot possess the kingdom of God'

The selection of perfective infinitives in negated sentences triggers a shift towards the epistemic reading of the modal verb. The very meaning of *ni magun* in (46) is not (47), but (48):

(47) 'flesh and blood are not able to overtake the realm of god'
(48) 'It is impossible that flesh and blood inherit the realm of god'

The speaker's stance is that he considers it as impossible that the proposition can be affirmed. An interesting side effect consists in the widening of scope. In (48) the negation scopes over the entire proposition, which is characteristic of epistemic readings of modals, as well as for clausal negation with wide scope, in contrast to negation with narrow scope. Padučeva (2008:201-202) claims for epistemic *močet* 'can' in Russian that it selects the perfective aspect in negated clauses. This is very close to the behavior of negated clauses with epistemic reading of the modal in Gothic, and it supports the conclusion that markedness values are part of the architecture of modality.

Another effect that sides with the selection of perfective aspect in negated clauses is a clear definiteness effect. This effect has been emphasized by Heindl (2009:130) for Modern Russian:

(49) On *ne stroil dom.*
he not built:IMPF house.
'He did not build **a** house.'

(50) *On ne po-stroil dom.*
he not PF-built house.
'He did not build **the** house.'

The selection of a specific aspect provokes a specific definiteness/indefiniteness effect. This effect can be used to encode different sorts of negation: propositional negation with wide scope and negation with narrow scope. Needless to say that the unmarked type of negation is negation with wide scope. For this very reason, perfective infinitives in negated sentences are less frequent than imperfective infinitives. In both types of constructions, in epistemic modal constructions as well as with clausal negation, the negation scopes over the proposition.

The definiteness effect in negation will help to explain hitherto unexplained records of *magan* + imperfective infinitive in non-negated sentences.

5.5. Root/deontic modals, aspect, and definiteness effects

In (51) and (52) the perfective verbs *ga-taujan* and *ga-hausjan* are expected for semantic as well as for syntactic reasons. They are construed as embedded infinitives of deontic modals. As the perfective aspect partners of *taujan* 'to do' and *hausjan* 'to hear' are well attested for Gothic, we are confronted with the question why the perfective aspect partners are not selected.

(51)	*ga-ulaubjats*	*þatei magjau*	*þata*	***taujan***?
	PF-believe:PRES.2PL	CONJ can:OPT.1SG	DET.ACC.SG.	do

'Do you believe that I can do/fullfill that'
[Matth. 9:28]

(52)	*hvas*	*mag*	*þis*	***hausjan?***
	who:NOM.SG.M	can:PRES.3SG	DET.GEN.SG	hear:IMPF

'who can hear/understand this'
[Joh. 6:60]

The intended semantics of the verbs chosen in the imperfective aspect is clearly perfective. Moreover, the deontic modal verb construction should, according to the rule, select the perfective aspect partner. An explanation for the counterintuitive selection of imperfective aspect partner was provided in Leiss (2000). There is evidence that perfective verbs regularly loose their *ga*-prefix in definite contexts. The reason for this is the functional equivalence of definiteness markers and perfectivity markers in Gothic and OGH (for more detail, see Leiss 2000 and 2008).

6. Covert coding of deonticity: conclusion and outlook

In sum, the presented findings are the following ones. First, there is a clear functional equivalence between the Gothic *ga*-prefix, the *to*-preposition English or its equivalents in Modern Germanic languages, and the definite article or demonstrative pronoun. Second, covert patterns of modality are made up by intricate patterns composed by definiteness effects, aspectuality and, as appears, telicity or directionality or whatever the function of the preposition *TO* might be. To understand the function of the preposition *TO* in non-grammaticalized quasi-modals or premodals with a root/deontic reading, it may help to take into account that quasi-modals/premodals/lexical modals such as *ga-sokjan* in Gothic are perfective verbs. This compares with the semimodals in modern Germanic languages, which are construed with the *TO*-infinitive. Third, alleged exceptions have proved to be marked constructions such as clausal negation and epistemic readings, all of which are encoded with the help of marked aspectual selection and the respective scope effects. Fourth, the results fully support Abraham's important interface generalizations on the affinities between deontic readings of modals and the perfective aspect, and epistemic readings of modals and the imperfective aspect, published in the last 20 years. Based on these insights, it was possible to uncover essential building blocks of complex patterns of covert coding of modality, - effects that were hitherto classified as exceptions to Abraham's generalizations concerning the modality-aspect interface. Finally, it may be time to propose the conclusion that the covert encoding of modality is strongly prevalent in aspect languages (see also Abraham/Leiss 2008, Kotin 2008, Kotin 2012, Leiss 2002), whereas overt encodings emerge as a consequence of dissolving systems of verbal aspect.

There are still open questions that need answers: Are there any hidden patterns of epistemicity in the older stages of Germanic languages? Kotin (2008) detected a large amount of covert encodings of root/deontic modality in Old Slavonic languages. Covert modality in the sense of Bhatt is clearly incompatible with epistemicity. The very reason is that Bhatt focuses on constructions with the auxiliaries *be* and *have* plus the embedded *to*-infinitive. In the present paper, emphasis was placed on the incompatibility of *TO*-infinitives with epistemic modal verb construals. As the preposition *TO* was shown to be functionally equivalent to the perfective aspectual prefixes, it is evident that epistemicity and covert modality constructions with *TO* exclude each other. Until now no patterns of covert coding of epistemic modality have been discovered for the older stages of Slavic and Germanic languages. It seems, however, that the effects of embedded imperfective infinitives in modal verb constructions in affirmative clauses, as well as those of perfective embedded infinitives in negated clauses, still have to be investigated in detail in order to understand the process of grammaticalization of modality in terms of **markedness** of functions rather than in terms of a **lack** of functions in former stages of languages. In the light of the findings above, there is good reason to assume that most of the covert patterns of epistemic modality are yet to be uncovered. This holds especially for the investigation of patterns of modality in diachrony.

Acknowledgments

I would like to thank the participants of the Workshop on Covert Patterns of Modality (held at 44th Annual Meeting of the Societas Linguistica Europaea, Universidad de La Rioja, Logroño, Spain, 8-11 September 2011) as well as the participants of the Workshop on modality (organized by Volker Gast and Ekkehard König at the University of Jena, Germany) for comments and discussion on the paper presented there. I am especially grateful to Werner Abraham, who commented upon most of the issues presented here in great detail, and to Sonja Zeman for help on formal matters.

List of abbreviations

List of abbreviations:
ACC = accusative, CONJ = conjunction (subordinated and coordinated), DMV = deontic modal verb, EMV = epistemic modal verb, F = feminine gender, FIN= final, IMPF = imperfective aspect, INF = infinitive, FUT = future tense, LMV = lexical modal verb, PAST = past tense, M = masculine gender, NOM = nominative, OPT = optative, POSS = possessive pronoun, PF = perfective aspect, PL = plural, SG = singular, 3SG = third person singular, 2PL = second person plural.

References

Abraham, Werner (1989): Syntaktische Korrelate zum Lesartwechsel zwischen epistemischen und deontisch/volitiven Modalverben. *Groninger Arbeiten zur Germanistischen Linguistik* 30, 145-166. [also as: http://gagl.eldoc.ub.rug.nl/FILES/root/1989-30/04/GAGL-30-1989-04.pdf. last download: 05.04.2012].

—. (1991): Modalverben in der Germania. In: Iwasaki, Eijirō (ed.): *Begegnung mit dem Fremden. Akten des VIII. Internationalen Germanistenkongresses*, Tokyo 1990. Bd. 4: *Kontrastive Syntax, kontrastive Semantik, Lexikologie, Lexikographie, kontrastive Pragmatik.* München: Iudicium, 109-118.

—. (1999): Über allgemeine Zusammenhänge zwischen Präpositionsinfinitiv, Futur, deontischer Modalität und Perfektivität: lokalistische Allativität. *Sprachwissenschaft* 24, 361-405.

—. (2002): Modal verbs: epistemics in German and English. In: Barbiers, Sjef / Beukema, Frits / van der Wurff, Wim (eds.): *Modality and its interaction with the verbal system.* Amsterdam, Philadelphia: Benjamins, 19-50 [Linguistik Aktuell / Linguistics Today 47].

—. (2004): The grammaticalization of the infinitival preposition – toward a theory of 'grammaticalizing reanalysis'. *Journal of Comparative Germanic Linguistics* 7/2: 111-170

—. (1995/2005). *Deutsche Syntax im Sprachenvergleich. Grundlegung einer typologischen Syntax des Deutschen.* Tübingen: Stauffenburg [Studien zur deutschen Grammatik 41].

—. (2012): (Inter)Subjektivierung oder Fremdbewusstseinsabgleich als synchrone und diachrone Wandelbegriffe? Begriffsschärfung und theoretische Einordnung. In: Ernst, Peter (ed.): *Jahrbuch der Gesellschaft für Germanistische Sprachgeschichte* 3. Berlin, Boston: de Gruyter.

Abraham, Werner / Leiss, Elisabeth (eds.) (2008): *Modality-aspect interfaces – implications and typological solutions.* Amsterdam, Philadelphia: Benjamins, 15-41 [Typological Studies in Language 79].

Diewald, Gabriele (1999): *Die Modalverben im Deutschen. Grammatikalisierung und Polyfunktionalität.* Tübingen: Niemeyer [Reihe Germanistische Linguistik 118).

Gelderen, Elly van (2004): *Grammaticalization as economy.* Amsterdam, Philadelphia: Benjamins [Linguistik Aktuell / Linguistics Today 71].

Götz, Ursula (2001): *uuvo mag thaz sîn.* Die unterschiedlichen Gebrauchsweisen der Präterito-präsentien im Althochdeutschen des 8.-10. Jahrhunderts. Unpublished Habilitationsschrift: University of Bamberg.

Heindl, Olga (2009): Negation, Modalität und Aspekt im Mittelhochdeutschen im Vergleich zum Slawischen. In: Abraham, Werner & Leiss, Elisabeth (eds.): *Modalität. Epistemik und Evidentialität bei Modalverb, Adverb, Modalpartikel und Modus.* Tübingen: Stauffenburg, 123-179 [Studien zur deutschen Grammatik 77].

Holl, Daniel (2010): *Modale Infinitive und dispositionelle Modalität im Deutschen* Berlin: Akademieverlag [studia grammatica; 71].

Kangasniemi, Heikki (1992): *Modal expressions in Finnish*. Helsinki [Studia Fennica Linguistica 2].

Kotin, Michail L. (2008): Zu den Affinitäten zwischen Modalität und Aspekt: Eine germanisch-slawische Fallstudie. *Die Welt der Slawen* 53, 116-140.

—. (2012): *Gotisch: Im (diachronen und typologischen) Vergleich*. Heidelberg: Winter.

Krause, Maxi (1997): Zur Modalisierung bei Otfrid. In: Desportes, Yves (ed.): *Semantik der syntaktischen Beziehungen. Akten des Pariser Kolloquiums zur Erforschung des Althochdeutschen 1994*. Heidelberg: Winter [Germanische Bibliothek, N.F., 3. Reihe: Untersuchungen 27].

Leiss, Elisabeth (1985): Zur Entstehung des neuhochdeutschen analytischen Futurs. *Sprachwissenschaft* 10, 250-273.

—. (2000): *Artikel und Aspekt. Die grammatischen Muster von Definitheit.* Berlin, New York: de Gruyter [Studia Linguistica Germanica 55].

—. (2002): Explizite und implizite Kodierung von Deontizität und Epistemizität: über die grammatische Musterbildung vor der Entstehung von Modalverben. *Jezykoslovlje* 3, 69-98.

—. (2008): The silent and aspect-driven patterns of deonticity and epistemicity. A chapter in diachronic typology. In: Abraham, Werner & Elisabeth Leiss (eds.): *Modality-aspect interfaces – implications and typological solutions*. Amsterdam, Philadelphia: Benjamins, 14-41 [Typological Studies in Language 79].

—. (2012a): Lexikalische versus grammatische Epistemizität und Evidentialität: Plädoyer für eine strikte Trennung zwischen Lexikon und Grammatik. In: Diewald, Gabriele / Smirnova, Elena (eds.): *Evidentialität und Modalität*. Trier: Wissenschaftlicher Verlag [Fokus 37], 149-169.

—. (2012b): Epistemicity, evidentiality, and Theory of Mind. In: Abraham, Werner / Leiss, Elisabeth (2012), 37-65

Miestami, Matti (2005): *Standard negation. The negation of declarative verbal main clauses in a typological perspective.* Berlin, New York: de Gruyter [Empirical Approaches to Language Typology 31).

Miestami, Matti / Van der Auwera, Johan (2011): Negation and perfective vs. imperfective aspect. *Cahiers Chronos* 22, 65-84.

Öhlschläger, Günther (1989): *Zur Syntax und Semantik der Modalverben des Deutschen.* Tübingen: Niemeyer [Linguistische Arbeiten 144].

Payawang, Surachai (2012): Muster der Informationsstruktur und der Muster der Kodierung des Deutschen und des Thailändischen aus der Perspektive der sprachlichen Invarianz. PhD Dissertation: Linguistisches Internationales Promotionsprogramm: University of Munich.

Padučeva, Elena (2008): Russian modals *možet* 'can' and *dolžen* 'must' selecting the imperfective. In: Abraham, Werner / Leiss, Elisabeth (2012), 197-211.

Piskorz, Jadwiga (2012): Die Grammatikalisierung eines neuen Perfekts im Polnischen. Ein Beitrag zur Entwicklungslogik des Perfekts. PhD Dissertation: Linguistisches Internationales Promotionsprogramm: University of Munich.

Scaffidi-Abbate, B. Augusto (1981): Möglichkeiten der Futurbezeichnung im althochdeutschen Tatian und anderen althochdeutschen literarischen Denkmälern. *Sprachwissenschaft* 6, 288-334.

Streitberg, Wilhelm (1910): *Gotisches Elementarbuch.* 3. und 4. verbesserte Auflage. Heidelberg: Winter [Germanische Bibliothek. Sammlung germanischer Elementar- und Handbücher I,2].

—. (1910/2000): *Die Gotische Bibel.* Band 1: *Der gotische Text und seine griechische Vorlage.* Band 2: *Gotisch-Griechisch-Deutsches Wörterbuch.* 6. und 7. Auflage 2000. Heidelberg: Winter [Germanistische Bibliothek 4].

Traugott, Elizabeth Closs (1989): The rise of epistemic meaning in English. *Language* 65, 31-55.

Tauscher, Elisabeth / Birnbaum, Ernst-Georg (1983): *Grammatik der russischen Sprache.* 15., unveränderte Auflage. Düsseldorf: Brücken-Verlag.

Ultan, Russell (1978): The nature of future tense. In: Greenberg, Joseph (ed.): *Universals of human language.* Vol. 3: *Word structure.* Stanford: Stanford University Press.

Ziegeler, Debra (2008): Propositional aspect and the development of modal inferences in English. In: Abraham, Werner / Leiss, Elisabeth 2008, 15-41.

Author's affiliation:
Elisabeth Leiss
Ludwig-Maximilians-Universität München
Department für Germanistik, Komparatistik, Nordistik, Deutsch als Fremdspache
Schellingsstr. 3/RG
80799 München

PART II:

(C)OVERT MODALITY AND EVIDENTIALITY

GERMAN *WOHL*: AN EVIDENTIAL?*

DAGMAR HAUMANN AND OLE LETNES
UNIVERSITY OF AGDER

Abstract: This paper advances the argument that the German modal particle *wohl*, in a number of contexts, displays evidential properties. This argument is backed up by data drawn from the *Norwegian-English-German Parallel Corpus*, where the translation equivalents of *wohl* are often evidential expressions. A grammaticalized marker of evidentiality, *wohl* is argued to be a weak evidential adverb in the spirit of Cardinaletti & Starke (1999). *Wohl* is shown to occupy the specifier position of the same designated functional projection in the higher inflectional layer of the clause that also hosts bona fide or strong evidential adverbs, e.g. *offensichtlich* "obviously". Supportive evidence for this analysis derives from the positions weak and strong evidential adverbs assume vis-à-vis other high sentence adverbs within the inflectional layer of the clause, and from the fact that both types of evidential adverbs are sensitive with respect to the illocutionary force of the clause (cf. Jacobs 1986; Abraham 1991, 1995; Zimmermann 2009 and others). The differences between *wohl* and strong evidential adverbs are also discussed. While the relative syntactic versatility of the elements under consideration follows from "deficiency" as defined by Cardinaletti & Starke (1999), their different scope properties and thus their interacting with the complementizer layer of the clause will be argued to follow from the presence vs. absence of features that encode the speaker's concern (cf. Bayer 2008; Bayer & Obenauer 2011; Abraham 2012, this volume).

1. Introduction

In this paper, we focus on the modal particle *wohl*. Starting out from a brief introduction to modal particles and their fuzzy categorial status in general (section 2), we review the properties of *wohl*, with a special focus on the categorization of unstressed *wohl* as a modal particle and modal

* We are grateful to the editors of the volume and two anonymous reviewers for their comments on an earlier version of this paper.

adverb. Following Cardinaletti & Starke's (1999) original proposal,[1] we suggest that unstressed *wohl* be viewed as a syntactically, referentially and prosodically deficient adverb (section 3). In section 4, we develop the leading argument that unstressed *wohl*, in a number of contexts, displays evidential properties. Supportive evidence for our claim derives from the analysis of data drawn from the *Norwegian-English-German Parallel Corpus*, that primarily contains fictional texts in the pertinent languages as well as their translations from and into these languages.[2] There is a tradition in particle research of contrasting German with other languages (cf. e.g. Aijmer 1996; Waltereit 2001; Fischer 2007). For the purpose of our analysis we partake in this tradition and take into consideration the various renderings of unstressed *wohl* in English, which lacks modal particles (see e.g. Aijmer 1996, 2009), and also in Norwegian, a language that has modal particles, but considerably fewer than German. Section 5 reviews evidential *wohl* vis-à-vis bona fide evidential adverbs, such as *offensichtlich* "obviously". We argue that *wohl*, like traditional evidential adverbs, occupies the specifier position of a designated functional projection in the inflectional layer of the clause and does not freely assume a number of positions in the middle field (pace Coniglio 2006, 2007; Abraham 2010, 2012; Cardinaletti 2011 and others). This section highlights the similarities between *wohl* and bona fide evidential adverbs with respect to their sensitivity to the illocutionary force of the clause (see among others Abraham 1995, 2012; Zimmermann 2009; Bayer & Obenauer 2011), as well as the differences that exist between *wohl* and traditional evidential adverbs with respect to syntactic versatility, scope and the expression of the speaker's concern with herself or the addressee in relation "to the propositional content of the utterance" (Bayer & Obenauer 2011: 450; see also Abraham 2012, this volume). Section 6 concludes the paper.

2. Modal particles – the Duden classification (2005)

German abounds in modal particles, and there are few languages, if any, that could match German in this respect. German modal particles have been a much debated issue for the past four decades (cf. for example Weydt 1969, 1979, 1989; Helbig 1977, 1990; König 1997), and the topic is still most controversial. We take the classification of "particle" in the

---

[1] See also Coniglio 2006, 2007; Grosz 2007 and Cardinaletti 2007, 2011 for recent adaptations of Cardinaletti & Starke's (1999) proposal.

[2] The *Norwegian-English-German Parallel Corpus* is a subcorpus of the *Oslo Multilingual Corpus* (OMC). For more detailed information, the reader is referred to http://www.hf.uio.no/ilos/english/services/omc/sub-corpora/.

fairly authorative *Duden Grammatik* (henceforth Duden) as our point of departure.[3] Duden (2005: 495-606) subsumes modal particles (cf. (1) below) under the label "particle" together with elements as diverse as degree particles, focusing particles, sentential negation, presequence particles, interjections and onomatopoetics ("PRT" in (1c) stands for the set of modal particles):

(1) a. Sie haben *ja* geraucht.
b. De har *jo* røykt.
c. They have *PRT* smoked.

Duden defines modal particles as follows (2005: 597):

> "Sie drücken sehr differenziert Einstellungen, Annahmen, Bewertungen und Erwartungen des Sprechers bezüglich des geäußerten Sachverhalts, teilweise auch seine Erwartungen an den Hörer aus. Abtönungspartikeln beziehen sich auf den ganzen Satz. Syntaktisch sind sie auf das Mittelfeld beschränkt [und sind] oft unbetont."
>
> ['They express very differentiatedly the speaker's attitudes, assumptions, evaluations and expectations with respect to the state of affairs uttered, and partly also the speaker's expectations with respect to the hearer. Modal particles take scope over the entire sentence. Syntactically, they are restricted to the middle field and are often unstressed.' (our translation)]

Traditionally, particles have been considered to be closely related to adverbs and, as is often the case, adverbs are subsumed under particles and vice versa. The reason for taking into consideration adverbs is that certain subsets of adverbs, notably disjuncts or sentence adverbs, obviously share interpretational properties with modal particles. Moreover, it is not always clear whether a given element is treated as a particle or an adverb, which is a corrollary of fuzzy and often also contradictory definitions (e.g. Helbig 1990; Helbig & Helbig 1990; Gast 2008).

Of prime interest for our investigation is the subset of sentence adverbs which in standard contemporary reference grammars of English, such as Quirk et al. (1985), are labelled disjuncts, which correspond to *Kommentaradverbien* in Duden. According to Duden, this subcategory comprises "evaluative" (*evaluativ*) and "validity related" (*geltungsbezogen*) adverbs, as shown in Table (2-1):

---

[3] *Modalpartikeln* are alternatively referred to as *Abtönungspartikeln* (cf. Duden 2005: 597).

Table 2-1. "Kommentaradverbien", adapted from Duden (2005: 593).

Kommentaradverbien ("commentary adverbs", "disjuncts", "sentence adverbs")	
evaluativ ("evaluative")	*Leider* / *Dummerweise* / *Natürlich* konnte sie nicht kommen. "*Regrettably* / *Unfortunately* / *Naturally*, she could not come." "Dessverre / *Dumt nok* / *Naturligvis* kunne hun ikke komme."
geltungsbezogen ("validity related", also: "Modalwörter", "modal disjuncts", "epistemic adverbs")	Er kann *offensichtlich* / *zweifelsohne* / *sicher* / *vielleicht* laufen. "He can *obviously* / *undoubtedly* / *certainly*/ *probably* walk." "Han kan *åpenbart* / *utvilsomt* / *sikkert* / *kanskje* gå."

Validity related adverbs relate to modality in that they express degrees of subjective certainties with respect to the truth of the proposition they take scope over. In other words, they are epistemic in nature. However, as can be seen in Table (2-1), Duden also subsumes adverbs like *offensichtlich* "obviously" under validity related adverbs, which many linguists would classify as evidential rather than as epistemic adverbs (cf. e.g. Bellert 1977; Fraser 1996; Frey & Pittner 1999; Cinque 1999: 13, 33f., 2004; Ernst 2002: 69ff., 2007). As can be read off the classification of validity related and evaluative adverbs, Duden does not distinguish between epistemic modality and evidentiality:

> "Von dieser Gruppe der evaluierenden Kommentaradverbien gilt es eine zweite Gruppe der so genannten epistemischen Adverbien (oft auch Modalwörter genannt) zu unterscheiden (*vielleicht*, *kaum*, *zweifelsohne*). Diese geben den Grad der Wahrscheinlichkeit an, mit der das bezeichnete Geschehen nach Ansicht des Sprechers bzw. der Sprecherin eintritt oder eingetreten ist, und betreffen damit den Wahrheitsgehalt des Satzes: *Vielleicht sind sie ja zu spät gekommen* (ob es so gewesen ist oder nicht, kann nur vermutet werden). Die Skala der Wahrscheinlichkeit reicht von 'überaus gewiss' bis 'wenig gewiss'." (Duden 2005: 593)

> ['It is essential to distinguish the so called epistemic adverbs, also known as "modal words" (*vielleicht* "probably", *kaum* "hardly", *zweifelsohne* "doubtlessly"), from this group of evaluative disjuncts. These adverbs specify the degree of probability with which the event, according to the speaker, will occur or has occurred and thus concern the truth value of the

proposition: *Vielleicht sind sie ja zu spät gekommen* "Probably they have PRT been late" (whether this has actually been the case or not, can only be guessed at). The scale of probability ranges from 'particularly certain' to 'little certain'.' (our translation)]

The following modal particles are among the 17 "most common" modal particles given in Duden:

Table 2-2. Modal particles in Duden (2005: 598).

Sie haben	*halt, eben, ja, doch, schon* *schon,* ***wohl,*** *übrigens,* *ja, aber, vielleicht*	geraucht
"they have	PRT	smoked"
"de har	PRT	røykt"

3. *Wohl* as modal particle and modal adverb

In the following, we focus on unstressed *wohl* in declaratives.[4] The reason for zooming in on this modal particle is twofold. First, some of the relevant literature classifies unstressed *wohl* both as modal particle and adverb. Second, and most importantly, there are cases in which this variant of *wohl* is clearly a marker of evidentiality, in fact a grammaticalized marker of that category (in other words, an evidential). To our knowledge, this fact has not been recognized until now.

First, we will look into some definitions of *wohl*, given in studies which consider two variants of *wohl*: a modal particle *wohl* and a homophonous adverb.[5]

Helbig (1990: 238) ascribes the following meaning to the modal particle (he uses the term "Abtönungspartikel"):

[4] According to Helbig (1990: 239ff.), *wohl* also occurs as a stressed modal particle, e.g. in *Er arbeitet wóhl (, aber nicht sehr fleißig)* "He works, all right, but not very busily". In this paper, we do not go any further into the stressed variant of the modal particle *wohl*. Unstressed *wohl* also appears in imperatives (e.g. *Gehst du wohl sofort wieder ins Bett!* "Go PRT to bed, immediately!"), in probe questions (*Wer hat den Brief wohl geschrieben?* "Who PRT has written the letter? ") and in yes-no questions (*Hat er das Buch wohl gelesen?* "Has he PRT read the book?"). It also occurs in probe questions which are rather intended as exclamations than questions (*Du willst dich wohl erkälten?* "You want PRT to catch a cold?").

[5] See also Thurmair (1989: 139ff.) and Doherty (1985: 81) for discussion.

> "[*Wohl*] [s]ignalisiert, daß der Sprecher die Richtigkeit der Aussage über das Zutreffen eines Sachverhalts nicht behauptet, sondern als sehr wahrscheinlich vermutet, kennzeichnet die Aussage durch den Bezug auf einen (**evidenzreichen**) Redehintergrund als Hypothese (die – da sie nur vorausgesetzt ist – weder bestritten noch bestätigt werden kann); drückt eine hypothetische Einstellung des Sprechers zur Aussage aus (die noch durch *werden* verstärkt werden kann) (= *vermutlich*, *wahrscheinlich*)." [our emphasis]
>
> ['*Wohl* signals that the speaker does not claim, but rather suspects the correctness of the state of affairs, marks the proposition, by the reference to a discourse (**rich in evidence**), as a hypothesis (which – as it is only presupposed – can neither be disputed nor confirmed); expresses a hypothetical approach on the part of the speaker (which can also be strengthened by *werden*) (= *vermutlich* "assumedly", *wahrscheinlich* "presumably").' (our translation and emphasis)]

This variant of *wohl* is illustrated by examples such as the following (taken from Helbig 1990: 238; our translations added):

(2) a. Diese Entscheidung ist *wohl* nicht akzeptabel.
b. Denne avgjørelsen er *PRT* ikke akseptabel.
c. This decision is *PRT* not acceptable.

(3) a. Sie hat *wohl* das Auto verkauft.
b. Hun har *PRT* solgt bilen.
c. She has *PRT* sold the car.

In their section on "Hypothesenindikator" ("indicator of hypothesis"), Helbig & Helbig (1990) provide the following definition of *wohl* as an adverb (the authors employ the term "Modalwort"):

> "Sprecher signalisiert, daß er hinsichtlich der Faktizität von p Zweifel hegt, daß er das Zutreffen von p aber für möglich hält. Er drückt eine hypothetische Einstellung zur Aussage aus, er behauptet nicht die Richtigkeit der Aussage über das Zutreffen des Sachverhalts, sondern kennzeichnet die Aussage (durch Bezug auf einen **evidenzreichen Redehintergrund**) als Hypothese (Es kann wohl sein, daß p. / Für Sprecher gilt: eher p als nicht p.)." (Helbig & Helbig 1990: 283 [our emphasis])
>
> ['The speaker signals that he doubts the facticity of p, but considers p possible. He expresses a hypothetical attitude with respect to the proposition, he does not claim the correctness of the statement as to whether the proposition is true, but marks (by relating the proposition to a **discourse**

rich in evidence) the statement as a hypothesis (It might WOHL be that p./ For the speaker, it holds: rather p than not p.).' (our translation and emphasis)]

Helbig & Helbig (1990) claim that *wohl* is used adverbially in the following (taken from Helbig & Helbig 1990: 283; our translations added):

(4) a. Er wird die Straßenbahn *wohl* verpasst haben.
b. Han har *muligens* kommet for seint til trikken.
c. He has *probably* missed the tram.

(5) a. Er denkt *wohl* noch nach.
b. Han tenker *PRT* fremdeles.
c. He is *PRT* still thinking.

Helbig & Helbig (1990: 284) concede that it is hard to draw a distinction between the unstressed modal particle ("Abtönungspartikel") *wohl* and the homophonous modal adverb ("Modalwort") in cases in which unstressed *wohl* occurs in declaratives. Reciprocally, in his account of modal particles, Helbig (1990: 239) underlines that it is difficult to draw the line between the unstressed modal particle *wohl* and the modal adverb *wohl* in declaratives.[6] Even though we do not agree with Helbig's (1990) and Helbig & Helbig's (1990) characterization of unstressed *wohl* in (4) and (5) as an adverb, we find it interesting that the concept of evidence occurs in both definitions. In other words, by using *wohl*, the speaker refers back to some given evidence in the discourse (cf. Helbig 1990: 238; Helbig & Helbig 1990: 283). If this can be backed up by relevant data, the unstressed modal particle *wohl* would be in the vicinity of evidential adverbs.

3.1 Distinctive properties

Table (3-1) summarizes the properties that are generally taken to distinguish between modal particles and modal adverbs (see e.g. Weydt 1969; Abra-

[6] For a (possible) distinction between *wohl* as a modal adverb ("Modalwort") and a modal particle ("Abtönungspartikel"), a question test like the one suggested in Helbig & Helbig (1990: 31) is not very illuminating. According to the authors, modal adverbs can constitute answers to yes-no questions, whereas modal particles can never be used to answer questions. Related to the examples (4) and (5) above, this would mean that the questions *Wird er die Straßenbahn verpasst haben?* ("Has he missed the tram?") and *Denkt er noch nach?* ("Is he still thinking?") could both be answered by "wohl". To us, "wohl" hardly qualifies as an acceptable answer to the two questions.

ham 1991; Jacobs 1991; Aijmer 1996; van Gelderen 2002; Fischer 2007; Grosz 2007; Zimmermann 2009; Egg 2010; Bayer & Obenauer 2011 on the formal properties of particles):

Table 3-1. Distinctive properties of "Modalpartikel" and "Modalwort".

	Particles ("Modalpartikeln")	Adverbs ("Modalwörter")
Syntax	restricted to the middle field[7]	susceptible to overt syntactic movement[8]
Reading	non-referential (no modification, no coordination)	referential (modification, coordination)
Prosody	phonetically weak	phonetically strong

In the following, we briefly illustrate these properties for the modal particle *wohl* and the modal adverb *wohl*. We follow Helbig (1990) and Helbig & Helbig (1990) in that both the modal particle *wohl* and the homophonous modal adverb express hypotheses and probabilities on the basis of a discourse rich in evidence.

However, as indicated in Table (3-1), the modal particle *wohl* and the modal adverb *wohl* differ on the syntactic, interpretive and prosodic level, as illustrated in (6)-(8) vs. (9)-(11).

The modal particle *wohl* is restricted to occurring in the middle field (6), resists modification (7) and it is phonetically weak, i.e. it cannot bear stress (8):[9]

---

[7] Bayer & Obenauer (2011: 471ff.) discuss strings as in (i) where the modal particle is contained within an interrogative constituent with which it raises to the left periphery:

(i) [*Wer wohl*] zur Beerdigung kommt? (LSC2TD)
who PRT to the funeral comes
"Who PRT will come to the funeral?"

(ii) [*Warum wohl*] floppt das Bildungspaket?
[http://blog.given-word.de/2011/04/17/warum-wohl-floppt-das-bildungspaket/]
why PRT flops the educational reform
"Why PRT does the educational reform flop?"

Note that, according to Bayer & Obenauer, modal particles are functional heads, Prt, which usually take vP/VP as their complement, but they may also be merged with a *wh*-constituent which then raises to SpecPrtP.

[8] These elements may raise to designated specifier positions in the left periphery of the clause, e.g. SpecFocP.

(6) a. Sie gehört *wohl* zu den Wohlhabenderen in der Gegend. (TB1TD)
she belongs PRT to the more well-to-do people in the district
"She is PRT one of the more well-to-do people in the district." (adapted from TB1TE)
b. **Wohl* gehört sie zu den Wohlhabenderen in der Gegend.
PRT belongs she to the more well-to-do people in the district
"She is PRT one of the more well-to-do people in the district."

(7) a. Sie dachten *wohl*, ich sei ein ganz normales Kind, das eben in die Pubertät gekommen ist. (CF1)
they thought PRT I was a quite normal child who PRT in the puberty come is
"They thought PRT I was quite a normal child who was going through puberty." (adapted from CF1TE)
b. *Sie dachten [*sehr wohl*], ich sei ein ganz normales Kind, das eben in die Pubertät gekommen ist.
they thought very PRT I was a quite normal child who PRT in the puberty come is
"They thought PRT I was quite a normal child who was going through puberty."

(8) a. Papa bekommt *wohl* eines Tages einen Herzinfarkt. (BV2TD)
daddy gets PRT one day a heart attack
"Daddy will PRT have a heart attack one day." (adapted from BV2TE)
b. *Papa bekommt *wóhl* eines Tages einen Herzinfarkt.
daddy gets PRT one day a heart attack
"Daddy will PRT have a heart attack one day."

Note that the strings in (6b), (7b) and (8b) all have a well-formed reading if and only if *wohl* is stressed, in which case *wohl* contradicts a proposition in the immediate context (cf. Meibauer 1994: 240; see also Weydt 1969: 56). However, the variant of *wohl* that allows for this reading is not the modal particle, but the homophonous epistemic, i.e. modal adverb:

(9) a. Sie gehört *wóhl* zu den Wohlhabenderen in der Gegend. (based on (6))

---

[9] The data in (6)-(8) are partly taken and/or adapted from the *Oslo Multilingual Corpus*. See section 4 for a brief description of the corpus and the source codes (cf. note 14).

b. *Wóhl* gehört sie zu den Wohlhabenderen in der Gegend.
ADV belongs she to the more well-to-do people in the district
"Certainly she is one of the more well-to-do people in the district."

(10) a. Sie dachten *wóhl*, ich sei ein ganz normales Kind, das eben in die Pubertät gekommen ist. (based on (7))
b. Sie dachten [*sehr wóhl*], ich sei ein ganz normales Kind, das eben in die Pubertät gekommen ist.
they thought [very ADV] I was a quite normal child who PRT in the puberty come is
"Very certainly they thought I was quite a normal child who was going through puberty."

(11) Papa bekommt (sehr) *wóhl* eines Tages einen Herzinfarkt. (based on (8))
daddy gets ADV one day a heart attack
"Daddy will (very) certainly have a heart attack one day."

3.2 The modal particle wohl vis-à-vis its adverbial cognates – a question of category

In their 1999 article, Cardinaletti & Starke propose a typology of structural deficiency in pronouns, which they argue holds true for adverbs as well (Cardinaletti & Starke 1999: 207ff.). The gist of their argument is that adverbs come in three flavors: (a) strong adverbs, which are positionally versatile, referential (whence they allow for modification and coordination) and can be stressed, (b) weak adverbs, whose distribution is highly limited and which are non-referential and phonologically weak, and, finally, (c) clitic adverbs, which differ from weak adverbs in that they are syntactic heads and as such interact with verb movement (cf. Cardinaletti & Starke 1999: 212f.; Cardinaletti 2011 for elaboration and modifications). Crucially, Cardinaletti & Starke's (1999) characterization of strong and weak adverbs rests on the same syntactic, interpretive and prosodic differences that, across the board, figure in the distinction between adverbs and modal particles (cf. Table 3-1). Given the striking similarities between weak adverbs and modal particles in terms of limited distribution, non-referentiality and phonological weakness, it is not surprising that Cardinaletti & Starke's (1999) initial proposal has been adapted to modal particles (cf. Cardinaletti 2007, 2011; Grosz 2007; Coniglio 2006, 2007). It is beyond controversy that most modal particles are both diachronically and synchronically related to adverbs: they evolved from adverbs through grammaticalizaiton and/or have a strong adverbial cognate (cf. Thurmair 1989; König et. al. 1990; Abraham 1991, 2001, 2012; Meibauer 1994; Diewald 1997; Wegener 1997; Molnár 2002; Diewald & Ferraresi 2008; Cardinaletti 2011, and many others). Thus, the modal particle *wohl* is both diachronically and synchronically related to the homophonous manner adverb (12) and the homophonous epistemic sentence adverb (13).[10] These elements, as opposed to the variant of *wohl* under consideration (14), may be stressed, may support modifiers and may precede the finite verb in a V2-structure (cf. also (6)-(8) vs. (9)-(11) above):[11]

(12) a. Ich fühlte mich überhaupt nicht *wóhl*. (LSC2TD)
"I was absolutely not feeling well!" (LSC2TE)
b. Ich fühlte mich nicht *besonders wóhl*.
"I was not feeling very well."
c. (*Besonders) wóhl* fühlte ich mich nicht.
"I was not feeling (very) well."

(13) a. Ich denke *wóhl* an ihre Veröffentlichung!
"I certainly am thinking of publishing it!" (TBE1TE)
b. Ich denke *sehr wóhl* an ihre Veröffentlichung! (TBE1)
"I very certainly am thinking of publishing it!"
c. (Sehr) *wóhl* denke ich an ihre Veröffentlichung!
"I (very) certainly am thinking of publishing it!"

(14) a. *"Da hast du *wóhl* Recht," sagte er zustimmend.
(adapted from JG3TD)
"you are PRT right", said he concedingly
""You are PRT right", he conceded."

---

[10] Note that the epistemic sentence adverb *wohl* has developed from the homophonous manner adverb through subjectification (cf. Traugott 1997, 2003). See also Swan (1991, 1997) for the development of English and Norwegian (epistemic) sentence adverbs from manner adverbs.

[11] Note that the examples in (14) would be semantically anomalous if *wohl* were stressed and/or modified, since stressed and/or modified *wohl* would contradict a proposition in the immediate context (cf. Meibauer 1994: 240), which, in turn, would not go well with the manner modification of the matrix verb *zustimmend* "concedingly".

b. *"Da hast du *sehr wóhl* Recht," sagte er zustimmend.
""You are very PRT right", he conceded."
c. *"(*Sehr*) *wóhl* hast du da Recht," sagte er zustimmend.
""Very PRT you are", he conceded."

As is argued by van Gelderen (2002), Roberts & Roussou (2003), Abraham (2012), Cardinaletti (2011: 510), Abraham & Leiss (this volume) and others, grammaticalized elements assume higher structural positions than the elements they developed from. We shall come back to this issue below (cf. section 5).

Vis-à-vis its adverbial cognates, the unstressed modal particle *wohl* is syntactically, referentially and prosodically deficient, i.e. it displays those properties that Cardinaletti & Starke (1999) identify for weak adverbs. Structurally, deficiency manifests itself in the absence of functional structure. Leaving technical details aside, weak adverbs (16) differ from strong adverbs (15) in that they lack the $C_{Adv}P$ layer of structure that hosts referential features. Both weak and strong adverbs, but not clitic adverbs (17), project a $\Sigma_{Adv}P$ layer that hosts prosody related features. In other words, "weak" elements are "peeled" strong elements, and clitics are "peeled weak elements" (Cardinaletti & Starke 1999: 195; Cardinaletti 2011: 509f.):

(15) strong adverbs [$C_{Adv}P$ ... [$\Sigma_{Adv}P$ ... [$I_{Adv}P$ ... [AdvP ...]]]]

(16) weak adverbs [$\Sigma_{Adv}P$ ... [$I_{Adv}P$ ... [AdvP ...]]]

(17) clitic adverbs [$I_{Adv}P$ ... [AdvP ...]]

We follow Cardinaletti & Starke's (1999) original lead and suggest that unstressed *wohl* be analyzed as a weak adverb (see also Cardinaletti 2007, 2011; Grosz 2007; Coniglio 2006, 2007). In the following, we argue that this element, in a number of contexts, displays evidential properties and thus should be analyzed as an evidential. Specifically, we argue that this variant of *wohl* (alongside Norwegian *visst*) be analyzed as a multiply deficient functional relative of orthodox evidential adverbs, such as *offensichtlich* "obviously". In other words, we argue that the variant of *wohl* under consideration is a grammaticalized marker of evidentiality.

4. *Wohl* as an evidential? Suggestive evidence from multilingual corpus data

Before turning to present and discuss the data that corroborate our claim that *wohl* can be a marker of evidentiality, some comments on evidentiality and evidentials are in order. One of the ongoing debates in modality research concerns the question of whether evidentiality and epistemicity represent two discrete categories (cf. for example Leiss 2009; Diewald & Smirnova 2010)[12] or rather mark the extremes of one scalar category (cf. Aijmer 1996; Traugott 1997; Gunkel 2000; Palmer 2001). In addition, as is suggested by Abraham & Leiss (this volume), the distinction between evidential and epistemic modality "may be blurred by different descriptive traditions". The stance we take is that evidentiality and epistemicity represent "entirely different cognitive areas" (de Haan 2001: 203) and must be distinguished on semantico-pragmatic and syntactic grounds. Semantico-pragmatically, they differ from epistemic expressions in that they state "the existence of a source of evidence for some information" (Aikhenvald 2003: 1). Conversely, epistemic expressions concern "the degree of certitude of the truth value, expressed in terms of possibility or necessity" (Ernst 2002: 73). Syntactically, they differ from epistemic expressions in that they occupy a higher position and thus outscope epistemic expressions (cf. Cinque 1999: 33, 135, passim; Nilsen 2000: 38, passim):

(18) a. … dass er *angeblich vielleicht* zurückgetreten ist.
b. … at han *angivelig sannsynligvis* har trukket seg. (Nilsen 2000: 38)
c. … that he *allegedly* has *probably* withdrawn.

(19) a. *… dass er *vielleicht angeblich* zurückgetreten ist.
b. *… at han *sannsynligvis angivelig* har trukket seg. (Nilsen 2000: 38)
c. *… that he *probably* has *allegedly* withdrawn.

[12] According to Diewald & Smirnova (2011: 82f.), "evidentiality – as a semantic domain as well as a grammatical category – has to be kept notionally distinct from other categories, in particular from modality and the grammatical category of mood […]. Without denying the fact that modality and evidentiality may merge under certain conditions, we propose to treat evidentiality as a distinct and discrete functional domain whose distinctive feature is INFORMATION SOURCE, whereas epistemic modality is primarily concerned with the speaker's evaluative attitude towards the proposition".

For our analysis, we searched the *Norwegian-English-German Parallel Corpus*,[13] a subcorpus of the *Oslo Multilingual Corpus* (OMC) for *wohl*, both in original German texts and texts translated into German from both English and Norwegian. We found that, in addition to the usual suspects, i.e. no translation at all, like in (20b, c) and epistemic adverbs (21b, c), *wohl* is often rendered by an evidential expression in both the English and Norwegian translation of a German text and also in the English and Norwegian original on which the German translation is based:[14]

(20) a. Ich fragte mich, was sie *wohl* zum Kreischen gebracht hatte. (WB1TD)
b. Jeg lurte på hva som **Ø** hadde fått dem til å skrike og rope slik. (WB1TN)
c. I wondered what had **Ø** made them scream. (WB1)

(21) a. Er wird *wohl* Urlaub machen. (PDJ3TD)
b. Han er her *sikkert* på ferie. (PDJ3TN)
c. It's *probably* just a holiday. (PDJ3)

While the relationship between German and Norwegian is relatively straightforward in the sense that both languages have comparable modal particles, the relationship between German and English (and Norwegian and English) is somewhat more intriguing, since English lacks modal particles and hence depends on translation equivalents (see Aijmer 1996; Waltereit 2001; Fischer 2007). Among these, the verb *seem* obviously plays a vital role. The corpus data reveal that English *seem* (22b)-(27b), Norwegian *visst* "certainly" (22c) & (23c),*vel* "obviously" (24c) & (25c) and *nok* "apparently" (26c) & (27c) figure as translation equivalents of *wohl*:

(22) a. Wir sind *wohl* alle beide Gewohnheitsmenschen, suchen uns Tag für Tag mit Vorliebe die gleichen Plätze aus. (KF1TD)
b. We both *seem* to be creatures of habit, prefer to use the same seats day after day. (KF1TE)

---

[13] Thanks to Hilde Hasselgård for granting us access to the OMC.

[14] We provide the source codes employed by the compilers of OMC, where the simple combination of letters followed by number(s) marks the original text, and TE, TD and TN its translation into English, German and Norwegian, respectively. Thus, for example, (20a, b) and (21a, b) are German and Norwegian translations of (20c) and (21c).

c. Vi er *visst* vanemennesker begge to, søker helst til de samme setene dag etter dag. (KF1)

(23) a. "Wie heißen Sie?" fragt sie dann, spürt *wohl* aber plötzlich, daß mich die Frage verwirrt und peinlich berührt, und unterbricht sich: "Nein, das geht mich nichts an!" (KF1TD)
b. "What's your name?" she asks, but *seems* to realize at once that the question makes me confused and ill at ease, so she interrupts: "No, that's really none of my business!" (KF1TE)
c. "Hva heter du?" sier hun så, men ser *visst* med en gang at spørsmålet gjør meg forvirret og ille til mote, og avbryter selv: "Nei, det har jeg da ingenting med!" (KF1)

(24) a. Diese Eigenschaft mußte *wohl* besonders betont werden. (UR1)
b. It *seems* that this fact had to be particularly emphasized. (UR1TE)
c. [...] det var *vel* denne egenskap som spesielt skulle fremheves. (UR1TN)

(25) a. Wenn Enthaltsamkeit überhaupt einen Sinn habe, dann den, Menschen, die sich ehrlich getrennt haben, aus reiner Not einander wieder in die Arme zu treiben; daran sei der Gesellschaft *wohl* eigentlich gelegen. (KF1TD)
b. If it were to serve any purpose at all, it must be to force unwilling separated couples into each other's arms again through sheer need; as a matter of fact, that *seemed* to be what society was interested in. (KF1TE)
c. Om den overhodet skulle tjene til noe, måtte det være å drive uvillige separerte tilbake i armene på hverandre av ren nød; det var *vel* også egentlig det samfunnet var interessert i. (KF1)

(26) a. " Ja, der Reichstag ist *wohl* durch seine Arbeit ziemlich überfordert, " bemerkt Petrén trocken. (HME3)
b. "Yes, the Riksdag *seems* to have too much to do," remarks Petrén drily. (HME3TE)
c. "Ja, arbeidet er *nok* litt for krevende for Riksdagen", sier Petrén tørt. (HME3TN)

(27) a. Meine Lust aufs Studium ist nicht so unermeßlich, wie sie *wohl* meint. (JUB1)

b. My desire to go to university is not as immense as she *seems* to think. (JUB1TE)
c. Lysten min på å studere er ikke så overveldende stor som hun *nok* tror. (JUB1TN)

We follow Cornillie (2009: 46) in assuming that evidentiality is not only expressed by garden variety evidential adverb(ial)s, but also "by more grammaticalized expressions such as evidential auxiliaries, e.g. English *seem*."[15] Given Faarlund, Lie & Vannebo's (1997: 825f.) characterizations of the three Norwegian modal particles under consideration, *visst* "certainly" stands out as the undisputedly clearest case of evidential marking:

> "[*Visst*] markerer at påstanden er *ei slutning ut frå visse objektive teikn*, at utsegna er eit referat, eller noko som dukkar opp i minnet." (Faarlund, Lie & Vannebo 1997: 826 [our emphasis])
>
> ['*Visst* marks that the statement is *an inference of certain objective signs*, that the utterance is reported or something that comes to mind.' (our translation)]

We take *vel* and *nok* to qualify as evidential markers, though less explicitly than *visst* (cf. Faarlund, Lie & Vannebo 1997). See also Cruschina (2010: 353f.) for the status of the Danish counterparts of *visst* (vist) and *nok* (nok) as evidentials, and Aijmer (1996) for the corresponding Swedish elements:

> "[*Vel*] blir brukt til å signalisere *at ein reknar med at innhaldet er sant*, samtidig som ein appellerer til mottakaren om ei stadfesting av at det er slik." (Faarlund, Lie & Vannebo 1997: 825 [our emphasis])
>
> ['*Vel* is used to signal *that one expects that the content is true*. At the same time one appeals to the receiver for confirmation that this is the case.' (our translation)]
>
> "[*Nok*] signaliserer *at sendaren sjølv reknar med at innhaldet i setninga er sant, utan å vere heilt sikker*." (Faarlund, Lie & Vannebo 1997: 825 [our emphasis])

---

[15] Cf. for example de Haan (2001, 2007), Speas & Tenny (2004), Aijmer (2009), Diewald (2004) and Diewald & Smirnova (2010, 2011) for similar qualifications. The classification of *seem* / *scheinen* etc. as an evidential is, however, disputed; see e.g. Leiss (2009, 2011) for arguments. In the present article, we will not address this controversy, as we premise that *seem* / *scheinen* can be considered a (grammaticalized) evidential marker.

['*Nok* signals that *the sender him-/herself expects the content of the utterance to be true without being entirely sure that this is the case.*' (our translation)]

The core property the elements under consideration share with each other and, as we claim, also with *wohl* is that they are inferential evidentials in the spirit of Diewald & Smirnova (2010) with specific evidence being derivable and derived from the discourse (cf. Helbig 1990; Helbig & Helbig 1990).[16]

Supportive evidence for our claim that *wohl* is an evidential comes from (28)-(31), where, in at least one of the Norwegian and English equivalents, *wohl* is rendered by an evidential expression, such as *apparently* and *åpenbart* in (28b, c), *visst* in (29b), *obviously* in (30) and *surely* in (31):[17]

(28) a. Angesichts von Rembrandts notorischer Streitsucht und der Passivität, die wir Saskia zuschreiben, paßten beide *wohl* gut zusammen, und die Ehe war durchaus befriedigend [...] (JH1TD)
b. Given the litigious nature that we know was Rembrandt's, and the passive disposition we attribute to Saskia, they *apparently* were well suited and the marriage probably was thoroughly satisfactory [...] (JH1)
c. I betraktning av den stridbare natur som vi vet at Rembrandt var i besittelse av, og den passive legning som vi tilskriver Saskia, passet de *åpenbart* godt sammen, og ekteskapet var sannsynligvis fullt ut tilfredsstillende [...] (JH1TN)

(29) a. "Nein, da hast du *wohl* Recht," sagte er zustimmend. (JG3TD)
b. "No, not many, certainly," he conceded. (JG3TE)
c. "Nei, det er *visst* ikke så mange av oss," vedgikk han. (JG3)

(30) a. Die Köchin meinte, daß der Lehnsmann *wohl* nicht mit dem Schießpulver gespart habe, als er feuerte. (HW2TD)

[16] See also Cornillie (2009: 46) for the inferential reading of the evidential *seem*.
[17] From the 35 occurrences of *wohl* that have an overt counterpart in both the English and Norwegian translation and/or source, that counterpart is an evidential expression in 14 cases in English (*seem* (10), *obviously* (3), *apparently* (1)) and in 32 cases in Norwegian (*vel* (19), *nok* (7), *visst* (5), *åpenbart* "obviously" (1)). The remaining cases are epistemic expressions: *no doubt* (8), *undoubtedly* (2), *doubtless* (1) and *certainly* (1) in English and *antagelig* "probably" (2) and *sikkert* "certainly" (1) in Norwegian.

b. The cook remarked that the sheriff *obviously* had not spared gunpowder when he fired his cannon. (HW2TE)
c. Kokka mente at lensmannen nok ikke hadde spart på kruttet, da han fyrte. (HW2)

(31) a. Ich hatte um den Schlüssel gebeten, doch er gab ihn mir nicht, er sagte, in diesen Tagen dürfe man *wohl* von mir verlangen, daß ich mich auf den Hintern setze und lerne. (JUB1)
b. I asked him for the key, but he wouldn't give it to me, saying that right now it *surely* wasn't too much to ask for me to stop fooling around and get down to some studying. (JUB1TE)
c. Jeg hadde bedt om å få nøkkelen, men han gav meg den ikke, han sa at disse dagene måtte man vel kunne forlange av meg at jeg satte meg ned og pugget. (JUB1TN)

Finally, data as in (32), where *wohl* patterns like a bona fide evidential adverb in linearly preceding an epistemic adverb, suggest that *wohl*, in the cases under consideration, be viewed as an evidential (cf. (18)):

(32) a. Die ausgeleierten Kordhosen [...] sprachen dafür, dass Herr Tinkl *wohl vielleicht* künstlerisch tätig sei. [http://www.haus-der-literatur.com/newsextra/fuellfederhalter.html]
the bulky corduroys spoke for that Herr Tink PRT probably artistically active be
"The bulky corduroys suggested that Herr Tink PRT was probably an artist."
b. Da ist es *wohl vielleicht* einfacher, eine günstigere Werkstatt zu finden oder auch eine billige Haftpflichtversicherung. [http://www.geldmarie.at/spartipps/billiger-tanken.html]
there is it PRT probably easier a less expensive garage to find or an inexpensive insurance
"It is PRT probably easier to find a less expensive garage or an inexpensive insurance."

Clearly, the analysis of *wohl* as an evidential raises the question of the relationship between *wohl* and traditional evidential adverbs (or evidential adverbials in general). Note that this question carries over to the relationship between *visst*, *vel* and *nok*, and Norwegian evidential adverbs:

(33) a. Det var *visst muligens* urinveisinfeksjon, det var det resultatet av urinprøven indikerte.
[http://forum.kvinneguiden.no/index.php?showtopic=531860]
that was PRT probably urinary tract infection, that was that the result of the urine sample indicated
"That was PRT probably a urinary tract infection, that was what the result of the urine sample indicated."

b. Jeg kan *visst sannsynligvis* ikke på onsdag likevel.
[http://www.nanowrimo.org/en/forum_comments/794523]
I can PRT probably not on Wednesday
"I PRT probably cannot make it on Wednesday."

In the remainder of this paper, we will briefly sketch the distribution and licensing of weak evidential adverbs vis-à-vis their strong counterparts.[18]

5. Evidential wohl vis-à-vis bona fide evidential adverbs

Adapting an essentially Cinquean (1999) analysis, we take evidential adverbs to occupy the specifier position of a designated functional projection in the higher part of the inflectional layer of the clause (the *middle field*, if you wish), which we label EvidP (cf. Haumann 2007: 352ff.). The internal make-up of three layers of the clause, i.e. the C(omplementizer)-layer, the I(nflectional)-layer and the L(exical)-layer, are depicted in (34). ForceP is the highest functional projection within the complementizer layer of the clause which encodes illocutionary force, TopP hosts topicalized elements and FocP focalized elements. ModP is the Rizzean (2004: 242f.) functional projection that hosts adverb(ial)s that, by being 'preposed', are made discourse prominent. FinP is the highest functional projection within the inflectional layer of the clause. EvalP hosts evaluative adverbs, EvidP evidential adverbs, EpiP epistemic adverbs and ReltP temporal adverbs. AspP* stands for Cinque's (1999: 106) set of functional projections that host aspectual adverbs:

(34) C-layer [ForceP [TopP [FocP [ModP [TopP
I-layer [FinP [… [EvalP **[EvidP** [EpiP [ReltP [AspP*
L-layer [vP […

[18] Since clitic adverbs are not relevant in connection with our analysis, the reader is referred to Cardinaletti & Starke (1999: 207ff.), Grosz (2007: 88f.) and Cardinaletti (2007: 95, n. 9; 2011: 501f.).

Since *wohl* behaves like traditional evidential adverbs in that it precedes epistemic adverbs (32) and follows evaluative adverbs (35), and in that it is sensitive to the illocutionary force of the clause containing it (cf. below), we assume that *wohl* occupies the same structural position as traditional evidential adverbs, i.e specEvidP hosts both strong and weak evidential adverbs:[19]

(35) a. Opfer hat es *glücklicherweise wohl* nicht gegeben.
[http://www.ureader.de/msg/14501254.aspx]
victims have it fortunately PRT not given
"Fortunately PRT, there were no victims."

b. Diese CD wird es *bedauerlicherweise wohl* nie in die Charts schaffen.
[http://www.dasorchester.de/de_DE/journal/showarticle,31082.html]
this CD will it unfortunately PRT never into the charts make
"Unfortunately PRT, this CD will never make it into the charts."

The same holds true for Norwegian:

(36) Det finnes produsenter som har levert gode varer i en årrekke [...] som *dessverre vel* ikke lenger finnes på det norske markedet. [www.vin-forum.no/forum/viewtopic.php?=1&t=38]
there finds producers that have delivered good goods for a number of years that unfortunately PRT not longer finds on the Norwegian market
"There are producers that have delivered good products for a number of years, which unfortunately cannot be found any longer on the Norwegian market."

Note that we do not follow Coniglio (2006, 2007), Abraham (2010, 2012), Cardinaletti (2011) and Coniglio & Zegrean (this volume) in assuming that

[19] Specifier analyses of modal particles differ mainly with respect to the merge site: while Coniglio (2006, 2007), Cardinaletti (2011) and Coniglio & Zegrean (this volume) assume that modal particles are specifiers of designated FPs that may be merged in various positions within the inflectional layer, Abraham (2012) takes modal particles to be merged as specifiers of vP, i.e. they "originate" in the lexical layer of the clause. A very different analysis is that proposed by Bayer & Obenauer (2011), where modal particles are functional heads that are merged with VP/vP and thus occupy a relatively low structural position.

modal particles can occupy a number of positions in the middle field. Rather we consider seemingly alternate orders of *wohl* and high sentence adverbs, as in (37), where *wohl* follows lower adverbs, to be the result of *wohl* functioning as a focus particle. This assumption is inspired by Belletti's (1990) observation, reported by Cinque (1999: 31f.), that high sentence adverbs, such as evaluative, evidential and epistemic adverbs, can function as focusing adverbs and take scope over the constituent they immediately precede. However, as is pointed out by Bayer & Obenauer (2011: 472f.), focus particles may also linearly follow the focal constituent they combine with, as is case in (37), where the aspectual adverbs *normalerweise* "usually" (habitual aspect) and *oft* "often" (frequentative aspect) bear focal stress, indicated by small caps:

(37) a. Es wäre NORMALERWEISE *wohl* sinnvoll, mal bei Alice anzurufen.
[http://www.ip-phone-forum.de/showthread.php?t=224337&page=1]
it would be usually PRT meaningful PRT Alice to call
"Usually, it would make sense to call Alice."
b. Es ist die Macht über Schicksale zu entscheiden, die OFT *wohl* verkannt wird.
[http://www.zeit.de/gesellschaft/familie/2011-08/index]
it is the power over destinies to decide that often PRT not-recognized is
"It is the power to decide over destinies that is often PRT not recognized."

Crucially, in the cases under consideration, *wohl* is not the weak evidential adverb, but a focus particle, i.e. a functional head that merges with a focal constituent (cf. Bayer 1996; Bayer & Obenauer 2011).[20] Given that the focal constituent that *wohl* is merged with "can be raised to the left of the particle due to a requirement of additional feature checking," as has been argued by Bayer & Obenauer (2011: 473), the linear order of "*aspectual adverb* > *wohl*" in (37) follows from the raising operation schematically indicated in (38), rather than from the weak evidential adverb *wohl* assuming a structural position lower than that occupied by adverbs expressing habitual aspect (37a) and frequentative aspect (37b):

[20] Note that under Bayer & Obenauer's (2011) analysis, all modal particles are functional heads that, in addition to standardly being merged with VP/vP, may be merged with *wh*-constituents (cf. Bayer & Obenauer 2011: 471ff.).

(38) a. $[_{\text{PrtP}}\ [_{\text{Prt'}}\ [_{\text{Prt}}$ wohl] **$[_{\text{AspP*}}$]**]]
b. $[_{\text{PrtP}}$ **$[_{\text{AspP*}}$]** $[_{\text{Prt'}}\ [_{\text{Prt}}$ wohl] ___]]

Supportive evidence for the analysis proposed derives from (39), where constituents of the type under consideration precede the finite verb in V2 structures (cf. Cinque 1991: 31; Bayer & Obenauer 2011:471ff. for discussion):

(39) a. [Normalerweise *wohl*] staut er sich oder er sucht sich einen Weg drumherum.
[http://www.betzgi.ch/de/veloreisen/odyssee/bericht/2009/laos-nord.html]
usually PRT dams-up it REFL or it searches itself a way around
"Usually PRT, it dams up or it moves around."
b. [Vielleicht *wohl*] heißt es deshalb man könne nach dem Glück streben, es aber niemals erlangen... ?
[http://www.zitate-online.de/literaturzitate/allgemein/16348/die-freude-steckt-nicht-in-den-dingen-sondern.html]
maybe PRT means it therefore one could after the luck strive, but never reach it
"Maybe PRT that's why we say that one can strive for luck but never find it."

We take the data presented in (37)-(39) to back up our analysis of the weak evidential adverb *wohl* as occupying specEvidP, i.e. the specifier position that is designated for evidential adverb(ial)s.

It has often been observed that both the weak evidential adverb *wohl* and its strong relatives interact with the illocutionary force of the clause (cf. Jacobs 1986; Thurmair 1989; Abraham 1991, 1995, 2010, 2012; Coniglio 2006, 2007; Zimmermann 2009; Egg 2010; Bayer & Obenauer 2011; Modicom, this volume; Coniglio & Zegrean, this volume), which is encoded in ForceP, the highest functional projection in the left periphery of the clause (cf. Rizzi 1997, 2004). Depending on whether the weak evidential adverb *wohl* or a strong evidential adverb, e.g. *offensichtlich* "apparently", occurs in a declarative (40) or an interrogative (41), evidence is located in the speaker or the hearer, respectively (cf. Speas & Tenny 2003; Zimmermann 2009).[21] Note that the oft-repeated claim that evidential adverbs cannot sit in the scope of interrogative operators (cf.

[21] See also Abraham (1991) for arguments that *wohl*, depending on the illocutionary force, takes the speaker (declarative) or the hearer (interrogative) as its epistemic reference point. See also Abraham (2010, 2012) for detailed discussion.

e.g. Jackendoff 1972: 84; Bellert 1977: 343f.) is far too strong. Evidential adverbs, as can be seen in (41), are acceptable in interrogatives if they imply that "the matter under consideration has not been definitely settled before" (Bellert 1977: 344):

(40) a. Es war dem Dreck {*wohl*, *offenbar*} nicht gewachsen. (adapted from UB1)
b. Det tålte {*visst*, *åpenbart*} ikke forurensningen. (adapted from UB1TN)
c. It {PRT, *apparently*} could not withstand the pollution. (adapted from UB1TE)
→ evidence is accessible to the speaker

(41) a. Was war dem Dreck {*wohl*, *offenbar*} nicht gewachsen? (based on (40))
b. Hva tålte {*visst*, *åpenbart*} ikke forurensningen?
c. What could {PRT, *apparently*} not withstand the pollution?
→ evidence is accessible to the hearer

Although illocutionary force, and thus presence of ForceP, is typically associated with root clauses, it is not restricted to them. As has been widely argued by Haegeman (2002, 2004, 2006, 2007, 2010), subordinate clauses fall into types: those that are subordinate in the traditional sense of the word, and those that display root properties, i.e. they accommodate modal particles and allow for internal topicalization and operator movement. The former comprise factive complement clauses, central adverbial clauses (e.g. temporals, locals) and restrictive relatives, while the latter comprise non-factive complement clauses, peripheral adverbial clauses (e.g. adversatives, concessives) and appositive relatives (see also Coniglio 2006, 2007; Abraham 2010, 2012; Coniglio & Zegrean, this volume for discussion). The two types of subordinate clauses differ with respect to the presence vs. absence of left peripheral functional projections as schematically indicated in (42), where "Sub" stands for "subordinating conjunction" (adapted from Haegeman 2002: 159).[22] While factive complement clauses, central adverbial clauses and restrictive relatives have a reduced left periphery (42a), non-factive and interrogative complement clauses, peripheral adverbial clauses and appositive relatives have a full left periphery (42b):

---

[22] Note that Rizzi's (1997, 2004) Force is split into a subordinating component, Sub, and the illocutionary force component, Force.

(42) a. Sub --- --- --- --- Fin (reduced left periphery)
b. Sub Force Top* Foc Mod* Fin (full left periphery)

All and only those subordinate clauses that have a full left periphery bear autonomous illocutionary force and are thus capable of licensing *wohl* and its strong adverbial relative (e.g. *offenbar* "obviously"),[23] as illustrated in (43) and (44) for non-factive vs. non-factive complement clauses (see among others Coniglio 2007: 114-34; Abraham 2010: 53ff.; 2012; Abraham & Leiss, this volume; Bayer & Obenauer 2011: 464ff.; Coniglio & Zegrean, this volume for a discussion of various modal particles):

(43) a. Die Köchin meinte, daß der Lehnsmann {*wohl*, *offenbar*} nicht mit dem Schießpulver gespart habe, als er feuerte. (adapted from HW2TD)
b. Kokka mente at lensmannen {*nok*, *åpenbart*} ikke hadde spart på kruttet, da han fyrte. (adapted from HW2)
c. The cook remarked that the sheriff {PRT, *obviously*} had not spared gunpowder when he fired his cannon. (adapted from HW2TE)

(44) a. *Sie fand heraus, daß der Lehnsmann {*wohl*, *offenbar*} nicht mit dem Schießpulver gespart hat. (adapted from (43))
b. *Hun fant ut at lensmannen {*nok*, *åpenbart*} ikke hadde spart på kruttet.
c. *She found out that the sheriff {PRT, *obviously*} had not spared gunpowder.

In light of the well-established fact that *wohl* is barred from occurring in subordinates clauses that have a reduced left periphery, such as factive complement clauses (44), we would like to come back to our discussion around examples as in (37) above. In (45), the bracketed complement clauses are governed by factive verbs, i.e. they have a reduced left periphery and should therefore not be able to accommodate *wohl*, viz. (44):

---

[23] Drawing on earlier work by Tenny (2000), Bayer (2001) and Ernst (2007) that highlight the dependency of high adverbs on Force, Haegeman (2010) discusses the non-availability of high sentence adverbs in a subset of adverbial clauses that lack a full left periphery, e.g. temporal clauses. Given the ill-formedness of the strong adverb variant of (44), it would seem that this observation extends beyond adverbial clauses.

(45) a. So gibt es auch Bürgerinnen und Bürger, die bedauern, [dass es *nun wohl* nicht zur Brückenlösung kommt].
[http://www.fehmarn24.de/ereignisse/beltquerung/ausstellungs-zentrum-auch-tunnel-1034512.html]
thus gives it female and male citizens who regret that it now PRT not to bridge-solution come
"There are citizens who regret that the bridge-solution is not an option any longer."

b. Wir sind sehr stolz, [dass wir *deutschlandweit wohl* die einzigen sind, die dieses schottische Bier importieren]
[http://www.unlicht.com/index.php?id=0&seite=2]
we are very proud that we across-Germany PRT are the only that this Scottish beer import
"We are very proud to be the only ones in Germany to import this Scottish beer."

In connection with (37), where *wohl* seems to sit in a position that is lower than its canonical position, we argued that *wohl* functions as a focusing adverb that is merged with a focal constituent. The fact that the strings in (45) are well-formed despite accommodating *wohl* and, at the same time, lacking ForceP suggests that *wohl* is not the weak evidential adverb (or modal particle), but again the homophonous focus particle that combines with sentential negation in (45a) and the [$_{DP}$ *die einzigen*] "the only ones" in (45b). We tentatively take this observation to support our initial claim that the weak evidential adverb *wohl* occupies the same structural position as garden variety evidential adverbs, specEvidP.

At various points, we have seen that *wohl*, as opposed to strong evidential adverbs, is confined to occurring in the inflectional layer of the clause; in specEvidP, to be precise. Strong evidential adverbs are susceptible to overt syntactic raising operations, e.g. raising to specModP, as illustrated in (46). The same holds for Norwegian *visst* vs. *åpenbart* "apparently" in (47):

(46) a. Der Staubsauger war dem Dreck {*wohl*, *offensichtlich*} nicht gewachsen. (adapted from UB1)
"The vacuum cleaner {PRT, *apparently*} could not withstand the dirt." (adapted from UB1TE)

b. *Offensichtlich* war der Staubsauger dem Dreck nicht gewachsen.

c. **Wohl* war der Staubsauger dem Dreck nicht gewachsen.

(47) a. Støvsugeren tålte {*visst*, *åpenbart*} ikke forurensningen. (adapted from UB1TN)
"The vacuum cleaner {PRT, *apparently*} could not withstand the dirt." (adapted from UB1TE)
b. *Åpenbart* tålte støvsugeren ikke forurensningen.
c. **Visst* tålte støvsugeren ikke forurensningen.

Thus, the relative distributional versatility of the elements under consideration is a corollary of their (non)deficiency. According to Cardinaletti & Starke (1999: 212), structural deficiency must be compensated for by "the deficient element [being] in the checking position of this feature" in *underived* structure (see also Grosz 2007). Under this view, what appears like *freezing* upon merge in specEvidP, would result from weak adverbs lacking referential features, which raising operations that target the left periphery (e.g. [PROMINENCE], [TOPIC] and [FOCUS]) are parasitic on. However, this explanation scratches only at the surface.[24]

Despite the similarities between weak and strong evidential adverbs that we have discussed so far, the two types of elements differ with respect to their relative scope properties and with respect to subjectivity, i.e. the expression of the speaker's attitude.

As we have seen in section 2, modal particles take scope over the entire proposition, i.e. they outscope even high sentence adverbs as well as topicalized and focalized constituents. In this respect, they differ from the garden variety evidential adverbs whose scope is computed in their base position. Even raising to the left periphery as in (46b) and (47b) does not affect the relative scope properties of *offensichtlich* / *åpenbart* "apparently". Their scope is computed under reconstruction in their base position (cf. Cinque 1999: 17ff. for "scope under reconstruction"). In other words, they do not take propositional scope, but scope over the chunk of structure that is c-commanded by specEvidP. Also, it has been mentioned in section 3.2 that grammaticalized elements assume higher structural positions than the elements they developed from (see among others van Gelderen 2002; Roberts & Roussou 2003; Abraham 2012; Cardinaletti 2011: 510; Abraham & Leiss, this volume).[25] Another consequence of grammaticalization

---

[24] Thanks to Werner Abraham for being insistent!

[25] This holds true in overt syntax. The weak evidential adverb *wohl* can be observed to sit in a higher position than the homophonous manner and epistemic adverb. Note that this qualification does not extend to cases in which the adverbial cognates have raised to the left periphery, as in (12c) & (13c), repeated here:

(i) *(Besonders) wóhl* fühlte ich mich nicht. (manner adverb, cf. (12c))
"I was not feeling (very) well."

is the "acquisition" of a new, more discourse related meaning. Thus, weak adverbs (or modal particles) can be argued to signal or lexicalize "the speaker's concern" with herself or the addressee in relation "to the propositional content of the utterance" (Bayer & Obenauer 2011: 450; see also Abraham 2012, this volume).

According to Abraham (2010, 2012-this volume), the distinction between strong and weak adverbs can be stated in terms of speaker deixis. While strong evidential adverbials have a simple deixis that encodes the source of the proposition, weak evidential adverbs (or modal particles in general) have a double deixis: one encoding the source of the proposition, and one identifying the speaker's concern with herself or the addressee in relation to the proposition. In other words, strong evidential adverbs are deictically less complex than their weak evidential relative *wohl*. Following Bayer (2008), Abraham (2012) represents the bundle of features that is constitutive of the speaker's assessment as <Sp(eaker)-concern>. Thus, the major difference between the weak evidential adverb *wohl* and its strong relatives, e.g. *offensichtlich* "apparently", lies in the presence vs. absence <Sp-concern>.

(ii) (Sehr) *wóhl* denke ich an ihre Veröffentlichung! (epistemic adverb, cf. (13c))
"I (very) certainly am thinking of publishing it!"

Given that *wohl* and its homophonous cognates are essentially members of different categories, they should be able to co-occur, with the weak adverb assuming a higher position, as shown for *wohl* and its manner cognate in (iii):

(iii) Du fühlst dich *wohl* [$_{\text{AdvP-manner}}$ *ganz wohl*] hier!
you feel REFL PRT very well here
"You seem to thrive here!"

The situation involving the epistemic adverb is slightly less straightforward. While the epistemic adverb freely co-occurs with its manner adverb cognate (iv), the co-occurrence of the epistemic adverb and grammaticalized *wohl*, i.e. the weak adverb, seems impossible (v):

(iv) Du fühlst dich [$_{\text{AdvP-epistemic}}$ (sehr) wóhl] [$_{\text{AdvP-manner}}$ ganz wohl] hier!
you feel REFL (very) certainly very well here
"You certainly thrive here!"

(v) *Du fühlst dich *wohl* [$_{\text{AdvP-epistemic}}$ *(sehr) wóhl*] überarbeitet.
you feel REFL PRT (very) certainly overworked
"You certainly seem to be overworked!"

However, in light of data as in (32) above (partly repeated here), where *wohl* precedes an epistemic adverb, the unacceptability of (iv) could be attributed to the avoidance of haplology:

(vi) Da ist es *wohl vielleicht* einfacher, eine günstigere Werkstatt zu finden oder auch eine billige Haftpflichtversicherung. (cf. (32b)).
"It is PRT probably easier to find a less expensive garage or an inexpensive insurance."

<Sp-concern> is a discourse relevant feature and as such it is represented in the left periphery of the clause, say the head of ForceP (cf. Bayer & Obenauer 2011; Abraham 2012). The major challenge, then, lies in the structural implementation of the relationship between <Sp-concern> in Force^0 and *wohl* in specEvidP. Depending on the syntactic framework one adopts, e.g. minimalist or preminimalist, the relationship between the feature bundle <Sp-concern> in Force^0 and *wohl* in specEvidP is established either via feature sharing-based agreement (48) or covert movement (49). Under feature sharing-based agreement, as advocated by Bayer & Obenauer (2011: 462f.), the probe, i.e. <Sp-concern> in Force^0, and the goal, i.e. *wohl* in specEvidP, would be marked as instances of the same kind, whereas under the covert movement analysis, as advocated by Abraham (1995, 2012, passim) and Coniglio (2006, 2007) among others, the 'link' would be established by *wohl* raising covertly to specForceP:

(48) $[_{\text{ForceP}}\ \text{Force}^0{}_{<\ldots\ \text{uSp–concern}>}\ [\ldots\ [_{\text{EvidP}}\ \textit{wohl}_{<\ldots\ \text{uSp–concern}>}\ [\ldots\ [_{\text{vP}}\ ]]]]]$

(49) $[_{\text{ForceP}}\ \textit{wohl}\ \text{Force}^0{}_{<\ldots\ \text{Sp–concern}>}[\ldots\ [_{\text{EvidP}}$ ~~*wohl*$_{<\ldots\ \text{Sp–concern}>}$~~ $[\ldots\ [_{\text{vP}}\ ]]]]$

Crucially, under both scenarios, *wohl* is linked to ForceP, the functional projection that encodes illocutionary force and constitutes the interface between the content of the proposition and the "articulation of discourse" (cf. Rizzi 1997: 283).

However, given that bona fide evidential adverbs interact with the illocutionary force of the clause (cf. Jacobs 1986; Thurmair 1989; Abraham 1991, 1995, 2010, 2012; Coniglio 2006, 2007; Zimmermann 2009; Egg 2010; Bayer & Obenauer 2011; Modicom, this volume; Coniglio & Zegrean, this volume), which is encoded in ForceP, one might consider splitting Force into two functional heads, one hosting illocutionary force and one hosting those features that encode <Sp-concern>.

We leave the details and consequences of such an analysis to further research.

6. Conclusion

The overall aim of the paper was to show that the unstressed modal particle *wohl* displays evidential qualities in a considerable number of contexts. In support of this claim, we provided data drawn from the *Norwegian-English-German Parallel Corpus* that show that evidential expressions figure in the translation equivalents of this variant of *wohl*, both from and into German. Our findings suggest that unstressed *wohl* be analyzed as an evidential, i.e. as a grammaticalized marker of evidentiality. Drawing on Cardinaletti & Starke (1999), Cardinaletti (2007, 2011),Grosz (2007) andConiglio (2006, 2007), we argue that *wohl* is a weak adverb; a weak evidential adverb, to be precise. We argue that *wohl*, like its strong evidential relatives, i.e. traditional evidential adverbs such as *offenbar* "obviously", occupies the specifier position of a designated functional projection in the inflectional layer, speEvidP, and does not display distributional versatility within the inflectional layer of the clause, as is argued by Coniglio (2006, 2007), Abraham (2010, 2012) and Cardinaletti (2011) among others. We suggest that seemingly alternative orders of *wohl* and high sentence adverbs are in fact instances of the homophonous focus particle *wohl* combining with focalized constituents. We highlight that, while *wohl* and *offenbar* "obviously" behave identically in a number of respects, such as their being sensitive to illocutionary force (e.g. Abraham 1995, 2012; Zimmermann 2009; Bayer & Obenauer 2011), *wohl* and bona fide evidential adverbs differ in a number of respects. First, and maybe trivially, *wohl* is restricted to occurring in its merge position, specEvidP, whereas traditional evidential adverbs may raise to the left periphery (provided they bear C-related features). Second, *wohl* takes scope over the entire proposition, whereas the scope of garden variety evidential adverbs is computed in their merge site (cf. Cinque 1999). Third, *wohl*, in the course of grammaticalization, has acquired a discourse related meaning (which Bayer 2008; Bayer & Obenauer 2011 and Abraham 2012, this volume refer to as "speaker concern"), that is absent in traditional evidential adverbs.

References

Abraham, Werner 1991. The grammaticalization of German modal particles. In: Traugott, E. C. & B. Heine (eds.). *Approaches to Grammaticalization* II. Amsterdam & Philadelphia: John Benjamins, 331-380.

—. 1995. Wieso stehen nicht alle Modalpartikeln in allen Satzformen? Die Nullhypothese. In: *Deutsche Sprache* 23: 124-146.

—. 2001. How far does semantic bleaching go? About grammaticalization that does not terminate in functional categories. In: Faarlund, J. T. (ed.). *Grammatical Relations in Change*. Amsterdam & Philadelphia: John Benjamins [Studies in Language Companion Series 56], 15-63.

—. 2010. Diskurspartikel zwischen Modalität, Modus und Fremdbewusstseinsabgleich (Theory of Mind). In: Harden, Th. & E.

Hentschel (eds.). *40 Jahre Partikelforschung*. Tübingen: Stauffenburg, 33-77.
—. 2012. What type of syntax does the representation of speaker deixis require? Templates vs. derivational structure? In: W. Abraham & E. Leiss (hg.) *Modality and Theory of mind elements across languages*, 67-108. Berlin: Mouton de Gruyter.
—. (this volume). (Inter)Subjectification of Foreign Consciousness / Other's Mind Alignment as synchronic and diachronic concepts of change? Conceptualizations and data fidelity. In: Abraham, W. & E. Leiss (eds.). *Patterns of (C)Overt Modality*. Cambridge: Cambridge Scholars.
Abraham, Werner & Elisabeth Leiss (this volume). Introduction. In: Abraham, W. & E. Leiss (eds.). *Patterns of (C)Overt Modality*. Cambridge: Cambridge Scholars.
Aijmer, Karin 1996. Swedish modal particles in a contrastive perspective. In: *Language Sciences* 18: 393-427.
—. 2009. *Seem* and evidentiality. In: *Functions of Language* 16: 63-88.
Aikhenvald, Alexandra Y. 2003. Evidentiality in typological perspective. In: Aikhenvald, A. & R. M. W Dixon (eds.). *Studies in Evidentiality*. Amsterdam & Philadelphia: John Benjamins [Typological Studies in Language 54], 1-31.
Bayer, Josef 1996. *Directionality and Logical Form. On the Scope of Focusing Particles and Wh-in-situ*. Dordrecht: Kluwer [Studies in Natural Language and Linguistic Theory 34].
—. 2001. Asymmetry in emphatic topicalization. In: Féry, C. & W. Sternefeld (eds.). *Audiatur Vox Sapientiae*. Berlin: Akademie Verlag [Studia Grammatica 52], 15-47.
—. 2008. *From Modal Particle to Interrogative Marker. A Study of 'denn'*. Ms. University of Konstanz.
Bayer, Josef & Hans-Georg Obenauer 2011. Discourse particles, clause structure, and question types. In: *The Linguistic Review* 18: 449-491.
Bellert, Irena 1977. On semantic and distributional properties of sentential adverbs. In: *Linguistic Inquiry* 8: 337-350.
Belletti, Adriana 1990. *Generalized Verb Movement: Aspects of Verb Syntax*. Torino: Rosenberg & Sellier.
Cardinaletti, Anna 2007. Für eine syntaktische Analyse von Modalpartikeln. In: Thüne, E.-M. & F. Ortu (eds.). *Gesprochene Sprache – Partikeln*. Frankfurt/Main: Peter Lang [Deutsche Sprachwissenschaft International 1], 89-101.
—. 2011. German and Italian modal particles and clause structure. In: *The Linguistic Review* 18: 493-531.

Cardinaletti, Anna & Michal Starke 1999. The typology of structural deficiency. In: van Riemsdijk, H. (ed.). *Clitics in the Languages of Europe*. Berlin / New York: de Gruyter, 145-234.
Cinque, Guglielmo 1999. *Adverbs and Functional Heads. A Cross-Linguistic Perspective*. Oxford: Oxford University Press [Oxford Studies in Comparative Syntax].
—. 2004. Issues in adverbial syntax. In: *Lingua* 117: 683-710.
Coniglio, Marco 2006. German Modal Particles in the Functional Structure of IP. In: *University of Venice, Working Papers in Linguistics* 16: 57-95. [http://lear.unive.it/bitstream/10278/204/1/2006-2s-Coniglio.pdf, accessed Oct 04, 2011]
—. 2007. German Modal Particles in Root and Embedded Clauses. In: *University of Venice, Working Papers in Linguistics* 17, 109-141. [http://lear.unive.it/bitstream/10278/142/1/Coniglio-WP-2007-pp109-141.pdf, accessed Oct 04, 2011].
Coniglio, Marco & Iulia Zegrean (this volume). Notes on overt and covert modality in Italian and Romanian. In: Abraham, W. & E. Leiss (eds.). *Patterns of (C)Overt Modality*. Cambridge: Cambridge Scholars.
Cornillie, Bert 2009. Evidentiality and epistemic modality. In: *Functions of Language* 16: 44-62.
Cruschina, Silvio 2010. On the syntactic status of sentential adverbs and modal particles. In: *Sprachtypologie und Universalienforschung* 4: 345-357.
de Haan, Ferdinand 2001. The relation between modality and evidentiality. In: *Linguistische Berichte*, Sonderheft 9: 201-216.
—. 2007. Raising as grammaticalization: the case of Germanic SEEM-verbs. In: *Rivista di Linguistica* 19: 129-150.
Der Duden. 2005. *Duden Grammatik der deutschen Gegenwartssprache, neue Rechtschreibung*. Mannheim: Bibliographisches Institut.
Diewald, Gabriele 1997. *Grammatikalisierung. Eine Einführung in Sein und Werden grammatischer Formen*. Tübingen: Niemeyer [Germanistische Arbeitshefte 36].
—. 2004. Faktizität und Evidentialität. Semantische Differenzierungen bei den Modal- und Modalitätsverben im Deutschen. In: Leirbukt, O. (ed.). *Tempus / Temporalität und Modus / Modalität im Sprachenvergleich*. Tübingen: Stauffenburg [Eurogermanistik. Europäische Studien zur deutschen Sprache 18], 231-258.
Diewald, Gabriele & Gisella Ferraresi 2008. Semantic, syntactic and constructional restrictions in the diachronic rise of modal particles in German: A corpus-based study on the formation of a grammaticalization channel. In: Seoane, E. & M. J. López-Couso (eds.). *Theoretical*

and Empirical Issues in Grammaticalization. Amsterdam & Philadelphia: John Benjamins, 77-110.

Diewald, Gabriele & Elena Smirnova 2010. Abgrenzung von Modalität und Evidentialität im heutigen Deutsch. In: Katny, A. & A. Socka (eds.). *Modalität / Temporalität in kontrastiver und typologischer Sicht*. Frankfurt/Main: Peter Lang [Danziger Beiträge zur Germanistik 30], 113-131.

Diewald, Gabriele & Elena Smirnova 2011. German evidential constructions and their origins. In: Mortelmans, T., J. Mortelmans & W. De Mulder (eds.). *In the Mood for Mood*. Amsterdam & New York: Editions Rodopi [Cahiers Chronos 23], 81-100.

Doherty, Monika 1979. Wohl. In: *Linguistische Studien* 60: 101-140.

Egg, Markus 2010. A unified account of the semantics of discourse particles. In: *Proceedings of SIGDIAL 2010: the 11th Annual Meeting of the Special Interest Group on Discourse and Dialogue*, 132-138.

Ernst, Thomas 2002. *The Syntax of Adjuncts*. Cambridge: Cambridge University Press [Cambridge Studies in Linguistics 96].

—. 2007. On the role of semantics in a theory of adverb syntax. In: *Lingua* 117: 1008-1033.

Faarlund, Jan Terje, Svein Lie & Kjell Ivar Vannebo 1997. *Norsk Referansegrammatikk*. Oslo: Universitetsforlaget.

Fischer, Kerstin 2007. Grounding and common ground: Modal particles and their translation equivalents. In: Fetzer, A. & K. Fischer (eds.). *Lexical Markers of Common Grounds*. Amsterdam: Elsevier [Studies in Pragmatics 3].

Fraser, Bruce 1996. Pragmatic markers. In: *Pragmatics* 6: 167-90.

Frey, Werner & Karin Pittner 1999. Adverbialpositionen im deutsch-englischen Vergleich. In: Doherty, M. (ed.). *Sprachspezifische Aspekte der Informationsverteilung*. Berlin: Akademie Verlag [Studia Grammatica 47], 14-40.

Gast, Volker 2008. Modal particles and context updating – the functions of German *ja*, *doch*, *wohl* and *etwa*. In: Letnes, O., E. Maagerø & H. Vater (eds.). *Modalität und Grammatikalisierung / Modality and Grammaticalization*. Trier: Wissenschaftlicher Verlag Trier [Fokus. Linguistisch-Philologische Studien 34], 153-77.

Grosz, Patrick G. 2007. German Discourse Particles are Weak Sentence Adverbs. In: Picchi, M. C. & A. Pona (eds.). *Proceedings of the XXXII Incontro di Grammatica Generativa. Firenze, 2-4 March 2006*. Alessandria: Edizioni dell'Orso, 79-91.

Gunkel, Lutz 2000. Selektion verbaler Komplemente: Zur Syntax der Halbmodal- und Phrasenverben. In: Thieroff, R., N. Tamrat & O.

Teuber (eds.). *Deutsche Grammatik in Theorie und Praxis*. Tübingen: Niemeyer, 111-121.

Haegeman, Liliane 2002. Anchoring to speaker, adverbial clauses and the structure of CP. *Georgetown University Working Papers in Theoretical Linguistics* 2: 117-180.

—. 2004. The syntax of adverbial clauses and its consequences for topicalisation. In: *Antwerp Papers in Linguistics* 107: 61-90.

—. 2006. Conditionals, factives and the left periphery. In: *Lingua* 116: 1651-1669.

—. 2007. Operator movement and topicalisation in adverbial clauses. In: *Folia Linguistica* 41: 279-325.

—. 2010. The internal syntax of adverbial clauses. In: *Lingua* 120: 628-648.

Haumann, Dagmar 2007. *Adverb Licensing and Clause Structure in English*. Amsterdam & Philadelphia: John Benjamins [Linguistik Aktuell / Linguistics Today 105].

Helbig, Gerhard 1977. Partikeln als illokutive Indikatoren im Dialog. In: *Deutsch als Fremdsprache* 14: 30-44.

—. 1990. *Lexikon deutscher Partikeln*. Leipzig: Verlag Enzyklopädie.

Helbig Gerhard & Agnes Helbig 1990. *Lexikon deutscher Modalwörter*. Leipzig: Verlag Enzyklopädie.

Jackendoff, Ray 1972. *Semantic Interpretation in Generative Grammar*. Cambridge, MA: The MIT Press.

Jacobs, Joachim 1986. Abtönungsmittel als Illokutionstypmodifikatoren. In: *Groninger Arbeiten zur Germanistischen Linguistik* 27: 100-111.

—. 1991. On the semantics of modal particles. In: Abraham, W. (ed.). *Discourse Particles. Descriptive and Theoretical Investigations on the Logical, Syntactic and Pragmatic Properties of Discourse Particles in German*. Amsterdam & Philadelphia: John Benjamins [Pragmatics and Beyond New Series 12], 141-162.

König, Ekkehard 1997. Zur Bedeutung von Modalpartikeln im Deutschen: Ein Neuansatz im Rahmen der Relevanztheorie. In: *Germanistische Linguistik* 136: 57-75.

König, Ekkehard, Detlef Stark & Susanne Requardt 1990. *Adverbien und Partikeln. Ein deutsch-englisches Wörterbuch*. Heidelberg: Julius Groos Verlag.

Leiss, Elisabeth 2009. The silent and aspect-driven patterns of deonticity and epistemicity. In: Abraham, W. & E. Leiss (eds.). *Modality-Aspect Interfaces. Implications and Typological Solutions*. Amsterdam & Philadelphia: John Benjamins [Typological Studies in Language 79], 15-41.

—. 2011. Lexikalische versus grammatische Epistemizität und Evidentialität: Plädoyer für eine klare Trennung von Lexikon und Grammatik. In: Diewald, G. & E. Smirnova (eds.). *Modalität und Evidentialität / Modality and Evidentiality*. Trier: Wissenschaftlicher Verlag Trier [Fokus. Linguistisch-Philologische Studien 37], 149-169.

—. (this volume). Covert encoding of modalty in Gothic, Old High German, and Middle High German. In: Abraham, W. & E. Leiss (eds.). *Patterns of (C)Overt Modality*. Cambridge: Cambridge Scholars.

Meibauer, Jörg 1994. *Modaler Kontrast und konzeptuelle Verschiebung: Studien zur Syntax und Semantik deutscher Modalpartikeln*. Tübingen: Niemeyer [Linguistische Arbeiten 314].

Modicom, Pierre-Yves (this volume). Shared knowledge and epistemic reductionism: the covert semantics of the German modal particles. In: Abraham, W. & E. Leiss (eds.). *Patterns of (C)Overt Modality*. Cambridge: Cambridge Scholars.

Molnár, Anna 2002. *Die Grammatikalisierung deutscher Modalpartikeln*. Frankfurt/Main: Peter Lang [Metalinguistica 12].

Nilsen, Øystein 2000. *The Syntax of Circumstantial Adverbials*. Oslo: Novus Press.

Palmer, Frank Robert 2001. *Mood and Modality*. Second Edition. Cambridge: Cambridge University Press [Cambridge Textbooks in Linguistics].

Quirk, Randolph, Sidney Greenbaum, Geoffey Leech & Jan Svartvik 1985. *A Comprehensive Grammar of the English Language*. London & New York: Longman.

Rizzi, Luigi 1997. The fine structure of the left periphery. In: Haegeman, L. (ed.). *Elements of Grammar*. Dordrecht: Kluwer, 281-337.

—. 2004. Locality and left periphery. In: Belletti, A. (ed.). *Structures and Beyond. The Cartography of Syntactic Structures,* Vol. 3. Oxford: Oxford University Press, 223-250.

Roberts, Ian & Anna Roussou 2003. *Syntactic Change. A Minimalist Approach to Grammaticalization.* Cambridge: Cambridge University Press [Cambridge Studies in Linguistics 100].

Speas, Peggy & Carol Tenny 2003. Configurational properties of Point of View roles. In: Di Sciullo, A.-M. (ed.). *Asymmetry in Grammar.* Volume 1: *Syntax and Semantics.* Amsterdam & Philadelphia: John Benjamins [Linguistik Aktuell / Linguistics Today 57], 315-344.

Speas, Peggy & Carol Tenny 2004. *The interaction of clausal syntax, discourse roles, and information structure in questions.* [http://www.linguist.org/ESSLI-Questions-Extended.pdf, accessed Oct 16, 2011]

Swan, Toril 1991. Adverbial shifts: Evidence from Norwegian and English. In: Kastovsky, D. (ed.). *Historical English Syntax*. Berlin / New York: de Gruyter [Topics in English Linguistics 2], 409-438.
—. 1997. From manner to subject modification: adverbialization in English. In: *Nordic Journal of Linguistics* 20: 179-95.
Tenny, Carol 2000. Core events and adverbial modification. In: Tenny, C. & J. Pustejovsky (eds.). *Events as Grammatical Objects*. Stanford: CSLI Publications, 285–334.
Thurmair, Maria 1989. *Modalpartikeln und ihre Kombinationen*. Tübingen: Niemeyer [Linguistische Arbeiten 223].
Traugott, Elisabeth Closs 1997. Subjectification and the development of epistemic meaning: The case of *promise* and *threaten*. In: Swan, T. & O. J. Westvik (eds.). *Modality in Germanic Languages: Historical and Comparative Perspectives*. Berlin / New York: de Gruyter [Studies and Monographs 99], 185-210.
—. 2003. From subjectification to intersubjectification. In: Hickey, R. (ed.). *Motives for Language Change*. Cambridge: Cambridge University Press, 124-139.
van Gelderen, Elly 2002. The syntax of mood particles in the history of English. In: *Folia Linguistica Historica* 22: 301-331.
Waltereit, Richard 2001. Modal particles and their functional equivalents: A Speech-Act Theoretic approach. In: *Journal of Pragmatics* 33: 1391-1417.
Wegener, Heide 1997. Zur Grammatikalisierung von Modalpartikeln. In: Barz, I. & G. Öhlschläger (eds.). *Zwischen Grammatik und Lexikon*. Tübingen: Niemeyer [Linguistische Arbeiten 390], 37-55.
Weydt, Harald 1969. *Abtönungspartikel. Die deutschen Modalwörter und ihre französischen Entsprechungen*. Berlin u.a.: Gehlen [Linguistica et Litteraria 4].
Weydt, Harald (ed.). 1979: *Die Partikeln der deutschen Sprache*. Berlin / New York: de Gruyter.
Weydt, Harald 1981. Methoden und Fragestellungen der Partikelforschung. In: Weydt, H. (ed.). *Partikeln und Deutschunterricht. Abtönungspartikeln für Lerner des Deutschen*. Heidelberg: Groos, 45-63.
Weydt, Harald (ed.). 1989: *Sprechen mit Partikeln*. Berlin / New York: de Gruyter.
Zimmermann, Malte 2009. Discourse particles in the Left Periphery. In: Shaer, B., Ph. Cook, W. Frey & C. Maienborn (eds.). *Dislocated Elements in Discourse*. Oxford: Routledge, 543-566.

OMC Oslo Multilingual Corpus.
[http://www.hf.uio.no/ilos/english/services/omc/]

COVERT MODALS AND (NON-)IMPLICATIVE READINGS OF *TOO/ENOUGH* CONSTRUCTIONS[1]

RUI MARQUES
UNIVERSIDADE DE LISBOA

Abstract: This paper is focused on the implicative and non-implicative readings of *too/enough*-constructions. Two lines have been explored in the literature concerning these readings, which Karttunen observed in 1971. The first one (cf. Meier 2003) proposes that the complement clause of the *too/enough* operators has a (possibly hidden) existential modal verb, while the second line (cf. Hacquard 2005) proposes that such constructions are at base implicative, the non-implicative reading following from the presence of a genericity operator reflected by imperfect morphology of the verb in languages such as French.

Taking into consideration a larger set of data, it becomes clear that the implicative or non-implicative readings in these constructions are conditioned by different constraints, both grammatical as pragmatic. The hypothesis that the *too/enough*-operators are at base implicative doesn't seem to be able to account for the new observed data. On the contrary, the hidden modal verb hypothesis seems to be compatible with such data.

1. Introduction

Karttunen (1971) observed that the predicates of the form *be enough* Adj *to* x or *be too* ADJ *to* x sometimes have an implicative reading and sometimes a non-implicative one. That is, in some cases, the predicate *be enough* Adj *to* x seems to imply that the infinitival clause[2] is true, as in

---

[1] This work was financed by Portuguese national funds, through the *Fundação para a Ciência e a Tecnologia* (FCT), project «PEst-OE/LIN/UI0214/2011».

[2] At least in Romance languages, the complement clause of the (equivalents of) *too/enough* operators can also be a finite clause, as in the following example, from Portuguese:

[1] A situação era suficientemente grave para que ele pedisse ajuda.
the situation was-IPFV enough serious for that he ask-SBJV help
'the situation was serious enough for him to ask for help.'

example (1a), while in other cases this inference does not follow, as in (1b):

(1) a. John was clever enough to leave early.
    b. John was clever enough to learn to read.

From (1a) one can easily infer that John left early, but (1b) does not indicate whether John actually learned to read. It only states that he had the necessary capabilities.

Similarly, the predicates of the form *be too* ADJ *to* x may be associated with an implicative reading, allowing the inference that the infinitival clause is false, while in other cases they have a non-implicative reading, not allowing such an inference. This is exemplified by (2a) and (2b), respectively:

(2) a. John was too stupid to call the cops.
    b. John was too stupid to be a regent.

The first sentence seems to allow the inference that John didn't call the cops, while (2b) does not state whether John became a regent or not.

The question of why *too/enough*-constructions sometimes display the implicative reading and sometimes the non-implicative one has not received much attention in the literature, though it didn't pass unnoticed after Karttunen's 1971 observation. The main purpose of this paper is to shed some light on the factors responsible for the implicative or non-implicative readings. A second purpose is to evaluate whether any of the descriptions of the semantics of *too/enough* taken into consideration can explain why some constructions with these operators trigger the implicative reading and others the non-implicative one.

The paper is organized as follows. On section 2, I will briefly present two proposals made in the literature that address the issue of (non-)-implicative readings in *too/enough*-constructions. Next, I will enlarge the set of considered data, trying to figure out grammatical and contextual factors that play a role in the surfacing of the implicative or of the non-implicative reading. In sections 5 and 6 I return to the proposals presented in section 2, evaluating their capability to describe the set of new data. Section 6 presents the main conclusions.

For simplicity, I will consider only cases where the complement is an infinitival clause.

2. Previous analyses

At least two lines have been pursued in the literature in order to explain the implicative or non-implicative readings of *too/enough*-constructions. The first one is defended by Meier 2003; the second one by Hacquard 2005. I will first summarize the main ideas of both proposals, after which I will observe data that seems to show that more is to be said about the implicative or non-implicative readings of *too/enough*-constructions.

2.1 The (hidden) modal verb proposal

Meier 2003 proposes that the complement of the *too/enough* operators has an existential modal operator, which is usually hidden, but can be realized, as in examples (3a) and (3b), which have the same meaning as (4a) and (4b), respectively:

(3) a. Bertha is old enough [to be able / to be authorized] to drive a car.
b. The food is too good for us to be allowed to throw it away.

(4) a. Bertha is old enough to drive a car.
b. The food is too good to throw (it) away.

Meier 2003 proposes that the truth conditions of these examples are as stated in the paraphrases (5a) and (5b):

(5) a. 'The value *v* such that Bertha is *v*-old is GREATER than or EQUAL to the MINIMUM of all values *v** such that, if Bertha is *v**-old, she *is able* [/ allowed / permitted] to drive a car.'

b. 'The value *v* such that the food is *v*-good is GREATER than or EQUAL to the MAXIMUM of all values *v** such that, if the food is *v**-good, we are allowed to throw it away.' (Meier 2003: 72)

Concerning the implicative / non-implicative readings, the author proposes that the duality of the readings follows from the interpretation of the sentences with respect to contexts with different characteristics. In the case of the non-implicative reading, the sentence is evaluated "against a (partially) idealistic background", while sentences with the implicative reading are evaluated preferably against a "totally realistic" or "fatalistic" background. In other words, in the case of sentences with the non-implicative reading the state of affairs described by the infinitival clause is verified in some ideal possible world, but not necessarily in the real world, while sentences with the implicative reading are evaluated with respect to a realistic context and the infinitival clause is taken to be true in the real world.

A less clear point of this proposal is what determines which context is taken into consideration when processing the sentences. That is, what leads to the consideration of a realistic or else of an idealistic background? At first sight, it seems defensible that the relevant background to be taken into consideration is provided by the context of assertion. For instance, consider sentence (1a), repeated as (6), which Meier presents to exemplify the non-implicative reading:

(6) John was clever enough to learn to read.

In a context where John is reading a paper and someone shows surprise for the fact that he is capable of reading, the assertion of (6) would lead to the consideration of a realistic background. In another context, as the one which Meier describes, where John comes from a poor neighborhood and never had the chance to learn to read, the sentence would be interpreted against a (partially) idealistic background, stating that in an ideal world where John had the chance to learn to read he could have learned.

However, if the implicative or non-implicative readings are purely pragmatic inferences that follow from the context of assertion, why does the non-implicative reading of (6) and the implicative reading of (1b), repeated below as (7), follow so easily when interpreting the sentences out of context? In other words, the fact that, out of context, in some sentences the implicative reading is the preferred one and in other cases the non-implicative reading is more natural suggests that these readings are not just pragmatically conditioned, but are somehow associated to grammatical features.

(7) John was clever enough to leave early.

Evidence that the implicative or non-implicative readings are not just conditioned by the context comes from Romance languages, as shown by Hacquard 2005, whose proposal I will briefly consider now.

2.2 The episodicity / genericity approach

Hacquard 2005 observes that in French the implicative reading is possible if the main verb is inflected in the *passé composé*, which expresses perfective aspect, but not if it is inflected in the *imparfait*, which expresses imperfective aspect. This is shown by examples (8) and (9):

(8) a. Jean a été assez rapide pour s'enfuir
Jean was-PFV[3] enough quick to REFL-escape

(#mais il ne s'est pas enfui).
(but he not REFL-has NEG escape)

'Jean was quick enough to escape (# but he didn't escape).'

b. Jean a été trop lent pour s'enfuir
Jean was-PFV too slow to REFL-escape

(#mais il s'est enfui).
(but he REFL-has escape)

'Jean was too slow to escape (# but he still escaped).'

(9) a. Jean était assez rapide pour s'enfuir
Jean was-IPFV enough quick to REFL-escape

(mais il ne s'est pas enfui)
(but he not REFL-has NEG escape)

'Jean was quick enough to escape (but he didn't escape).'

b. Jean était trop lent pour s'enfuir
Jean was-IPFV too slow to REFL-escape

(mais il s'est enfui)
(but he REFL-has escape)

'Jean was too slow to escape (but he still escaped).'

Hacquard 2005 proposes that the *too/enough* operators are at base implicative, the non-implicative reading following from the presence of a genericity operator, whose presence is reflected by imperfective morphology.

Simplifyingly, Hacquard's proposal is that in *too/enough* sentences the degree which is taken into consideration is sufficient and necessary to fulfill the state of affairs described by the infinitival clause. In the case of

[3] List of abbreviations used in the paper: PFV – perfective; IPFV – imperfective; SBJV – subjunctive; REFL – reflexive pronoun; NEG – negation particle; COND – conditional.

(8a), with perfective aspect, the sentence has the meaning paraphrased as (10a) and the presupposition stated in (10b):

(10) a. Jean had the degree of quickness sufficient & necessary for him to escape.

b. There is a degree of quickness sufficient & necessary for him to escape.

In the case of (9a), with imperfective aspect, she assumes that the *imparfait* is a reflection of a genericity operator and proposes that the meaning of (9a) is as stated in (11):

(11) GEN[w](∃d: ∀w' ∈ Acc(w) J. is d-quick in w' ↔ J. escapes in w'; J. is d-quick in w)
'In every normal world where there is a degree of quickness that guarantees his escape, Jean has that degree of quickness.'

This association between aspect and implicative or non-implicative readings is also observable in Portuguese, as shown by the following examples:

(12) a. Ele foi suficientemente esperto para aprender a ler
he was-PFV enough smart to learn to read

(# mas nunca aprendeu).
(# but never learned)

'He was smart enough to learn to read (# but he never learned).'

b. Ele foi demasiado preguiçoso para se levantar cedo
he was-PFV too lazy to REFL get up early

(# mas levantou-se às 06.00h).
(# but got up-REFL at-the 6 AM)

'He was too lazy to get up early (# but he got up at 6 AM).'

(13) a. Ele era suficientemente esperto para aprender a ler
he was-IPFV enough smart to learn to read

(mas nunca aprendeu).
(but never learned)

'He was smart enough to learn to read (but he never learned).'

b. Ele era demasiado preguiçoso para se levantar cedo
he was-IPFV too lazy to REFL get up early

(mas naquele dia levantou-se às 06.00h).
(but in-that day got up-REFL at-the 6 AM)

'He was too lazy to get up early (#but that day he got up at 6 AM)'

In (12), with the main verb inflected in the *pretérito perfeito do indicativo*, which conveys perfective aspect, the implicative readings arise (as shown by the impossibility of continuation of the discourse as indicated), while examples (13), with the main verb inflected in the *pretérito imperfeito do indicativo*, which conveys imperfective aspect, have the non-implicative reading.

However, as I will try to show in the next section, aspect doesn't seem to be the only factor responsible for the implicative or non-implicative readings.

3. Further data

In the literature on the implicative and non-implicative readings of *too/enough*-constructions only cases where these operators are linked to an adjective were taken into account. However, (the equivalents of) these operators can also occur in association with a noun, a verb or an adverb, as shown by the examples (14)-(16):

(14) a. A Maria teve *tempo* suficiente para acabar o artigo.
the Maria had-PFV time enough to finish the paper

'Maria had time enough to finish the paper.'

b. O bolo esteve demasiado *tempo* no forno
the cake was-PFV too much time in-the oven

para não estar queimado.
to not be burned

'The cake was in the oven too long not to be burned.'

(15) a.

A	Ana	*estudou*	o	suficiente
the	Ana	studied-PFV	the	enough

para	ter	uma	boa	nota	no	exame.
to	have	a	good	score	at-the	exam

'Ana studied enough to achieve a high score at the exam.'

b.

A	inflação	*subiu*	demasiado
the	inflation	raised-PFV	too much

para	não	serem	tomadas	medidas.
to	not	be	taken	measures

'Inflation raised too much for not taking action.'

(16) a.

O	João	correu	suficientemente	*depressa*
the	João	ran-PFV	enough	fast

para	ganhar	a	corrida.
to	win	the	race

'John ran fast enough to win the race.'

b.

A	Ana	esteve	demasiado	*perto*	dos	leões
the	Ana	was-PFV	too	close	of-the	lions

para	não	se	assustar.
to	not	REFL	scared

'Ana was too close to the lions not to be scared.'

When attention is turned to these cases, Hacquard's proposal that the operators *too/enough* are at base implicative, the non-implicative reading following from the presence of a genericity operator, is hardly tenable. In fact, it is very easy to find examples where the main clause has perfective aspect[4] and an episodic reading, yet, nevertheless, the reading being non-implicative. This is clearly true of the examples (14a) and (15a). These

---

[4] Hacquard 2005 only considers cases of the *passé composé*, a verbal form that expresses perfectivity, but not other verbal forms that also express perfectivity; in other words, somewhat simplifyingly, she only considers cases of perfectivity in the past. For simplicity, in this paper I will simply use the term 'perfective aspect', though I am not considering all the verbal forms that express perfectivity, only those of the *passé compose*, in French, or the *pretérito perfeito do indicativo*, in Portuguese.

sentences do not indicate that the complement of *enough* is true. They can be continued by the negation of the infinitival proposition:

(14') a. A Maria teve tempo suficiente para acabar o artigo,
the Maria had-PFV time enough to finish the paper

mas não o acabou.
but not it finished

'Maria had time enough to finish the paper, *but she didn't finish it.*'

(15') a. A Ana estudou o suficiente
the Ana studied-PFV the enough

para ter uma boa nota no exame.
to have a good score at-the exam

mas teve uma nota péssima.
but had a score bad

'Ana studied enough to achieve a high score at the exam, *but she had a bad score.*'

In the other examples of (14)-(16), it may be harder to see the non-implicative reading, but this possibility seems to exist. In fact, it is possible to continue each of these sentences as follows:

(14') b. ..., mas surpreendentemente ainda nem está cozido.
…, but surprisingly yet not-even is cooked

(portanto, deve haver algum problemacom o forno).
(thus must have some problemwith the stove).'

'The cake was in the oven too long not to be burned, but surprisingly it is not even cooked yet (so, something must be wrong with the stove).'

(15') b. ..., mas duvido que o Governo faça alguma coisa.
…, but doubt that the Government does any thing

'Inflation raised too much for not taking action, but I doubt that the Government will do anything concerning that.'

(16’) a. ...; só não ganhou porque foi desclassificado.
...; only not won because was disqualified

‘John ran fast enough to win the race; he didn’t win only because he was disqualified.’

b. ..., mas surpreendentemente esteve sempre muito calma.
..., but surprisingly was always very calm

‘Ana was too close to the lions not to be scared; but surprisingly she was always very calm.’

Even when the *too/enough* operators are combined with adjectives, it is possible to have perfective aspect in the main clause (as well as episodicity) and the non-implicative reading. This is shown by the underlined sentence of the following example:

(17) Foi então que a Ana gritou e *o grito foi*
was then that the Ana shouted and the scream was-PFV

suficientemente alto para se ouvir na sala ao lado

enough loud to one hear at-theroom at-theside

mas como a sala estava vazia, ninguém a ouviu.
but as the room was-PFV empty, nobody her heard

‘That was when Ana shouted and *the scream was loud enough to be heard in the next room*, but, since the room was empty, nobody heard her’

Thus, Hacquard’s generalisation that the constructions with the operators *too/enough* have the implicative reading if the main clause has perfective aspect does not seem to be confirmed. Though Hacquard 2005 is right in that the implicative reading is blocked if the main clause has imperfective aspect (cf., e.g., the contrast between (12) and (13), above), perfective aspect in the main clause seems to be a necessary condition for the implicative reading, but not a sufficient condition. The question that emerges, then, is which additional factors are responsible for the existence or the blocking of the implicative reading.

4. Grammatical and pragmatic constraints

The data considered in the previous sections shows that, when the main clause has perfective aspect, there are three possibilities:

(i) The sentence has easily the non-implicative reading; cf., e.g., (15a), repeated as (18):

(18) A Ana *estudou* o suficiente
the Ana studied-PFV the enough

para ter uma boa nota no exame.
to have a good score at-the exam

'Ana studied enough to achieve a high score at the exam.'

(ii) The sentence may preferably have the implicative reading, but the non-implicative reading is not blocked; cf., e.g., (19), below; the first member of the coordination is easily interpreted as conveying the information that Ana won the race. Yet, it is possible to add information that cancels such an inference:

(19) A Ana correu suficientemente depressa para ganhar
the Ana ran-PFV enough fast to win

a corrida e teria ganho
the race and *have*-COND *won*

se não tivesse tropeçado e caído.
if not had stumble and fall

'Ana ran fast enough to win the race and she would have won it had she not stumbled and fallen.'

(iii) The sentence can only have the implicative reading; cf., e.g., (20); continuing the discourse with the negation of the truth of the infinitival clause[5] leads to oddity:

(20) A Ana foi suficientemente corajosa
the Ana was-PFV enough brave

para entrar na gruta
to enter in-the cave

---

[5] Or with the assertion of its truth, in the case of constructions with *too*, as in the following example:

[2] A Ana foi demasiado medrosa para saltar (# mas saltou).
the Ana was-PFV too fearful to jump (# but jumped)
'Ana was too fearful to jump (# but she jumped).'

(# mas não entrou / # mas não a deixaram entrar).
(# but not entered / # but not her allow to-enter).'

'Ana was brave enough to enter the cave (# but she didn't enter / # but she wasn't allowed to enter).'

On the one hand, these facts show that the implicative reading is not just pragmatically conditioned, since otherwise it should be possible to create a context where cases as (20) could have the non-implicative reading. On the other hand, the facts show that in some cases the (non-)implicative reading is context dependent; the context can be manipulated in order to achieve the otherwise unnatural non-implicative reading (cf. (19)). Thus, it seems that the inference concerning the truth value of the infinitival clause is dependent both on grammatical and on pragmatic factors. The identification of the factors that, in addition to the perfective aspect in the main clause, are responsible for the (non-)implicative reading is the main purpose of this paper, and it is the one to which I will turn now.

One factor that seems to be a necessary condition for the implicative reading is the temporal overlap between the state of affairs described in the main clause and the one described by the infinitival clause:

(21) a. Ele foi suficientemente corajoso para entrar
he was-PFV enough brave to enter

na gruta (# mas não entrou).
in-the cave (# but not entered)

'He was brave enough to enter the cave (# but he didn't enter).'

b. Ele foi demasiado cobarde para entrar na gruta
he was-PFV too coward to enter in-the cave

(# mas entrou).
(# but entered)

'He was too coward to enter the cave (# but he entered).'

(22) a. No último encontro, ele foi humilhado
in-the last meeting, he was-PFV humiliated

o suficiente para agora recusar o convite
the enough to now refuse the invitation

para um novo encontro (mas parece que já
for a new meeting (but appears that already

se esqueceu, porque está a pensar aceitar).
REFL forgot since is at think to-accept)

'In the last meeting, he was humiliated enough to refuse now the invitation for a new meeting (but apparently he already forgot, since he is planning to accept the invitation).'

b. Ele foi demasiado criticado para estar contente
he was-PFV too criticized to be happy

(mas parece não se ter incomodado
(but seems not REFL have bothered

com as críticas e continua bem disposto).
with the criticism and continues cheerful)

'He was too criticized to be happy (but he seems to have not been bothered by the criticism and he continues in a good mood.'

Sentences (21a) and (21b) have the implicative reading, as shown by the oddity of the continuations in parentheses, contrary to (22a) and (22b), which have the non-implicative reading (i.e., the complement clause of *enough* is not given to be true and the complement of *too* is not necessarily taken to be false). Using φ to represent the infinitival clause, d as a degree variable and x as the referent of the subject of the main clause, sentences (21a) and (21b) indicate that there is a point in the past where x was d-ADJ *while* φ; while sentences (22a) and (22b) make reference to a degree that x had at a time interval prior to the one where φ is (or may be) verified. Thus, the contrast between (21) and (22) suggests a relation between temporal overlapping and implicative readings.

However, temporal overlapping is not a sufficient condition, though it seems to be a necessary one for the implicative reading. For instance, in the following example, which has the non-implicative reading, the main clause refers an amount of time during which the state of affairs considered in the infinitival clause could occur:

(23) a. Ele teve tempo suficiente para fazer o trabalho
he had-PFV time enough to do the job

(mas não o fez).
(but not it did)

'He had time enough to do the job (but he didn't do it).'

Therefore, temporal overlapping and perfective aspect in the main clause seem to be two necessary conditions for the implicative reading, but, as shown by example (23), even if both of them are fulfilled, the implicative reading is not obligatory. In other words, they are necessary, but not sufficient conditions for the implicative reading.

Both the conditions, temporal overlap and perfective aspect in the main clause, are of semantic nature. Before turning into pragmatic, or contextual, conditions that appear to favor the implicative reading, let us consider another semantic factor that seems to play a role in favoring the implicative reading: the presence of perfective aspect also in the infinitival clause. Consider the following examples:

(24) a. Ele cometeu um crime suficientemente grave
he committed-PFV a crime enough serious

para *ter sido* condenado a dez anos de prisão.
to have been sentenced to ten years of prison

'He committed a crime serious enough to *have been* sentenced to ten years in prison.

b. Ele cometeu um crime suficientemente grave
he committed-PFV a crime enough serious

para *ser* condenado a dez anos de prisão.
to be sentenced to ten years of prison

'He committed a crime serious enough to *be* sentenced to ten years in prison.'

Out of context, (24a) is easily interpreted as conveying the justification for the conviction to ten years in prison; i.e., as expressing the information that he was sentenced to ten years in prison because of the crime he committed. Thus, the construction seems to have the implicative reading: the infinitival clause is taken to be true. Sentence (24b), on its side, can have the same interpretation, but it can as easily be interpreted as expressing solely the information that the penalty for the crime he committed is ten years in prison, not the information that he was, in fact, sentenced to ten years in prison.

Nevertheless, perfective aspect in the infinitival clause does not guarantee the implicative reading either. In fact, also (24a) can have the non-implicative reading. For instance, imagine a context of an historical investigation where the speaker is trying to figure out what happened to a prominent member of the court who vanished before the French Revolution. In such a context, the speaker may assert (24a) without implying the truth of the infinitival clause. By asserting (24a), the speaker adds to the common ground one hypothesis of what happened to such person, and he may continue the sentence with, for instance, *maybe he was sentenced in fact and died in prison*, or with *but we know that he was never sentenced*; *but the records do not show that he was ever sentenced*, and so on.

Thus, perfective aspect in the infinitival clause is a factor that may lead to prefer the implicative reading if the sentence is interpreted out of context, but it is not a sufficient condition (nor a necessary one; cf., e.g., (20)) for the implicative reading either.

Apart from these semantic factors, there is also information external to the meaning of the clause that seems to favor the implicative or non-implicative readings. Concerning this dimension of interpretation, there are at least three issues that appear to be relevant for the emergence of the (non-)implicative reading.

The first issue is the kind of text which the sentence is part of, or the role played by the speaker when asserting the sentence. As observed when considering example (24a), the non-implicative reading is easily obtained if the speaker is making inferences or raising hypotheses. However, if the sentence is part of a narrative text, where the speaker is telling a story, the implicative reading would be preferred, given the expectation that the speaker tells what happened. Still, there is not a systematic relationship between narration and the implicative reading. The speaker may continue his discourse by negating the inference that the infinitival proposition is true without changing his role of story teller.

A more significant aspect which conditions the (non-)implicative reading concerns the kind of attitude that relates the speaker and the infinitival proposition. To see this, let us consider the following examples:

(25) a.

Ele	teve	coragem	suficiente	para	saltar
he	had-PFV	courage	enough	to	jump

(# mas	não	saltou).
(# but	not	jumped)

‘He had enough courage to jump (# but he didn’t jump).’

b.

Ele	foi	demasiado	cobarde	para	saltar
he	was-PFV	too	coward	to	jump

(# mas	saltou).
(# but	jumped)

‘He was too coward to jump (# but he jumped).’

(26) a.

Ele	teve	tempo	suficiente	para	telefonar	para	casa
he	had-PFV	time	enough	to	phone	to	home

(mas	não	quis).
(but	not	wanted).’

‘He had time enough to phone home (but he didn’t want to).’

b.

A	festa	foi	demasiado	barulhenta	para	as	crianças
the	party	was-PFV	too	noisy	for	the	children

não	acordarem	(mas	surpreendentemente	não	acordaram).
not	wake up	(but	surprisingly	not	woke up).’

‘The party was too noisy for the children not to wake up (but surprisingly they didn’t wake up).’

In the case of (25a) and (25b), which have the implicative reading, the speaker expresses his opinion concerning a state of affairs, saying that to jump was a courageous thing to do and not to jump was a coward decision. On the contrary, in the case of (26a) and (26b), the speaker’s attitude towards the infinitival proposition is neutral. The speaker just describes a state of affairs, remaining silent as to what is his opinion concerning it. In other words, sentences (25a) and (25b) are cases of evaluative modality (cf. Rescher 1968), contrary to (26a) and (26b).

The *too/enough*-constructions that combine evaluative modality and past tense with perfective aspect in the main clause are among the cases where the implicative reading is systematic. In fact, in these cases, the inference that the infinitival proposition is true, with *enough*, or that it is false, with *too*, cannot be cancelled by discourse continuation. Another case where the implicative reading appears to be indefeasible is shown by the following examples, which illustrate the last factor that I will consider as playing a role in the existence of the (non-) implicative reading:

(27) a. A Ana teve inteligência suficiente para resolver
the Ana had-PFV intelligence enough to solve

a equação (# mas não a resolveu).
the equation (# but not it solved).'

'Ana had enough intelligence to solve the equation (# but she didn't solve it).'

b. O tribunal teve demasiadas dúvidas para o condenar
the Court had-PFV too-many doubts to him sentence

(# mas condenou-o).
(# but sentenced him)

'The Court had too many doubts to sentence him (# but sentenced him anyway).'

The reason for the non-implicative reading to be excluded in these cases can be perceived by contrasting them with the following similar constructions:

(28) a. A Ana teve tempo suficiente para telefonar para casa
the Ana had-PFV time enough to phone to home

(mas não telefonou).
(but not phoned)

'Ana had time enough to phone home (but she didn't phone).'

b. O processo teve demasiadas testemunhas
the process had-PFV too-many witnesses

para ser rápido (mas acabou por ser célere).
to be fast (but ended by be fast)

'The process had too many witnesses to be fast (but, in the end, it was fast).'

The meaning of both the sentences (27) and (28) involves the consideration of a degree or quantity: a degree of intelligence that allows the solution of the equation, an amount of time that a phone call takes, and so on. This degree or quantity is related to the state of affairs described by the infinitival clause. Roughly, *enough*-constructions indicate that the considered degree or quantity (i.e., the degree of intelligence that Ana had in the case of (27a); the amount of time that she had in the case of (28a)) was sufficient to realize the state of affairs described by the infinitival clause (solve the equation, phone home), while *too*-constructions indicate that such degree is sufficient to not realize the state of affairs described by the infinitival clause. This information is part of the truth conditions of both the sentences (27), which have the implicative reading, and (28), which have the non-implicative one. The reason for this disparity of readings, I propose, is related to world knowledge. More precisely, in the case of (27), the realization of the state of affairs described by the infinitival clause is dependent on particular circumstances, contrary to what happens in the case of (28). To make this point clearer, let us consider first the contrast between (27a) and (28a). Both sentences refer to a degree or amount that allows Ana to solve the equation and to phone home, respectively. Any phone call takes a minimum amount of time, no matter what the circumstances are. For instance, regardless whether the call is an international or a local one; whether the phone call is a short or a long conversation, and so on, any phone call takes at least the time of dialing the number, the connection to be established, and so on. On the contrary, the minimum degree of intelligence necessary to solve an equation varies according to the circumstances. It depends on the degree of difficulty of the equation, on the mathematical knowledge of the person who is trying to solve it, and so on. Similarly, both (27b) and (28b) make reference to a number (of doubts and of witnesses, respectively) that is an obstacle to the realization of the state of affairs described by the infinitival clause. In the case of (28b) this number is, to a great extent, independent of particular conditions; any process in the court with more than a certain number of witnesses is expected to take long. On the contrary, in the case of (27b), the amount of doubts that prevents the judges from making a guilty verdict is dependent on the kind of doubts, their relevance to the trial at stake, and so on; it is not the same amount under any circumstance.

In sum, the considered data show that there are several factors that play a role in the emergence of the implicative reading. Two necessary conditions for this reading to emerge are the use in the main clause of a verbal form that expresses perfectivity, as Hacquard 2005 observes, and temporal overlapping between the state of affairs described by the main clause and by the infinitival clause. When these two conditions are satisfied, the implicative reading seems to be the only available one if the main clause expresses evaluative modality (that is, if the information is expressed that the state of affairs described by the infinitival clause is subject to some evaluation on the part of the speaker) or if the realization of the state of affairs described by the infinitival clause is dependent on particular circumstances. Finally, two other factors were identified that may favor the implicative reading or the non-implicative one, but which are neither necessary nor sufficient conditions for any of these readings: the existence of perfective aspect in the infinitival clause and the role of the speaker (i.e., whether the speaker is telling a story or playing some other role, such as making inferences or raising hypotheses, when asserting the sentence). Given these observations, I will now return to the analyses of Hacquard 2005 and of Meier 2003, with the purpose of trying to figure out whether any of these analyses proves to yield a better description of the observed data.

5. Back to the basic implicative hypothesis

Hacquard 2005 proposes that *too/enough-construction*s are basically implicative, the non-implicative reading being a consequence of the presence of a genericity operator, which is reflected by imperfective morphology. This hypothesis doesn't explain the fact that in many cases the constructions describe an episodic (i.e., non-generic) state of affairs and have the non-implicative reading. However, it is a fact that a tense form that signals imperfectivity (the *imparfait* in French and the *pretérito imperfeito* in Portuguese) blocks the implicative reading in constructions that would have such reading if a perfective tense were used. This is verified in the examples repeated below, where only the first member of each pair of sentences has the implicative reading:

(29) a

A	Ana	*foi*	suficientemente	corajosa
the	Ana	was-PFV	enough	brave
para	entrar	na	gruta	
to	enter	in-the	cave	

b

A	Ana	*era*	suficientemente	corajosa
the	Ana	was-IPFV	enough	brave
para	entrar	na	gruta	
to	enter	in-the	cave	

'Ana was brave enough to enter the cave.'

(30) a. Ele *foi* demasiado cobarde para entrar na gruta
he was-PFV too coward to enter in-the

b. Ele *era* demasiado cobarde para entrar na gruta
he was-IPFV too coward to enter in-the cave

'He was too coward to enter the cave.'

(31) a. A Ana *teve* inteligência suficiente
the Ana had-PFV intelligence enough

para resolver a equação.
to solve the equation.'

b. A Ana *tinha* inteligência suficiente
the Ana had-IPFV intelligence enough

para resolver a equação.
to solve the equation.'

'Ana had enough intelligence to solve the equation.'

(32) a. O tribunal *teve* demasiadas dúvidas para o condenar
the Court had-PFV too-many doubts to him sentence

b. O tribunal *tinha* demasiadas dúvidas para o condenar
the Court had-IPFV too-many doubts to him sentence

'The Court had too many doubts to sentence him.'

This fact is explained by Hacquard 2005 on the basis of the assumption that the *imparfait*, in French, signals genericity. But, given that the absence of genericity doesn't guarantee that *too/enough*-constructions have the implicative reading, another explanation must be offered for the fact that examples like (29)-(32) have the implicative reading if the *pretérito perfeito* is used and the non-implicative one with the *pretérito imperfeito*.

As seen above, examples like (29) and (30) involve evaluative modality. That is, the speaker expresses an opinion concerning a state of affairs (saying that to enter the cave was / would be a courageous or a coward attitude). In these cases, the implicative reading (which emerges with the *pretérito perfeito*) only apparently is linked to the presence of the *too/enough* operators. In fact, the implicative reading in constructions combining evaluative modality and perfective aspect in the main clause is also observed with predicates like *to have the misfortune of*, *to have the pleasure of*[6], as shown by the following examples, which allow the inference that the complement clause is true:

(33) a.

Tive	o	prazer	de	ser	apresentado	à	Maria.
had-PFV	the	pleasure	of	be	introduced	to-the	Maria.

'I had the pleasure to be introduced to Maria.'

b.

A	Ana	teve	o	azar	de	chegar	atrasada.
the	Ana	had-PFV	the	misfortune	of	arrive	late

'Ana had the misfortune to arrive late.'

c.

A	Ana	teve	coragem	para	entrar	na	gruta.
the	Ana	had-PFV	courage	to	enter	in-the	cave.'

'Ana had the courage to enter the cave.'

Thus, the implicative reading of sentences like (29) might be the manifestation of a more general regularity and be independent of the presence of *too/enough* operators.

Let us now consider cases such as (31) and (32). Apart from the fact that, when the *pretérito perfeito* is used, the sentences describe a single event that happened in the past (i.e., the sentences have an episodic interpretation), contrary to what is verified with the *pretérito imperfeito*, there are other differences related to the temporal interpretation of each case. This will be illustrated on the basis of the examples repeated below:

(34) a.

A	Ana	*tinha*	inteligência	suficiente	para
the	Ana	had-IPFV		intelligence	enough

resolver	a	equação.
to solve	the	equation.'

'Ana had enough intelligence to solve the equation.'

---

[6] Karttunen 1971 uses the term 'implicative predicates' to designate this kind of predicates which allow the inference that their complement clause is true if the main clause is affirmative and false if the main clause is negative. Other examples of implicative predicates are *manage*, *bother*, *get*, *venture*, *happen*, among others (cf. Karttunen 1971, 341).

b. A Ana	*teve*	inteligência	suficiente	para
the Ana	had-PFV	intelligence	enough	

resolver	a	equação.
solve	*the*	*equation.'*

'Ana had enough intelligence to solve the equation.'

Sentence (34b) describes an eventive situation – the one of Ana solving an equation –, while (34a) describes a stative situation – the one of Ana being *d*-intelligent. Moreover, in (34a) two states of affairs are considered – the one of Ana having a certain degree of intelligence and the one of Ana solving an equation –, while in (34b) these two states of affairs are part of single event: the one of Ana solving an equation. These facts are reflected in the temporal location of the states of affairs described by the main and infinitival clauses. In the case of (34a), the time span occupied by 'Ana being *d*-intelligent' starts before the time interval that can be occupied by the event of 'Ana solving the equation'. In other words, if Ana solves the equation, this state of affairs occurs at a time interval that follows a temporal point where Ana is *d*-intelligent:

(35) There is a time interval *i* which includes t' (t' < t_0); Ana is *d*-intelligent at *i* and Ana solves the equation at a time interval *i*' (*i*' > t')

In this sense, the state of affairs described by the infinitival clause is futurate with respect to the one described by the main clause. That is, if Ana solves the equation, this event takes place at a time preceded by the beginning of the state of Ana being *d*-intelligent. On the contrary, in (34b), the state of affairs of Ana being *d*-intelligent doesn't have to begin prior to her solving the equation (she might have had an unusual moment of brain activity that allowed her to solve the equation and that started during the exercise of solving the mathematical problem). In other words, the main clause of (34a) appeals to the consideration of a time interval which begins before Ana solves the equation, contrary to (34b), where only the time interval occupied by the event of Ana solving the equation is taken into consideration.

This temporal information might be more relevant for explaining why (34b), but not (34a), has the implicative reading than Hacquard's proposal of episodicity *vs* genericity. In fact, as seen in the previous section, when there is no temporal coincidence between the states of affairs described by the main and the infinitival clauses, the non-implicative reading of *too/enough*-constructions is observed. This is shown by, e.g., (36):

(36) a No último encontro, ele foi humilhado
in-the last meeting, he was-PFV humiliated

o suficiente para agora recusar o convite
the enough to now refuse the invitation

para um novo encontro (mas parece que já
for a new meeting (but appears that already

se esqueceu, porque está a pensar aceitar).
REFL forgot since is at think to-accept)

'In the last meeting, he was humiliated enough to refuse now the invitation for a new meeting (but apparently he already forgot, since he is planning to accept the invitation).'

b. Ele foi demasiado criticado para estar contente
he was-PFV too criticized to be happy

(mas parece não se ter incomodado
(but seems not REFL have bothered

com as críticas e continua bem disposto).
with the criticism and continues cheerful)

'He was too criticized to be happy (but he seems to have not been bothered by the criticism and he continues in a good mood.'

Although in these examples the main verb is inflected in the *pretérito perfeito* and in (34a) it is inflected in the *pretérito imperfeito*, in both cases lack of temporal coincidence between the states of affairs described by main and subordinated clause exists. Thus, the contrast between examples as (34a) and (34b) might be the manifestation of a more general regularity, leading to question the Hacquard's explanation of the contrast.

Nevertheless, even if the explanation for the non-implicative reading of (34a) might be as proposed above, an analysis along these lines does not explain why (34b) has the implicative reading. In fact, temporal overlapping between main and subordinated proposition doesn't guarantee the implicative reading, as shown by the following example:

(37) A Ana gritou suficientemente alto para
the Ana screamed-PFV enough loud to

ser ouvida na sala ao lado
be heard in-the room at-the next

(mas como a sala estava vazia, ninguém ouviu).
(but as the room was empty, nobody heard)

'Ana screamed loud enough to be heard in the next room (but since the room was empty, nobody heard her).'

If the scream is heard, it is heard during its existence (i.e., there is temporal overlapping), but the sentence has the non-implicative reading, as shown by the possibility of continuing the discourse as indicated. So, the question remains why has (37) the non-implicative reading and (34b) the implicative one. Hacquard's proposal that *too/enough*-constructions are at base implicative accounts for the implicative reading of (34b), but predicts, contrary to facts, that (37) has also the implicative reading. Let us now consider the hypothesis of a hidden modal verb.

6. Back to the hidden modal hypothesis

According to Meier 2003, the operators *too* and *enough* take as their complement a proposition modalized by a (possibly hidden) weak modal verb. A strong argument that she presents for sustaining this hypothesis is the fact that this modal verb can be realized without changing the meaning of the sentence. In fact, (34b) and (37) are equivalent to (38) and (39), respectively:

(38) A Ana teve inteligência suficiente
the Ana had-PFV intelligence enough

para *poder* resolver a equação.
to be able to-solve the equation

'Ana had enough intelligence to be able to solve the equation.'

(39) A Ana gritou suficientemente alto
the Ana screamed-PFV enough loud

para *poder* ser ouvida na sala ao lado
to be able to be heard at-the room at-the next

(mas	como	a	sala	estava	vazia,	ninguém	ouviu).
(but	as	the	room	was	empty,	nobody	heard)

'Ana screamed loud enough to be able to be heard in the next room (but since the room was empty, nobody heard her).'

This hypothesis of the hidden modal verb may account for the truth conditions of *too/enough*-constructions, as Meier 2003 shows, but it doesn't by itself, explain why (34b) and (38) have the implicative reading, contrary to (37) and (39). However, I think that an analysis that assumes a hidden modal verb is more promising in accounting for the implicative *vs.* non-implicative readings than the hypothesis that *too/enough*-constructions are at base implicative. In what follows, I will sketch the lines of a possible account of the (non-) implicative reading in *too/enough*-constructions on the basis of the assumption that these operators take a modalized complement.

According to Meier 2003, the truth conditions of (38) and (39) will be (40) and (41), respectively (cf. Meier 2003: 72):

(40) The amount *v* such that Ana was *v*-intelligent is GREATER than or EQUAL to the MINIMUM of all values *v** such that, if Ana was *v**-intelligent, she *could* solve the equation.

(41) The amount *v* such that Ana screamed *v*-loud is GREATER than or EQUAL to the MINIMUM of all values *v** such that, if Ana screamed *v**-loud, she *could* be heard in the next room.

The modal verb expresses the information that there is a possible world where the proposition under its scope is verified. In (38) the subordinated clause indicates that there is a possible world where Ana solved the equation, and the subordinated clause of (39) indicates that there is a possible world where Ana was heard. As for the main clauses, they are asserted and describe reality. Thus, the whole construction (39) indicates that, in the real world, there is a time prior to utterance time where Ana screamed *d*-loud and that this situation evolved into one where she was heard at the next room. Similarly, (38) indicates that, in the real world, there is a time prior to utterance time where Ana was *d*-intelligent, and this situation is part of a larger one where she solved the equation. Because of the presence of the modal verb, the possible world where the state of affairs described by the subordinated proposition is verified doesn't have to be the real world (i.e., the subordinated clause is not asserted). The sentences will be true if such state of affairs is verified in some possible world and the state of affairs described by the main clause is verified in reality.

This can be best seen in a diagram that represents an historical modal base (cf. Werner 2006), which is based on the branching time model of the relationship between time and possible worlds:

(42) For any world w and time t, $\cap$ f (w,t) = the set of worlds which are identical to w up through time t. (cf. Portner 2009: 233)

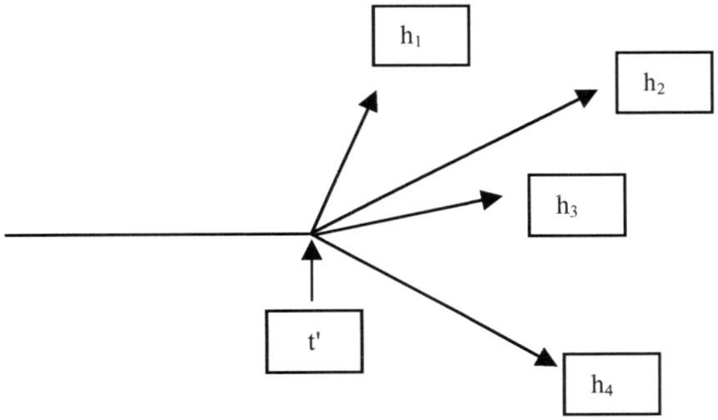

Figure 6-1 – Historical modal base.

Suppose h_2 is the real world and t' is a point where the state of affairs described by the main clause in (38) or (39) takes place. The state of affairs described by the infinitival clause is observed in one of the possible ramifications of t'. That is, the complex sentence describes a state of affairs that starts in the real world and finishes in some possible world which is identical to the real one up to t' (i.e., the infinitival clause describes a state of affairs that can be verified in h_2, the real world, or else in h_1, h_3 or h_4).

All that is to be explained is why in the case of (38) the inference follows that the possible world where the infinitival proposition is verified is the real one, while in (39) it doesn't have to be (the sentence can be true if the infinitival proposition is verified in h_2, or else in h_1 or any other possible world different from the real one after t'). This is where world knowledge plays a role.

In the case of (39), the relevant states of affairs are 'to scream *d*-loud' and 'the scream to be heard next room'. World knowledge tells us that in any normal circumstance if a scream is loud to at least a certain degree, then it can be heard in the surrounding space. Thus, when interpreting (39), one has to consider one possible ramification of t' and *any* of the ramifications can be chosen. Thus, 'the scream was heard' does not have to be observed in the real world.

By contrast, in the case of (38), the fact that someone is *d*-intelligent doesn't guarantee that in any possible world such person solves an equation. The capability of solving the equation depends also on its degree of difficulty, on the mathematical skills of the person, and so on. That is, contrary to what is verified in (39), it is not the case that in any normal world the infinitival clause can be verified. To be at least *d*-intelligent is a necessary condition for solving the equation, but the solving also depends on other circumstances. Thus, the ramifications of t' in the case of (38) are less than in the case of (39). The interpretation of sentence (38) requires the consideration of a particular possible world (one where Ana has certain mathematical knowledge, where she is focused on solving the equation, and so on), while the infinitival clause of (39) can be verified in any normal world.

Likewise, in constructions with the *too* operator, the implicative reading is dependent on whether the non realization of the state of affairs described by the infinitival clause is natural in any normal world or only in particular possible words:

(43)

O	tribunal	teve	demasiadas	dúvidas
the	Court	had-PFV	too many	doubts

para	o	(poder)	condenar
to	him	(be able)	to sentence

(# mas	acabou	por	condená-lo).
(# but	ended	by	sentence him)

'The Court had too many doubts to (be able to) sentence him (# but sentenced him anyway).'

(44)

O	processo	teve	demasiadas	testemunhas
the	process	had-PFV	too many	witnesses

para	(poder)	ser	rápido
to	(be able to)	be	fast

(mas	acabou	por	ser	célere).
(but	ended	by	be	fast).'

'The process had too many witnesses to (be able to) be fast (but, in the end, it was fast).'

In the case of (43), the amount of doubts that prevent the court to produce a guilty verdict depends on particular circumstances (what is the nature of the doubts, etc.). On the contrary, in the case of (44), if a process has at least *n* witnesses, it is expected to take long in *any* normal world. Thus, when processing the infinitival clause of (43), one has to consider a particular possible world, while in the case of (44) any possible world can be considered.

Nevertheless, the fact that a particular possible world has to be picked out doesn't guarantee that the chosen one is the real word. In other words, if sentences such as (38) and (43), which have the implicative reading, lead to the consideration of a particular ramification of t', in Figure 1, something must assure that the chosen ramification is the one modeling reality, instead of some other. I assume that some principle of economy operates, such that if a particular possible world has to be chosen when interpreting the infinitival clause the chosen world is the one that was considered in the interpretation of the main clause.

To some extent, there is some similarity between constructions as (38) and (43) and cases of modal subordination, as the following example:

(45) A tornado might hit the city. The building will be destroyed.

The second sentence of (45) is interpreted, roughly, as describing a state of affairs in the same possible world as the first sentence. The same happens in the case of (38) and (43), where the possible world considered in the interpretation of the subordinated clause is the same as the one considered in the interpretation of the main clause.

7. Conclusion

The main purpose of this paper was to identify the factors that lead to the implicative reading in some *too/enough*-constructions and to the non-implicative reading in other constructions. The second purpose was to figure out which of the considered analysis (the basic implicative proposal of Hacquard 2005 and the hidden modal proposal of Meier 2003) gives a more accurate account of the observed facts.

Concerning the first item, the observation was made that several conditions appear to play a role in the emergence of the implicative reading. Some of them are necessary, but not sufficient, conditions for the implicative reading; others may favor the implicative reading, but do not force it; and only in two cases was the implicative reading observed to be systematic: (i) when the main clause has perfective aspect and evaluative modality, or (ii) when the main clause has perfective aspect and the realization of the state of affairs described by the infinitival clause is dependent on particular conditions. The first case was observed to be not exclusive of *too/enough*-constructions. Rather, it appears to be the manifestation of a more general regularity. As for the second case, the idea explored in this paper was that the (non-)implicative reading is dependent on the number of possible worlds that form the modal base. For instance, in a (non-implicative reading) construction with the predicate *to be loud enough to* φ, the constituent *loud enough to* φ refers to a degree of loudness that allows φ in any normal possible world, while in an implicative reading construction, with, e.g., the predicate *to be intelligent enough to* φ, the degree which allows φ is different from world to world, since φ depends on other circumstances as well.

As for the second item, the observation was made that the hidden modal proposal seems to allow a more reasonable account of the facts. One criticism made in the literature (cf. Hacquard 2005) to this proposal is that it predicts the (non-)implicative readings to be contextually conditioned. Although Hacquard is right in that grammatical factors are relevant for the (non-)implicative readings, such readings don't appear to be constrained purely on grammatical factors, contextual information also playing a role. This fact is compatible with the contextual dependency of modal verbs.

References

Karttunen, Lauri 1971. Implicative Verbs. *Language* 47/2: 340-358.

Hacquard, Valentine 2005. Aspects of *Too* and *Enough* Constructions. In: Efthymia Georgala & Jonathan Howell (eds.): *Proceedings of SALT XV*. Ithaca, NY: Cornell University, 80-97.

Meier, Cécile 2003. The meaning of *too*, *enough* and *so ... that*. *Natural Language Semantics* 10/4: 69-107.

Portner, Paul 2009. *Modality*. New York: Oxford University Press.

Rescher, Nicolas 1968. *Topics in Philosophical Logic*. Dordrecht: Reidel.

Werner, Tim 2006. Future and non-future modal sentences. *Natural Language Semantics* 14/3: 235-255.

COVERT MODALITY IN CHECHEN

ZARINA MOLOCHIEVA
UNIVERSITY OF CALIFORNIA, BERKELEY
MAX PLANCK INSTITUTE FOR EVOLUTIONARY ANTHROPOLOGY

Abstract: This paper provides a survey of the distribution of the inceptive suffix *-d.ala* in Chechen and shows that its semantics depends on the valence and Aktionsart of the verb it occurs with. The inceptive meaning is diachronically basic, and the modal meaning is derived, since the inceptive meaning is not available to all verbs and since hinges upon the Aktionsart type imposed by deadjectival derivation. The syntactic constraints on the modal meaning then suggest the diachronic developments by which the modal meaning may have arisen. Thus aspect and Aktionsart provide an entry point for the rise of covert modality.

1. Introduction[1]

Chechen belongs to the Nakh branch of the Nakh-Daghestanian family spoken in the Northeastern Caucasus. Chechen is an ergative, case-using, head-final language. The word order is SOV. There are four gender classes, V, J, D, B, marked as prefix (or infix) on the verb.

In Chechen, every noun has a gender. Gender markers occur on the verb as initial prefix or infix placed between deictic prefixes and verbal stem (a). Only 30% of the verbs show gender agreement. The nominative argument is an agreement trigger, regardless of whether its function is A, S, or O.[2] The intransitive verbs agree in gender with the subject, whereas transitive verbs agree with the direct object (1a-b).

[1] Acknowledgements: Hans Rausing Fund for Documentation of Endangered Languages (SOAS) IGS0057; NSF BCS 0966675; Max Planck Institute for Evolutionary Anthropology, Leipzig. I am also thankful to Johanna Nichols, to the two volume editors, and to two anonymous reviewers for helpful comments on this paper.

[2] Based on Dixon (1979).

(1a)	so	dwa-**v**-oedu
	1SG.NOM(**V**)	dwa-**V**-go.PRS
	'I (male) go away.'	

(1b)	as	xudar	**d**-u'-u
	1SG.ERG	porridge.NOM(**D**)	**D**-eat-PRS
	'I eat porridge.'		

In continuous tenses (which consist of a converb and auxiliary), the auxiliary agrees in gender with the subject in the nominative case, whereas the converb agrees with the direct object (1c).

(1c)	so	xudar	**d**-u'u-sh	**j**-u
	1SG.NOM(J)	porridge.NOM(**D**)	**D**-eat-CVBsim	**J**-be.PRS
	'I (female) am eating porridge.'			

Chechen has special verbs to express modal meanings such as *mega* 'may / can / is possible' and *d.ieza* 'should, must'. These verbs can be used with all transitive and intransitive verbs to express necessity. Expression of ability and possibility ('can', 'be able') is more complicated. Most of the verbs can take the inceptive[3] suffixed auxiliary *-d.ala* ('INCP'). Whereas this suffix can add an inceptive meaning to all verbs, its modal meaning emerges only from some verbs. Where and when it can have modal meaning is one of the thorniest problems of Chechen syntax, which this paper aims to clarify. Another goal is to use the synchronic distribution to reconstruct an origin for the modal meaning, and below I suggest that an aspect-like or Aktionsart-like meaning gave rise to a modal meaning in certain contexts. For this sort of developmental trajectory see Abraham (1999, 2004).

1.1 The suffix *-d.ala*

The primary meaning of the independent verb *d.ala* is 'give'. This verb can be suffixed to the infinitival stem of verbs of different types, taking the tense inflection of the independent verb 'give': *lo* 'give:PRS', *d.alla* 'give:PRF', *lur d.u* 'give:FUT AUX'.[4] The lexical verb is in the infinitive

---

[3] *Inceptive* means the beginning of an action.

[4] Chechen verbs show 35 regular ablaut classes of the stem vowel; there are four grades of the stem: infinitive, perfective stem 1 (used in perfective tenses), perfective stem 2 (used in evidential perfective tenses), and imperfective stem; there are a number of irregular verbs as well; the stems of such verbs are

form, and all TAM categories are borne by the inceptive suffix (2a-d). The suffix *-d.ala* with a small number of verbs expresses the beginning of an action (Section 2).

(2a) Infinitive form:
*d.axa-**d.ala*** (D.go:INF-D.INCP:INF) 'be able to go'

(2b) Present:
*d.axa-**lo*** (D.go:INF-D.INCP:PRS) 'is able to go'

(2c) Past:
*d.axa-**d.alla*** (D.go:INF-D.INCP:PRF) 'has been able to go'

(2d) Future:
*d.axa-**lur d.u*** (D.go:INF-D.INCP:FUT AUX) 'will be able to go'

1.2 Intransitive and transitive verbs with *-d.ala*

Transitive and intransitive verbs behave differently with the inceptive suffix. Some intransitive verbs cannot be used with it. The transitive verbs fall into a few subcategories as regards their behavior with the inceptive, and dative-subject verbs mostly do not allow it. For transitive and intransitive verbs that cannot take the suffix, the same modal meaning is expressed lexically with the verbs *mega* 'may' and *d.ieza* 'should'.

Intransitive verbs

The subject of the one-argument verb is in the nominative case and the verb agrees in gender with the subject. The inceptive does not change the case of the subject of intransitive verbs (3a, 3b). In (3b) the inceptive indicates that the subject is able to perform the action.

(3a)	so	taxana	baazar	voedu
	1SG.NOM	today	market.ADV	V.go.PRS

'Today I'm going to the market.'

(3b)	so	taxana	baazar	**vaxa-lo**
	1SG.NOM	today	market.ADV	V.go:INF-INCP.PRS

'Today I can go to the market / I'm able to go to the market.'

---

suppletive; the verb *d.ala* is one of the irregular verbs (Nichols & Vagapov 2004: 685-687).

Not all one-argument verbs allow *-d.ala*. For instance, it is not possible with verbs such as *d.ala* 'die', **daladala* and *twousa* 'fall asleep', **twousad.ala*. Instead, such verbs are used with the modal verb *mega* 'may' to express the same meaning (4).

(4) ahw dwa-vizha-vohw dwa-twousa
2SG.ERG DX-V.lie.down-V.CAUS.CVB DX-fall.asleep.INF

mega iza
may.PRS 3SG.NOM
'If you put him to bed, he may fall asleep.'

There is no obvious category that unites these verbs and precludes the inceptive. They have different Aktionsart types.

Transitive verbs
The A-argument of transitive verbs is in the ergative case and the O is in the nominative case. The inceptive suffix changes an ergative A-argument to allative.[5] Also, the valence of the verb changes from transitive (ergative A, nominative O) to ambitransitive where the obligatory A becomes optional and the S/O is still nominative. (6) is inceptive of (5), and (7) is the inceptive without the A argument.

(5) as kiexat **doeshu**
1SG.ERG letter.NOM(D) D.read:IPFV.PRS
'I'm reading the letter.'

(6) soega kiexat **d.iesha-lo**
1SG.ALL letter.NOM(D) D.read:INF-INCT.PRS
'I can read the letter. / I am able to read the letter.'

The omission of the allative agent can change the semantics (cf. 4-5). (4) means that the agent is able to read the letter; without the allative argument it means that the letter is readable; see (5). However, not all verbs allow this meaning; (7c below does not).

[5] One of the locative suffixes; the speech and transmission verbs take usually an indirect allative objects

(7) kiexat **diesha-lo**
letter.NOM(D) D.read-INCP.PRS
'The letter is readable.'

In (8), there is no overt agent present. However, the modality reading implicates an agent, while the inceptive meaning does not. Such constructions are ambiguous and can mean either that an agent opens the door (transitive verb with null-Agent which can be anaphoric or arbitrary) or the door opens by itself (one-argument verb with only a subject).

(8) niaw **hwa-jella-lo**
door.NOM(J) DX-J.open-INCP.PRS
'The door is openable. / (Someone) is able to open the door.'
[null A, anaphoric or arbitrary]

While (8) can have both meanings, there are verbs which allow only the meaning that the agent is able to perform the action. For instance, (9b) means that an unspecified agent is able to eat the porridge (cf. 9a-b). With the negation it means 'The porridge is not edible or A is not able to eat the porridge' (9c).

(9a) soega xudar **da'a-lo**
1SG.ALL porridge.NOM(J) D.eat-INCP.PRS
'I can eat the porridge. / I am able to eat the porridge.'

(9b) xudar **da'a-lo**
porridge D.eat-INCP.PRS
'(Someone) can / is able to eat the porridge.'
[null A, anaphoric or arbitrary]
(*'The porridge is edible.')

(9c) xudar **ca-da'a-lo**
porridge NEG-D.eat-INCP.PRS
'(Someone) cannot eat the porridge.'
[null A, anaphoric or arbitrary]
(*'The porridge is not edible.')

To express the meaning 'edible, can be eaten' a progressive tense form of the verb *mega* 'can' must be used (10).

(10)

xudar	da'a	**mega-sh**	**du**
porridge.NOM(D)	D.eat.INF	can-CVBsim	D.be.PRS

'The porridge is edible.'

Similarly, the verb *d.a* 'do' suffixed with the inceptive means only that the agent is able to perform the action (11a-c). It cannot mean 'The work is doable'; though again there are progressive constructions (not shown here) that make that meaning possible.

(11a)

as	wyyrenna	bolx	**bo**
1SG.ERG	in.the.morning	work.NOM(B)	B.make.PRS

'I work in the morning.'

(b)

soega	wyyrenna	bolx
1SG.ALL	in.the.morning	work.NOM(B)

ca-bala-lo
NEG-B.make-INCP.PRS
'I cannot work in the morning.'

(c)

bolx	**bala-lo**
work.NOM(B)	B.make-INCP.PRS

'(Someone) is able to work.' (*'The work is doable.')

Dative subject verbs

A number of verbs with experiencer subjects take the dative on those subjects in Chechen. Dative subject verbs behave differently. Some of them cannot be used with the inceptive suffix *-d.ala*, for instance, *bwaergd.aa* 'notice', *iesha* 'need', *xaza* 'hear', *ga* 'see', *d.ouza* 'recognize', *motta* 'think, seem'. One of the dative subject verbs can take the inceptive suffix but it changes its lexical semantics, for example, *xa'a* 'know' with the inceptive suffix gives *xa'ad.ala* 'get to know', i.e. 'notice'.

1.3 Verb with dative and allative subject

There is only one dative-subject verb which can be used with the inceptive without changing its lexical meaning: *waama* 'learn, *waama-d.ala* 'be able to learn' (12-13). It takes either dative or allative as its subject case.

(12)	suuna	jaaz-da='a	diesha='a	sixxa	weema
	1SG.DAT	write-D.make=and	D.read=and	quick	learn.PRS

'I learn to write and to read quickly.'

(13)	suuna / soega	jaaz-da='a	diesha='a
	1SG.DAT/1SG.ALL	write-D.make=and	D.read=and

	sixxa	waama-lo
	quick	learn-INCP.PRS

'I can learn to write and to read quickly.'

In Chechen, this is probably the only example of an inceptive whose A argument can be either dative (as with the unsuffixed verb) or allative (as with the former ergative subject of a transitive inceptive verb). As mentioned above, the A-argument of an inceptive verb is usually in the allative, whereas the S-argument is in the nominative. Apart from this usage, the allative marks indirect objects and causees in causative constructions (see below). Most verbs of saying take allative indirect objects (14). The G-argument of ditransitive verbs also takes the allative or dative case (15) (see Daniel et al. 2010).

(14)	as	**cynga**	diicira / eelira	(…)
	1SG.ERG	3SG.ALL	tell / say.WPST	

'I told / said to him…'

(15)	as	**cynga** / cunna	axcha	della
	1SG.ERG	3SG.ALL/DAT	money.NOM	D.give.PRF

'I gave (loaned) him the money.'

In causative constructions, a causee is always in the allative case (16).

(16)	**deega**	tyyra	diic-iti-ra	k'ant-as
	father.ALL	story.NOM	D.tell-CAUS-WPST	boy-ERG

'The son got (his) father to tell a story.'

2. No modal meaning for the homophonous verb-forming suffix *-d.ala*

2.1. Inceptive-semelfactive verbs

The inceptive suffix *-d.ala* can affect the Aktionsart of the verbs without adding a modal meaning. I use the term *inceptive-semelfactive* for those semelfactive verbs which emphasize the onset of a state, e.g. 'to start to do something'. The input verbs are stative and have no onset or endpoint. The inceptive suffix changes the following verbs to inceptive-semelfactive: *qiera* 'fear', *qierad.ala* 'take fright, get scared'; *d.iela* 'laugh', *d.ielad.ala* 'start laughing', *d.ieza* 'like, love', *d.ieza-d.ala* 'fall in love' as in (17)-(18). One stative verb, *laza* 'hurt', exceptionally takes a different inceptive suffix *-d.aala* (*lazad.aala* 'start to hurt') whose primary meaning as an independent verb is 'finish' (19a). This is the only verb that takes *-d.ala* as its inceptive suffix (19b).

(17)	juxa	cu	k'ant-ana	i	jow	**jieza-lo**
	then	DEM	boy-DAT	DEM	girl.NOM(J)	J.love-start.PRS

'And then this boy fell in love with this girl.'

(18)	as	ziezag-ash	del-cha
	1SG.ERG	flower-PL.NOM(D)	give-CVBtemp
	jiela-jeli-ra		jow
	J.laugh:INF-J.INCP-Rem.WPST		girl.NOM(J)

'The girl laughed when I gave flowers to her.'

(19a)	so	bolx	bi-na	**vaella**
	1SG.NOM(V)	work.NOM(J)	B.make-PRF	
	V.finish.PRF			

'I have finished working.'

(19b)	san	korta	**laza-baella**
	1SG.GEN	head.NOM(B)	hurt-B.finish.PRF

'I've got a headache.'
(Lit. 'I've gotten a headache (and still have one)'.)

Inherently, the verbs such as *qiera* 'fear', *d.iela* 'laugh', *d.ieza* 'like, love' cannot form the perfect (*dieza*, PRF **diezna* 'love', *diela* **diella* 'laugh' *qiera* **qierna* 'be afraid of'), but they can use the inceptive-semelfactive verb in the perfect instead (20a-b).

(20a)	*k'ant-ana	jow	**jiez-na**
	boy-DAT	girl.NOM(J)	J.love-PRF
	Intended reading: 'The boy liked the girl.'		

(20b)	k'ant-ana	jow	jieza-jella
	boy-DAT	girl.NOM(J)	J.love-J.INCP.PRF
	'The boy fell in love with the girl.'		
	(*'The boy was able to like the girl.')		

2.2. Deadjectival verbs

The same suffix derives intransitive change-of-state verbs from adjectives: *douxa* 'warm', *d.oux-d.ala* 'get warm', *waerzha* 'black', *waerzhad.ala* 'get dark'; *k'ai* 'white', *k'ai-d.ala* 'get white', *ghial-d.ala* 'get tired' (21a-b).

(21a)	xi	**douxa**	du
	water.NOM(D)	D.warm	D.be.PRS
	'The water is warm.'		

(21b)	xi	sixxa	**doux-deli-ra**
	water.NOM	quick	D.warm-D.INCP-WPST
	'The water got warm quickly.'		

The derived verbs can appear in impersonal constructions expressing weather conditions: *shiallo* 'It's getting cold', etc. These inceptives are paired with transitives taking a different suffix. Neither the inceptives nor the transitives have modal meaning (22a-b).

(22a)	**shial-lu-sh**	ju
	get.cold-INCP-CVBsim	J.be.PRS
	'It's getting cold.' (*It can get cold.)	

(22b) nana xudar
mother.NOM(J) porridge.NOM(D)

shial-die-sh jara
cold-D.make-CVBsim J.be.PST
'Mother was cooling the porridge.'
(*'Mother was able to cool the porridge.')

3. The modal verbs *mega* 'can' and *d.ieza* 'should'

Of the two lexical verbs of modality mentioned in Section 1 *mega* 'can' can be used both with verbs that cannot take the inceptive suffix and those that can (23a).

(23a) so txousa **mega**
1SG.NOM fall.asleep.INF can.PRS
'It could be that I'll fall asleep. / I'll probably fall asleep.'
(*'I am able to sleep.')

mega can also have this meaning with verbs that are able to take *-d.ala* (23b-c).

(23b) so qaana bazaar vaxa **mega**
1SG.NOM(V) tomorrow market.ADV V.go.INF can.PRS
'Maybe I (male) will go to the market tomorrow.'
(*'I am able to the market tomorrow.')

(23c) so baazar vaxa-lo
1SG.NOM(V) market.ADV V.go-INCP.PRS
'I (male) can go to the market.' ('I am able to go to the market.')

The verb *mega* can also express permission. Then the subject must be in the dative case (24a-b).

(24a) suuna bazaar vaxa **mega**
1SG.DAT(V) market V.go.INF can.PRS
'I can go to the market. / I am allowed to go to the market.'
(*'I am able to go to the market.')

(24b)

suuna	xudar	da'a	**mega**
1SG.DAT	porridge.NOM(D)	D.eat.INF	can.PRS

'I can eat the porridge. / I am allowed to eat the porridge.'
(*'I am able to eat the porridge.')

The other modal verb, *d.ieza* 'should, must', has three different possibilities for its subject case, with a difference in meaning. The subject can be in the ergative, dative or genitive (genitive is less used than dative). Nichols (2011:478) uses the term *case attraction* for similar phenomena in Ingush. In (25a) the subject case is assigned by the infinitive (this is case attraction), whereas in (25b) it is assigned by *d.ieza* 'must'. In (25c) it is assigned by *d.ieza* in the sense 'should'. Constructions with case attraction (here, ergative subject assigned by 'bring') imply that the subject has a moral obligation to perform the action (25a). In (25b-c) the obligation is not moral but more practical or pragmatic.

(25a)

as	xi	daa	**dieza**
1SG.ERG	water.NOM	D.bring.INF	D.should.PRS

'I should bring water.' (*'I am able to bring water.')

(25b)

suuna	xi	daa	**dieza**
1SG.DAT	water.NOM	D.bring.INF	D.should.PRS

'I must bring water. (I need to bring water.)'
(*'I am able to bring water.')

(25c)

xi	daa	**dieza**	**sa**
water.NOM	D.bring.INF	D.should.INF	1SG.GEN

'I must bring water. (I'm supposed to bring water.)'
(*'I am able to bring water.')

4. Epistemic modality

The modal verbs *d.ieza* 'must' and *mega* 'may' can also express deductive and speculative epistemic modality respectively (in the terms of Palmer 1986). According to Palmer (1986:51), there are four ways in which the speaker may indicate that his statement is not based on fact: (a) the speaker is speculating about it; (b) the speaker is presenting it as a deduction; (c) the speaker has been told about it; (d) it is based on sensory evidence which may be incorrect. In Chechen, constructions with the modal verb *d.ieza* 'must' express a deductive meaning, where the speaker makes assumptions based on evidence or previous experience. For instance, in (26a) the speaker came home and saw that somebody had cooked and the speaker knows that Seda usually comes home at that time. He assumes that she must have come home and cooked (Molochieva 2011:243).

(26a)	Sieda	**c'a-je'a-na**	**xila**	**jieza**
	Seda.NOM(J)	home-J.come:PFV1-CVBant	be.INF	J.must.PRS

'Seda must (already) have come.'

The assumption can also be made even if the speaker does not have visible evidence. For example, the speaker knows that his friend's son is sixteen years old and should already have received his high school diploma; see (27b). The speaker has not seen the son and does not know whether he has really graduated from school, but makes an inference based on the age of the boy.

(27b)	*ceera*	*k'ant*	***diesh-na***
	they.GEN	boy.NOM(V)	study:IPFV-CVBant
	vaella	***xila***	***vieza***
	V.finish:PFV1.CVBant	be.INF	V.need.PRS

'Their son must have finished school.'

The speculative modality of *mega* 'is possible' expresses the speaker's attitude toward an assumption based on general knowledge. For instance, in (28) the speaker makes an inference based on his general knowledge of the time when Seda comes home. The assumption is based on generally available information.

(28)	*jaalx*	*dael-cha*	*Sieda*
	six	D.finish-CVBtemp	Seda.NOM(J)
	c'a-je'a-na	***xila***	***mega***
	home-J.come-CVBant	be.INF	may.PRS

'At six o'clock Seda may have already come home (she is usually at home at this time).'

The modal verbs can express probability, possibility, and also the speaker's judgment when they are used with a past infinitive as (27b-28), whereas to express permission and necessity the modal verbs are used with an untensed infinitive as in (24a)-(25c).

5. Conclusions

To express necessity, permission and possibility, Chechen uses the modal *d.ieza* 'must' and *mega* 'may, can' which can also be used to express epistemic modality as in European languages (e.g. English, German). However, unlike the European languages where the verb *can* indicates possibility, permission and ability, in Chechen it never expresses ability. The inceptive suffix can have both modal meaning and the non-modal inceptive meaning. The modal meaning of the suffix is derived, since it is not available to all types of verbs.

The verbs where the inceptive has only pure inceptive meaning and no modal meaning (inceptive-semelfactive and deadjectival verbs: Section 2) are the key to reconstruct the history of the inceptive. Since with the other verbs the inceptive can have pure inceptive as well as modal semantics, it must be that an inceptive meaning is the original one and the modal meaning was historically secondary. This is supported by the behavior of the cognate suffix in more distantly related Batsbi, where it also derives inceptive verbs from adjectives but in its deverbal functions is semantically different from Chechen and Ingush, and has meanings like 'involuntarily, unawares, spontaneously' (Holisky & Gagua 1994:7). This would mean that covert modality has arisen from Aktionsart semantics, as has been supported in detail for other languages by Abraham (1999, 2004, 2005, this volume), Abraham & Leiss (eds.) (2008, 2009).

Abbreviations

ADV = adverb, ant = anterior, ALL = allative, AUX = auxiliary, CAUS = causative, CVB = converb, DAT = dative, DEM = demonstrative, DX = deictic prefix, ERG = ergative, FUT = future, GEN = genitive, INF = infinitive, INCP = inceptive, IPFV = imperfective, NOM = nominative, PFV = perfective, PL = plural, PRF = perfect, PRS= present, PST = past, SG = singular, sim = simultaneous, temp = temporal, V, J, B, D = gender agreement markers, WPST = witnessed past.

References

Abraham, Werner 1999. Über allgemeine Zusammenhänge zwischen Präpositionsinfinitiv, Futur, deontischer Modalität und Perfektivität: lokalistische Allativität. *Sprachwissenschaft* 24: 361-405.

—. 2004. The grammaticalization of the infinitival preposition. *Journal of comparative Germanic linguistics* 7: 111-170.

—. 2005. Event arguments and modal verbs. In C. Maienborn & A. Wöll-stein (eds.) *Event arguments: Foundations and applications*, 243-276. [Linguistische Arbeiten 501]. Tübingen: Niemeyer.

Abraham, Werner & E. Leiss (eds.) 2008. *Modality-aspect interfaces. Implications and typological solutions,* XI-XXIV. Amsterdam / Philadelphia: John Benjamins. [Typological Studies in Languages 79].

Abraham, Werner & E. Leiss (eds.) 2009. *Modalität. Epistemik und Evidentialität bei Modalverb, Adverb, Modalpartikel und Modus.* Tübingen: Stauffenburg. [Studien zur deutschen Grammatik 77].

Daniel, Mikhail, Zaira Khalilova, & Zarina Molochieva. 2010. Ditransitive constructions in East Caucasian: a family overview. In Malchukov, Andrej, Haspelmath, Martin & Comrie, Bernard (eds.) *Studies in Ditransitive constructions: A Comparative Handbook*, 277-316. Berlin / New York: de Gruyter.

Dixon, Robert, M. W. 1979. Ergativity. *Language* 55: 59-138.

Holisky, Dee Ann & Rusudan Gagua. 1994. Tsova-Tush (Batsbi). In Rieks Smeets (ed.) *The Indigenous Languages of the Caucasus.* Vol. 4, 147-212. Delmar, NY: Caravan Books.

Molochieva, Zarina. 2011. Tense, Aspect, and Mood in Chechen. PhD thesis. University of Leipzig.

Nichols Johanna & Arbi Vagapov. 2004. *Chechen-English and English-Chechen dictionary.* London / New York: Routledge.

Nichols, Johanna. 2011. *Ingush Grammar.* Berkeley / Los Angeles: University of California Press.

Palmer, Frank R. 1986. *Mood and Modality.* Cambridge: Cambridge University Press.

SHARED KNOWLEDGE AND EPISTEMIC REDUCTIONISM: COVERT SEMANTICS OF THE GERMAN MODAL PARTICLES

PIERRE-YVES MODICOM
UNIV. PARIS-SORBONNE

Abstract: The contribution advocates the use of the category of covertness in the semantic description of grammatical items. After a short presentation of the two different kinds of covertness we distinguish (resp. epistemological and structural covertness), it is shown that resorting to this notion makes it possible to propose a monosemic account of apparently polysemic *signifiants*. The two examples discussed here are the German modal particles *ja* ("yes") and *wohl* ("well"), both of which are related to commitment and Theory of Mind. While *ja* is often said to be either a marker of consensus between speech act participants or an exclamative marker, we demonstrate the existence of a unique meaning, which can become covert depending on the illocutionary type of the sentence. Then, we prove that *wohl* is a strong commitment marker involved in covert evidential patterns. Thus, we can reduce the so-called "weak commitment" value of *wohl* to an external interpretative bias.

1. Basic features of German Modal Particles

German modal particles (hence GMPs) form a class of modal items which have now been extensively studied under various perspectives. The aim of this paper is to show that the semantics of GMPs has much to do with the problem of covertness in language. The study will make the case for internalism and reductionism as a means for identifying external impediments responsible for core features being covert. Consequently, we will underline the relevance of silent categories which seem to have caught little attention in the study of these modal particles up to now, such as the interplay between commitment and evidentiality. Thus, we hope to explore the complex realm of modal features and their combinations throughout all types of *signifiants*. After the general presentation of the status and functions of GMPs as well as of our understanding of the notion of covertness (this part), the analysis will focus on two items: The first step will be devoted to *ja* ("yes") and will present the positional regularities of the particle in the topology of the German sentence, which make the case for an interpretation of *ja* as a modal marker. In a second phase of the analysis of *ja*, we will argue that the alleged two meanings of the particle can be reduced to one and the same. The following part will present the GMP *wohl* ("well"), for which two readings are proposed, as well. There, too, we will reduce those two readings to one and the same. We argue that in both cases, semantic features pertaining to modality combine with other factors, such as the illocutionary type, and yield a variety of interpretations which make the modal meaning of GMPs covert in the sense defined in this introductory part.

German modal particles have been studied along pragmatic, semantic, and syntactic lines since the end of the 1960s (most notably by Weydt 1969), after being long considered mere "filling words" (*Füllwörter*) deprived of strict, systematic conditions of usage. Indeed, they do not alter the truth conditions of the proposition they are embedded in. For example, sentences (1a) to (1d) have the same truth conditions as (1):

(1) Ich mag ihn sehr,
1SG like him much

aber	er	ist		ein bisschen	übergeschnappt.
aber	er	ist	Ø	ein bisschen	über-ge-schnapp-t.
but	3SG	is	NO.PRT	a bit	over-PTCP-snatch-PTCP

"I like him much, but he is a little crazy."

(1a) Ich mag ihn sehr, aber er ist *ja* ein bisschen übergeschnappt.
"yes"
~ "I like him much, but he is a little crazy, as you know."

(1b) Ich mag ihn sehr, aber er ist *wohl* ein bisschen übergeschnappt.
"well"
~ "I like him much, but he seems to be a little crazy."

(1c) Ich mag ihn sehr, aber er ist *schon* ein bisschen übergeschnappt.
"already"
~ "I like him much, but he is a little crazy, I must say."

(1d) Ich mag ihn sehr, aber er ist *eben* ein bisschen übergeschnappt.
"plainly"
~ "I like him much, but he is a little crazy, altogether."

GMPs form a class of morphemes whose extension and exact value are still discussed intensively, even though a scientific consensus has been reached on several basic features (see, for instance, Thurmair 1989, or the summary in Ormelius-Sandblom 1997). These are the characteristics about which there is a (quasi-)unified stance:

(i) GMPs are all phonologically identical with non-modal homonymes. Thus, for example, the GMP *ja* is identical with the *yes*-interjection *ja*, whereas *wohl* corresponds to the adverbial *wohl*, "well" and *eben* with the adjective *eben* "even" and with the temporal adverb *eben*, "just now, a short time ago". Nevertheless, this homonymy has to be reduced to a segmental one, since GMPs tend to exhibit a prosodic feature of their own (see point ii).

(ii) A feature making the case for grammaticalization hypotheses is the strong tendency of those GMPs to lose the lexical accent still presented by their non-modal cognates. Yet, this loss is not systematic and some particles present a merely weakened accent. This point will be discussed in section 2.

(iii) GMPs cannot be syntactical heads, at least in traditional accounts. For a discussion on this point, see Struckmeier (to appear).

(iv) GMPs cannot occupy the topical position preceding the finite verbal form in assertive matrix sentences.

(v) GMPs are subject to strong usage restrictions in illocutionary dependent clauses (see Coniglio 2011).

(vi) When GMPs scope over the whole proposition, which is the standard case, they occur before the structural position where the global negator *nicht* appears or would have appeared.

(vii) More generally, GMPs occur at the juncture of *theme* and *rheme* (Abraham 1991)

(viii) GMPs are not part of the propositional content, but, much rather, they mark illocutionary values supporting the felicity conditions of the appropriate speech act.

(ix) Finally, the meaning of GMPs is heavily dependent on the state of knowledge of the addressee (on this point, see Abraham 2010, Egg 2010, Evans 2009, Gast 2008, König 1997).

The perspective we defend here relies on the following assumptions, shared by most of the recent literature on the topic and justifying the integration of GMPs to the domain of modality:

(a) Each GMP has a precise meaning corresponding to one special distribution of propositional attitudes (knowledge, disbelief, surprise, inferability, wish, ...) among the speech act participants.
(b) GMPs fulfill an epistemic modal function which is correlated with their syntactic position at the juncture of theme and rheme, a field where many other modal markers are to be found in German.

It is possible to isolate a number of GMPs forming a coherent and complete system pertaining at the distribution of knowledge between the speaker and the hearer in assertive as well as in interrogative sentences (*ja*, *wohl*, *doch*, *schon*, *denn*, *eigentlich*, *eben*, *halt*). Under the perspective defended here, these GMPs could be ordered according to just two criteria: First, the speaker's epistemic stance with respect to *p*, the propositional content of her utterance (whether *p* is true or not, and if so, whether it is absolutely true or only restrictedly so); and second, the speaker's evaluation of the hearer's supposed knowledge.[1] Given these two criteria, the relationship between GMPs and the concept of modality is relatively clear. The question of covertness, on its part, has more to do with the specific thesis that shall be defended in the present contribution. We have two reasons to consider GMPs relevant for the study of covert patterns of modality. The first has to do with the way those morphemes are commonly interpreted. The second is related to the problem of covert evidentiality within modal phenomena, i.e. the evidential values or interpretations triggered by apparently modal markers. Those two distinct problems are to be addressed respectively as EPISTEMOLOGICAL and as STRUCTURAL COVERTNESS. A similar distinction can be found in Abraham & Leiss (this volume) under the opposition of "undiscovered" and "silent" phenomena.

The most frequent problem of covertness regarding GMPs is related to epistemological covertness. It must be noticed that the modal value of these morphemes has often been questioned or restricted, if not completely

[1] Another question regards the *evolution* of the speaker's evaluation of what is part of the Common Ground (CG) and what is not. This issue has been addressed among others by König (1997) or Gast (2008) in terms of relevance under the name of "context updating" or "CG updating". See Evans (2009) for a panorama of such "engagement and expectation" strategies, one of which has been represented more systematically by Abraham (2010) within the framework of Foreign Consciousness Alignment.

denied[2]. This may be illustrated by the naïve descriptions delivered by many native speakers, who often consider those particles to be devoid of meaning, but also in much more accurate accounts by linguists who privilege external(ist) analyses leading to a multiplicity of values. The unstable terminology used in this domain epitomizes this tendency: GMPs are also called *Abtönungspartikeln* (roughly: "modulation particles"), *discourse particles,*[3] *illocution particles* or (much more relevant in our perspective) *epistemic particles*. The main reason for such problems of classification is the ubiquity of some GMPs: They can appear in sentences of several illocutionary types where their meaning seem to differ considerably. This is mainly the case for *ja* and *wohl*. Especially *wohl* is subject to contradictory interpretations (strong commitment of the speaker v. distancing) depending on the syntactic and pragmatic context. This surface-bound polysemy has also been a problem for hypotheses about the grammaticalization of GMPs which postulate the persistence of a common core meaning (see Abraham 1991). The present contribution makes the case for a partly pragmatic or Gricean (Grice 1975), systematic account for the meaning of those particles. Thus, we want to restore the modal status of GMPs behind the superficial plurality of values.

The second aspect of covertness is a much more intrinsic one, since it has to do with the interplay of several semantic and functional categories within a unique *signifiant*. We assume this *signifiant* to exhibit only one of the several features at stake at the level of the *signifié*. In other words, silent categories are embedded in and intertwined with an overt one. As regards GMPs, structural covertness is exemplified by the presence of evidential features within modality, which questions the status of both categories and raises the question of their subsumption under one macro-category of epistemological marking (see Guentchéva & Landaburu 2007). As regards *ja* and *wohl*, we intend to show that their semantic opposition relies mainly on evidential constraints: It appears that *wohl* bears an additional inferential value which can be gained in a strict compositional way if we combine modality with other syntactic and semantic features. Thus, *wohl* exhibits covert evidential inferential features, whereas *ja* is a canonical case of GMP marking intersubjective alignment. More

---

[2] Accounts denying the modal value of GMPs can usually be quickly identified insofar as they tend to name them "Abtönungspartikeln". The most prominent – and valuable – study based on such premises is the seminal monography of Weydt (1969).

[3] This latter term is extremely problematic, since it is possible to distinguish another class of discourse markers which are not GMPs and therefore deserve the name of *discourse particles*. On this point, see Detges & Waltereit (2009).

generally, structural covertness can be interpreted as a symptom for the pervasiveness of the categories of modality and evidentiality. An evidential account is at the same time the condition for a unified description of all values, since inferential marking has dramatic consequences on the interpretation of *wohl* as a strong resp. weak commitment marker.

2. Modal reductionism: the case of *ja*

This section is devoted to the problem of epistemological covertness, i.e. to the semantic opacity of *ja* to the speaker, and above all to the multiplicity of values entailed by externalist accounts. The analysis advocates modal reductionism: *Ja* is to be described as a monosemic modal particle. In accordance with the literature, we consider that the modal value of GMPs is related to commitment as well as to Theory of Mind. Consequently, modality is tightly linked to the management of the common ground (CG, see König 1997, Gast 2008, Egg 2010 for similar accounts in the framework of relevance theory). On this basis, the demonstration of the advantages of modal reductionism will follow two steps. First, a short positional account will show how GMPs are fully integrated to the set of grammatical(ized) markers of modal meaning in German. Therefore, the modal value of *ja* has to be regarded as its core semantic and functional feature, and not as a secondary phenomenon. GMPs only exist as markers of informational status, i.e. as epistemic particles. In a second step, possible counterexamples will be discussed in order to show how apparently non-modal features are only external, usage-bound regularities and can be reduced to the postulated CG value.

2.1 Intersubjectivity and Epistemicity: On the role and place of Modal Particles

The first argument for modal reductionism is based on their well-known morphological status as *Doppelgänger* of non-modal morphemes. GMPs are provided with their modal and illocutionary features iff they receive precise syntactic and prosodic properties. As we shall see, this is not a coincidence: The syntactic and prosodic constraints are positively correlated to the conversion of the non-modal items to epistemic clitics. For prosodic reasons, such cliticized morphemes move to the positional field where modal markers are to be found in German. Following the syntactic and positional account by Abraham (1991), we assume that the basic lexemes have been grammaticalized at the juncture of theme and rheme, a position described by Zemb (1984: 97ff., 1978: 403ff.) as the *pheme*, i.e. as the main place for modal evaluation. This field is centered on the global negation *nicht*, but it also contains sentence adverbs and evaluative markers, as illustrated in (2).[4] In this theory, modality is not reduced to epistemicity, since some of the evaluative markers are clearly axiological (such as *leider*, "unfortunately") and rather pertain to deonticity.

(2)	Das Wetter ("the weather") heute ("today") in der Normandie ("in N.")	leider ("unfortunately")	unbeständig sein dürfte ("might be changeable")
	TH	PH	RH (*basic order*)

→ Heute dürfte das Wetter in der Normandie leider unbeständig sein. (Zemb 1978: 397)
"Unfortunately, the weather in Normandy might be changeable today."

A later position usually coincides with scope reduction: The GMP is placed immediately before the main focused element of the sentence, just as in example (3). Such positional rules are common to GMPs and to the negator *nicht*, suggesting a strong correlation between the use of GMPs and the evaluation of how valid the proposition is. Consequently, topological phenomena seem to support the hypothesis that GMPs primarily encode propositional attitudes. This scenario is confirmed by corpus data. The following examples have been collected in summer 2010 from radio interviews. To prevent possible dialectal variations from distorting the results, three geographically distinct broadcasters have been taken into account, respectively the national network DeutschlandRadio (*Deutschlandfunk-DeutschlandradioKultur*, glossed DLF-DRK), and two regional corporations, the Broadcasting Corporation of the South-West (*Südwestrundfunk*, glossed SWR) and the Bavarian Broadcasting Corporation (*Bayerischer Rundfunk*, BR). It turns out that in the

[4] It is not our aim to discuss the highly difficult question of how to combine Zemb's account of the theme/rheme distinction with Functional Sentence Perspective. In this paper, we use the concepts in the meaning of the Prague School. We just use Zemb's concept of *pheme* as a useful hint at the presence of a third, modal field between theme and rheme.

overwhelming majority of assertive sentences, *ja* occurs at the end of the chain of enclitics after the finite verb. This position could be a sign of grammaticalization, the loss (or weakening) of the lexical accent turning the morphemes into clitic elements, which could then be integrated in the clitic chain, which may result from the Wackernagel movement.[5] The position at the end of the clitic chain leads to a superficial ambiguity, since it most often coincides with the juncture of theme and rheme, especially in a strictly information-structural perspective:[6] Pronouns being generally thematic, the first element coming after them is likely to be at the border of both fields. This is confirmed by one fact underlined in the literature: GMPs with global meaning appear immediately before the negation and other modal markers. Consequently, points (vi) and (vii) of the list of features exposed in the introduction appear to be tightly correlated. This could provide a first scenario for the grammaticalization of non-modal items into GMPs.

Table 2-1. Statistical survey of the positions of GMPs in verb-second assertive sentences.

Position of the GMP in verb-second sentences	DLF-DRK	SWR	BR	overall
Beginning of the pheme	258	97	87	442
Other	11	0	0	11
- before focus particle	4	-	-	4
- others	7	-	-	7

We consider the 11 cases of later GMPs to be linked with a reduction of the scope to a strongly focalized element. In four cases, this is beyond any doubt because of the presence of a focus particle, e.g. in (3):

[5] The Wackernagel movement is a hypothetical cross-linguistic generalization of the "Wackernagel Law" first identified in 1892 in Indo-European languages, mainly Greek. According to this law, clitics – above all pronominal elements – tend to concentrate behind the finite verbal form. This concentration is often described as a "movement" due to its origin in diachronic (Indo-European) linguistics as an explanation for the emergence of verb-front structures with accumulation of enclitics. Even though Germanic languages are among those where phenomena corresponding to this law can be observed, no "movement" can be attested in synchrony.

[6] As opposed to the logical account proposed by Zemb (1978, 1984).

(3) Die Hilfsorganisationen, sie legen sehr viel Wert auf Unabhängigkeit und sie führen ihre Erfolge *ja* auch auf diese Unabhängigkeit zurück (DLF 22.07.2010)

Sie führ-en	ihr-e	Erfolg-e	*ja*	auch
they lead-3PL	their-ACC.PL	success-PL	*ja*	too

auf dies-e	Un-abhängig-keit	zurück
to this-ACC.FEM	in-dependent-NMLZ	back(CVB)

"The relief organizations are very much attached (lit. "attach much value") to their independence and they bring their successes in connection *ja* to this independence, *as well.*"

Another example illustrates that reduction of scope to the mere following adjunct or argument, namely a sentence where *ja* occurs twice, once with propositional scope and once with reduced scope:

(4) Nun bietet sich *ja* eine Erklärung für die vielen Naturereignisse *ja* geradezu an, und nicht erst seit heute. (DRK 12.08.2010)

Nun biet-et=sich=*ja*	ein-e	Erklärung
now offer-3SG=REFL=*ja*	INDEF:ART-NOM.FEM.SG	explanation

für d-ie	viel-en	Natur-ereigniss-e
for the-ACC.PL	many-ACC.PL	nature-event-PL

ja=geradezu	an
ja=immediately	CVB

"Now, there is (lit. "proposes itself") *ja* an explanation for the many natural phenomena *ja* immediately, and [this] not just since today."

In six of the other seven cases, the GMP is placed immediately before a post-verbal subject, as in (5):

(5) Das Hamburger Debakel in der Abstimmung über die Schulreform verantwortet *ja* eine grüne Kultusministerin! (DLF 20.07.2010)

D-as	Hamburg-er	Debakel	in d-er Abstimmung über die
he-ACC.N	H.-ADJ	disaster	in th-DAT.FEM vote on the-ACC.

Schul-reform	verantwort-et=*ja*
school-reform	be.responsible.for-3SG=*ja*

ein-e	grün-e	Kultus-minister-in!
INDEF.ART-NOM.FEM	green-NOM.FEM	culture-minister-FEM

"It's [notoriously] a Green culture minister who is responsible for the disaster with the vote on school reform in Hamburg!"

The last example, which even some native speakers would judge unacceptable, is a sentence where the particle occurs before the final, non-finite verb form, which itself introduces indirect speech. Since it is a passive sentence with an empty subject, one can assume that the verb form is the single element transmitting new information:

(6) ?Es wurde nach den Anschlägen in New York *ja* festgestellt, dass man einen erweiterten Sicherheitsbegriff ansetzen muss. (DLF 22.07.2010)[7]

Es wurde-Ø	nach d-en Anschlag-¨e-n	in NY
it PASS:PAST-3G	after the-DAT.PL attack-PL-DAT	in NY

ja=fest-ge-stell-t,	dass…
ja=CVB-PTCP-set-PTCP	COMP…

"After the terrorist attacks in New York, it was *ja* remarked that one had to resort to a broadened security concept."

The results from our small corpus support the thesis that *ja* is properly speaking at the juncture or theme and rheme, therefore at the heart of the *pheme*. When the scope of GMPs is global, they cliticize at the end of the verbal phrase: Their position corresponds to the default value of the

---

[7] It might also be relevant to remind here that for Zemb (1984), tense adjuncts are thematic per default and are generally placed before the pheme.

theme/rheme boundary, exemplified by the global negation *nicht*. Cases of scope reduction are always linked to a reduction of the rheme. Correspondingly, cliticization no longer occurs at the default position but, iconically, at the beginning of the focal field. Thus, there appears to be a strong correlation between the position of GMPs inside the clause and the marking of informational structure, viz. the modal status of the new information conveyed in the proposition. Together with the cliticized form of GMPs, these regularities suggest that GMPs, in contrast to their non-modal cognates, are grammaticalized markers and that they encode propositional attitudes and CG updating. Thus, they seem to pertain to epistemic modality. Moreover, their place in the topology of the German sentence relates them to markers of propositional attitudes such as *leider* ("unfortunately"), evidential adverbs such as *offensichtlich* ("manifestedly") or other sentence adverbs such as *vielleicht* ("maybe"), which also appear at the juncture of theme and rheme and represent the different types of modality. Those features seem to converge and invite us to regard GMPs as proper modal markers.

2.2 A case for reductionism

Considering this topological and prosodic base, we can now ask whether all the usage values identified for a given GMP can be subsumed under one modal feature. Unlike what many accounts postulate, we assume that modal reductionism should be privileged. In this perspective, epistemological covertness becomes a major factor to account for apparent counterarguments. The standard felicity conditions for an utterance containing a proposition under the scope of *ja* are well-described: Both speech act participants have to agree about the propositional content, *p*. The nature of that consensus is still a matter of debate and it remains unclear if both speech act participants have to know *p* or if the speaker just expects the hearer not to contradict her. Adapting recent reflections on the so-called "distribution of propositional alternatives" (see Paillard 2009), according to which every proposition is located in a system of possible oppositions and alternatives, we opt for the following definition:

(7) DEF *ja* (*p*): any alternative $\neg p$ to *p* has already been excluded from the paradigm of contextually possible propositions pre-existing between the speech act participants before the assertion of *p*.

In other words, *ja*-assertions implicate *p* to be without any possible alternative in the CG (or much rather: it implies no propositions $\neg p$ to be normally derivable from the CG). In contrast to this, standard illocutions are felicitous when the speaker is ruling out $\neg p$ from the CG by the very act of asserting *p*. An even more radical solution would be to dub *ja* (*p*) as the marker for the absence of real CG-updating when *p* is asserted, since the possibility of $\neg p$ is supposed to have already been ruled out by both the speaker and the hearer. Thus, we are rather supportive of accounts focusing on the absence of contradiction, whereas interpretations where *p* is already known are not to be ruled out: They just represent a special case. Consequently, *ja* can be described as a marker of strong commitment involving both speech act participants. Corpus examples confirm that general intuition: The GMP *ja* is often used in sentences whose propositional content is a proverb or is presented as obvious or self-evident. There is also a strong compatibility with generic sentences.

(8) Zeit ist *ja* bekanntlich relativ. (DRK 12.08.2010)
Zeit ist *ja* bekannt-lich relativ
time is *ja* known-ADV relative
"Time is relative, as everybody knows."

(9) Recht haben und Recht bekommen sind *ja* immer zweierlei (DRK 29.07.2010)
Recht hab-en und Recht bekomm-en sind *ja* immer zweier-lei
right have-INF and right receive-INF are *ja* always two-ADV
"To be right and to get one's rights are notoriously not the same."

The claim defended here is that it is possible to derive all contextual and external values which can be assigned to *ja* (*p*) from that one modal feature. We consider an external value (EV) to have been reduced to an internal one (IV) if it is possible to decompose EV into the combination of IV with a predictable pragmatic bias B. B does not alter the semantics of the item, but can explain how any linguistic sign bearing the semantic feature IV is likely to occur in contexts triggering the implicature of EV. For instance, we can trivially derive the privilege of sentences where *p* is already known by both speech act participants from definition (7), which is restricted to the absence of contradiction. The assertion of reciprocal strong commitment has very peculiar truth conditions: The speaker not only has to be sure of *p*, but also of the hearer's attitude to *p*. If the speaker expects the hearer not to contradict her, she must have concrete evidence leading her to that assumption, and the status of *p* as a notorious part of the CG or as a self-evident truth would be an extremely reliable reason for such an assumption. Thus, sentences where *p* is already known by both speech act participants are most likely to be felicitous under the scope of *ja*. Nevertheless, this has nothing to do with modality nor with the core meaning of *ja*, but it is the contingent consequence of an external bias.

Most other values of *ja* can be inferred from the internal modal feature when it is combined with conversational hazards, especially with the maxim of quantity as Grice (1975) puts it. For instance, corpus studies signal a frequent use of *ja (p)* in contexts where *p* is clearly backgrounded and presented as the mere base for further developments, as in (10).

(10) Es gibt *ja* auch den Vorschlag, Medikamente erst mal vorläufig zuzulassen. Wäre das eine Möglichkeit? (BR, Samstagsforum 12.06.2010)

Es ge<i>b-t=*ja* auch d-en Vorschlag,
it give<3SG.PRES>-3SG=*ja* too the-ACC.MASC proposal,

Medikament-e erst-mal vorläufig zu-zu-lassen.
medicament-PL first-time provisory into-INF-let.

"There is *ja* also the possibility to authorize medicaments temporarily at first. Would that be a possibility?"

It is thus a textual theme. Yet, we do not need to postulate the existence of a "backgrounding particle" or a "thematic particle" *ja*, even though that would be perfectly possible under a strict externalist perspective. We can propose reduction in three steps:

(i) It is trivial that the felicity conditions of *ja*-utterances are exactly what should make those utterances irregular according to Grice's principles.
(ii) We can expect a consensual proposition to be rather on the background than on the foreground of the conversation, due to its lack of conversational relevance.
(iii) If *ja* scopes over propositions being such matters of consensus, then there is no wonder to see that *ja* occurs very often in situations where *p* is backgrounded. Thus, it is superfluous to postulate a specific value, since the core feature exhausts the meaning and the pragmatics of the problematic examples. There is consequently no need to specify the value of *ja* beyond that of a marker of assumed shared commitment between speaker and hearer.

So far, there is no real problem of epistemological covertness, since the value of *ja* as a thematic particle has apparently never been advocated for in the literature. Yet, other cases where a reduction would also be possible seem to present greater difficulties, most notably the so-called "exclamatory *ja*". This last type is all too often presented as distinct from the "usual" modal value. This leads to the division of *ja* into two GMPs with different semantic features according to the illocutionary type of the utterance: An assertion type modifier, corresponding to what we have seen so far (ASSERT*ja*), is being opposed to an exclamation marker (EXCL*ja*). Even though this distinction might look relevant, we argue that it relies on an external, pragmatic bias. Here, too, a reduction similar the one proposed for (10) is perfectly possible. Meanwhile, it should not be overseen that the alternative between a mono- and a polysemic account is directly relevant for the issue of covert modality: If the distinction between ASSERT*ja* and EXCL*ja* is to be maintained, then *ja* is not primarily a modal marker, but a marker of illocutive force. If a common function is postulated for both forms in this dual perspective, the illocutive force can hardly be defined with respect to the distribution of knowledge but, much more vaguely, in terms of vivification or expressivity. According to such accounts, the modal value of ASSERT*ja* would necessarily be a secondary phenomenon without clear explanation, so that both usages remain basically irreducible and divided along purely pragmatic lines. This would make a unified modal account impossible. Polysemic, illocutionary-based depictions of *ja* include above all the first works on this topic, especially by Harald Weydt (see for instance Hentschel/Weydt 1994: 283).[8]

(11)	Du	bist ja	ein guter Koch!
	du	bist=*ja*	ein-Ø gut-er Koch!
	you	be:2SG:PRES=*ja*	INDEF.ART-NOM good-NOM.MASC cook!
	"You're *ja* a good cook!"		

Under this perspective, what we gloss EXCL*ja* is supposed to be part of a distinct sub-system of exclamatory particles together with *vielleicht* and *aber*. For Weydt, *ja* is the exclamatory particle par excellence, whereas *aber* and *vielleicht* mark the quantitative resp. qualitative origin of the surprise. Thus, EXCL*ja* would be a marker of exclamatory illocution and could be compared with the prosodic pattern of exclamatory sentences in

[8] Weydt (e.g. Hentschel/Weydt 1994:283) seems to be perfectly aware of the premises implied by such a qualification, if we consider the fact that he has preferred using the term *Abtönungspartikel* rather *modal particle* since his 1969 work.

German, which play the same role of sentence type marker. There are indeed arguments for such a reading. The comparison between (10) and (11) reveals one similar feature: In both sentences, *p* is a matter of consensus since no further contestation is expected. Yet, there is also a great difference: In (11), this no-contestation rule is linked to the sheer lack of interaction with the hearer. Apparently, no general agreement is necessary between the speech act participants: The fact that $\neg p$ is ruled out could just be related to the logical base of any assertion ["if *p*, then $\neg(\neg p)$"] rather than to definition (7). This is especially true if we regard exclamations as expressions of surprise, as is the case in Hentschel/Weydt 1994. Under this view, the distinction of both particles seems to be confirmed. Yet, following Olbertz (2009), we can distinguish mirativity from exclamation: Exclamation pertains to an expressive function of language whose main value is to highlight the speaker's own propositional stance on the proposition – it is thus a highly pragmatic category (Olbertz calls exclamation a type of illocution). Mirativity, on its turn, is a semantic category. It deals with the proposition's inferability in context. Mirative forms mark surprise and are not restricted to exclamative sentences: In some languages, "mirativity can be expressed in both declarative and interrogative utterances" (Olbertz 2009:71). Thus, the so-called "exclamatory *ja*", if it is defined by a semantic feature of "surprise", as assumed by Hentschel/Weydt, needs not be an exclamatory morpheme. It is much rather a "mirative particle". This shows that we have to better distinguish between the value of the illocutive type and that of the particle, and thus to determine whether the difference between (10) and (11) can be reduced to that between assertion and exclamation. If this reduction to the sole opposition of illocutionary types provides a sufficient account for the difference between (10) and (11), then the alleged mirative feature of the particle would prove to be an illusion resulting from the confusion between exclamation and mirativity, and the non-contestation feature shared by both (10) and (11) could become predominant for the analysis of *ja*. This would pave the way to a unified account. Such a reductionist assumption is encouraged by the comparison of (10) and (11) with (10b) and (11b), where the GMP is lacking. The difference in terms of "interaction-friendliness" is roughly the same with and without the GMP:

(10b) Es gibt auch den Vorschlag, Medikamente erst mal vorläufig zuzulassen. Wäre das eine Möglichkeit? (BR, Samstagsforum 12.06.2010)

Es ge<i>b-t auch d-en Vorschlag,
it give<3SG.PRES>-3SG too the-ACC.MASC proposal,

Medikament-e erst-mal vorläufig zu-zu-lassen.
medicament-PL first-time provisory into-INF-let.

"There is also the possibility to authorize medicaments temporarily at first. Would that be a possibility?"

(11b) Du bist ein guter Koch!
Du bist Ø ein-Ø gut-er Koch!
you be:2SG:PRES a good-NOM.MASC cook!
"You're a good cook (indeed)!"

Assuming that the hearer's viewpoint in (11) is backgrounded, and that this backgrounding is preserved in (11b), then the difference between (10) and (11) resp. (10b) and (11b) might just be a question of sentence type. We are now provided with a hypothesis for the reduction of EXCL*ja* to the particle defined under (7): The specific features attributed to the particle result from the combination of the modal meaning of *ja* with the illocutive idiosyncrasies of exclamation. The first consequence of this assumption is the necessity to correct the definition (7) in order to be able to combine it with several illocutionary types.

Considering that GMPs encode propositional attitudes related to the distribution of knowledge, it is possible to imagine a characterization of the two interacting viewpoints as purely informative roles. One plausible characterization would be "a speech act participant in charge with the main assertion of the modal evaluation of *p*" vs. "a speech act participant in respect to whose propositional stance the evaluation of *p* has to be situated". For reasons of convenience, they will henceforth be called the "holder" and the "interpreter".[9] We assume no additional constraint on the

[9] Those instances should be taken as idealizations. The term of *interpreter* should be taken as an allusion to Davidson's theory of the "triangulation of knowledge" introduced for the study of epistemicity by Leiss (2008). The interpreter is not primarily the empirical, external second person of interaction but much rather she is the representation of a real or possible counterpart of the holder by the holder herself (Theory of Mind), and our whole study aims at showing that she is not a

instantiation of those roles into the respective speech act participants, most notably on the number of speech act participants involved. This instantiation occurs along different lines depending on the illocutionary type of the sentence: In an assertive utterance, the holder is the speaker and the interpreter is the hearer. Those roles are inverted in a question. Given what we have seen about the expressive function of exclamation as an interaction-unfriendly type of illocution having to do with the speaker's regulation of her own propositional stances, it follows that in exclamatory utterances, the speaker can play both roles (holder and interpreter), whereas the hearer is just a possible, non-necessary candidate for the role of interpreter. We can now correct (7) into (12):

(12) DEF *ja*(*p*): any alternative $\neg p$ to *p* has already been excluded from the paradigm of contextually possible propositions pre-existing between the speech act participants before the assertion of *p*: the holder asserts the truth of *p* and assumes the interpreter not to disagree with her.

This new definition allows us to proceed to the reduction: First, we have to concentrate on the characteristics of exclamation as a highly expressive type in which the speaker comments upon her own propositional stance. In such an illocutive pattern, *ja*(*p*) is possible for two reasons: (i) It would mark the speaker's strong commitment to *p* and highlight the fact that her personal conviction is strong enough to provide *p* with the status of an intersubjectively valid assertion: The speaker claims both epistemic roles for herself; (ii) It would be highly compatible with the expressive (self-mirroring) function of that utterance type. At this stage, the reduction is fulfilled: If *ja* occurs in an exclamatory sentence, both epistemic roles are played by the speaker. This yields the value which is traditionally attributed to the particle EXCL*ja*. Far from undermining the modal accounts for GMPs, the case of *ja* is therefore a good example for the necessity to radicalize our modal readings by purging them of their pragmatic elements. In this respect, we can say that pragmatic roles recover the epistemic ones and are an epistemological obstacle. We can now move to the non-epistemological, structural aspect of modal covertness.

---

secondary figure but a primary point of the epistemic system of coordinates as the holder. Of course, the holder herself is the interpreter's interpreter.

3. The metamorphoses of *wohl*

We now focus on *wohl* ("well"). When it is not a GMP, *wohl* can occur as a lexical item with the meaning of its English cognate "well":

(13) Das hast du *wohl* gemacht!

Das	ha(b)-Ø-st	du	*wohl*	ge-mach-t
this	have-PRST-2SG	2SG	*well*	PCTP-do-PTCP

"This is well done!"

In the following, we base on the distinction between knowledge-holder and knowledge-interpreter to make the following distinction: Whereas *ja* points to the interpreter of the asserted propositional content, the assertive value of *wohl* is always centered on the epistemic standpoint of the knowledge-holder. This means that the most prominent semantic feature of *wohl* is not related to intersubjective alignment, but the modal evaluation of the proposition by the knowledge-holder. We defend the thesis that this difference can account for the apparent plurality of meanings of *wohl* under a reductionist perspective.

3.1 Weaknesses of the mainstream account

The second GMP we are faced with, *wohl* is a much more complex case. Traditionally, the literature on GMPs presents two particles identified as *wohl*. They are not strictly homonymous because of a prosodic difference: The stressed *wohl* (14) is supposed to highlight the status of the proposition as common shared knowledge, whereas the unstressed particle (15) is a weak commitment marker sometimes compared to a sentence adverb.[10]

[10] An argument for such a reading would be the possibility to use *wohl* in preverbal position with a meaning very close to that of the weak commitment marker. Yet, postulating an identity between both forms, which would make a sentence adverb of the second *wohl*, is problematic given the fact that preverbal *wohl* normally occurs when p is followed by another proposition *q* linked to *p* by an adversative marker, typically *aber*, so that it can also be supposed that *wohl* ... *aber* ... is a grammaticalized form of its own, having lost its synchronic link to the GMP, even though this link is certainly real in diachrony.

(14) Von Oktober bis März ist *wohl* primär Winterreifenzeit. (BR 17.10.2009)

Von Oktober bis März	ist=*wohl*
from October to March	be:3SG:PRES=*wohl*

primär	Winter-reifen-zeit
primarily	winter-tyre-time.

"Clearly, from October to March, it's basically time for winter tyres."

(15) Das ist sehr komplex, aber es sollen *wohl* die meisten Geldautomaten von der Chip-Erkennung auf die Erkennung des Magnet-Streifens umgestellt worden sein. BR 09.01.2010

Es=sollen=*wohl*	[die meisten Geldautomaten]
EXPL=should=*wohl*	[most of the cash dispensers]

um-<ge>-stell-<t>	worden sein
converted<PART>	AUX.PASS.PERF be.

"This is very complex, but most of the cash dispensers are apparently supposed to have already been converted from chip recognition to magnetic recognition"

As Abraham (1991) notices, the meaning of the first GMP can easily be derived from the core lexeme because a modal reinterpretation of "well" would be expected to have a strong corroborative value. Unfortunately, the path to a weak commitment marker is not so obvious. Yet, this dichotomy can be criticized for at least two reasons:

(i) The distinction between stressed and unstressed items presupposes clear criteria of what lexical accent should be. In German, lexical, pragmatic and syntactic accent are all a combination of pitch, intensity and length variation. This formal identity makes it difficult to rule out the hypothesis that the difference could be a matter of contrastive (pragmatic) and not of lexical accent. As we shall see later, the hypothesis of a prosodic focus could lead more easily to a unified account.

(ii) To our knowledge, there is no example of clearly stressed *wohl* with a weak commitment value. Yet, there are examples of sentences where *wohl* does not exhibit the weak commitment feature even though it seems difficult to identify it with the stressed particle.

This suggests that the unstressed *wohl* can mark both stances. One of those examples can be found in Stefan Zweig's short story *The Star above the Forest* (*Der Stern über dem Walde*). Even though the source is a written text, the prosodic status of the particle seems to be relatively clear since most native speakers would be reluctant to set an accent on *wohl* here:

(16) Er strich nach dem Souper über die zerknüllten Tischtuchfalten vor ihrem Platze mit so zärtlichen und kosenden Fingern, wie man *wohl* liebe und weichruhende Frauenhände streichelt.

…wie man *wohl*	lieb-e	und	weich-ruh-end-e
…how one *wohl*	loved-ACC.PL	and	light-rest-PRS.PTCP-ACC.PL

Frauen-hand-¨e	streichel-t.
woman-hand-PL	caress-3SG

"After dinner, he stroke the crumpled folds of the tablecloth before her sit with so sweet and delicate fingers, such as one caresses *wohl* only beloved and gentle women hands."

Zweig is alluding to something he presents as general knowledge (cf. the use of *man*, "one", and the use of present tense with the value of a general truth): The felicity conditions and the degree of commitment are very close to what we would know from *ja*. Indeed, *ja* would also be felicitous here, even though the epistemic coloration would be slightly different. Another example comes from the very famous ballad by Heine, *Die Grenadiere*, where supposing weak commitment would lead to a radical misunderstanding of the text. The poem is centered on the blind faith of a dying soldier convinced that Napoleon will come back once. The last line of the following gloss shows the metric pattern of the verse, with 0 standing for unstressed syllables and 1 for stressed ones, confirming that there is no stress on *wohl*.

(17) So will ich liegen und horchen still,
Wie eine Schildwacht, im Grabe,
Bis einst ich höre Kanonengebrüll,
Und wiehernder Rosse Getrabe.

<u>Dann</u> reitet mein Kaiser *wohl* über mein Grab,
Viel Schwerter klirren und blitzen;
Dann steig' ich gewaffnet hervor aus dem Grab –
Den Kaiser, den Kaiser zu schützen.

Dann	reit-et	mein-Ø	Kaiser	*wohl*	über
then	ride-3SG	my-NOM.MASC	emperor	*wohl*	over
0 1	0	0	1 0	0	1 0

mein-Ø	Grab
my-ACC.NEUTR	tomb
0	1

„So I want to lie and to hear in silence, just as a sentinel, in my grave, til once I can hear canonades and the noise of neighing horses. (§) **<u>Then</u> my Emperor is *wohl* riding above my grave**, many swords are tinkling and clashing, then I'm standing up, already armed, and leaving my grave, to protect my Emperor, my Emperor."

Both examples (16) and (17) suggest that *wohl(p)* can mark a consensual status of *p*. Consequently, *wohl* can present a bi-affirmative value such as *ja*. Yet, it is undisputable that most of the time, the "unstressed" *wohl* corresponds to a lower degree of commitment. Thus, we should select the "strong commitment" value of *wohl* as the basic internal feature and derive the lower degree of commitment from the higher one. For this goal, two postulates are introduced:

(i) *Wohl* has only one internal modal value, marking the acceptability of *p* for both the holder and the interpreter, viz. the speaker and the hearer.

(ii) The place of *wohl* within the system of GMPs is made epistemologically unclear by a silent (i.e. structurally covert) evidential value. The interpretation in terms of weak commitment, yielding a secondary modal value, is an external, context-bound bias proceeding from the structurally covert evidential value as well as from cross-linguistically attested rules of pragmatic bleaching.

3.2 Delayed validation and epistemic roles

The key to the explanation of those phenomena can be found in the analysis of Zimmermann (2008:205ff.), corroborated by corpus data collected by Kwon (2005:166-171):

> First, we find that the epistemic reference point of *wohl* in declarative clauses is the speaker (cf. Abraham 1991). This means that ***wohl*** in declaratives expresses uncertainty on the part of the speaker. (...) The picture changes with interrogatives. Here, the epistemic reference point of *wohl* is undetermined as long as it is not the speaker alone. Rather, an interrogative clause containing *wohl* indicates that the addressee does not know the answer for sure. (Zimmermann 2008:205)

(18) Was ist *wohl* die Hauptstadt von Tansania?
Was ist=*wohl* d-ie Haupt-stadt von T.?
what be.3SG.PRES=*wohl* the-NOM.FEM head-city of T.?
"What do you presume is the capital of Tanzania?"
(quoted after Zimmermann 2008:206)

In line with the information-distributional categories sketched for *ja*, we can describe the semantics of *wohl* as follows: In *wohl(p)*, the epistemic standpoint of the interpreter is constructed only secondarily; fundamentally, *wohl* encodes the epistemic standpoint of the knowledge-holder, whereas *ja* is oriented to the interpreter. This orientation to the holder could also explain why the meaning of *wohl* is perceived as less polyphonic as that of *ja*: *Wohl* is much more introverted. The same is true for the corresponding non-modal lexemes: *Wohl* deals with the degree of relevance of the proposition itself, whereas *ja* is a yes-interjection. Therefore, *wohl* is rather oriented to the proposition and *ja* rather to its intersubjective validity: The key concept here is that of Theory of Mind (ToM), which stands for the alignment of the speaker on the supposed propositional attitude of others, and more especially of the hearer (see Abraham 2010 for discussion). In the case of *wohl*, the representation of the interpreter's ToM is constructed secondarily from the idea of strong commitment: Objective or third-personal truth can be interpreted as acceptable to the "second person" (cf. Davidson 2001). Given its core lexical meaning, the primary modal meaning of *wohl* is probably a rather speaker-oriented confirmation (e.g. of *p* meeting some truth-conditional requirements). Besides, as Kwon

(2005:167) points out, unstressed *wohl* is often used in questions to orient the hearer's answer (to a *yes* in a standard question, to a *no* in an interro-negative sentence). This suggests that *wohl* marks the holder's commitment to *p*.

Such an orientation is a very favorable ground for evidentiality, for reasons linked to pragmatic implicatures. Once again, we can resort to the conversational rules postulated by Grice (1975): The Gricean maxim of quality entails the assumption that the speaker is strongly committing herself to *p* when there are no other overt indications. On a commitment scale, the default value is high. As a consequence, expressions coding this strong commitment tend to be structurally redundant: According to the rule of quantity, they should be avoided. Therefore, highlighting one's commitment could undermine the idea that *commitment to* p *should have been self-evident*. To put it in a more casual way, if a marker suggests explicitly that the holder believes in what she says, then this means that the truth of the propositional content was (to say the least) not self-evident. Either there might have been reasons not to believe it, or the reasons for such a belief are not beyond any doubt. This feature paves the way to inferential semantics. The question is now whether we can find empirical data confirming this hypothesis.

3.3 A compositional account for covert evidentiality

3.3.1 Restrictions of selection

According to the reductionist hypothesis, the interpretation of *wohl* as a weak commitment marker can be accounted for thanks to covert evidentiality. The weak commitment feature need not be present in the core meaning of the morpheme. This claim can explain some tendencies which are left uncommented in mainstream literature. If *wohl* reinforces the speaker's commitment to the proposition that would be left unasserted without the use of the GMP, we can expect *wohl* to take primarily irrealis propositions in its scope.[11] Indeed, Grimm's dictionary (Vol. 30, 1062) already pointed at this tendency, which is confirmed in our small corpus: *Wohl* preferably scopes over future, conditional or hypothetic propositions; it is also very frequently used in sentences containing a modal verb. In those sentences, *wohl* validates *p* as acceptable even though the proposition

[11] Future tense as well as conditional and hypothetic constructions can be associated with an irrealis modal meaning. Consequently, they are representative for the class of propositions over which we suppose *wohl* to scope in the cases where a "weak commitment"-interpretation occurs.

does not rely on direct evidence but rather on individual reckoning of inference. This is conform to what we could predict from the Gricean bias just described: Commitment is mediated by reflection, hearsay or inference. This is the point where we can postulate covert evidentiality within modality. Among 11 sentences with unstressed *wohl*-forms, 6 had a modal verb, 2 an epistemic adverb and 2 were at the future tense. Moreover, the last one dealt with rumors about unpublished opinion polls, representing the other context typical for evidential marking: hearsay.

(19) Aber es geht ja *wohl* eher bergab, nicht bergauf. Die Zeitung schreibt „unter 40 Prozent". (DLF 27.07.2010)

Aber	es geh-t=ja=*wohl*	eher berg-ab,	
but	it go-3SG=ja=*wohl*	rather mountain-downwards,	

nicht berg-auf.
not mountain-upwards.

"But manifestedly, it seems to go rather downwards, not upwards. The paper writes 'under 40 percent'."

Remember also the example by Heine (17): *p* is undoubtedly an inference from *q*, namely from the fact that the speaker hears the Emperor's horse. The example by Zweig (16) resorts to a general truth with an impersonal subject, a context which is far from any direct cognitive accessibility of evidence – the criterion in respect to which evidentiality is constructed in German and in many other languages.[12] This suggests that the unstressed *wohl* is part of an evidential pattern: "strong commitment + no direct evidence" means "inferential". More specifically, inferentiality can be marked by a construction "strong commitment + irrealis".

Thus, weak commitment is simply a possibility induced by pragmatic implicatures. It is realized only if the proposition is already deprived of the default value of strong commitment. The example from Zweig (16) shows that a proposition without any peculiar restriction of commitment can also

[12] Haumann & Letnes (this volume) detect a strong bias towards evidential interpretations of *wohl(p)* in their study based on translations into Norwegian and English. Their examples also show two strong preferences for the proposition under *wohl*: on the one hand and as we have just seen, irrealis marking, and on the other hand many propositions having to do with Theory of Mind and conjectures on other people's propositional attitudes, which are always part of indirect knowledge since they can only be inferred from observed behaviour.

be selected by *wohl* and does not suffer any degradation. On the other hand, the example by Heine (17) shows that an irrealis proposition, when it is marked by *wohl*, can gain a strong epistemic status. In other words, neither weak commitment nor inferential marking are part of the stable meaning of the unstressed *wohl*. Weak commitment is just an irregular external implicature, whereas the inferential status is constituted by the presence of a strong commitment marker scoping over an irrealis proposition. The frequency of that evidential meaning is due to pragmatic regularities (the mentioned Gricean rules) entailing a selection privilege for irrealis clauses under the scope of *wohl*. This is the reason why we can speak of covert evidentiality within modality here: There is nothing evidential in the core meaning of *wohl*, nor in the fact that a proposition is marked as irrealis, but the co-construction of both appears to be an evidential pattern in German. In a narrow meaning, we can even say that the hypothesis (ii) formulated in 2.1. goes too far: there is no "silent evidential value" in *wohl*: This covert evidentiality is already interpreted from a construction. Now, this presupposes that the core modal meaning of *wohl* has been left intact. A first argument for this affirmation is delivered by (16) and (17), which prove that the core meaning can still be present without restrictions. Thus, we are faced with a two-stage interpretation process: The first stage corresponds to the covert inferential pattern and the second to the implicature of weak commitment on the basis of inferentiality. This suggests that in the case of *wohl*, we are not faced with structural silent categories, but with two layers of epistemological covertness.

3.3.2 Strong commitment defended; prosodic aspects

Our thesis is that *wohl* reinforces the speaker's commitment to irrealis propositions: In the contexts we are faced with, modality appears at several morphologic and syntactic levels and there can be important interactions between them; *wohl* is generally used either in a proposition in an irrealis tense (future, subjunctive II) or in co-construction with a modal verb (*x soll / muss / mag wohl* p) which is already carrying a dimension of epistemic distance to the propositional content of *p*.

(20) Der dich so anrührte, musz *wohl* der könig und dein bräutigam selber sein, sonst hätte ers nimmer gewagt. (Grimm Dictionary, 30:1062)

D-er	d-ich so	an-rühr-te-Ø,
REL-NOM.MASC	2SG-ACC so	CVB-touch-PAST-3SG

muss=*wohl*	d-er König [...] sein.
must=*wohl*	the-NOM.MASC king [...] be.

"He who touched you so, must *wohl* be the king and your groom himself, else he wouldn't have dared it."

The higher scope of the particle tends to suggest that the particle here legitimates the assumption (*wohl(mag(p))* = one has to take it into account that it is possible that *p*). Actually, the meaning of *wohl* has not changed. What has been altered is the set of conditions for the selection of *p*, which tends to be restricted to irrealis propositions. We have explained how a unified modal account of *wohl* as a strong commitment marker oriented to the knowledge holder can pave the way to silent evidentiality and often (but not always)[13] trigger the assertive weakening in conversational context.

We have not considered the stressed *wohl* so far, so that we now have to ask two questions: (i) Is a unified account for both particles possible, given that there is no trace of evidentiality in the stressed form? (ii) How can the latter difference be accounted for? As can be inferred from what has already been said, we take the modal-evidential account for *wohl* to be compatible with a unified semantic description of *wohl*. It is even the best way to succeed in such an attempt. Since we reduced so-called weak commitment to covert, compositional evidentiality involving the selection of irrealis propositions, we just have to explain how the path to this selectional privilege can be blocked. We have seen that this path is linked to Grice's laws. For the purpose of unifying the semantics of *wohl*, we propose the following thesis: We regard this evolution as a case of pragmatic bleaching, whereas the stressed *wohl* is the naked modal form with its original meaning. Now, we can observe that (i) the form preserved from bleaching is also the one which bears an accent and (ii) there is no difference between the phonetic realizations of pragmatic and lexical

[13] The irregularity of this implicature is itself a sign that those interpretations are biased by questions of contextual salience and should rather not be integrated to the internal semantic make-up of the GMP.

accent in German.[14] A pragmatic accent would focus on the hearer's attention to the holder's modal evaluation of *p* as a mutually acceptable proposition. In this case, prosodic focus can preserve the original meaning of *wohl*. On the other hand, the absence of such a prosodic focus has left the way free for a restriction of selection to irrealis propositions. This hypothesis could be supported by cross-linguistic data: In French, sentence adverbs coding commitment such as *sans doute* "undoubtedly" or *sûrement* "certainly" are generally admitted to mark the fact that the speaker refuses to endorse *p* as a personal certitude – *sans doute* even represents the contrary of its compositional meaning, namely the fact that there are some doubts about the validity of *p*. The same is true for German, where *zweifelsohne* "without doubt" and *bestimmt* "certainly" are often subject to the same pragmatic weakening. If we look at the precise meaning of *sans doute* or *sûrement*, we nevertheless have to consider two restrictions: (i) Those markers have kept their strong commitment value when they are focused upon, especially with a pragmatic accent or as sentence-equivalent. (ii) Even when they bear no accent, they do not just mark weak commitment. They also add *p* to the CG under the restriction that the speaker has no direct access to the evidence. In other words, *sans doute (p)* marks the fact that *p* is an assumption per default: either a postulate or a proposition that seems to be more plausible than any $\neg p$. *p* is signaled to have been validated only after a phase of mental reckoning considering possible alternatives. The pragmatic implicature "weak commitment" is due to the fact that such a reckoning phase is possible only if the proposition would have failed to match the standard for the default level of strong commitment, i.e. if *p* would have been left unasserted without the intervention of the modal and inferential marker. We regard such a phenomenon as strictly parallel to what happened to *wohl* – therefore explaining the similarities of that particle with sentence adverbs.

3.4 Different semantic levels: the compositional solution

Far from undermining the modal account of *wohl*, the stressed particle rather confirms the assumptions made before. The overall semantics of *wohl* can be depicted as follows:

[14] Both rely on a similar elevation of pitch and intensity (see section 2.1.).

(i) The modal conversion of "well" entails the emergence of a GMP marking the fact that *p* matches the requirements of validity in the eyes of the knowledge-holder. Thus, *p* is supposed to be objectively acceptable. The logical consequence of this is that the interpreter is supposed to share such a positive epistemic attitude to *p*, third-personal truth being defined as truth accessible for other minds. This is the core semantic value of *wohl*, which is completely preserved in accentuated uses.

(ii) When *wohl* is not focused upon, the main informative value of the utterance is in the proposition. But given the felicity conditions of a *wohl*-marked proposition, this contradicts with Grice's laws: The speech act is felicitous iff *p* is a proposition whose truth value had not been asserted yet. This entails a restriction of selection: When it is under the scope of the unstressed *wohl*, *p* is preferably a proposition for which no evidence is directly accessible to the knowledge-holder. This corresponds to irrealis semantics. Thus, the modal morpheme marks commitment to propositions with an inferential status: Covert evidentiality appears within modality. There is neither grammaticalization nor diachronic change in the sense of Construction Grammar here: The meaning of *wohl* is still the same and the restriction of selection is synchronic and partly external, so that *wohl* + *irrealis* is not a grammaticalized "evidential construct": Strong modal commitment to a proposition for which there is no accessible evidence is the very definition of an inference or of a postulate. In sum, evidentiality here can be gained in a strictly compositional way.

(iii) An external, conversational bias derives weak commitment from inferential marking. Such a bias is context-bound and not part of the primary value of the GMP. *Wohl* is an affirmative modal marker which frequently occurs in co-construction with irrealis propositions because of conversational regularities. This causes a covert evidential meaning.

4. Conclusion

We can notice that we are faced with several types of covertness: First, *wohl* presents the epistemological covertness we had already been faced with in the case of *ja*, where the plurality of external uses and constructions seemed to cast a shadow on strict modal values. The external meaning of "weak commitment" is recovering both the compositional inferential meaning and the core modal value, which are nevertheless at the basis of the whole interpretation. Second, evidentiality and modality are shown to be intimately interwoven: Evidentiality can be gained compositionally out of a primarily modal pattern. The ubiquitousness of modality and evidentiality is exemplified by the fact that inferential meaning can be expressed in a construction involving a grammaticalized modal enclitic combined with a semantic feature of the proposition, namely an irrealis status – i.e. another modal feature. This irrealis value is sometimes marked overtly (e.g. by a conditional tense) but sometimes it has to be inferred out of the logical implications of the context. Another feature interacting in the construction of modal meaning is the sentence type: In the case of *ja*, we saw that the core modal meaning of the clitic becomes epistemologically opaque if it is combined with an exclamatory sentence. The variations of *wohl* also rely on whether the GMP is used in a declarative or in an interrogative sentence. Sensitivity to the illocutionary type becomes even more crucial if we adopt a definition of modal roles in terms of knowledge and not of speech acts (knowledge-holder and interpreter). We hope to have shown (i) that GMPs are not multifarious items and (ii) that covert modality, as regards those particles, may be reduced to the epistemological type. We have also tried to demonstrate that they basically always function in co-construction with other linguistic signs, sometimes without any morphematic *signifiants*: sentence type, realis or irrealis status, or selectional restrictions. Such signs are also laden with modal relevance, so that the final modal meaning of an utterance appears to be a construction of several features distributed in diverse categories. This result confirms the high degree of pervasiveness presented by the category of modality. Yet, we hope that the analysis of *wohl* can make the case for a strictly compositional account of those co-constructional patterns. In such a perspective, we can wonder if there is still any place left for the concept of structural covertness: If strict compositionality is preserved, should not we link our difficulties for understanding it to the linguistic approaches rather than to intrinsic factors? Modal eliminativism seems to culminate in the reduction of structural covertness to mere epistemological obscurity.

Acknowledgements

Thanks are due to the volume editors and to the anonymous reviewers, who considerably helped ameliorating previous versions of this paper.

References

Abraham, Werner. 1991: Discourse particles in German: How does their illocutive force come about? In W. Abraham (ed.): *Discourse particles. Descriptive and theoretical investigations on the logical, syntactic and pragmatic properties of discourse particles in German.* Amsterdam: Benjamins. 203-252.

—. 2010: Diskurspartikeln zwischen Modalität, Modus und Fremdbewusstseins-abgleich (Theory of Mind). In Th. Harden & E. Hentschel (eds.). *40 Jahre Partikelforschung*. Tübingen: Stauffenburg. 33-70.

Coniglio, Marco. 2011. *Die Syntax der deutschen Modalpartikeln: ihre Distribution und Lizenzierung in Haupt- und Nebensätzen.* Berlin: Akademie.

Davidson, Donald. 2001: *Subjective, intersubjective, objective*. Oxford: Clarendon Press.

Detges, Ulrich & Waltereit, Richard. 2009: Diachronic pathways and pragmatic strategies: different types of pragmatic particles from a diachronic point of view. In M.-J. M. Hansen & J. Visconti (eds.): *Current trends in diachronic semantics and pragmatics*. Bingley: Emerald [Studies in pragmatics 7]. 43-61.

Egg, Markus. 2010: A unified account of the semantics of discourse particles. In *Proceedings of SIGDIAL 2010*. University of Tokyo. 132-138.

Evans, Nicholas. 2009: *The Grammar of expectation*, Talk at the Ludwig-Maximilians-Universität Munich, December 2009 (Ms.).

Gast, Volker. 2008: Modal particles and context updating. The functions of German *ja*, *doch*, *wohl* and *etwa*. In O. Letnes & H. Vater (eds.): *Modality and grammaticalization*. Trier: Wissenschaftlicher Verlag. 153-177.

Grice, H. Paul. 1975: Logic and conversation. In P. Cole and J. L. Morgan (eds.): *Syntax and semantics: speech acts.* Vol. 3. New York: Academic. 41-58.

Guentchéva, Zlatka & Landaburu, Jon (eds.). 2007: *L'énonciation médiatisée II. Le traitement épistémologique de l'information. Illustrations amérindiennes et caucasiennes*. Louvain / Paris: Peeters.

Hentschel, Elke & Weydt, Harald. 1994: *Handbuch der deutschen Grammatik*. Berlin / New York: de Gruyter.

König, Ekkehard. 1997: Zur Bedeutung von Modalpartikeln im Deutschen: Ein Neuansatz im Rahmen der Relevanztheorie. In *Germanistische Linguistik* 136. 57-75.

Kwon, Min-Jae. 2005: *Modalpartikeln und Satzmodus. Untersuchungen zur Syntax, Semantik und Pragmatik der deutschen Modalpartikeln.* Munich, PhD Thesis.

Leiss, Elisabeth. 2008: Drei Spielarten der Epistemizität, drei Spielarten der Evidentialität und drei Spielarten des Wissens. In W. Abraham & E. Leiss (eds.): *Modalität. Epistemik und Evidentialität bei Modalverb, Adverb, Modalpartikel und Modus*. Tübingen: Stauffenburg [Studien zur deutschen Grammatik 77]. 3-24.

Olbertz, Hella. 2009: Mirativity and exclamatives in functional discourse grammar: evidence from Spanish. In E. Keizer & G. Wanders (eds): *The London papers I,* Special Issue of *Web papers in Functional Grammar* 82. 66-82.

Ormelius-Sandblom, Elisabet. 1997: The Modal particle *schon*: its syntax, semantics and pragmatics. In T. Swan & O. J. Westvik (eds.): *Modality in Germanic languages*. Berlin / New York: de Gruyter [Trends in Linguistics – Studies and Monographs 99]. 75-131.

Paillard, Denis. 2009: Prise en charge, commitment ou scène énonciative. In *Langue Française* 162: *La notion de prise en charge en linguistique*. 109-128.

Struckmeier, Volker. to appear: "*Ja doch wohl* C? Modal particles in German as C-related elements". To appear in *Studia Linguistica.*

Thurmair, Maria. 1989: *Modalpartikeln und ihre Kombinationen*. Tübingen: Niemeyer.

Weydt, Harald. 1969: *Abtönungspartikel. Die deutschen Modalwörter und ihre französischen Entsprechungen.* Bad Homburg v.d.H. / Berlin / Zürich: Gehlen [Linguistica et litteraria 4].

Zemb, Jean-Marie. 1978: *Vergleichende Grammatik Französisch-Deutsch*, Bd. I: *Comparaison de deux systèmes*. Mannheim: Dudenverlag.

—. 1984: *Vergleichende Grammatik Französisch-Deutsch*, Bd. II: *L'économie de la langue et le jeu de la parole*. Mannheim: Dudenverlag.

Zimmermann, Malte. 2008: Discourse particles in the left periphery. In B. Shaer, Ph. Cook, W. Frey & Cl. Maienborn (eds.): *Dislocated elements in discourse. Syntactic, semantic, and pragmatic perspectives*. London: Routledge. 200-231.

ON THE DEVELOPMENT OF EPISTEMIC 'FEAR' MARKERS: AN ANALYSIS OF MANDARIN *KONGPA* AND CANTONESE *TAIPAA*

FOONG HA YAP, WINNIE CHOR AND JIAO WANG
HONG KONG POLYTECHNIC UNIVERSITY
OPEN UNIVERSITY OF HONG KONG
UNIVERSITY OF DELAWARE

Abstract: This paper examines how 'fear' verbs develop into epistemic mood markers in Chinese. Diachronic, syntactic and discourse data converge to show that Mandarin *kongpa* and Cantonese *taipaa* have grammaticalized to serve as subjective epistemic and inferential markers equivalent to English *probably*. Within the interactional domain, these epistemic 'fear' markers have further extended to serve pragmatic hedging functions such as marking speakers' doubt, reservation or hesitation, either as a means for the speaker to qualify his or her epistemic stance or for the speaker to express consideration for the addressee's face wants. This paper also addresses how the degree of grammaticalization influences the status of these epistemic markers in terms of their classification as overt or covert grammatical constituents.

1. Introduction

Like any other language, Chinese is rich in linguistic strategies that encode speakers' stance, i.e. speakers' expression of mood, attitude, perspective, evidentiality (or source of information), in short, their expression of their thoughts, feelings, viewpoints, and evaluations of others and situations around them. Among the better-known stance marking strategies in Chinese are its sentence final particles. Another extensively discussed group of stance marking strategies are its adverbials, such as *lian* and *dou* with their counterexpectation reading (in the sense of English 'even'), and concessive *danshi* and *buguo* (both meaning 'however'). Besides these better-known 'overt' stance-marking strategies, Chinese, again like other languages, also has 'covert' ones, which previously have not been included among the list of grammaticalized stance markers. One such 'covert' stance marker in Chinese is the 'fear' epistemic adverbial, realized as *kongpa* in Mandarin and as *taipaa* in Cantonese, both equivalent in meaning with the English epistemic adverb *probably*, as seen in (1a) and (1b) respectively.

(1) a.

將來	外國	人	要起	罪魁	來，
jiānglái	*wàiguó*	*rén*	*yàoqǐ*	*zuìkuí*	*lái*
future	foreign	people	request.up	chief.criminal	come

恐怕	一	個	也	跑不掉	。
kǒngpà	*yī*	*gè*	*yě*	*pǎobudiào*	
fear	one	CL	also	run-NEG-RESULT	

'In future, if the foreigners request for the chief criminal, **probably** nobody can escape.'
(*Wénmíngxiǎoshǐ* 文明小史, by Lǐ Bóyuán, early 20th century)

b.

佢	睇怕	會	身敗名裂	。
keoi^{5}	***tai***^{2}***paa***^{3}	*wui*^{5}	*san*^{1}*baai*^{6}*ming*^{4}*lit*^{6}	
3SG	look.fear	FUT	body.failure.name.break	

'He will **probably** lose both fortune and honour!'
(Contemporary Cantonese)

In this paper, we will examine how these 'fear' epistemic adverbials develop, and how the functions of Mandarin *kongpa* and Cantonese *taipaa* extend beyond the epistemic ('degree of certainty') domain into the inferential (logical reasoning) domain, as seen in (2a) and (2b) respectively. We will also further examine the pragmatic functions of *kongpa* and *taipaa* in different social contexts, including the marking of speakers' doubt or reservation, and their efforts at pragmatic softening, as in (2c).

(2) a.

抻麪，	你	知道	嗎	？
chēnmiàn	*nǐ*	*zhīdào*	*ma*	
hand-pulled.noodle	2SG	know	Q	

這	個	外地	人	恐怕	也	不	知道。
zhè	*gè*	*wàidì*	*rén*	***kǒngpà***	*yě*	*bù*	*zhīdào*
this	CL	non-local	people	fear	also	NEG	know

'As for the Beijing hand-pulled noodles, you know what, non-locals **probably** don't know about it either.'
(*Data from 1982 Běijīng Dialectal Survey* 1982 年北京話調查資料)

b.

恐怕	又	是	上次	那	個	學生	作弊！
kǒngpà	*yòu*	*shì*	*shàngcì*	*nà*	*gè*	*xúeshēng*	*zuòbì*
fear	again	COP	last.time	that	CL	student	cheat

'It seems that it **might be** the same student who cheated last time.'

c.

您	的	受傷	可能	使	對方
nín	*de*	*shòushāng*	*kěnéng*	*shǐ*	*duìfāng*
2SG.HON	GEN	get.hurt	may	cause	opposite.party

終生	不安，	這	恐怕	也	是	一	種
zhōngshēng	*bùān*	*zhè*	***kǒngpà***	*yě*	*shì*	*yī*	*zhǒng*
whole.life	uneasy	this	fear	also	COP	one	CL

傷害	。
shānghài	
wound	

'The fact that you got hurt may lie heavy on the opposite party. This is **probably** also a kind of hurting.'
(from *Academia Sinica Balanced Corpus of Modern Chinese*)

Another objective in this paper is to contribute to discussions on the distinction between 'overt' and 'covert' modality. Many of the papers in this volume identify the notion of 'covertness' with the notion of 'null elements'. Our focus here is slightly different though not incompatible. Specifically, we seek to highlight the role of grammaticalization in providing a language with 'overt' modal cues. We will show that while some lexical expressions can encode epistemic modal values, in the early stages of grammaticalization their epistemic strengths often compete with referential or predicational content, and thus their contribution to the modal interpretation of an utterance comes through via secondary (or muted) channels. However, with increasing grammaticalization, in part due to frequent usage, we see significant gains in epistemic strength, particularly in situations where semantic extensions pave the way for syntactic reanalysis. Often, the process of syntactic restructuring occurs as 'covert operations'. These operations are often invisible to the untrained eye, and often give rise to ambiguous or multiple interpretations. Native speakers of the language are often unaware of these ongoing covert changes, but as the forces of change gather strength, new grammatical and pragmatic functions often 'suddenly' become visible. Essentially, what happens in the parlance of language acquisition and language processing research is this: When frequency of use escalates, it can give rise to a 'flip' or 'switch' effect, and what was covert then suddenly becomes overt. A new marker is born. But as with each newborn, the genesis is not achieved in a flash. Gestation takes time.

Covertness then can be understood as *a fluid process, often still in a state of flux*, while overtness can on the other hand be defined as *a relatively stable outcome or resultant state*. This paper provides an account of one such journey from covertness to overtness. More specifically, it tells the story of how certain lexical verbs meaning 'fear' in two Sinitic languages develop into overt markers of epistemicity that still retain reflexes of its etymology, and hence its close association with meanings related to adversity.

We discuss the development of these 'fear' verb constructions as follows. In section 2, we identify the etymology and functions of the 'fear' expression *kongpa* in Mandarin and *taipaa* in Cantonese. In section 3, we analyze the syntactic and pragmatic environments that facilitate the development of these 'fear' expressions as epistemic adverbials. In section 4, we consider other possible realizations of these 'fear' constructions besides their subjective use as a marker of speaker's epistemic and inferential stance, focusing in particular on their intersubjective use as a pragmatic marker that signals speakers' doubt or reservation, and pragmatic softening efforts. Section 5 discusses the notion of 'covert modality' in terms of the semi-lexical and quasi-modal status of *kongpa* and *taipaa*, drawing attention to degree of grammaticalization in determining whether these 'fear' expressions in Mandarin and Cantonese (and arguably in other languages as well) are still covert, or whether they have become overt markers of speakers' epistemic stance. Section 6 concludes the paper.

2. Etymology and functions of Mandarin *kongpa* and Cantonese *taipaa*

Both Mandarin *kongpa* and Cantonese *taipaa* are epistemic stance adverbials derived from the verb 怕 'fear' (pronounced as *pa* with tone 4 in Mandarin, and *paa* with tone 3 in Cantonese). Mandarin *kongpa* 恐怕 is formed via combination of two fear verbs, *kong* 恐 and *pa* 怕.[1] The fear verb *kong* 恐, attested in Old Chinese as seen in (3), is no longer used in modern Mandarin. The 'fear' verb *pa* 怕 emerged in Middle Chinese, as seen in (4a), and continues to be highly productive to this day, as seen in (4b).[2]

(3)

子	曰：	學	如	不	及，	猶	恐	失	之。
zǐ	*yuē*	*xué*	*rú*	*bù*	*jí*	*yóu*	***kǒng***	*shī*	*zhī*
master	say	learn	as.if	NEG	reach	as if	fear	lose	3SG

'The Master said, "Learn as if you could not reach your object, and were always **fearing** also lest you should lose it."
(*Analects* 8.17, 5th century BC, *transl.* James Legge)

(4) a.

如何	此	貴	重，
rúhé	*cǐ*	*guì*	*zhòng*
why	this	expensive	significant

卻	怕	有	人	知。
què	***pà***	*yǒu*	*rén*	*zhī*
nonetheless	fear	EXIST	people	know

'Why is it so expensive and significant? I nonetheless **fear** that somebody knows (of its existence).'
(*Lìchūn* 麗春 'Beautiful Spring', by Tu Fu, 712-770 AD, Tu 1999: 877)

---

[1] In written Chinese, a disyllabic word combined with two synonymous morphemes is often formed with one morpheme from the colloquial stratum and one morpheme from classical / formal Chinese. In the case of *kongpa* 恐怕, *pa* 怕 is the colloquial morpheme, while *kong* 恐 is the literary morpheme.

[2] The verb *pa* 怕 'fear' is arguably derived from Old Chinese **p^ha 怖 'fear' (Wang 1982: 176).

b. 總算 我們 怕了 他們。
zǒngsuàn wǒmen pàle tāmen
after.all 1PL fear-PFV 3PL
'After all, we **are afraid** of them.'
(*Luòtuóxiángzi* 駱陀祥子 'Rickshaw Boy', by Laǒshè, 1936)

Cantonese *taipaa* 睇怕, on the other hand, is formed via combination of a perception verb *tai* 睇 'look, see, watch, read' and the 'fear' verb *paa* 怕. Both verbs were attested in the Cantonese film corpus of the mid-20th century and are still widely used in present-day Cantonese, as seen in (5a) and (5b) respectively.

(5) a. 媽媽 怕醜 喎！ 你 睇下 ！
ma^4*ma*^{1} *paa*^{3}*cau*^{2} *wo*^{4} *lei*^{5} ***tai***^{2}*haa*^{5}
mother afraid.ugly SFP 2SG see-CL
'Mummy is shy! **Look**!'
(from the film *May Heaven Bless You* 天官賜福, 1958)

b. 你 唔使 怕 㗎！
lei^5 *m*^{4}*sai*^{2} ***paa***^{3} *gaa*^{3}
2SG NEG.need fear SPR
'You don't need to **be afraid**!'
(from the film *One Queen and Three Kings* 一后三王, 1963)

The disyllabic form *kongpa* was attested as a lexical verb meaning 'fear' in Late Middle Chinese during the Tang period (7th – 9th century), as seen in (6a). The text is a satirical poem depicting a scene in which local officials were using the farmers' oxen to transport sand from the riverbanks to pave the roads in the city in order to flatter a newly appointed prime minister, treating him almost like an emperor. This was done at the height of the ploughing season, when the oxen should have been deployed in the fields. The poem thus sarcastically describes the fear among the local officials that they may not be doing enough to prepare for a grand welcome for the prime minister. Lexical verb uses of *kongpa* are not very productive but are still attested in the 20th century, as seen in (6b).[3]

---

[3] Lexical noun uses of *kongpa* in the sense of psychological fear were attested slightly later, in Early Modern Chinese during the Ming period (14th – 17th century), as seen in (i) and (ii) below.

(6) a.

昨	來	新	拜	右	丞相	，
zuó	*lái*	*xīn*	*bài*	*yòu*	*chéngxiàng*	
yesterday	come	new	take.office	right	prime.minister	

恐怕	泥	塗	污	馬	蹄	。
kǒngpà	*ní*	*tú*	*wū*	*mǎ*	*tí*	
fear	earth	besmear	dirty	horse	hoof	

‘The prime minister, who has just assumed office, arrived yesterday. There was **fear** (< ‘Government officials feared’) that the earth would besmear the horse’s hooves.’
(*Guānniú* 官牛 ‘Official Cow’, a poem by Bái Jūyì, 772-846 AD, Tang dynasty, Bái 1979: 85)

b.

但是	他們	也	不	恐怕	戰爭
dànshì	*tāmen*	*yě*	*bù*	***kǒngpà***	*zhànzhēng*
however	3PL	also	NEG	fear	warfare

‘They, however, also do not **fear** of warfare.’
(*The Victory of Bolshevism*, Bolshevism 的勝利, by Lǐ Dàzhaō, 1918)

Liú (2011) noted that toward the end of Late Middle Chinese, *kongpa* came to increasingly express a weaker sense of ‘fear’. As illustrated in (7a) and (7b) from the late Song period (10th – 13th century), *kongpa* was frequently used in the sense of ‘worry’. Toward the end of the Song period (13th century), as seen in (7c), a subjective epistemic reading equivalent to the English subjective expression ‘I’m afraid’ began to emerge from the

(i)

有	恐怕	之	意
yǒu	***kǒngpà***	*zhī*	*yì*
have	fear	GEN	meaning

‘Have the feeling of **fear**.’
(*Qiánhànshū pínghuà* 前漢書平話, 1321 - 1323 AD)

(ii)

我們	也	有	些	恐怕
wǒmen	*yě*	*yǒu*	*xiē*	***kǒngpà***
1PL	also	have	CL	fear

‘We also somehow **fear** (it).’
(*Xīyóubǔ* 西遊補, early 17th century)

more general sense of 'fear, worry and anxiety'. This usage continues to be productive to this day, as shown in (7d).

(7) a.

門	人	過往	人	多，
mén	*rén*	*guòwǎng*	*rén*	*duō*
door	people	pass	people	many

恐怕	驚	他	驢	。
kǒngpà	*jīng*	*tā*	*lǘ*	
worry	frighten	3SG	donkey	

'Since there are so many people passing by the house, he **worries** (this) will frighten his donkey.'
(*Dūnhuáng Biànwénjí Xīnshū* 敦煌變文集新書, 10th century)

b.

如	此	用	功夫	，
rú	*cǐ*	*yòng*	*gōngfu*	
like	this	use	time	

恐怕	輕	費了	時月	。
kǒngpà	*qīng*	*fèile*	*shíyuè*	
worry	frivolously	waste-PFV	hour.month	

'If (we) spend time like this, I **worry** (we will just) frivolously waste our time.'
(*Thematic Discourses of Master Zhū* 朱子語類, 1270 AD; Lí 1986: 2424)

c.

問	喪	禮	制度	節目，
wèn	*sāng*	*lǐ*	*zhìdù*	*jiémù*
ask	funeral	ritual	institution	procedure

曰：	恐怕	《儀禮》	也	難	行	。
yuē	***kǒngpà***	*Yílǐ*	*yě*	*nán*	*xíng*	
say	fear	*book.title*	even	hard	practise	

'Asking about the procedure of the ritual of funerals: (Master Zhū) says, "**I'm afraid** it is even hard to practise (the details as prescribed in) *Yílǐ*."'
(*Thematic Discourses of Master Zhū* 朱子語類, 1270 AD; Lí 1986: 2275)

d.

不好意思，	打擾	了，	衹	耽誤	你
bùhǎoyìsi	*dǎrǎo*	*le*	*zhǐ*	*dānwù*	*nǐ*
excuse.me	disturb	SFP	only	delay	2SG

一	分鐘	想	和	你	說
yī	*fēnzhōng*	*xiǎng*	*hé*	*nǐ*	*shuō*
one	minute	want	with	2SG	say

幾	句	話，	如果	現在	不	說，
jǐ	*jù*	*huà*	*rúguǒ*	*xiànzài*	*bù*	*shuō*
several	CL	word	if	now	NEG	say

我	恐怕	就	再也	沒有	機會	和
wǒ	***kǒngpà***	*jiù*	*zàiyě*	*méiyǒu*	*jīhuì*	*hé*
1SG	fear	then	never.ever	NEG.have	chance	with

你	說	了。
nǐ	*shuō*	*le*
2SG	say	SFP

'Excuse me, I would like to talk with you and I shall not keep you long. **I'm afraid** I will never get a chance to talk to you if I lose this opportunity.'
(*Life of Chinese Artists in Beijing* 中國北漂藝人生存實錄)

Epistemic and inferential uses of *kongpa* with the meaning 'probably' were attested sporadically from the Song period (10th – 13th century), but did not become productive until the Qing period (see Table 3-1 in section 3 for further discussion). An example of epistemic *kongpa* from the Ming period is shown in (8),[4] and an example of inferential *kongpa* from the Qing period is shown in (9).[5] These grammaticalized uses of *kongpa*

---

[4] Norman (1988) refers to early Ming as Old Mandarin, late Ming and early Qing as Middle Mandarin, and late Qing as Early Modern Mandarin.

[5] Epistemic use of the monosyllabic 'fear' verb *pa* was attested somewhat later in the 18th century, as seen in the example below. Note that it is the speaker (*wo* 'I'), not the subject (*ta* 's/he'), who worries. The usage of *pa* here is thus a subjective epistemic usage.

他	怕	不	也	有	二十五	六	歲，
tā	***pà***	*bù*	*yě*	*yǒu*	*èrshíwǔ*	*liù*	*suì*
3SG	fear	NEG	also	have	twenty-five	six	year.old

within the epistemic (degree of certainty) and inferential (logical reasoning) domains require a first person subject *wo* 'I', yielding the subjective interpretation *wo kongpa* 'I'm afraid', with the implicit understanding that the fear, anxiety, or worry is linked to some prior negative personal experience(s), or to admonition(s) gained through hearsay or shared wisdom, or to logical inferences based on available evidence.

(8) 恐怕 它 是 姻緣 未 斷 ，
kǒngpà *tā shì yīnyúan wèi duàn*
fear 3SG COP destiny.of.marriage not.yet break

三言兩句 成合 了。
sānyánliǎngjù chénghé le
a.few.sentences form PFV

'**Probably** because the destiny that joins them together remains unbroken, they (eventually) got married with a few sentences (by the matchmaker).'
(*Xiǎosūntú* 小孫屠, Ming dynasty, 14th - 17th century; cited in Liú 2011)

(9) 我 恐怕 他 後來 改了 口。
wǒ ***kǒngpà*** *tā hòulái gǎile kǒu*
1SG afraid 3SG afterwards change-PFV saying
'**Probably (< 'I'm afraid')** he may have changed his mind afterwards.'
(*Xǐngshìyīnyuánzhuàn* 醒世姻緣傳, Qing dynasty, late 17th cent.)

In present-day Mandarin, *kongpa* 恐怕 is no longer frequently used as a lexical verb to express 'a psychological state or feeling of fear', as is evident from the infelicity of (10a) and (10b) below. Instead, *kongpa* has largely grammaticalized into an epistemic stance adverbial, as seen in (11).

他 對 人 自 說 二十一 歲。
tā duì rén zì shuō èrshíyī suì
3SG face people self say twenty-one year.old
'He **probably** (< '**I'm afraid**') is even twenty-five or twenty-six years old, yet he tells others that he is twenty-one years old.'
(*Rúlínwàishǐ* 儒林外史, Chapter 26, by Wú Jìngzǐ, 1701 - 1754 AD)

As an epistemic marker, as noted above, *kongpa* indicates high likelihood or probability of an undesirable event occurring, or an unwelcome change of situation emerging. In other words, we see a semantic extension whereby *kongpa* comes to further express feelings of unease, based on prior personal experience or shared information, which paves the way for extensions beyond the psychological domain to the epistemic and inferential domains.

(10) a. * 我 恐怕 老鼠。
* *wǒ* ***kǒngpà*** *lǎoshǔ* (Modern Chinese)
1SG fear mouse
'I'm **afraid** of mice.'

b. * 我 覺得 恐怕。
* *wǒ juéde* ***kǒngpà*** (Modern Chinese)
1SG feel fear
'I **fear** (it).'

(11) 我 恐怕 要 遲到。
wǒ kǒngpà *yào chídào* (Modern Chinese)
1SG afraid will be.late
'I'm afraid (*I am afraid) I will be late.'
= 'I **probably** will be late.'

As highlighted in (11) above, this subjective feeling is expressed in the first person *wo kongpa* 'I'm afraid'. This 'first person' (= speaker) stance is evident from the epistemic interpretation of *ni* ***kongpa*** *yao chidao* in (12) below, which native speakers interpret (parenthetically) as 'You, **I'm afraid**, will be late' > 'You **probably** will be late', and never as '*You're afraid* you'll be late'. Similarly, a subjective 'first person' (= speaker) epistemic interpretation emerges for *ta* ***kongpa*** *yao chidao* in (13) in the sense of 'S/he, **I'm afraid**, will be late' > 'S/he **probably** will be late', and never in the sense of '*She's afraid* s/he'll be late.' Both (12) and (13) thus confirm that *kongpa* is first-person (speaker) oriented, and that it does not refer to the stance of the second or third person subject.

(12) 你 恐怕 要 遲到。
nǐ ***kǒngpà*** *yào chídào* (Modern Chinese)
2SG afraid will be.late

'You, **I'm afraid (*I am afraid)**, will be late.'
= 'You **probably** will be late.'
≠ 'You're afraid you'll be late.'

(13)

他	恐怕	要	遲到。
tā	***kǒngpà***	*yào*	*chídào*
3SG	afraid	will	be.late

'S/he, **I'm afraid (*I am afraid)**, will be late.'
= 'S/he **probably** will be late.'
≠ 'S/he's afraid s/he'll be late.'

Unlike Mandarin *kongpa*, the Cantonese disyllabic epistemic adverbial *taipaa* was never used as a lexical verb to express 'a psychological state or feeling of fear'. That is to say, it started out from its very inception as an epistemic marker. This is not surprising, given that *taipaa* is partly comprised of a perceptual evidential component *tai* 'look, see, watch, read', which readily facilitates an epistemic ('apparently' > 'probably') interpretation, as in (14) below.

(14) a.

噉	我	睇	呢	個	怕	唔	係	嘑！
gom2	*ngo5*	***tai2***	*li1*	*go3*	***paa3***	*m4*	*hai6*	*la3*
conn	1SG	see	this	CL	fear	NEG	COP	SFP

人	有	相似	啫！
jan4	*jau5*	*soeng1ci5*	*ze1*
human	EXIST	similar	SFP

'In this case, **I'm afraid / probably** this one/guy is not (the person that we are looking for). They merely look similar to each other.'
(from the film *Lover in Disguise* 化身情人, 1965)

b.

我	睇	都	怕	重	要	攞	一	百	緡
ngo5	***tai2***	*dou1*	***paa3***	*zung6*	*jiu3*	*lo2*	*jat1*	*baak3*	*man1*
1SG	see	also	fear	still	need	take	one	hundred	dollar

至	夠	嚊！
zi3	*gau3*	*bo3*
only.then	sufficient	SFP

'**I'm afraid / Probably** we still need a hundred dollars more (to pay the fee)!'
(from the film *Face of Demolition* 危樓春曉 , 1953)

c. 如果 你 做唔到 ，
jyu4gwo2 lei5 zou6m4dou3
if 2SG do-NEG-SUCCESS

我 睇怕 你 會 身敗名裂 嚕 ！
ngo5 ***tai2paa3*** *lei5 wui5 san1baai6ming4lit6 bo3*
1SG look.fear 2SG FUT body.failure.name.break SFP

'In case you fail (to do so), you will **probably (< 'I'm afraid')** lose both fortune and honour!'
(from the film *Thief Captures Thief* 小偷捉賊記, 1962)

d. 如果 你 話 循 法律 手續 去 解決 ，
jyu4gwo2 lei5 waa6 ceon4 faat3leot6 sau3zuk6 heoi3 gaai2kyut3
if 2SG say follow legal procedure to solve

我 睇怕 你 契媽 呢 世 都 唔使 旨意
ngo5 ***tai2paa3*** *lei5 kai3maa1 li1 sai3 dou1 m4sai2 zi2ji3*
1SG look.fear 2SG godmother this life also NEG.need able

收返 呢 筆 錢。
sau1faan1 lei1 bat1 cin2
collect-back this CL money

'If you solve (this problem) by following legal procedure, your godmother will **probably** not be able to receive the sum of money in this life.'
(from the film *A Gimmicky World* 綽頭世界, 1963)

Cantonese disyllabic *taipaa* 睇怕 emerged relatively late, with only 2 tokens of *tai ... paa* (discontinuous constituents) and another 2 tokens of *taipaa* (fused form) compared to 264 tokens of monosyllabic *paa* 怕 attested in a corpus of Cantonese films from the 1940s – 1960s, as exemplified in (14) above. There were in fact more tokens of disyllabic *hungpaa* 恐怕, the Cantonese equivalent of Mandarin *kongpa* (with 6 tokens of *hungpaa* to 2 tokens of *taipaa* in the film corpus).[6] Older Cantonese texts available to us yielded 27 tokens of *hungpaa*, 10 of which occur in *Huājiānjì* 花箋記 and 6 tokens in the first 58 songs of *Yuèōu* 粵謳, both Cantonese opera lyrics from the 17th century and 19th century respectively, but these older texts yielded no tokens of *tai* ... *paa* nor *taipaa*. It is worth noting that Cantonese *hungpaa* served almost a similar range of functions as Mandarin *kongpa*, namely, (i) lexical verb 'fear', (ii) epistemic adverbial expression 'I'm afraid' or 'probably', and (iii) pragmatic marker of speaker's doubt or reservation, as well as pragmatic softening 'perhaps' (equivalent to Cantonese *waakze* 'perhaps'), as seen in (15) below.

(15)	恐怕	唔	彀	估	亞	
	Hung pa	im	kăw	koo	a	(original romanization)
	hung^{2}paa^{3}	*m^{4}*	*gau^{3}*	*gu^{2}*	*aa^{3}*	(present-day Cantonese)
	fear	NEG	sufficient	guess	SFP	

'**I'm afraid / Probably / Perhaps** there is not a sufficient quantity.'
(Morrison 1828/2001: Part III, Section XXII Trade)

Both epistemic adverbials *hungpaa* and *taipaa* are attested in present-day Cantonese, with *hungpaa* conveying a stronger sense of fear and worry (if needed) than *taipaa*. While *taipaa* is often interchangeable with *hungpaa*, the perception verb *tai* 'look, see, watch, read' in *taipaa* often induces a more reflective and inferential interpretation. In this regard, *taipaa* serves a triple function of marking attitude (fear), epistemicity (probability) and evidentiality (inference). Intimations of evidentiality are more indirect and much weaker in the case of *hungpaa*. This subtle difference between *taipaa* and *hungpa* within Cantonese also holds as we compare the functions of Cantonese *taipaa* with those of Mandarin *kongpa*. That is, Mandarin *kongpa* does not have as strong an inferential evidentiality interpretation as Cantonese *taipaa*.

In sum, diachronic evidence indicates a development from lexical to epistemic use, with the 'fear' verb *kongpa* in Mandarin attested in Late Middle Chinese during the Tang period (7th – 9th century), and epistemic and inferential uses of *kongpa* attested sporadically from the Song period and becoming more productive from the Qing period (14th – 17th century)

[6] We wish to thank Dr. Andy Chin for generous access to the *Linguistic Corpus of Mid-20th Century Hong Kong Cantonese Movies* (1940s to 1960s). See also Chin (2011) for more details pertaining to this corpus.

onward. Cantonese epistemic adverbial *taipaa* is a more recent development, with examples attested in movies from the mid-20th century, as in (14) above.

3. Syntactic and pragmatic factors facilitating the emergence of epistemic *kongpa* and *taipaa*

In this section, we will examine the syntactic environments and pragmatic motivations that give rise to the development of Mandarin *kongpa* and Cantonese *taipaa* as epistemic adverbials. As seen in (16), Mandarin *kongpa* can occur as a complement-taking psych verb with the meaning 'fear', and as seen in (17), an epistemic and subjective sense could emerge in contexts where the possibility of a negative outcome gives rise to a more general sense of anxiety, unease, displeasure or disappointment. Crucially, this subjective epistemic interpretation comes from a combination of first person subject *wo* 'I' and the psych verb *kongpa* 'fear', yielding the stance adverbial *wo kongpa* 'I fear' > 'probably', which scopes over an erstwhile complement clause that is now 'insubordinated' (see Evans 2007) and reanalysed as the main clause.[7] Note that the first person subject need not be overtly realized to yield a subjective epistemic interpretation, as seen in (18).

(16) 我 恐怕 他 會 用 卑鄙 的 手段 。
wǒ kǒngpà *tā huì yòng bēibǐ de shǒuduàn*
1SG fear 3SG FUT use disgusting GEN means
'**I fear** s/he will use dirty tricks.'

(17) 我 恐怕 他 不 會 來 了。
wǒ kǒngpà *tā bú huì lái le*
1SG fear 3SG NEG FUT come SFP
'**I'm afraid / Probably** s/he won't come.'

(18) 恐怕 他 不 會 來 了。
kǒngpà *tā bú huì lái le*
fear 3SG NEG FUT come SFP
'**I'm afraid / Probably** s/he won't come.'

[7] See also Thompson and Mulac (1991), *inter alia*, on similar developments of English *I think* as epistemic parentheticals.

The emergence of subjective epistemic stance adverbial *wo kongpa* 'I fear' / 'I'm afraid' / 'I worry' > 'probably', which requires the merger of the first person subject *wo* 'I' with the complement-taking psych verb *kongpa* 'fear', is highlighted in (i) and (ii) below:

(i) [$_{\text{CP2}}$ [$_{\text{IP2}}$ *(wǒ)* [$_{\text{VP}}$ ***kǒngpà*** [$_{\text{CP1}}$ [$_{\text{IP1}}$ *tā bú huì lái*] *le*]]]]
(ii) [$_{\text{CP2}}$ [$_{\text{IP2 Sentence adverbial}}$ ***(wǒ) kǒngpà*** [$_{\text{CP1}}$ [$_{\text{IP1}}$ *tā bú huì lái*] *le*]]]

Note that aspectual *le* in sentence final position can function as an interactional particle that signals the completion of the speaker's turn and tacitly invites the addressee to take his or her turn on the conversational floor (see Su 2011).

As seen in (19) below, the subjective epistemic adverbial expression *(wo) kongpa* 'I'm afraid' > 'probably' can be right-dislocated to form an epistemic utterance tag. The tag-like (rather than sentence final particle) status of *(wo) kongpa* in this right-dislocated epistemic construction is confirmed by its post-*le* position, and the frequent occurrence of an extended pause (signalled here by a comma) between interactional sentence final particle *le* and epistemic utterance tag *(wo) kongpa.*

(19) 他 不 會 來 了 (，) (我) 恐怕。
tā bú huì lái le (,) **(*wǒ*)** ***kǒngpà***
3SG NEG FUT come SFP 1SG fear
'S/he won't come, **probably / I'm afraid**.'

A number of previous studies (Simpson & Wu 2002; Lin 2008; Cheung 2008) have posited a Comp-to-Spec analysis for the emergence of right-dislocated utterance tags and sentence final particles similar to the epistemic adverbial expression *(wo) kongpa.*[8] Typological evidence also

[8] Simpson and Wu (2002) posited a Comp-to-Spec analysis for evidential and counterexpectation marker *kong* in Taiwanese Southern Min. Lin (2008), Hsieh (2005), Sybesma (2008), and Cheung (2008) pursued similar albeit improved analyses for sentence final particles and utterance tags in other Sinitic languages as well, including Mandarin and Cantonese. Sybesma (2008) make the important observation that there are two different CP layers for the grammaticalized particles such as the 'say' constructions under discussion here. The present study likewise recognizes two different types of complementizers derived from the 'say' verbs in Cantonese (and potentially many other Chinese varieties; see for example Chappell 2008, to appear 2012): one is the head-initial factive-type complementizer (similar to English complementizer *that*), while the other is the left-periphery evidential complementizer (equivalent to either English hearsay evidentials *They say* and *It is said* or English inferential evidentials *Evidently* and *Apparently*). In this paper, we

indicates that some Sinitic utterance-final stance expressions are realized as utterance tags (e.g. Taiwanese evidential and counterexpectation marker *kong* (derived from utterance verb 'say')), and some of these utterance tags grammaticalize further into sentence final particles (e.g. Cantonese evidential and counterexpectation marker *wo* (< *waa* 'say'); see Yap & Ahn 2011). As noted above, utterance-final *(wo) kongpa* in Mandarin is still an utterance tag, and its derivation from utterance-initial *(wo) kongpa* via right-dislocation (or Comp-to-Spec raising from a formal syntactic perspective) is highlighted in the syntactic reanalyses from (iii) (=(ii) above) to (iv) and then (v) below:

(iii) [$_{CP2}$ [$_{IP2\ \text{Sentence adverbial}}$ ***(wǒ) kǒngpà*** [$_{CP1}$ [$_{IP1}$ *tā bú huì lái*] *le*]]]
(iv) [$_{CP2}$ [$_{CP1}$ [$_{IP1}$ *tā bú huì lái*] *le*] [$_{IP2\ \text{Sentence adverbial}}$ ***(wǒ) kǒngpà*** t_{CP1}]]
(v) [$_{CP2}$ [$_{CP1}$ [$_{IP1}$ *tā bú huì lái*] *le*] [$_{IP2\ \text{Utterance tag}}$ ***(wǒ) kǒngpà***]]

Note that the utterance tag *(wo) kongpa* is syntactically incomplete unless legitimized by an (inter)subjective illocutionary force, as represented by the syntactic constituent [$_{CP2}$] as shown in (v) above.[9] As seen in (20) below, the speaker's intersubjective stance conveyed by the utterance tag *(wo) kongpa* is often accompanied by a response (or 'uptake') by the addressee.

(20) A: 他 不 會 來 了 (，) 恐怕 。
tā bú huì lái le (,) ***kǒngpà***
3SG NEG FUT come SFP fear
'S/he won't come, **probably (< I'm afraid)**.'

---

argue that it is the latter type (i.e. the left-periphery hearsay and inferential evidentials) that participate in right-dislocation to give rise to utterance tag and sentence final particle 'say' evidentials and counterexpectation markers *waa* and *wo* in Cantonese (and arguably also in other Chinese varieties).

[9] Note that in the case of utterance-final epistemic and inferential marker *(wo) kongpa*, native speakers of Mandarin still consider it as an utterance tag, while interestingly in the case of utterance-final evidential and counterexpectation marker *wo3*, native speakers of Cantonese consider it as a sentence final particle. In the case of the latter, we suggest that sentence final particle *wo3* is a complementizer of CP_2 rather than CP_1. That is, evidential and inferential *wo3* belongs to the 'higher CP layer' within the analysis posited in Hsieh (2005) and Sybesma (2008).

B:	别	理	他。
	bié	*lǐ*	*tā*
	do.not	mind	3SG
	'Don't mind about him/her.'		

A similar syntactic development involving right dislocation is also evident for Cantonese epistemic stance expression *(ngo) taipaa*, which is available as a sentential adverb in utterance-initial position as seen in (21), and as an epistemic utterance tag in utterance-final position as in (22).

(21)	（我）	睇怕	佢	唔	會	嚟	嘞。
	(ngo^{5})	***tai^{2}paa^{3}***	*keoi^{5}*	*m^{4}*	*wui^{5}*	*lai^{4}*	*lak^{3}*
	1SG	look.fear	3SG	NEG	FUT	come	SFP
	'**I'm afraid / It looks like / Probably** s/he won't come.'						

(22)	佢	唔	會	嚟	嘞	（我）	睇怕	。
	keoi^{5}	*m^{4}*	*wui^{5}*	*lai^{4}*	*lak^{3}*	***(ngo^{5})***	***tai^{2}paa^{3}***	
	3SG	NEG	FUT	come	SFP	1SG	look.fear	
	'S/he won't come, **I'm afraid / it looks like / probably**.'							

An interesting difference between Mandarin *kongpa* and Cantonese *taipaa* is the similative 'it looks like' interpretation that is more readily available for Cantonese *taipaa*, given that its first morpheme *tai* 'look, see, watch, read' is a perception verb. Thus, the epistemic reading for Cantonese *taipaa* emerges not only from its '**fear** (that something will happen)' reading but also from its similative '**it looks like** (something will happen)' reading. This to some extent accounts for the greater ease with which Cantonese *taipaa* can also yield a neutral epistemic interpretation, as opposed to the more 'fear-oriented' and generally negative interpretation, expectation, or assumption which is often associated with Mandarin *kongpa*.

As epistemic stance adverbials, both Mandarin *kongpa* and Cantonese *taipaa* can also occur as parenthetical epistemic markers in clause-medial position. As illustrated in (23a) and (24a), clause-medial *kongpa* in Mandarin and clause-medial *taipaa* in Cantonese are always interpreted in the first person subjective epistemic sense of (23b) and (24b), that is, in the sense of '*I'm* afraid' (> 'probably'), and not in the non-first person objective sense of '*s/he's* afraid'.[10]

[10] Recall also example (11) in section 2 earlier.

(23) a. 他 恐怕 不 會 來 了。
tā ***kǒngpà*** *bú huì lái le*
3SG fear NEG FUT come SFP
'S/he **probably** won't come.'

b. 他 我 恐怕 不 會 來 了。
tā ***wǒ kǒngpà*** *bú huì lái le*
3SG 1SG fear NEG FUT come SFP
'(S)he, **I'm afraid**, won't come.'
(speaker's subjective epistemic stance)
≠ 'S/he's afraid she won't come.'

(24) a. 佢 睇怕 唔 會 嚟 嘞。
keoi^{5} ***tai***^{2}***paa***^{3} *m*^{4} *wui*^{5} *lai*^{4} *lak*^{3}
3SG look.fear NEG FUT come SFP
'S/he **probably** won't come.'

b. 佢 我 睇怕 唔 會 嚟 嘞。
keoi^{5} ***ngo***^{5} ***tai***^{2}***paa***^{3} *m*^{4} *wui*^{5} *lai*^{4} *lak*^{3}
3SG 1SG look.fear NEG FUT come SFP
'(S)he, **I'm afraid**, won't come.'
(speaker's subjective epistemic stance)
≠ 'S/he's afraid she won't come.'

Parenthetical epistemic marker *(wo) kongpa* in clause-medial position arises via insertion or adjunction. This is made possible when utterance-initial *(wo) kongpa* is first reinterpreted as an adjunctive subjective epistemic sentence adverbial, as seen in (vi) (= (iii) above). Once it develops into an epistemic adverbial, *(wo) kongpa* can be inserted or adjoined in clause-medial position as a parenthetical epistemic marker, as seen in (vii) below.

(vi) [$_{CP2}$ [$_{IP2\ \text{Sentence adverbial}}$ ***(wǒ) kǒngpà*** [$_{CP1}$ [$_{IP1}$ *tā bú huì lái*] *le*]]]
(vii) [$_{CP2}$ [$_{CP1}$ [$_{IP1}$ *tā* [$_{\text{Parenthetical epistemic marker}}$ ***(wǒ) kǒngpà***] *bú huì lái*] *le*]]

Worth noting is that regardless of its syntactic position (i.e. utterance-initial, medial, or final), epistemic marker *(wo) kongpa* is strongly associated with subjective meaning (in the sense of '*I'm afraid* that X will happen' > '*I think* X *probably* will happen') and often also with intersubjective functions such as marking the speaker's sensitivity to the potential impact of his or her utterance on the addressee. Similar associations exist for Cantonese *taipaa* as well.

In sum, our syntactic analysis suggests a development in which utterance-initial *(wo) kongpa* extends into new syntactic positions, namely utterance-final position and utterance-medial position. These two extensions develop via different syntactic mechanisms: Utterance-final *kongpa* appears to have involved right-dislocation to become an utterance tag, while utterance-medial *kongpa* appears to have emerged via adjunction within the erstwhile complement clause that is now reanalysed as the main clause (involving a process of clausal insubordination; see Evans 2007) to form a parenthetical epistemic marker (see also Thompson & Mulac 1991). The former (i.e. utterance tag *kongpa*) has the potential of further developing into a sentence final particle, but as we shall see from the frequency distribution data below, *kongpa* has not (yet) developed into a sentence final particle.

Diachronic evidence, as shown in Tables 3-1 to 3-3 (see Yang, Wong & Yap 2012 for more detailed discussion), supports the above syntactic analysis. From Table 3-1, based on frequency studies from Middle Chinese to Early Modern Chinese, we see a semantic extension of *kongpa* from lexical 'fear' to epistemic and inferential uses, with a significant shift toward the grammaticalization of *kongpa* as an epistemic and inferential marker occurring in the Qing period (late 17th to early 20th century). In terms of syntactic position, *(wo) kongpa* extended from an utterance-initial position to an utterance-medial (i.e. parenthetical) position. Interestingly, although utterance-final *(wo) kongpa* is grammatical in Mandarin Chinese (with equivalents in other Sinitic varieties), no utterance tag tokens were attested in our corpus, which suggests that right-dislocation of *kongpa* constructions may be a relatively marked choice. This would help explain why utterance-final *kongpa* remains as a tag construction instead of further developing into a sentence final epistemic particle, as sometimes happens in other languages, for example Malay *kot* (< *kut* < *takut* 'fear') (see section 5 for more detailed discussion).

In Cantonese, the use of *taipaa* 睇怕 as epistemic as well as inferential marker is a fairly recent phenomenon, with examples attested from the 20th century, as noted earlier in section 2. Emerging later after two other 'fear' verbs – namely, *paa* 怕 and *hungpaa* 恐怕 – had acquired epistemic uses, *taipaa* 睇怕 bootstrapped on these older and more grammaticalized counterparts and started off right away as a subjective epistemic marker meaning 'probably' without developing a lexical use as a psych verb. Since its first morpheme *tai* 睇 is derived from a perception verb meaning 'look, see, watch, read', *taipaa* 睇怕 also readily developed an inferential evidential function in all three syntactic positions: utterance-initial, utterance-medial, and utterance-final (see also Wong, Yang & Yap, forthcoming, for a more detailed diachronic analysis).

Table 3-1: Frequency distribution of the functions of utterance-initial Mandarin *kongpa* from the 8th to early 20th century (based on tokens from the Middle Chinese and Early Modern Chinese subcorpus in the Center for Chinese Linguistics Corpus (CCLC), Peking University; findings from Yang, Wong & Yap 2012).

Functions of *kongpa*	**Period in which *kongpa* was attested**					
	Tang & Five Dynasties (618-960)	Song (960–1279)	Yuan (1279–1368)	Ming (1368–1644)	Qing (1644–1911)*	Total no. of tokens
Lexical verb expressing anxiety ('I'm afraid')	20	16	155	578	603	1372
Epistemic marker 'probably'	0	1	1	2	92	96
Inferential marker 'it seems to be'	0	1	0	1	15	17
Total no. of tokens sampled in the present study **	20	18	156	581	710	1485

*Note: For the Qing period, we culled every other token of *kongpa* from the total 1,420 tokens, which thus yields 710 tokens for this analysis.
** Note 2: There were a total of 2,195 tokens of *kongpa* in the entire corpus.

Table 3-2: Frequency distribution of the functions of Mandarin *kongpa* in different syntactic positions (based on tokens from the Contemporary Mandarin subcorpus in the Center for Chinese Linguistics Corpus (CCLC), Peking University; findings from Yang, Wong & Yap 2012).

Functions of *kongpa*	Syntactic position of *kongpa*			
	Utterance-initial	Utterance-medial	Utterance-final	Total no. of tokens of *kongpa* sampled in the present study
Lexical verb expressing anxiety ('I'm afraid')	2	10	0	12
Epistemic marker 'probably'	428	512	0	940
Inferential marker 'it seems to be'	26	22	0	48
Total no. of tokens of *kongpa* sampled in the present study*	456	544	0	1000

* Note: There were a total of 10,554 tokens of *kongpa* in the entire corpus. We culled every tenth token of *kongpa* from the online corpus.

Table 3-3: Frequency distribution of the functions of Mandarin *wo kongpa* in different syntactic positions (based on tokens from the Contemporary Mandarin subcorpus in the Center for Chinese Linguistics Corpus (CCLC), Peking University; findings from Yang, Wong & Yap 2012).*

Functions of *wo kongpa*	Syntactic distribution of *wo kongpa*			
	Utterance-initial	Utterance-medial	Utterance-final	Total no. of tokens of *wo kongpa*
Lexical verb expressing anxiety ('I'm afraid')	155	30	0	185
Epistemic marker 'probably'	45	13	0	58
Inferential marker 'it seems to be'	0	0	0	0
Total no. of tokens sampled	200	43	0	243

*Note: Table 3-3 with tokens of *wo kongpa* is a subset extracted from Table 3-2.

In this section, we have seen both syntactic analyses and frequency distributions converging with diachronic findings which show that lexical 'fear' verbs in Mandarin and Cantonese have developed into epistemic markers meaning 'probably', with additional extensions into inferential (logical reasoning) and pragmatic hedging functions. In the next section, we will elaborate on the pragmatic uses of epistemic marker *(wo) kongpa* in Mandarin discourse, i.e. its subjective and intersubjective uses, which can also be seen in the case of epistemic marker *(ngo) taipaa* in Cantonese (see Wong, Yang & Yap, forthcoming).

4. (Inter)subjective uses of *kongpa* and *taipaa*

Developed from its epistemic sense, *kongpa* in Mandarin and *taipaa* in Cantonese have both acquired a more subjective colour, coming to also express subjective and intersubjective functions, such as signalling the speaker's doubt or reservation, as well as the speaker's pragmatic softening stance, as seen in the following examples.

In (25), we have a situation involving a wealthy man from the Qing period being imprisoned because he had offended the royal family, and a prison official was commenting about this incident. In reply to the official's comment, the speaker remarked that the situation was not as simple as the official had thought. By using *kongpa*, the speaker signals his doubt or reservation about the official's interpretation of the events.

(25) 事情 恐怕 沒 那麼 簡單 。
shìqíng ***kǒngpà*** *méi nàme jiǎndān*
matter fear NEG so simple
Lit. 'The matter, I'm afraid, is not that simple.'
'**I'm afraid** it's not that simple.'
(*Qiáojiādàyuàn* 喬家大院 'The Grand Courtyard of the Qiáo Family', by Zhū Xiùhǎi, 2006)

In (26) below, taken from a contemporary article from a newspaper in Mainland China, the writer was commenting that explicit guarantees of good service are better than a beautiful motto. The writer prefaces his remark with a statement using *kongpa* to signal his doubt and reservation about whether the hotel staff members would be able to properly interpret the meaning of the motto *binzhirugui*, which is used within the hotel industry to emphasize the importance of making a guest feel at home. In this case, *kongpa* is used to signal lack of certainty, which can be traced back to the meaning of fear that is sometimes still found in the epistemic use of *kongpa*.

(26) 恐怕 飯店 的 員工 也 未必 說得清楚
kǒngpà *fàndiàn de yuángōng yě wèibī shuōdeqīngchǔ*
fear hotel GEN staff also not.necessary say-DEG-clear

"賓至如歸" 是 甚麼 。
bīnzhìrúguī shì shénme
guest.come.like.return COP what

'**I'm afraid** that not even the staff in the hotel (let alone the guests) can clearly explain what *binzhirugui* means.' (*binzhirugui* is a motto within the hotel industry that emphasizes the importance of making a guest feel at home)
(*Rènmín Rìbào* 人民日報 *Peoples' Daily*, January 1994)

Kongpa is also often used as a pragmatic softener in cases where the speaker is 100% certain about the outcome of the situation, but wishes to mitigate its potential negative impact on the addressee. This function of *kongpa* is illustrated in (27) below, where the speaker knows he cannot possibly spare time for a meeting with the addressee, but makes an effort to remedy the situation, and at the same time politely using *kongpa* to take care of the addressee's face wants when turning down the addressee's request for a meeting. In this way the speaker mitigates an otherwise potentially face-threatening situation.

(27) 我 現在 很 忙， 今天 恐怕 不 行 了，
wǒ xiànzài hěn máng jīntiān ***kǒngpà*** *bù xíng le*
1SG now INT busy today fear NEG okay SFP

我 叫 秘書 盡快 給 你 安排
wǒ jiào mìshū jìnkuài gěi nǐ ānpái
1SG ask secretary as.soon.as.possible give 2SG arrange

個 時間 好 吧？
gè shíjiān hǎo ba
CL time good SFP

'I'm very busy now. **I'm afraid** I'm not able to meet with you today. I'll ask my secretary to arrange another time for you as soon as possible, okay?'
(*Huánnǐ Qiánshēngyuán* 還你前生緣, by Cén Kǎilún)

Similar intersubjective uses are found for Cantonese *taipaa*, which suggests that epistemic markers derived from 'fear' verbs tend to be well-suited for pragmatic hedging functions. Not discussed here but mentioned earlier in section 3, epistemic 'fear' expressions are also amenable for inferential marking functions (see also Yang, Wong & Yap 2012). We suggest, to a large extent, this is because psychological states of fear and worry tend to direct our attention to possible negative outcomes and encourage us to assess the worrisome situation for possible interventions. In this regard, we thus see psychological realities influencing discourse patterns and the development of a language's grammar.

5. Covert modality and degree of grammaticalization

In this section, we discuss the notion of 'covert modality' in terms of the lexical vs. grammatical status of Mandarin *kongpa* and Cantonese *taipaa*, drawing attention to degree of grammaticalization in determining whether these 'fear' expressions in Mandarin and Cantonese (and arguably in other languages as well) are still covert, or whether they have become overt (in the sense of highly grammaticalized) markers of the speakers' epistemic stance.

We will begin this discussion with reference to a highly grammaticalized subjective epistemic marker, namely Malay *kut* 'probably'. As seen in (28) below, *kut,* or its phonological variant *kot* (the latter often found in internet communications), prefers the utterance-final position. The subjective epistemic marker *kut* is derived from the epistemic expression *(aku) takut* '(I) fear'/ '(I'm) afraid'), which occurs in utterance-initial position (28a), utterance-medial (i.e. parenthetical) position (28b), and utterance-final position (28c). As seen in (28d) and (28e), the reduced phonological form *kut* cannot co-occur with the first person subject, yet it still retains the subjective epistemic interpretation '(I think) probably' (< 'I fear').

(28) a. ***(Aku) takut*** *dia ni akan nangis nanti.*
1SG fear 3SG DEM.PROX will cry FUT (<wait)
'**I'm afraid** s/he will cry.'

b. *Dia ni,* ***(aku) takut****, akan nangis nanti.*
3SG DEM.PROX (1SG) fear will cry FUT
'S/he, **I'm afraid**, will cry.' / 'S/he **probably** will cry.'

c. *Dia ni akan nangis nanti,* ***(aku) takut.***
3SG DEM.PROX will cry FUT (1SG) fear
'S/he will cry, **I'm afraid / probably**.'

d. *Dia ni akan nangis nanti* ***(*aku) kut.***
3SG DEM.PROX will cry FUT (1SG) probably
'S/he will cry, **probably**.'

e. *Dia ni akan nangis* ***(*aku) kut*** *nanti*
3SG DEM.PROX will cry (1SG) probably FUT
'S/he will cry **probably**.'

With reference to the examples (28d) and (28e), note that utterance-final *kut* could occur not only **after** but also **before** the future marker *nanti* (< 'wait'). This indicates that temporal adverbial *nanti* could adjunctively occupy utterance-final position and scope over the entire clause modulated by attitudinal and epistemic marker *kut*. Crucially for our present discussion, this further suggests that *kut* has grammaticalized beyond the utterance tag stage and has become more highly integrated into the preceding clause, thus assuming the status of a sentence final particle.

Similar phenomena of clausal integration are not uncommon in Sinitic languages either. Indeed, subjective and evaluative expressions signalling the speaker's stance are often integrated into the preceding clause and develop into sentence final particles. Examples in Classical and Modern Chinese include mitigative particles such as *eryi*, *bale*, *haole*, *suanle* and *xingle* (see Yap, Wang & Lam 2010).

In the case of utterance-final *kongpa*, however, native speakers still perceive it as an utterance tag rather than as a sentence final particle. An interesting question is why this is so. Frequency of use appears to be one factor. Even in Contemporary Mandarin, as noted earlier from the frequency distribution data in section 3, *kongpa* still occurs more often in the utterance-initial and utterance-medial positions, leaving the utterance-final position as the more marked and less frequent option, and hence less ready for reanalysis as a sentence final marker. In other words, the infrequent occurrence of *(wo) kongpa* in utterance-final position would not help bring about the integration of utterance tag *kongpa* to the preceding main clause to form a monoclausal structure. As such, unlike utterance-final *kut* in Malay, utterance tag *kongpa* in Mandarin is not sufficiently primed to be reinterpreted as a sentence final particle.

In addition to frequency of use, phonological considerations appear to be important as well. Note that while utterance tags could be phonologically more substantial, as in the case of *(wo) kongpa*, sentence final particles generally need to be phonologically reduced in length. The monosyllabic 'fear' epistemic marker *pa* 怕 should have been a good candidate for reanalysis as a sentence final particle. However, although phonologically shorter than epistemic utterance tag *kongpa*, epistemic marker *pa* 怕 has in fact not been phonologically favoured in utterance-final position, perhaps partly due to competition with an existing and highly productive sentence final particle *ba* 吧, which has rather similar phonological properties.

Sentence final particle *ba* 吧 is not attested in colloquial Cantonese; even so, the monosyllabic epistemic marker *paa* 怕 in Cantonese remains as an utterance tag and has not developed into a sentence final particle. Compared to Malay utterance-final *kut*, which has already developed into a sentence final particle, Cantonese utterance-final *paa* 怕 is therefore less grammaticalized. This, we suggest, is because Cantonese *paa* 怕 is still semantically transparent and is still highly productive as a stance adverbial in the utterance-initial and utterance-medial positions.

In addition, given the availability of both monosyllabic epistemic marker *paa* 怕 and speculative epistemic marker *gwaa* 啩 ('I guess' or 'I suppose' > 'probably') as sentence final epistemic markers, the epistemic and inferential uses of disyllabic *taipaa* appears to be in no hurry to develop into yet another sentence final epistemic particle. Added to this semantic congruity (or similarity) constraint is the 'youthfulness' or 'lexical transparency' of *taipaa* as a grammatical marker. We thus see several factors contributing to the ease and degree of productivity with which an utterance tag further grammaticalizes into a sentence final particle, with 'frequency of use' being facilitative, and 'phonological and/or semantic similarity' often being inhibitive.

Although the degree of grammaticalization helps to determine the classification of epistemic 'fear' markers as either 'overt' or 'covert' modal markers, often it is also advances (or lack thereof) in linguistic research that determine the choice of terminology. Native speakers, often unaware of these terminological subtleties, have little difficulty in interpreting the modality of each utterance. Rather, that with which the linguist is yet unfamiliar often falls under the rubric of 'covertness', while that which we have defined (often by tacit consensus) we sometimes refer to as 'overt' markers; often, with things we find familiar, the term 'overt' doesn't even come to mind. What the present study contributes to our current focus on 'covert modality', then, is to shed light on some modal markers that have been understudied, and in so doing elevate their status to 'overt' modality markers, at least in the sense of being recognized as licit grammatical markers with modal and pragmatic functions.

6. Conclusion

In this paper we have traced the development of 'fear' verbs into epistemic mood markers meaning 'probably', using diachronic, syntactic and discourse data for Mandarin *kongpa* and Cantonese *taipaa*. Our analysis shows that within the logical domain, an inferential function often emerges as well, while in the pragmatic domain, these 'fear' epistemic markers often further develop into pragmatic hedgers or 'tone softeners' that signal the speakers' doubt, reservation, or hesitation, which are often used to mitigate any potential threat to the addressee's face wants. We have also compared the grammaticalization of these two Sinitic 'fear' epistemic markers with a similar marker in another language, namely Malay *kut*, which has grammaticalized even further, going beyond the utterance tag structure to develop into a sentence final particle. We considered a number of factors that could have given rise to differences in degree of grammaticalization (and hence potentially differences in the use of terminology such as 'overt' vs. 'covert' modality markers) and have identified frequency of use, as well as phonological and semantic (dis)similarities, as possible contributing factors.

Acknowledgment

We wish to gratefully acknowledge generous research funding support from the Research Grants Council of Hong Kong (General Research Fund, PolyU 5513/10H) to the first author for the project "Stance Marking in Asian Languages: Linguistic and Cultural Perspectives". We also wish to gratefully acknowledge generous research funding support from the Faculty of Humanities Dean's Reserve to the first and second authors for the project "Clause-medial Particles in Chinese". We are also greatly indebted to Vivien Ying Yang and Tak-Sum Wong for assisting with the diachronic analysis of Mandarin *kongpa* and Cantonese *taipaa* tokens used in this study. We further wish to thank Professor Samuel Hung-nin Cheung for access to his *Early Canton Dialect Database* and to Dr Andy Chi-on Chin for access to *A Linguistic Corpus of Mid-20th Century Hong Kong Cantonese Movies*. We would also like to express our thanks to the editors, Werner Abraham and Elisabeth Leiss as well as two anonymous reviewers, and to Henry Yung-Li Chang, Hongyong Liu, Li-May Sung and Sze-Wing Tang, for their valuable comments and suggestions.

References

A Linguistic Corpus of Mid-20th Century Hong Kong Cantonese Movies. 2011. The Hong Kong Institute of Education. Distributed by Dr Andy Chin.

Anonymous. 1824. *Courtship: in Verse* (*Huājiānjì*) (Peter Perring Thoms, Trans.). Macao: The Honorable East.

Bái, Jūyì. 1979. *Bái Jūyì Jí* [Bái Jūyì's collection] (Xuéjié Gù, Annotated). Peking: Zhonghua Book Company.

Chappell, Hilary. 2008. Variation in the grammaticalization of complementizers from *verba dicendi* in Sinitic languages. *Linguistic Typology* 12(1): 45-98.

Chappell, Hilary. (to appear 2012). Intersubjectivity in Sinitic: From verbs of saying to attitudinal discourse markers. In Hubert Cuyckens, Lobke Ghesquière & Daniël Van Olmen (eds), *Aspects of Grammaticalization: (Inter)Subjectification, Analogy and Unidirectionality*. (Trends in Linguistics Studies and Monographs). Berlin: Mouton de Gruyter.

Cheung, Yam-leung Lawrence. 2008. The Negative *Wh*-Construction. Unpublished doctoral dissertation. UCLA, California.

Chin, Chi-on. 2011. The construction and application of a linguistic corpus of mid-20th century Cantonese. Presented at the *16th International Conference on Yue Dialects*, The Hong Kong Polytechnic University, December 15-16.

Eastern Linguistics. 2012. Comparative Linguistics, EISU. January 31, 2012. <http://www.eastling.org/>

Evans, Nicholas. 2007. Insubordination and its uses. In: I. Nikolaeva (ed.), *Finiteness*, 366−431. Oxford: Oxford University Press.

Hsieh, Feng-fan. 2005. Atoms and particles. Ms., MIT.

Jiu, Ji-yung. 1828. *Yuèōu*. Canton: Dēngyúngé.

Lí, Jìngdé. 1986. *Zhūzǐ Yǔlù* [Thematic discourses of Master Zhū] (Collated by Xīngxián Wáng). Peking: Zhonghua Book Company.

Lin, Tzong-Hong Jonah. 2008. Complement-to-specifier movement in Mandarin Chinese. Unpublished Manuscript, National Tsing Hua University, Hsinchu.

Liú, Xiǎoyǐng. 2011. The diachronic evolution of lexical meaning and TCFL vocabulary teaching – Take *kongpa* as an example. *Journal of Hebei University (Philosophy and Social Science)* 36(3): 61−64.

Morrison, Robert D. D. 2001. *Vocabulary of the Canton dialect*. London: Ganesha Publishing Limited. [First ed. published in Macao: East India Company's Press, 1828.]

Norman, Jerry. 1988. *Chinese*. Cambridge: Cambridge University Press.

Project on the Electronic Version of Chinese Classics. 2012. Yanzi Academy. January 20. <http://www.cnculture.net/ebook/>.

Retrieval System for the Corpus of CCL. July 20, 2009. Center for Chinese Linguistics, Peking University. January 30, 2012 <http://ccl.pku.edu.cn:8080/ ccl_corpus/>

Simpson, Andrew & Wu, Zoe Xiuzhi. 2002. IP-raising, tone sandhi and the creation of particles: Evidence for cyclic spell-out. *Journal of East Asian Linguistics* 11(1): 1–45.

Su, Lily I-wen. 2011. How intersubjectivity works in conversation: The use of *le* in spoken discourse. Paper presented at the Workshop on *Stance Marking Across Languages: Typological, Diachronic and Discourse Perspectives*, Hong Kong Polytechnic University, July 18-20, 2011.

Sybesma, Rint. 2008. Generative syntax and sentence-final particles in Chinese. In Yang Shen & Shengli Feng (eds), *Contemporary Linguistic Theories and Related Studies on Chinese*, pp. 364–374. Beijing: Commercial Press.

Thompson, Sandra A. & Mulac, Anthony J. 1991. A quantitative perspective on the grammaticalization of epistemic parentheticals in English. In Elizabeth Traugott & Bernd Heine (eds), *Approaches to Gramamaticalization, Volume II: Types of Grammatical Markers*, 313-339. Amsterdam: John Benjamins.

Tu, Fu. 1979. *Dù Shī Xiángzhù* [A detailed annotation of Tu's poem] (Zhàoáo Qiú, Annotated). Peking: Zhonghua Book Company.

Wang, Li. 1982. *Túngyuán Zìdǐan* [A dictionary on cognates]. Peking: Commercial Press.

Wong, Tak-Sum, Yang, Ying & Yap, Foong Ha. (forthcoming). On the semantic extensions of 'fear' expressions *paa*, *hungpaa* and *taipaa* in Cantonese: diachronic and discourse perspectives. Unpublished manuscript, Hong Kong Polytechnic University, Hong Kong.

Yang, Ying, Wong, Tak-Sum & Yap, Foong Ha. 2012. A diachronic study of epistemic *kǒngpà* in Mandarin discourse. Paper presented at the 6th Conference on Language, Discourse and Cognition, National Taiwan University, May 4–6.

Yap, Foong Ha & Ahn, Mikyung. 2011. Verbal and nominal pathways in the development of 'SAY' as a sentence final particle. Poster presented at the *9th Annual Meeting of the Association for Linguistic Typology* (ALT-9), University of Hong Kong, July 21-24, 2011.

Yap, Foong Ha, Wang, Jiao & Lam Tsz-Kwan. 2010. Clausal integration and the emergence of mitigative and adhortative sentence-final particles in Chinese. Special Issue on Stance Phenomena in Chinese: Diachronic, Discourse and Processing Perspectives. *Taiwan Journal of Linguistics* 8(2): 63-86.

TOWARDS A COMPOSITE DEFINITION OF NOMINAL MODALITY

DEBRA ZIEGELER
PARIS III (SORBONNE NOUVELLE)

"When you can measure what you are speaking about and express it in numbers you know something about it; but when you cannot measure it, when you cannot express it in numbers your knowledge is of a meagre and unsatisfactory kind; it may be the beginning of knowledge but you have scarcely progressed in your thoughts to the stage of science whatever the matter may be."
—Lord Kelvin (1883)

Abstract: The possibilities for the categorisation of nominal modality across languages present a phenomenon that has, to present knowledge, rarely been discussed in the literature, most likely for the fact that such modality does not appear to be marked by any dedicated form-function correspondences. It has been observed, though, that in many languages, there is no particular encoding used to determine the difference between specific and non-specific nominals (e.g. Von Heusinger 2002). However, in Colloquial Singaporean English, the absence of specificity is frequently marked by the use of a bare NP (singular or plural), as opposed to the use of the numeral determiner 'one' and the plural -s to mark nouns with specific reference; i.e., countability marking is not completely grammaticalised in Singapore and Indian English to include non-specific indefinites in its scope. In this way, it is seen that there is a correlation between absence of specific reference, indefiniteness, and the absence of countability; what is not countable is not marked as such. The observed, variable absence of countability in Singapore and Indian English, creoles and in the history of English, is thus realised as a covert, sub-modality specific to generic nominals in standard English, and with implications for a more accommodating description of the entire field of modality itself.

1. Introduction

It is one of the aims of modern cognitive linguistic theory to try to establish a tighter cohesion between language form and the reality to which it refers, and to examine the possibilities that are evoked by the assumption of non-arbitrariness between linguistic form and linguistic function, and ultimately, linguistic form and the general reality of reference to events and entities in the real world. Such relationships are never more compellingly in focus than in the categorisation of nominals cross-linguistically, and the functions laid down by presence or absence of determiners and other modifiers. Previous research in the cognitive arena and in other fields has accepted the presence across languages of a type of nominal aspect existing alongside the more familiar categories of verbal aspect; the studies of, for example, Langacker (1987), Rijkhoff (1991), or Huumo (2010) have brought to light the ontological nature of aspectual distinctions that could be analogised from the verbal domain to the nominal domain, in English and other languages. The possibility of extending the domain of modality to include nominals as well as verbs has not, to present knowledge, been the subject of any kind of in-depth analysis, and yet, there seems to be no apparent reason for maintaining that modality should be exclusively a study associated with temporal factors. The analogy of modality in nouns thus regards the potential existence of the referents of nominals in the same way as verbal modality represents the potential existence of reference to events. The most interesting grammatical domain in which to study the overlap between verbal and nominal modality is predicted to be that of genericity, for two reasons: first, that genericity (across languages) is a feature of nominals as much as of the verbal propositions predicated of them, and second, that genericity is a separate category that has been shown in previous studies (e.g., Ziegeler 2006a) to be a historical source context for emerging verbal modality, due to the nature of the nominal entities participating in such contexts. The present study will therefore examine the domain of generics in the light of the nominal participants with which the verb phrase interacts in such constructions, particularly in the contrasts between Old English, the contact dialects of new Englishes and standard present-day English dialects. It will be noted that in the contrasting means of marking nominal referents in generic constructions across contact dialects of English, there is an equivalence between reference to generic entities in such constructions and measurability constraints imposed by the language system. Thus, the relationships between measurability, countability, and actualisation are held to question in the present account.

The prospect of expanding the category of modal meanings unrestrainedly should not go unchecked. In many earlier studies, e.g. Nuyts (2006), the category of modality (with special reference to English modality) is seen to have proliferated into a multitude of grammaticalised forms across languages, what he (justifiably) labels a 'supercategory'. The present study will examine a possible sub-category of modality that has been overlooked in Nuyts' study, but not, apparently in early accounts of the 1970s and 1980s (e.g. Jackendoff 1971; Givón 1981); that is, the category of nominal reference. In this respect, it is not intended to restrict the assumptions claimed to apply only to nouns and nominal entities, but to observe how far such claims contribute to the modality of the entire construction in which they are found; the manner in which this will be undertaken will become clearer as the study progresses. In the meantime, what is crucial to the study is that the definition of modality needs a great deal more refinement in order to cover the needs of increasing numbers of descriptive, typological analyses and also the evidence that contact data brings to light, as will be seen in the comparisons of contact English dialects in the present study.

The paper will first consist of a brief overview of the current and most popular definitions of modality, introducing a new definition that accommodates the fact that modality is a conceptual domain extending well beyond the verb phrase (section 1), and is relevant to generic constructions. It will then outline some of the past discussion on the relation between generic constructions and the nominal entities contained in them (section 2), illustrating also the ways in which such features are treated in creoles and contact English varieties, such as Jamaican English, Indian English and Singapore English (section 3). Data from such languages will enable a clearer picture to be presented of the category of modality as a nominal feature of languages. Finally the diachronic grammaticalisation of indefinite reference in English nouns (section 4) will be shown to entail the 'co-grammaticalisation' of the countability distinction, as a sub-category of measurability in nominals (section 5). A suggestion for a composite approach to the study of modality in nouns is therefore proposed, in which nominal modality is seen as a covert category, a by-product emerging from the coalescence of the distinctions of (discourse) reference as a functional domain, the morphosyntactic domain of countability, and the semantic domain of referent identification.

2. Current approaches to the definition of modality

The definition of modality has been a contentious issue for several decades, and at least since Palmer (1986) launched one of the most comprehensive research studies to date, primarily with a focus on English and Indo-European languages. His definition of modality was a semantic or notional one, while mood was defined as its formal expression across languages. The definition of mood has often in the past embraced terms such as the subjunctive, the indicative, and others such as imperatives, but some authors reject the grammatical category of mood as necessarily expressing the semantic domain of modality (see, for example, Narrog (2005: 167). A reason for this may be in the fact that mood, insofar as it refers to an inflectional system across languages, may often in fact be so highly grammaticalised that its original semantic functions have become somewhat opaque compared to what can be expressed in other modal forms. This possibility lies at the heart of the explanation of 'renewal' of the subjunctive mood in English and other languages by the grammaticalisation of modal auxiliary verbs (see Hopper and Traugott 2003: 123).

With regard to the definition of the semantic field of modality the explanatory possibilities are even greater. Palmer (2003) rejects the notions of factuality and non-factuality in favour of more speaker-oriented definitions such as assertion and non-assertion, and Lyons (1995) along with Bybee et al. (1994) referred to speaker commitment again as essential to the definition of modality. The role of the speaker in the expression of a proposition has been persistently used as a means of describing modality in a number of other accounts, e.g. Nuyts (to appear) who refers to this as the broader of two possible ways of describing modality, which include the speaker's use of tense and aspect as well. The other is linked to earlier logical accounts of a possibility and necessity distinction, something which is less likely to be adopted for much of the crosslinguistic work done nowadays since it cannot account for more specific modal categories. However, Van der Auwera (2001) and Van de Auwera and Plungian (1998) had embraced the possibility-necessity distinction as being essential for examining the typological tendencies of many languages, with the evidence that certain semantic values are especially noticeable as not grammaticalised crosslinguistically, e.g., modal forms expressing *possible-not*. Thus it may often be the case that the logical modal distinctions of possibility and necessity, which date back as far as Aristotle, will underscore the ways in which modality is manifest across languages, and may in fact have grammatical significance.

De Haan (2006: 28) provides a much looser definition of modality, considering an element modal if it has modal meanings, such as obligation, permission and prohibition. Given the recent debate over the modal status of auxiliaries like *will* (see, e.g., Klinge 2005: 183, and Depraetere and Williams (eds.) 2010), we are left wondering just how far such a definition may be extended. However, De Haan's (2006) exemplification of the crosslinguistic representation of modality is exhaustively covered, and leaves the reader in no doubt as to the candidature of a possible modal form in any language. As well as the classical categories of mood in Latin and Classical Greek, which include the subjunctive, the indicative and the optative, marked as affixes on the verb, he includes examples of other modal affixes such as the following, from Tamil (cited in Asher 1979: 170):

(1) Tamil (Dravidian)

avan	*peeca-**laam***
3SG	speak-PERM

'He is allowed to speak.'

He also discusses modal adverbs, such as *probably, necessarily* and *maybe* in English and modal adjectives, found in Russian (2006: 38):

(2) Russian

ja	***dolžen***	*idti*	*v*	*voksal*
I-NOM	must-MASC	go-INF	to	station-ACC

'I must go to the station.'

In (2), *dolžen* is an adjective, declined in agreement with the subject, which is always nominative.

Amongst other crosslinguistic modal morphemes he lists are modal tags (not mentioned by Nuyts 2006), such as *I think, I guess* (these were described by Brinton (1996) as epistemic parentheticals), noting that in Tok Pisin, some tags have grammaticalised into adverbs (*ating* - 'maybe', cited in Keesing 1988). Modal particles such as *denn, doch* in German were also mentioned (these are also discussed in Letnes and Haumann (this volume) for Norwegian as well as German, and for German by Modicom (this volume). Modal particles are found prolifically in Chinese languages, as De Haan (2006) and also Foong (this volume) note, and not least, in English dialects in contact with Chinese such as Singapore English, e.g., *leh, meh* – where they are often used to express various shades of certainty and uncertainty (see, e.g. Lim (2007).

De Haan does not mention in very great detail the rare cases of modal marking on nouns, which had been mentioned by Evans (1995, 2003). The use of a 'modal proprietive' marker on nouns in Kayardild and Lardil (northern Tangkic, Queensland), is discussed by Evans (2003: 207) as expressing a modal case on most nouns in the two languages via factors of either government in oblique constructions or agreement in subordinate clauses (where the modal agreement is spread over all the elements of the clause). The following example illustrates one use of the modal proprietive case (Evans 2003: 208):[1]

(3) *dangka-a burldi-ju* *yarbuth-u*
man-NOM hit-POT bird-M.PROP

thabuju-karra-ngun-u *wangal-ngun-u*
brother-GEN-INSTR-M.PROP boomerang-INSTR-M.PROP

'The man will / can hit the bird with brother's boomerang.'

This is the only crosslinguistic example of nominal modality cited in De Haan, and given the nature of the marking in (3), it is unlikely that it represents any kind of modal sense in the nominals: *thabuju* 'brother' and *wangal* 'boomerang' refer to entities obviously already in existence, and therefore not strictly speaking modal in themselves. The modality marked on the nouns is, as suggested by Evans, a factor of pure grammatical agreement, not a function of a semantic feature. However, the data does tend to broaden the general definition of what may and may not be described as modal, and raises the question of how best to define such a wide-ranging feature of grammatical systems across languages.

It is generally the case that definitions are often made with a particular data analysis in mind, and the present study is no exception to this weakness. While it is not denied in the present case that modality is highly subjective, subjectivity is at the same time not considered to be a key factor in the definition. The principle use of modality is always to express variations in the truth or factuality of an utterance, and levels of uncertainty pertaining to the factual status of an utterance; the same definition has been proposed by Narrog (2005: 184). Narrog backs his definition in suggesting that all that is expressed by labels such as 'irrealis'

[1] Abbreviations: GEN = genitive, INSTR = instrumental, M = modal function (of case), NOM = nominative, POT = potential, PROP = proprietive (Evans 2003: 206). Proprietive case refers to meanings of intention and purpose on the elements on which it is marked.

is that "... they all boil down to one thing, namely whether a state of affairs is 'actual' or 'existent' at a specific point or interval of time" (2005: 183). In the present study, the necessity for actuality as distinguishing realis modality from irrealis modality will be further refined to refer to actuality at the moment of speaking. In particular, Narrog rejects the likelihood of definitions based on "speakers' attitudes" as being flimsy and in fact, unreliable, using examples from Japanese which demonstrated that markers expressing speakers" attitudes and evaluations could be found in Japanese, but belonged to non-modal categories such as voice, aspect and inherent honorification. But there could be questions of circularity as well. It is not always the case that speaker attitudes coincide with variations in the factuality of a proposition; however, at the same time, variations in the factuality of a proposition are almost impossible to find unless coloured by speakers' attitudes, or subjectivity, whether such attitudes are shared with other interlocutors or not. The involvement of subjectivity, then, seems to presuppose that differences of factuality are dependent on speakers' beliefs.[2]

Thus subjectivity is as implicit in the expression of non-modal utterances as modal ones, so it does not help us to involve it as a term definitional of modality, as Narrog suggests. Modality is the expression of the abstract (Cotte 2002), and abstract notions are necessarily more subjective than non-abstract ones, so the question of subjectivity/objectivity in modality then becomes difficult to circumvent.[3] Abstraction from reality is at the same time modification of factuality, so a representation of modality as variation in the speaker's *commitment* to the truth of a proposition may be seen instead as an ancillary element contributing to modality descriptions. Speaker commitment may or may not be grammaticalised; it can be specific to the moment of utterance, or specific to the use of a particular grammatical device in a language. Whatever the case, it is clear that modality requires a stronger definition than is currently available, to cover all the possible domains of grammaticalised speaker commitment to factuality. In the present study, it is proposed to proceed with the understanding that modality may simply refer to any type of potentiality expressable through a linguistic device, whether or not the potentiality is

[2] Scope does not allow for further discussion on the topic of subjectivity in modality, an area of research which is attracting an increasing amount of interest (see, e.g., Abraham, this volume, or Nuyts (2012; to appear).

[3] This definition is not to suggest that possibility is a focal semantic characteristic of modality, to the exclusion of all other semantic characteristics, only that the expression of modality in the majority of cases involves the expression of the potential as a basic element of meaning.

encoded directly, as with modals of innate possibility, or indirectly, as with modals expressing socially-imposed possibility. In making such a proposal, it is intended to suggest that potentiality aligns with non-factuality, and that it is essential to distinguish between truth and actuality: the difference (as noted in Ziegeler 2006b: 85) is that the truth of a proposition need not coincide with its actualisation, which is tied to a particular time reference. Many earlier attempts to redefine modality in terms of factuality (e.g. Narrog 2005) do not investigate in detail the need to link time reference with modality in a more specific and principled way. Truth, on the other hand, can be timeless, as is shown in generic statements, but generic statements are not linked to actualisation; because of this, they are susceptible to modalisation.

It is evident, then, that the modality of nominals is a category that has not been at the centre of a great deal of attention in recent research efforts to refine the definition of modality. In discussing the definitions of modality as associated with speaker commitment and subjectivity, it is not necessarily the case that the inclusion of nominal modality as a sub-category should be overlooked. However, the more primitive notion of potentiality (of existence of events and entities) may be more useful as an approach to the present study. As noted earlier, the potentiality inherent in the truth conditions of generics is proposed as a compelling point of departure from which to investigate the modality of nouns, as it is the nominals in such contexts that were seen to contribute most to the meanings of potentiality in the early development of modal verbs. The following sections will investigate the ways in which this type of modality may be manifest in generics.

3. Generics

Generics and habituals frequently occupy a morphosyntactic middle ground between realis and irrealis across languages, in some languages being encoded in the same way as realis modality, in others like irrealis modal constructions (see, e.g. Cristofaro 2004), thus creating an ambivalent grammatical category that reflects the universal conceptual indeterminacy of such contexts. Since they express inherent truths not necessarily coincidental with the moment of speaking, they possess a modified truth value associated with implicit inductive reference to events that are believed to have taken place at times prior to the moment of speaking (Krifka et al. (1995: 54-5). That such reference is only implicit, though, is perceivable in the fact that generics can refer to events that have not yet even occurred, as indicated by Laca (1990) in examples like

(4) This machine crushes oranges.

which can be uttered as a true statement even when the machine has not yet crushed a single orange, i.e., it lacks the support of temporal experience. The non-actualisation of generic statements means that they are generally also lacking in the identification of the events they refer to; in this way, they align with more prototypical forms of verbal modality marking the potentiality of events that, since they have not occurred, also have no identification in the speaker's mind either.

Generics are described by Krifka et al. (1995: 122) as not a uniform concept, in that they distinguish between habituals as qualifications over situations (as in (4)), and other types of generics as generalisations over individuals (see (5-6) below). This means that generics and habituals may be considered as the spatial and temporal counterparts of each other: generics referring to single events or states distributed over multiple participants of the same kind, thus spatially-distributed genericity, and habituals as multiple events of the same kind performed by a single participant, thus temporally-distributed genericity (see also, Langacker 1997: 191). Carlson (2006) makes no distinction between habituals and generics at all, except in terminology, and Bybee (1994: 237) finds no grammatical differences between the expression of generics and that of habituals in a crosslinguistic survey of 76 languages. Krifka et al. (1995) also describe varying degrees of genericity: characterising sentences, which allow for exceptions, such as:

(5) A potato contains vitamin C, amino acids, protein and thiamine.

and universally quantified kind-referring sentences, such as

(6) The potato was first cultivated in South America.

which do not (Krifka 1995: 3-4). Carlson (2006) defined generic reference as noun-phrase reference used in expressions of generalisation, so it would seem that generic constructions are essentially determined by the noun phrases contained in them. He also mentions that generic reference is usually used to make statements about kinds, using the definite article, as in (6). This is the only means of generically referring to kinds that employs a specific determiner, according to Krifka et al. (1995: 34). In all such cases, though, there is an element of non-identification that distinguishes a generic statement from any other: either non-identification of the participants involved (as in (5-6)), or of the situations referred to (as in (4)).

It was emphasised above that generics are susceptible to modalisation because although they express truths and facts, the facts they express are not spatio-temporally anchored, and have no actualisation at the moment of speaking. Krifka et al. (1995: 61) claimed that all generics are modal since they make assertions about open-ended sets of entities (e.g. *A lion has a mane*). However, as we have seen above in (4), not all generics refer to open-ended sets of entities; in (4), the reference is to an open-ended set of events instead. Nevertheless, such claims may call for a hypothesis of generic modality as a semantic category defined on principles of indefiniteness (see also Leiss's 2008 discussions). Thus, either the subject, *a lion*, may be indefinite (as in Krifka et al.'s example), or in the case of (4), the event (*crushes oranges*). Traditional philosophy has regarded nominal definiteness as aligned with uniqueness of reference (see, e.g. Abbott (2010) citing Russell (1917), so the open-endedness of a set can imply also a non-uniqueness of reference to the individuals that comprise it. Definiteness distinctions have also been described as discourse-based phenomena (e.g. Hopper 1987). However, the argument that chains of textual referential distinctions of definiteness should be explained as a discourse phenomenon has been challenged more recently as lacking anchorage to extra-linguistic reality (Bach 2008: 30), and such arguments necessitate invoking relationships of 'extension' to referents in the real world. If it were considered instead that assertions about open-ended sets of entities in generics referred to a general indefiniteness of quantification, rather than discourse-related indefiniteness, the problem of dealing with a satisfactory definition of discourse-related definiteness may be avoided altogether, and habitual generics could also be accommodated, as those referring to an indefinite/open-ended quantification of events. However, whether such assumptions may lead to a reduction of the definition of modality to the level of an indefiniteness notion alone is a topic for further investigation and exploration.

3.1 Morphosyntactic problems

If generics are perceived to be inherently modal in character, a further problem is that there is no way of determining how the modality is formally grammaticalised. If it is because they make assertions about open-ended sets of entities, as Krifka et al. (1995) suggested, then it must be assumed that the NP participants in a generic construction contribute in some way to the modal meaning of the entire construction. As early as Jackendoff (1971: 305), it was questioned what syntactic elements in a generic construction actually supply the generic meaning. Having dismissed the possibility of present tense or any aspectual element because of the availability of generic modals such as *can*, Jackendoff arrived at the conclusion that genericity was a property of the surface subject; thus in (7b) there is a generic statement, but not in (7a), e.g. (1971: 305):

(7) a. A rhinoceros eats small snakes. I saw it yesterday. (specific)
b. A rhinoceros eats small snakes. I saw one doing just that yesterday. (generic)

A specific rhinoceros is understood as one that is identified to the speaker (see below). However, (7a) seems a rather odd way of referring to a specific rhinocerous – it would appear more natural to use a presentative construction to introduce a specific subject, such as *There is a rhinocerous that eats small snakes*. Furthermore, the statement in (7a) is, like (4), a habitual, and thus is still generic even though the subject is specific. Thus it remains problematic to suggest that the meaning of generics can be located in the specificity distinctions of the subject NPs alone; in addition, the subject's generic nature in (7b) cannot be used to isolate the modality of generics, if (7a) is a habitual generic.

Allan (1980: 551) also questioned the capacity for generics to have a form-function correspondence, suggesting that the only identifying element they contained was the scope of their reference – noun phrases used generically can otherwise be considered formally identical to non-generics. The problem of attributing the modality in a generic construction to the semantics of the subject NPs is equally perplexing in Allan's comparison between: *The lion is hungry* and *The lion is carnivorous*, as the generic meaning can be derived from the predicate meaning – the generic statement is defined by its content, a law-like statement that holds for all times, not a temporary state. Nevertheless, the syntax of the two constructions is identical, so generics in English, at least, need to be identified also by the properties of their predicates. Most importantly, Allan stresses that generic predicates must always range over countable entities; this means that the predicate implies the indefinite and non-specific quantification of its subject. In such cases, the subject of a generic statement, whether a bare plural, a definite singular or an indefinite singular, always refers either to an unidentified, but replicable entity, or collectively to the kind to which it belongs (the entire class of entities).

Cohen (1999: 40) discusses the restrictions on the use of indefinite singulars to express genericity, which may also suggest that the subject NP in a generic construction is a doubtful candidate for the derivation of the modality attributed to it. He proposes that certain generic constructions cannot be entirely interchangeable with other means of expressing genericity, for example:

(8) a. The dinosaur is extinct.
b. Dinosaurs are extinct.
c. *A dinosaur is extinct.

Cohen attributes the anomaly of (8c) to the fact that the predicate, *extinct*, requires a kind or genus as its argument, i.e., it must refer to the entire category of dinosaurs, which is only possible for the definite determiner in (8a) and the bare plural (8b). He also cites Jespersen (1927) whose original claim was that indefinite singulars referred only to a representative of a kind, not to the entire kind itself. A similar argument was put forward by Krifka et al. (1995: 13), e.g. in (9):

(9) *A madrigal is popular

an example first attributed to Lawler (1973). Jespersen's claim that indefinite singulars referred only to a representative of a kind seems to be supported by such an example, since popularity cannot be ascribed to all exemplars of the kind, *madrigal*. For this reason, the introduction of a modal verb renders the construction more probable: *A madrigal can be popular*, but does not remove the fact that the example expresses genericity. Krifka et al. (1995) claim, though, that indefinite singulars are linked to characterising sentences, and thus, *A football hero is popular* is acceptable because the notion of being popular is essential to footballers, though not to madrigals. In (9), then, the predicate does not necessarily represent a characterisation of madrigals (though the use of a possibility modal such as *can* also rules out an essential characterising sense). Krifka et al. (1995) emphasise the need to distinguish between kind reference and characterising predication as two different types of generic expressions, but it would seem that the predicate in (9) is disallowed because of the fact that it refers only to a changeable state of affairs, and cannot be justified for all madrigals as a timeless characteristic, in the same way as *The lion is hungry* refers to a changeable state (Allan's (1980) example above). Thus the predicate semantics still contributes significantly to the interpretation of a generic, and hence, to its modality. In the same way, reinforcement with possibility modals such as *can* offers the kind of timelessness that is otherwise missing in such examples.

What this means though, is that indefinite singular generics cannot always be held to have the same scope as bare plurals or definite singulars. Genericity, as a semantic category, then, must be seen to schematize over either universals expressing necessary distribution or existentials expressing possible but representative distribution, and (9) is a viable cancellation diagnostic; in other words, it stands as a failed representative generalisation. Krifka et al. (1995: 34) classify examples such as (8a) as specific in reference but kind-referring, hence universal (thus not all generic nouns are non-specific), whereas indefinite singular generics are non-specific, but may be either kind-referring or not, depending on what is expressed in the predicate – either a universal statement or a mere tendency. If anything, indefinite singular generic statements may be considered in terms of 'sub-generics': they fall into the category of generics simply because they happen to share a common semantic denominator of non-specificity of reference, and it is at such a point of semantic overlap that they can function in some cases to express possible genericity. However, this does not bring us any closer to the possibility of determining the morphosyntactic ingredients that serve to express the modalisation of generic constructions. Even bare plural subjects may not always express generic statements; for example, in news reports:

(10) Police use a water cannon on rioters after **protests** turned violent in Rome, Italy on Sunday.
[http://www.guardian.co.uk/world/picture/2011/oct/17/italy-occupy-movement]

Carlson (2006) supplies similar examples, but bare plurals can occur elsewhere in the clause, as in *rioters* as well, and they are not generic nominals. Thus we have seen that it is not possible to determine the semantics of generics consistently in the three subject types prototypically associated with a generic construction, the definite singular NP, the indefinite singular, and bare plural, since the same subject types may be found elsewhere in non-generic constructions. Therefore, if the nominal participants in a generic construction contribute in some way to the modality of a generic, there still remains the additional problem of how such modality is grammaticalised. What the two examples in (10) do have in common, though, is their absence of referentiality to an identified set of entities. This means that they share with the archetypical generic nominal a non-specificity of reference, and it is this category of noun reference which now requires closer attention.

3.2 Specificity in nominals

Specific reference had been discussed in the context of creoles since Bickerton (1981), amongst others, but also in reference to African languages by Givón (1973, 1978, 1981). Givón had referred to the presence of a referential/non-referential distinction, rather than a specific/non-specific one, and with almost the same definition: that the nominal expression should have non-empty references; i.e. "to 'exist' within a particular universe of discourse" (1978: 293). In the same paper, he draws attention to the fact that ambiguity between referential and non-referential reference can be found under the scope of a POSSIBLE or NEG(ATIVE) modality; in all other cases, the nominal must be interpreted referentially (1978: 294). In his 1973 study, Givón goes to great lengths to elucidate all the possible grammatical environments in which non-referential nominals may be interpreted. It is not the aim of the present paper to dispute the early work of Givón, though it may be worth quoting the following claim made in Givón (1973: 120):

> "It is thus the modality of propositions and the speaker's commitment to believing in the reality of the events they describe, which determines the speaker's ability to use and interpret nominals nonreferentially, suggesting a natural link between propositional modality and non-reference of nominals within the scope of non-assertives."

Givón does not suggest that the non-referential nominal is rendered modal by being in the scope of modality, only that modality scope renders the nominals non-referential. Givón's studies are amply supported with data from a range of languages, though it is only in his 1981 paper that he approaches the category of generics with any curiosity. However, the attribution of the non-referentiality of certain nominals to the modal contexts which have scope over them does not help to determine the source of modality in generics: generics may contain no marking for modality whatsoever, and yet the nominals found in them are frequently non-specific. It is questioned, then, whether non-specifics found in such contexts are in fact autonomously represented as nominal modals.

The distinction of specific reference leaves many more mysteries in its wake. Geurts (in press) succinctly summarises the consensus on the definition of specificity as outlined in Kasher and Gabby (1976), Fodor and Sag (1982), Manga (1996), Kratzer (1995), Yeom (1998), and van Rooy (1999) as referring to the knowledge of the speaker of a particular NP referent, distinguished from a definite NP by the fact that the hearer does not know the identity of the referent. He adds that there are no linguistic devices dedicated to the function of expressing the speaker's knowledge alone, in this respect, and refers to Haspelmath's (1997) claims of the number of languages available in which the same indefinite NP can signal the knowledge of the referent by the speaker as the absence of speaker-knowledge of the referent; e.g. German *irgendein*, which can be used specifically or non-specifically, as can English indefinite articles (Geurts, in press: 4):

(11) Wilma hat vor, irgendeinen Schweden zu heiraten
Wilma intends some-or-other Swede to marry.

The English translation: 'Wilma intends to marry a Swede', is thus equally ambiguous between specific and non-specific. However, it is arguable in classic cases such as (11), in English as well as in German, what form of specificity is actually under consideration: the absence of a social identity (i.e. the name of the Swede) need not imply that the particular individual in mind did not have an identity in the speaker's mind (the speaker might be cognizant of the individual without actually being aware of his name). The fact is that specificity always implies existence (past or present), whereas non-specificity can, but need not imply the existence of the referent. If so, it may offer grounds for a definition of nominal modality.

Geurts' main argument is that specificity should not be considered a distinct feature of many languages, as it is encoded in the same way as either an indefinite or a definite expression, e.g. in Lillooet Salish (citing Matthewson 1999) where the indefinite article can only appear in the scope of what are commonly referred to as negative polarity items. The presentative function of the article across languages though, be it definite or indefinite, is usually specific; this is due to the nature of the information structure of the utterance, as Geurts points out. Thus, there is therefore no hard-and-fast crosslinguistic rule determining whether specificity should be encoded in the same way as definites or in the same way as indefinites, specifics seem to be at an intermediate point between the two discourse categories, as is shown in many languages (see also Givón 1978).

Von Heusinger (2002) characterises specificity as existentially presupposed (2002: 246), and disambiguated (in English) by the use of *a certain*. The fact that *a certain* can be used to paraphrase a specifically-referring NP only serves to indicate that non-specifics, on the other hand, must be *not* existentially presupposed, and are therefore uncertain in terms of existence. This is what had been claimed by Lyons (1977: 190-1), when he stated that non-specifics do not always refer to the existence of their referents. Von Heusinger (2002) attempts to seek out a more rigorous semantic definition of specifics, suggesting that the speaker's knowledge of the referent is inadequate as a definition (after all, if this is not overtly encoded, how does one know what the speaker has in mind?). It could be argued that *a certain* reinforces the lost sense of specificity that the indefinite article once had historically (see below). Von Heusinger isolates the specificity distinction in (English) NPs as dating back to Baker (1966) and Fillmore (1967), also citing Givón's (1978) use of the term 'referentiality' to mean the same thing. However, his own explanation of the term 'specific' is upheld by discourse representation theories (as is Geurts', to a certain extent), and he suggests that the use of a non-specific nominal is an indication that it cannot be linked to a previously established discourse referent (2002: 252). He approaches the problem of definition by maintaining that specificity is just a matter of linking the referent to another already introduced referent in the discourse, or to the speaker.

Thus, it appears that the category of specific vs. non-specific nominals is something of an overlay on other, marked distinctions such as definiteness, and that some languages align specificity with definite markers while others align it with indefinite markers. Von Heusinger (2002: 254) claims that there are no articles dedicated to specific distinctions alone in any Indo-European languages. We have seen that there are at least two accounts which indicate a discourse-pragmatic explanation for the use of specificity distinctions; such accounts cater for the distributional occurrences of specific vs. non-specific markers across languages, and the same observational approaches were put forward by Givón (1981). However, with regard to the many uses of specific indefinite articles such as in English, it could be questioned why an indefinite article is even actually used, when it only renders ambiguous the referentiality of the NP in question to the hearer, as in the English translation of (11):

(12) Wilma intends to marry a Swede.

As noted for (7), the specificity needs to be disambiguated by supplementary information, e.g.:

(13) I was introduced to him at Wimbledon last year.

One might then ask, if the speaker needs always to clarify the identity of the indefinite referent, why bother using the indefinite article in the first place? Under a Gricean account, the speaker would be accused of being under-informative. However, if the speaker is adhering to the Quantity 1 maxim (Grice 1975), and supplying as much information as known, then the information in (13) should not be required. But there is a reason for using an indefinite specific, and that is if the speaker may not *intend* to disclose the identity of the referent, in other words, it serves as a means of withholding information, and flouting the Quantity 2 maxim for whatever reason (e.g., in (12) the Swede may be someone unmentionable, or simply have an unpronounceable name, or the speaker may wish to focus on his nationality rather than his identity). It could be argued, then, that the use of specific indefinites may be somewhat restricted in today's English, a fossil of a historically older system that must have once held more salience in discourse than it does in the present day. Notwithstanding, the evidence from non-specifics illustrates that they are not always associated with generic constructions, as in (12), though their meanings remain generic even outside of such constructions. Moreover, the definition of non-specifics as relating to the absence of the identity of the referent is in accord with their generic semantics, which, as noted above, refer to generalisations over individuals. This indicates that non-specific NPs may provide the source of generic meaning in generic constructions and, if they are taken as referring to existentially uncertain entities, the source of generic modality as well. In summary, then, the following hypotheses may be proposed at this stage:

(14) i. Nominal modality is covert in non-specific indefinites, and is associated with their semantics of non-identification;
ii. Modality is covert in non-specific indefinites, but not just because such nominals are tied to the scope of propositional modality.

However, the following question remains:

iii. How is nominal modality grammaticalised, if non-specific indefinites are indistinguishable from specific indefinites?

In seeking the answers to such questions, it is appropriate to consider some of the data from contact languages and creoles, since it will be seen that the ambiguities of specificity distinctions are to be found much less frequently in such languages than in standard dialects of English.

4. Indefinite determiners in creole systems

In discussing specificity distinctions in nominals, it should also be noted that only count nouns are eligible for classification as specific indefinites (at least in English); that bare mass nouns are inherently non-specific, e.g. in

(15) There is water on the floor

water is non-specific. However, this is not because it is not known to the speaker, but because of its non-individuable characteristics. In order to make it specific, a determiner such as *some* might be used, though even then, the specificity is usually only present when there is contrastive stress placed on *some*. This raises the question of individuation as a necessary ingredient for determining specificity, and for this reason it is also useful to study the evidence from pidgins and creoles, which often have a rigorous system for marking individuation in nominals, without necessarily an accompanying indefinite article system. Such patterns are illustrated in Mufwene (1981) and more recently, Stewart (2011), in the case of Jamaican Creole, where non-individuation may apply to either count or mass nouns, as shown in the following examples (Mufwene 1981: 229-230):

(16) ***Buk** de aal uova di tiebl ina im afis*
'There are books all over the table in his office.'

In (16) the absence of plural marking on *buk* indicates that non-specific plural count nouns in Jamaican Creole are considered as non-individuable, in the same way as mass nouns:

(17) ***Wata** de aal ouva di tiebl ina im afis*
'There is water all over the table in his office.'

In order to express singular individuation, either the determiner *di* or *wan* may be used, depending on whether the speaker wishes to express definite or indefinite individuation:

(18) ***Di/wan buk** (de) pan di tiebl ina im afis*
'The book is on the table in his office.'
'There is a book on the table in his office.'

Definite plurals may also be individuated using the plural marker *dem*:

(19) ***Di*** *buk dem de aal uova di tiebl ina im afis*
'The books are all over the table in his office.'

These examples do not necessarily suggest that there is no article system in Jamaican Creole, only that there is an implicit system for marking specific vs. non-specific distinctions in indefinite reference that aligns the formal expression of non-specific plural forms with mass nouns, due to their absence of potentiality for individuation. Mufwene, however, did not mention the likelihood of specificity distinctions, though these seem to emerge as a natural consequence of the need to distinguish individuation in the language, suggesting, further, that specificity overlaps with individuation in nouns. Patrick (2004) notes that the specificity distinction in Jamaican Creole is linked with tense and time reference, so that past temporal expressions all have specific referents (Leiss 2008 has observed similar correlations between perfective aspect and definiteness in Gothic and Old High German). Patrick (2004) further states that bare NPs are always generics though some bare NPs in the scope of past time reference can be specific. Similar evidence is supplied in Stewart (2011), who supplies one example of a singular non-specific (which she refers to as a singular generic), left as a bare nominal, just as for non-specific plurals (2011: 373):

(20) Waya a paizn ting
wire BE poison thing
'Wire is a poisonous thing.'

The single example is taken from Bailey (1966: 27).[4]

Additional examples are found in Hawaiian Creole, as Janson (1984) discusses, suggesting that the numeral *one* (*wan*) was introduced in the functional role of a new indefinite article, but did not replace the indefinite article with non-specific nouns because of the inappropriateness of using a numeral in cases where no specific referent can be counted (1984: 297). Again, we see an interesting overlap between specificity and individuation: specific indefinites being marked by *wan* and non-specifics aligning with bare mass nouns in having zero-marking, even if they are count nouns. Janson, however, finds varying patterns occurring in other creoles, and

---

[4] Patrick (2004) notes that in equatives like (20), the copula is *a*, a reduced form of the older form *da*, and that this varies with *is / was* in the mesolect. He also notes that the zero copula does occur but that Rickford (1996) shows that the copula has a more than 80% frequency of occurrence. However, he cites Bailey (1966) as mentioning that it is omitted in predicative NPs.

uses the data from Seychelles French Creole and Papiamentu to argue against the monogenesis hypothesis of Bickerton (1981) that a specific/non-specific distinction is universal across creoles. Instead, he proposed that there cannot be a single, universal explanation to the presence or absence of articles in creoles, as indeed there are many non-creole languages which do not have an article system (such as Russian). In one example, he provides evidence from Cameroon English Pidgin (from Todd 1979) to suggest that the language does not have any marker for indefinite nouns, whether specific or non-specific. However, he notes that, sometimes a determiner *sohm* is preposed in front of a noun (Janson 1984: 312):

(21) *trohki si* ***sohm*** *bush dia*
'Tortoise saw a wild deer' (Todd 1979: 44)

This item is not explained further, though it does appear as an optional nominal determiner under his listing of indefinite singular nouns (1984: 313). Janson continues to insist that the specific/non-specific distinction is not encoded; however, the paradigm is almost identical to Mufwene's (1981) noun classifications in Jamaican Creole: indefinites (singular or plural) are left unmarked except for an optional marker in the singular, in this case, *sohm*, and definites are always marked with a definite article *di*.

Although Janson's work pre-empts grammaticalisation studies to some extent, it does not ignore historical universals, and he is aware of the development of indefinite articles in Indo-European languages from numeral sources meaning 'one', and definite articles from demonstrative sources meaning 'this' or 'that'. It is only later that we see that Bickerton's early monogenesis hypothesis might have survived had it been better structured in terms of a comparative, historical appeal to grammaticalisation universals. For the same reason, Janson might have provided a more convincing argument if he had investigated the sources of the indefinite article in Old English, and found that a form meaning 'one' had co-existed alongside a form *sum* (= 'a certain' – see Quirk and Wrenn 1957) both of which had a function of marking specificity in the discourse (see below). Thus, the use of the optional determiner *sohm* in Cameroons English Pidgin in (21) could represent a specific indefinite that is reminiscent of one used in the early historical development of the English language itself. If these were the sources of the now grammaticalised determiner forms in present-day English, it would not be surprising to see the same patterns of development emerging in a new language like a creole. Universals do have a strategy, and all other things being equal, in the redevelopment of a new language, it would not be unexpected that the same grammaticalisation sources should be found, neutral to time differences, since grammaticalisation strategies are universal in diachrony as well as across languages (see, e.g. Heine and Kuteva 2002).

4.1 Colloquial Singapore English

Colloquial Singapore English (Singlish) is not a creole in the technical sense, though it has been noted as possessing many of the prototypical attributes of a creole, to the extent that it was labelled a 'creoloid' in earlier studies by Gupta (1991, 1994), who distinguished it as a contact variety of English, used as a lingua franca in a community of diverse language mixing. Input to the dialect may be said to have come from at least 10 different southern Chinese dialects, of which Southern Min and Cantonese are believed to have had the most influence in the past, but others such as Malay and a number of south Indian languages can also be said to have had a significant input (see, e,g., Ho and Platt (1993), Alsagoff and Ho (1998), Bao (2001, 2010), Deterding et al. (2003), amongst many others. CSE is spoken alongside a more educated variety, Standard Singapore English, which is claimed to vary little from any other standard variety (Gupta 1994), though it must be said that it is nevertheless in regular contact with the more colloquial sub-variety, as well as Mandarin Chinese, endorsed and institutionalised in the past 20 years as the prescribed Chinese dialect for interaction amongst the majority Chinese population.

The contact situation has the effect of creating a sub-variety which is rich in lexical borrowings, discourse particles and grammatical features (see, e.g., Alsagoff and Ho (1998), reflecting those of the other local languages that were once spoken quite profusely on the tiny, Southeast Asian island-nation, a trading port of around 4 million inhabitants. For this reason, it is also difficult to determine the origin of certain features, such as the absence of plural marking on some nouns (Alsagoff and Ho 1998: 143):

(22) She queue up very long to buy **ticket** for us.

Rather than describing this feature as an absence of plural marking, Alsagoff and Ho intuitively refer to the use of *ticket* in (22) as of non-count or mass usage, suggesting that many nouns that are not quantified can be used as either count nouns or non-count nouns in CSE, i.e. number marking is not obligatory. What they actually mean though, is that there is no countability requirement in CSE for unquantified NPs. Similarly, they suggest that CSE often treats singular count nouns as non-count by the omission of an article (1998: 144):

(23) She got **car** or not?
'Does she have a car?'

though they do not venture any further to explain the reason why this may be so.

In Ziegeler (2003, 2010b) many similar examples of zero-plural count nouns were listed, e.g. in listings of commercial goods for sale (Ziegeler 2003), where specifically-quantified items are marked for plural, e.g. *All items*, but those of unknown quantity are only variably marked: *and many more item*, *belt*, *wallet*, *shirt*, *jacket* (but nevertheless, *bags*). The tendency to leave specifically-unquantified nominal referents unmarked for plurality is found in many other situations, e.g., in a traffic warning sign (Ziegeler 2010b: 57):

(24) BEWARE OF PEDESTRIAN

in which the noun *pedestrian* refers to not one, but a potentially limitless number of unknown pedestrians that may cross the road from time to time.

In other examples, the singular noun was left unmarked (2010b: 59):

(25) a. I use **plastic spoon** to scoop my honey & put my honey jar in **cool dry place**.
b. Yesterday i went for **foot and back massage** @ Suntec n [and] bought **one** set of this honey.
(source: http://www.flowerpod.com.sg/forums/index.php?showtopic=8627, 4/8/05)

In (25) there is no indefinite article preceding *plastic spoon*, *cool dry place* or *foot and back massage*.

The data from CSE led to the hypothesis that the omission of plural marking on unquantified nouns and the absence of indefinite articles in certain contexts were attributable to the fact that in both cases, the resulting bare nominal form was non-specific or generic and was thus treated as uncountable, indicating the correlation in such dialects between absence of reference and absence of measurability. In such cases, the form takes on the appearance of a non-count noun (as suggested by Alsagoff and Ho 1998), but actually it is zero-marked for number because of its non-specific reference. In fact, the CSE speaker is actively signalling the non-specificity of the nominal by leaving it bare, whether singular or plural. It would appear that the same distinctions are to be found in Jamaican Creole, as in (16) and (17).

On the other hand, it wasobserved as long ago as Platt, Weber and Ho (1984) that Singapore English marks specificity with the use of *one*, exactly as in Hawaiian Creole and Jamaican Creole discussed above; (25b) clearly illustrates one example of the usage, in which the speaker is referring to a specific set of honey products. The use of a *one* for this purpose, however, is becoming relatively infrequent, as a recent study shows (Ziegeler, 2010c), occurring not much more than once per 10,000 words in both the ICE-Singapore and the ICE-India, though it is often difficult to discern from written texts whether the usage is simply contrastive (enumerating a single item rather than several) or specific (in which case spoken usage would not carry any contrastive stress). The example in (25) does not appear to reflect numerical contrast; other examples can be found in both the ICE-Singapore and the ICE-India:

(26) <ICE-SIN:S1A-085#281:1:A>
But Kallang got **one** Fun world or what lah
'But there is a Fun World at Kallang!'

(27) <ICE-IND:S1A-020#32:1:A>
Like uh District Industries Corporation ... industries ... there is uh **one** corporation called uh Karnataka State Financial Corporation

In both these examples, the use of the specific is constrained to presentative functions, *got* being the verb often used in CSE to mean 'there is / are', influenced by the Chinese contact languages, in which a possessive verb is used to express existence, e.g. *yoŭ* 'have' in Mandarin; (see also Heine (1997) for more crosslinguistic examples). The presentative use of *one* in Indian English, another new variety of contact English, is also believed to be related to substrate factors (Sharma 2005).

Thus the specific-non-specific distinction in Jamaican Creole, CSE and to a certain extent, in Indian English as well, is clearly defined in terms of the use or non-use of the linguistic coding for countability, either singular or plural. It can be said that CSE is transnumeral (Heine and Kuteva 2005: 134), though, as with most cases it exhibits variability with respect to number marking, and variation can occur even in the same context and with the same speaker (or writer). Bare plural generic nouns referring to merchandise in commercial usage are frequently left unmarked in Singlish

(Ziegeler 2003), as mentioned, though this is not categorical either, indicating that the dialect is constantly in a state of change and development. The same patterns of marking for specificity are also observable in English diachronic data, as the next section explains.

5. Generic and specific indefinite nouns in the history of English

It has long been noted that in Old English, non-specific nouns were not marked with a determiner, as Quirk and Wrenn (1957: 71) observe, who suggest that if the use of the definite determiner was variable enough, the use of an indefinite article was even rarer. They refer to the numeral *an* 'one' which sometimes functioned to express 'a strong indefiniteness', a function which it shared with *sum* (= 'certain', e.g. (1957: 71):[5]

(28) *æt wæs an cyning*
'here was a (unique) king'

The use of *an* 'one' or *sum* 'some, a certain' to express specificity in Old English was also noted by Hopper (1987), and Hopper and Martin (1987), who distinguish the two markers by the fact that while *an* may occur anywhere, *sum* almost always occurs in the beginning of the discourse (Hopper and Martin 1987: 299). They note that the use of *an* / *a* with subsequent mentions in the discourse (i.e., specific), in their sample, falls from 56% in Old English to 10% in the 20th century, illustrating a shift to (non-specific) positions previously occupied by zero, and the decline in its referential function.[6] The following examples of *sum* and *an* occurring with specific-reference nominals in Old English are taken from the *Helsinki Corpus*:[7]

[5] Quirk and Wrenn (1957) did not provide the source details for their examples.
[6] Note that Hopper and Martin (1987), like Geurts (to appear), and Von Heusinger (2002), had discussed the significance of discourse representation as a means of determining the difference between specific and non-specific uses of nominals.
[7] Translations for the Old English examples, unless otherwise indicated, are taken from the original series of the Early English Text Society.

(29) Wæs **sum** munuc & mæssepreost in nehnesse his cetan eardigende, þæs noma wæs Hamgels
'There was a monk and priest living in the neighbourhood of his hut, whose name was Hamgels'
(850-950) *Bede's Ecclesiastical History.* (Ed. Miller), R 13.434.8.

(30) & mon geseah swelce hit wære **an** gylden hring on heofonum brædre þonne sunne
'and people saw, as it were, a golden ring in the heavens, broader than the sun'
(850-950) *Alfred's Orosius, Part* I. (Ed. Sweet), p. 234, R 10.234.8.

Non-specifics indefinites were often left bare:

(31) Secggaþ Siones dohtrum þæt heora cining cymeþ, milde & monþwære, & biþ sittende ofor **eoselan** folan þæs nytenes.
'Say to the daughters of Sion that their king cometh, meek and humble, sitting upon [an] ass, (even) the foal of the animal.'
(950-1050) *The Blickling Homilies.* (Ed. Morris), p. 79.

(32) He wæs **byrnende leohtfæt & lyhtende**
'He was [a] burning and [a] shining lamp.'
(950-1050) *The West Saxon Gospels.* (Ed. Skeat). R 5.35.

The absence of the indefinite article preceding an attributive predicate in Old English is also noted in Hopper (1987: 143). However, plural, non-specific indefinites and generics were nevertheless marked for plurality, as is seen in the Old English version of the book of *Genesis*:

(33) and ealle eorðan **nytenu**; Fleogende **fuglas,** and **sæfiscas**, þa farað geond ða sæwegas
'and all earthly beasts; flying birds and sea-fishes, and whatsoever goes through the paths of the sea'[8]
(950-1050). *The Old Testament.* (Ed. Crawford), R 8.8.

[8] Translations for this text were adapted from the 1611 King James version of *The Holy Bible* (British and Foreign Bible Society).

In (33) the plural nouns are preceded by the quantifier *ealle* 'all'. Without a quantifier, though, the bare plural form is still used when the reference is generic or non-specific:

(34) On Egypta lande ne cymð næfre nan winter, ne **renscuras**, ac on middan urum wintra beoð heora feldas mid **wyrtum** blowende, & heora orcyrdas mid **æpplum** afyllede.
'In Egypt the winter never comes, nor rain-showers, but in the middle of our winter their fields are blowing with crops, and their orchards are filled with apples.'
Ælfric's De Temporibus Anni.
(Ed. Henel, R 4.53.

Such cases were clearly non-specific in reference, and yet still marked for replicability using the plural form, suggesting that a countability system was in evidence for plurals, specific or non-specific, but that singular, non-specific nouns were not always marked for countability in the same way. Allan (1980: 51) claims that countability is defined by the head constituent of a NP falling within the scope of a denumerator, and he lists English denumerators as the following set: *one*, *a*, *each*, *every*, *either*, *three* (or any number), *several*, *many*, *both*, *(a) few*, but not *no*, *some*, or *all*. But then he goes on to suggest that if plurality is marked on the head noun of a NP, it is countable also, so if *all* does not function as a denumerator, there must be another reason why *all* co-occurs with plural count nouns (as in (33)). It is not clear from such claims whether a denumerator is a necessary or just a sufficient diagnostic for countability. What is important in Allan's study though, is the suggestion that countability must be indicated in English where the audience knowledge of it cannot be assumed (1980: 565); this means that non-specific indefinites must be marked for countability, unlike in CSE or Jamaican Creole, which do not have the same rule, as we have seen. It appears also that only plural indefinite non-specifics were marked for countability in Old English, whereas in present-day English, countability must be marked, perhaps redundantly, on both singular and plural non-specifics, using the indefinite article for singulars.

However, certainly by early Middle English, the numeral 'one' began expanding its range of uses to include indefinite singular nouns that could be classed as non-specific:

(35) nim þanne **anne** linnenne clað. & do hine eal wate on þan wætere.
'Take then a linen cloth, and make it all wet in the water.'
(1150-1250) *Peri Didaxeon.*
(Ed. Cockayne), P. 84.

In (35), the noun phrase, *anne linnenne clað* is expressed using *an* as a non-specific indefinite (it is unlikely that it could be glossed as a numeral 'one', since there is no presupposition of numerical contrast derivable from the context). The same text contains examples of the same noun without an indefinite determiner, even co-occurring with the indefinite article in the same clause:

(36) wryng þanne þur **linne clæþ**. & do hyt on **an** glæs fæt.
'Wring (it) then through a linen cloth and put it in a glass vessel.'
(1150-1250) *Peri Didaxeon.*
(Ed. Cockayne), P. 94.

Such variation is to be expected in a situation of overlap in grammaticalisation in which a new change is in progress and in the process of ousting an old form of usage (see, e.g. Heine, Claudi and Hünnemeyer 1991, Heine 1993). Traugott and Dasher (2002: 36) note a similar example in Old English, in which the noun is left bare in the Old English text, *Lacnunga*, p. 100: *wring þurh linenne clað*, which is glossed by them as 'squeeze (the medication) through *a* linen cloth' (my emphasis), with the non-specific indefinite, *linenne clað*, unmarked by any determiners in the original. The use of the non-specific *an* is found more often in the Middle English text, as it is written as a series of medical instructions for treatment of various ailments, and therefore the imperative mood also appears quite frequently, creating a non-assertive context which would be appropriate for non-specific indefinites (according to Givón 1973). Another non-assertive context in which non-specific uses of *an* appeared was that of interrogatives:

(37) Hwa durste slepen hwil his deadliche fa heolde **an** itohe sweord up on his heaued?
'How dare he sleep while his deadly enemy held a drawn sword at his head?'
(1150-1250) *Ancrene Wisse.*
(Ed. Tolkien), P. 166.

At this stage, the developing indefinite article also appears marked by the loss of the final nasal before a consonant:

(38) Ich am **an** ancre. **A** nunne. **A** wif iweddet. **a** meiden. **a** wummon ...
'I am a recluse. A nun. A wedded wife. A maiden. A woman ...'
(1150-1250) *Ancrene Wisse.*
(Ed. Tolkien), P. 163.

As noted earlier, *an* is not found in predicative positions in Old English (e.g. (32)); (38) represents then a later stage of its development. Von Heusinger (2002) claims that predicative uses of the indefinite (or definite) article are all non-specific, so the use appearing in this particular text is indicative of the grammaticalisation of the numeral *an* from strictly specific functions to become a non-specific, indefinite article in a relatively short period of time.[9] No prototypical generic functions appear in the data at this stage, though some examples appear in later Middle English texts that could be considered to be generic in nature:

(39) for it is a greet shame to **a** man to have **a** povere herte and **a** riche purs
(1350-1420) *The Riverside Chaucer.*
(Ed. Benson), P. 233.C2.

Although (39) does not express a law-like statement in the scientific sense, it is generic in that the use of the non-specific NPs *a man*, *a povere herte*, and *a riche purs* refer to a quantifiably indefinite range of referents, i.e., they have maximal scope; furthermore, the statement is not grounded in time or space. There are many similar examples in Chaucer; it can be estimated that the indefinite article had generalised to co-occur with most non-specifics by the 15th century.

---

[9] De Swart and Zwarts (2009: 282) cite examples of predicative uses of bare nouns in today's English such as *Anne is head of department*; such examples are non-referential because they are not verb arguments. However, *department* is also bare, the obvious reason being that in both cases, the identity of the noun is not required. Predicative uses of indefinite articles, which they cite as not generally occurring in the bare predicative NPs of German, Dutch and French, could suggest a functional redundancy in English relative to the other languages, since the countability of the predicate is obvious from the context.

6. Discussion

The data from Old and Middle English are interesting for the fact that they reflect, in most cases, the gradual emergence of the indefinite article system developing out of the numeral 'one', as discussed in Givón (1981), Hopper (1987) and Hopper and Martin (1987). More recently, the same development has been noted as a crosslinguistic phenomenon, described by Heine (1997b), Heine and Kuteva (2002) and Heine and Kuteva (2006) as a universal pathway of grammaticalisation applicable to Albanian, Turkish, German, French, Ewe, Moré, Hungarian, Lezgian, Tamil, and Easter Island (Heine and Kuteva 2002: 220-1). In these languages, the numeral marks both specific indefinites as well as non-specifics. In Heine (1997b: 72-4), a five-stage sequence of changes is observed to take place in the grammaticalisation of the indefinite article from the numeral 'one' crosslinguistically. The five stages are the following (1997b: 72-4):

Stage 1: The numeral, in which specific indefinite reference may be left unmarked.
Stage 2: The presentative marker, introducing a new participant into the discourse.
Stage 3: The specific marker, when the form develops a discourse function in marking any nominal participant that is known to the speaker but presumably not to the addressee (this means that in many cases non-specific reference is marked in opposition by bare nominals.
Stage 4: The non-specific marker, no longer restricted to marking specific reference, but used whenever an indefinite singular nominal is referred to.
Stage 5: The generalised article, not restricted to determining singular count nouns but possible with plural and mass nouns also e.g. Spanish: *unos hombres* (one Masculine-Plural men: 'some men').

From the historical data above, we can see that Stage 2 was already underway in Old English (ex. 28), Stage 3 was also found, as illustrated in (30), and (35) and (37) illustrate the later expansion of its functions to Stage 4 in Middle English, which includes the category of indefinite singular generics (Stage 5 does not apply to English, which happened to recruit the counterpart Old English indefinite, *sum*, 'some', to generalise over non-specific plurals instead, as seen in the gloss above). It may be argued that indefinite singular sub-generics should be included at Heine's (1997b) Stage 4, but evidence from the Helsinki Corpus shows their possible appearance as a later stage of development (e.g. (39) – more evidence is required to determine exactly when). From the point of view of the data from creoles and from Colloquial Singapore English, it is clear that as far as the indefinite article is concerned, the expansion of the functions of the indefinite article lags slightly behind those of the historical data, with some speakers in some contexts leaving non-specific indefinites unmarked (e.g. (23 - 25)). It could be the case that the 'lag' is due to the fact that such contact languages are new by comparison to their more established lexifiers, and thus are undergoing the same developmental patterns in the grammaticalisation of certain forms, but at a different rate – accelerating over a few generations the processes that have taken hundreds of years in the diachronic model (see Heine and Reh 1984: 87). Thus it is the 'newness' of such languages that makes them appear to be retreating to earlier stages of grammaticalisation for some items, while in fact, they are actually in the process of recapitulating earlier, universal developmental stages.

In terms of the stages shown by present-day English relative to the new varieties, though, there is an additional level of meaning that has been accrued in the expansion of the indefinite article to non-specifics, and this is the covert level of modalisation of reference, as proposed in (14). In isolating such a development, it is intended to proceed on the understanding of modality as in section 1 as encoding any kind of potentiality through a linguistic device, and that truth values that appear without actualisation at the moment of speaking are amongst the meanings that are most akin to the notion of potentiality as a defining feature of modality; i.e., they provide factuality without actuality. Thus it could be argued that actualisation has a role to play in discriminating modal from non-modal utterances. It was argued earlier that Krifka et al.'s (1995) definition of generic modality as justified by reference to open-ended sets of participants suggests otherwise an alignment of modality with indefiniteness, verbal or nominal. As such, though, it also implies a definition of modality based on the non-actualised potentiality of existence.

In the same way, an indefinite singular generic noun forms the basis for an inductive inference concerning the entire class of its kind, as noted above, though it may be said that the indefinite singular generic is not a fully-qualified candidate for generic functions, as there are certain restrictions on its use that are not present in the case of the bare plural generic or the definite singular generic (see, e.g., (9)). The sub-generic function of the indefinite article, used non-specifically, nevertheless, may be understood as a type of nominal modality, since it implies the possible existence of its referent (in the same way as full generics by referring to open-ended sets), and in this way acts as a quantifier over the factuality of the noun phrase it is found in. If we consider again the points raised in Mufwene (1981) and Stewart (2011), it is possible to conclude that mass nouns are treated morphologically in the same way as bare plurals in Jamaican Creole and Bantu. The reasons for this can be either that bare plurals or unquantified plural count nouns are perceived as conceptually equivalent to mass nouns, or that there is some other common semantic reason to explain their formal representation. The reason that Mufwene supplies is that of non-individuation.

However, in CSE, as well as in Jamaican Creole, as we have seen, non-specific singular count nouns are also left unmarked for quantity. For this reason it may be concluded that non-specific singulars and zero-plurals in such languages are simply determined to be *non-denumerable*, or uncountable (hence the appearance in many commercial situations of examples such as *noodle* (see Ziegeler 2010b). Items which are considered uncountable are not marked for plural, in the same way as in most varieties of English, *sand* and *rice* are considered to be equivalent to mass nouns, because of their consistency of non-denumerable units (see also Langacker 2002: 71). Languages such as CSE, though labelled transnumeral, could instead be considered to have a count system, since number is marked only on actual referents, rather than a countability system as for standard English, which extends the count system to include unactualised and *potentially denumerable referents*, hence, modal nouns. Thus, in using an indefinite article with non-specific reference, the speaker is signalling a certain amount of predictability of the existence of the referent which it determines, in the same way as modifying a declarative speech act with modal auxiliary forms signals the predictability of the proposition contained in it.

It is therefore in the countability system of English, rather than the reference system, that a grammatical form of covert modality may reside, since the speaker, as Allan (1980) noted, is required to mark countability even on referents with no certainty of existence. Such distinctions are made manifest in the contrasts drawn by languages such as CSE, in which the system of numeration only applies to nouns that have actualisation. Non-actualised NPs in such dialects often remained unmarked for quantification, whether singular or plural, thus attributing them with a property of immeasurability. Countability then becomes the means of distinguishing reference from non-reference, in English and in the other languages we have examined, though in standard English countability is aligned with non-reference as well as reference. Non-specific reference in English, then, constitutes a form of "false quantification" over abstract entities, ascribing to the countability system a function of creating potential existence in a possible world, in the same way as verbal modality supplies a measurement of the potential existence of an event. Note that the provision of nominal modality in the form of generic possibility does not suggest the absence of existence altogether, merely its uncertainty, the inevitable result of inferences derived from referring to an unidentified entity in the discourse.

Thus, in the historical data, it can be seen that there are three coalescing domains from which the grammaticalisation of nominal modality may be seen to emerge as a by-product: one, the functional domain of discourse reference distinctions, which refers to the extension of the determiner *one* to non-specific environments marking indefiniteness as a text function, another, the morphosyntactic domain of countability distinctions, which extends to falsely quantify nouns that have uncertain existence in the real world (the countability domain includes plural non-specifics), and a third, the semantic domain of referent identification distinctions in nominals which refers to their non-specificity in the speaker's world of reference. The non-specific indefinite article, like plural morphology on generic (bare) plurals, functions to express simultaneously uncertainty of reference in the discourse context and at the same time the false quantification of a potentially realisable entity. This process may be labelled a 'co-grammaticalisation' since it involves the development of a formal marking for indefiniteness at the same time as the modality of nominals is grammaticalising in the extension of countability distinctions to non-referential entities. The grammaticalisation of nominal modality as a by-product of the coalescence of the three interlocking domains can be illustrated as in Figure 1:

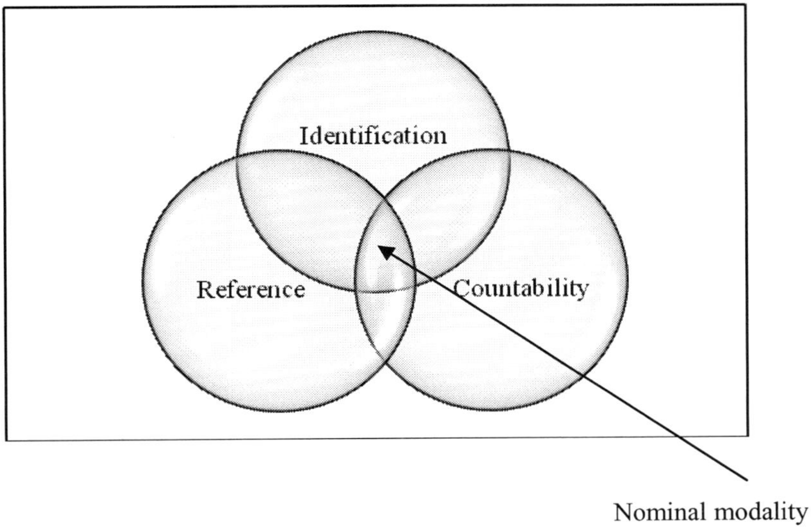

Fig. 1. Grammaticalisation of nominal modality (in English) as a by-product of the generalisation of countability distinctions to refer to unidentified referents in the discourse.

The data from languages such as CSE, though, differs from the historical patterns shown in that numeration is restricted to specific nouns only, singular or plural, or at least with a certain amount of variability according to the needs of the user. The numeration system in such languages is also affected by that of the contact languages, such as Chinese, which do not mark number in the same way, having a numeral classifier system. The development of nominal modality in such languages will similarly be influenced to a certain extent by the contact languages, and nominal modality may not be so prevalent: modal quantification is not a category of such systems, and countability is not grammaticalised to the same extent. Thus the coalescence seen in Figure 1 is shown less frequently in languages such as CSE and Indian English, or at least, only as far as variability permits, as the grammaticalisation of countability may be still emerging.

Bisang (1998) discusses countability in mathematical psychology as the mapping of objects onto numbers; thus without objects there can be no measurability. The viewpoint of the contact languages surveyed is just that: that measurability requires the actualisation of objects. In the indefinite reference system in English, an illusion is created of measuring what is not actually there, thus a more subjective and more abstract system of reference is required than is possible in many other languages. In the data shown, it seems that such a system emerged as a gradual development through time, possibly coinciding with other changing events in the grammatical system of English.

7. Conclusions

The words of Lord Kelvin at the beginning of the present study may now be considered again, with the possibility that he was correct in suggesting that if you cannot measure something, then it has no significance. We have seen in the above examples that there is a correlation in some languages between measurability in nominals and specificity of reference, and specificity of reference is defined by speaker knowledge (as distinct from what is generally known as the 'common ground' or shared knowledge between speaker and hearer). Modality derives from the speaker's need to abstract from reality, and in doing so, she is using the tools that are traditionally used to express the reality of an entity, those of quantification. While nominals were quantified with a range of determiners in Old English, they were not individuated for singularity unless they were known to the speaker. Thus knowledge of the existence of the referent presupposed its countability; what was not known was not countable.

The present paper has also attempted to answer the question posed earlier, and that is, assuming that nominal modality is associated with non-specific, generic indefinites, how may it be grammaticalised when such categories are not formally distinguished from specific indefinites? The distinction of generic participants is dependent on the construction itself, though there is no single attribute in a generic construction (in English at least) that may be held to define it alone: the formal representation of the participants, as well as the verbal morphology, is the same as is found in other, non-generic expressions. The generic construction is defined by its context, it is a semantic expression that describes properties applying to an indefinite number of participants. Nominal modality is therefore a complex by-product of the grammaticalisation of countability over unidentified (generic) nominal referents, and is not represented as having an independently motivated form-function correspondence. Moreover, it is the open-ended nature of generic statements that leads to inferences of potential existence and nominal modality. At the same time, the generic construction is modalised either by the non-identification of the nominal participants it possesses or by the non-identification of the open-ended sets of events to which it refers in habituals.

In the contribution of nominal reference to the sharper definition of modality as a general category across languages, it is therefore associated with the presence of generic meanings both in nouns as well as in the constructions in which they appear. Modality can be seen to emerge as an abstraction from the conditions of unactualised, timeless truth associated with generics, and producing inferences of probability relating to the future – for the existence of potential events or potential entities. The sense of timelessness derives as much from the nominal participants as from the nature of the predicates. In the present paper, we have discovered that marking for reference is inextricably linked to the speaker's needs to quantify existence, since it is only in existing referents that countability first appears, only later to be marked as a category on non-existent referents, or referents of uncertain existence. Thus, while non-specific reference may constitute aform of covert modality, countability marking is its only means of expression in terms of mood. According to Givón (1981: 51), "having quantity implies existence, [and] having existence implies connotation / genericity". When countability is applied to referents that have no actualisation in the real world, we may form an analogy with other categories known to the language system, such as modality. Note that in doing so, we are not entering into a debate on the existence or non-existence of non-extensional entities in the real world, but simply describing the ways in which language regards existence; i.e., through forms of measurability. Whether or not this corresponds to any scientific intuitions, as we might understand from Lord Kelvin, or is simply a convenient artifact of increased speaker-subjectification, is a question for future research and a far broader range of cross-linguistic surveys to undertake. The possibilities are limitless.

References

Abbott, Barbara 2010. *Reference*. Oxford: Oxford University Press.

Abraham, Werner (this volume). (Inter)Subjectification or Foreign Consciousness / Other's Mind Alignment as synchronic and diachronic concepts of change? Conceptualizations and data fidelity.

Allan, Keith 1980. Nouns and countability. *Language* 56, 3: 541-567.

Alsagoff, Lubna & Ho Chee Lick 1998. The grammar of Singapore English. In: J.A. Foley, T. Kandah, Z.M. Bao, A-F. Gupta, L. Algasoff, C. L. Ho, L. Wee & W. Bokhorst-Heng (eds.): *English in New Cultural Contexts. Reflections from Singapore*, 127-151. Singapore: Oxford University Press [Singapore Institute of Management].

Asher, N. 1979. *Tamil*. Amsterdam: North Holland.

Bach, Kent 2008. On referring and not referring. In: Jeanette K. Gundel & Nancy Hedberg (eds.): *Reference. Interdisciplinary Perspectives*, 13-58. New York: Oxford University Press.

Bailey, Beryl 1966. *Jamaican Creole Syntax. A Transformational Approach.* Cambridge: Cambridge University Press.

Baker, C.L. 1966. Definiteness and Indefiniteness in English. Unpublished Masters Thesis, University of Illinois.

Bao, Zhiming 2001. The origin of empty categories in Singapore English. *Journal of Pidgin and Creole Languages* 16: 275-319.

—. 2010. A usage-based approach to substratum transfer: the case of four unproductive features in Singapore English. *Language* 86, 4: 792-820.

Bickerton, Derek 1981. *Roots of Language*. Ann Arbor: Karoma.

Bisang, Walter 1998. Grammaticalization and language contact, constructions and positions. In: Anna Giacalone Ramat & Paul Hopper (eds.): *The Limits of Grammaticalization*, 13-57. Amsterdam / Philadelphia: Benjamins.

Brinton, Laurel J. 1996. *Pragmatic Markers in English: Grammaticalization and Discourse Functions* [Topics in English Linguistics 19]. Berlin / New York: de Gruyter.

Bybee, Joan 1994. The grammaticalisation of zero: asymmetries in tense and aspect systems. In: William Pagliuca (ed.): *Perspectives on Grammaticalization*, 235-254. Amsterdam / Philadelphia: Benjamins.

Bybee, Joan, Revere D. Perkins & William Pagliuca 1994. *The Evolution of Grammar: Tense, Aspect and Modality in the Languages of the World.* Chicago: University of Chicago Press.

Carlson, Gregory 2006. Generic reference. In: Brown, Keith (ed.): *Encyclopedia of Language and Linguistics*, 2nd edition. Amsterdam: Elsevier (pre-print version).

Cohen, Ariel. 1999. *Think Generic!* Stanford: CSLI Publications.

Cotte, Pierre 2002. Le possible, le nécessaire et la volonté. Paper presented at the 2002 ALAES, Institut Charles V, 1 fev. 2002. (Available at: http://www.univ-pau.fr/ANGLAIS/alaes/modaux.html).

Cristofaro, Sonia 2004. Past habituals and irrealis. In: Yuri A. Lander, Vladimir A. Plungian & Anna Yu Urmanchieva (eds.): *Irrealis and Irreality*, 256-272. Moscow: Gnosis.

De Haan, Ferdinand 2006. Typological approaches to modality. In: Frawley (ed.), 27-69.

Depraetere, Ilse & Chris Williams (eds.) 2010. Special issue on future time reference in English. Cambridge: Cambridge University Press (*English Language and Linguistics* 14, 2).

De Swart, Henrietta & Joost Zwarts 2009. Less form – more meaning: why bare singular nouns are special. *Lingua* 119: 280-295.

Deterding, David, Adam Brown & Ee Ling Low (eds.) 2003. *English in Singapore: Research on Grammar*. Singapore: McGraw Hill.

Evans, Nicholas 1995. *A Grammar of Kayardild, with Historical-Comparative Notes on Tangkic*. Berlin / New York: de Gruyter.

Evans, Nicholas 2003. Typologies of agreement: some problems from Kayardild. *Transactions of the Philological Society* 101: 203-34.

Fillmore, Charles 1967. The syntax of pre-verbs. *Glossa* 1: 91-125.

Fodor, W. A. & I. A. Sag 1982. Referential and quantificational indefinites. *Linguistics and Philosophy* 5: 355-398.

Foong, Ha Yap (this volume). Expressing mood and modality in Chinese: how we also do it without modal auxiliaries.

Frawley, William (ed.) 2006. *The Expression of Modality*. Berlin / New York: de Gruyter.

Geurts, Bart (in press). Specific indefinites, presupposition, and scope. To appear in: R. Bäuerle, U. Reyle & T. E. Zimmerman (eds.), *Presupposition and Discourse.*

Givón, Talmy 1973. Opacity and reference in language: an inquiry into the role of modalities. In: J. Kimball (ed.): *Syntax and Semantics 2*, 95-122. New York: Academic Press.

—. 1978. Definiteness and referentiality. In: J. H. Greenberg, C.A. Ferguson & E.A. Moravcsik (eds.): *Universals of Human Language.* Vol. IV, 291-330. Stanford: Stanford University Press.

—. 1981. On the development of the numeral 'one' as an indefinite marker. *Folia Linguistica Historica* II/1: 35-55.

Grice, H. Paul 1975. Logic and conversation. In Peter Cole & Jerry Morgan (eds.): *Speech Acts* [Syntax and Semantics 3]. 113-128. New York: Academic Press.

Gupta, Anthea Fraser. 1991. Almost a creole: Singapore Colloquial English. *California Linguistic Notes* 23: 9–21.

—. 1994. *The Step-Tongue. Children's English in Singapore*. Clevedon: Multilingual Matters.

Haspelmath, Martin 1997. *Indefinite Pronouns*. Oxford: Oxford University Press.

Haumann, Dagmar & Ole Letnes 2011. German modal particles and their (im)possible counterparts in English and Norwegian. Paper presented at the Workshop on Covert Modality, 44th Annual Meeting of the Societas Linguistica Europaea, Universidad de La Rioja, Logroño, 8-11 September 2011.

Heine, Bernd 1993. *Auxiliaries. Cognitive Forces and Grammaticalization.* New York: Oxford University Press.
—. 1997. *Cognitive Foundations of Grammar*. New York: Oxford University Press.
Heine, Bernd & Tania Kuteva 2002. *World Lexicon of Grammaticalization.* Cambridge: Cambridge University Press.
Heine, Bernd & Tania Kuteva 2005. *Language Contact and Grammatical Change*. Cambridge: Cambridge University Press.
Heine, Bernd & Tania Kuteva 2006. *The Changing Languages of Europe*. Oxford: Oxford University Press.
Heine, Bernd & Mechthild Reh 1984. *Grammaticalization and Reanalysis in African Languages*. Hamburg: Helmut Buske.
Heine, Bernd, Ulrike Claudi & Frederike Hünnemeyer 1991. *Grammaticalization. A Conceptual Framework.* Chicago: University of Chicago Press.
The Helsinki Diachronic Corpus of English Texts (electronic version). Department of English, University of Helsinki.
Ho, Mian Lian & John T. Platt 1993. *Dynamics of a Contact Continuum.* Oxford: Clarendon.
Hopper, Paul J. 1987. Emergent grammar. *Proceedings of the thirteenth Annual Meeting of the Berkeley Linguistics Society* 13: 139-57.
Hopper, Paul J. & Janice Martin 1987. Structuralism and diachrony: the development of the indefinite article in English. In: A. G. Ramat, O. Carruba & G. Bernini (eds.): *Papers from the seventh International Conference on Historical Linguistics*, 295-304. Amsterdam / Philadelphia: Benjamins.
Hopper, Paul J. & Elizabeth C. Traugott 2003[1993]. *Grammaticalization.* Cambridge: Cambridge University Press.
Huumo, Tuomas 2010. Nominal aspect, quantity and time: the case of the Finnish object. *Journal of Linguistics* 46: 83-125.
The ICE Corpus: The International Corpus of English. http://ice-corpora.net/ice/avail.htm.
Jackendoff, Ray S. 1971. Modal structure in semantic representation. *Linguistic Inquiry* 2, 4: 479-514.
Janson, Tore 1984. Articles and plural formation in creoles: change and universals. *Lingua* 64: 291-323.
Jespersen, Otto 1927 (= Jespersen, Otto. 1922-31). *A Modern English Grammar on Historical Principles*, Vol. IV. Heidelberg: Carl Winters.
Kasher, A. & D. M. Gabbay 1976. On the semantics and pragmatics of specific and non-specific indefinite expressions. *Theoretical Linguistics* 3: 145-190.

Keesing, Roger 1988. *Melanesian Pidgin and the Oceanic Substrate.* Stanford: Stanford University Press.

Kelvin, Lord 1883. *Popular Lectures and Addresses*. Vol. 1 (Personal volume). Available online: http://zapotopi.net/kelvin/quotes.

Klinge, Alex 2005. Where there is a *will*, there is a modal. In: Alex Klinge & Henrik Høeg Müller (eds.): *Modality: Studies in Form and Function*, 169-186. London: Equinox.

Kratzer, Angelika 1995. Scope or pseudoscope? Are there wide-scope indefinites? In S. Rothstein (ed.): *Events and Grammar*, 163-196. Dordrecht: Kluwer.

Krifka, Manfred, Francis Jeffrey Pelletier, Gregory N. Carlson, Alice ter Meulen, Godehard Link & Gennaro Cherchia 1995. Genericity: An introduction. In: Gregory N. Carlson & Francis Jeffrey Pelletier (eds): *The Generic Book*, 1–24. Chicago: University of Chicago Press.

Laca, Brenda 1990. Generic objects: Some more pieces of the puzzle. *Lingua* 81: 25–46.

Langacker, Ronald W. 1987. Nouns and verbs. *Language* 63: 53-94.

—. 1997. Generics and habituals. In: A. Athanasiadou & R. Dirven (eds.): *On Conditionals Again*, 191-122. Amsterdam / Philadelphia: Benjamins.

—. 2002. *Concept, Image and Symbol.* Berlin / New York: de Gruyter.

Lawler, J. 1973. Studies in English generics. *University of Michigan Papers in Linguistics* 1(1). Ann Arbor: University of Michigan Press.

Leiss, Elisabeth 2008. The silent and aspect-driven patterns of deonticity and epistemicity. A chapter in diachronic typology. In: Werner Abraham & Elisabeth Leiss (eds.): *Modality-Aspect Interfaces. Implications and Typological Solutions*, 15-41. Amsterdam / Philadelphia: Benjamins.

Lim, Lisa 2007. Mergers and acquisitions: on the ages and origins of Singapore English particles. *World Englishes* 26: 446-473.

Lyons, John 1977. *Semantics II.* Cambridge: Cambridge University Press.

—. 1995. *Linguistic Semantics. An Introduction.* Cambridge: Cambridge University Press.

Manga, L. 1996. *An Explanation for Ergative versus Accusative Languages: An Examination of Inuktitut.* Doctoral thesis: University of Ottawa.

Matthewson, L. 1999. On the interpretation of wide-scope indefinites. *Natural Language Semantics* 7: 79-134.

Mufwene, Salikoko 1981. Non-individuation and the count/mass distinction. *Papers from the Regional Meeting of the Chicago Linguistics Society*, 221-238.

Modicom, Pierre-Yves (this volume). Shared knowledge and epistemic reductionism: covert semantics of the German modal particles.

Narrog, Heiko 2005. On defining modality again. *Language Sciences* 27: 165-192.

Nuyts, Jan 2006. Modality: overview and linguistic issues. In: Frawley, William (ed.), 1-26.

—. 2012. Notions of intersubjectivity. Forthcoming in *English Text Construction* (special issue on intersubjectivity).

—. (to appear). Analyses of the modal meanings. To appear in: Jan Nuyts & Johan van der Auwera (eds.): *Handbook of Modality*. Oxford: Oxford University Press.

Palmer, Frank R. 1986[2001]. *Mood and Modality*. Cambridge: Cambridge University Press.

—. (2003). Modality in English: theoretical, descriptive and typological issues. In: Roberta Facchinetti, Manfred Krug & Frank R. Palmer (eds.): *Modality in Contemporary English*, 1-17. Berlin / New York: de Gruyter.

Patrick, Peter 2004. Jamaican Creole morphology and syntax. In: Bernd Kortmann, Edgar W. Schneider, Clive Upton, Rajend Methrie & Kate Burridge (eds.): *Handbook of Varieties of English*. Vol. 2: *Morphology and Syntax*. Berlin / New York: de Gruyter (draft version).

Platt, John T., Heidi Weber & Mian Lian Ho 1984. *The New Englishes*. London: Routledge & Kegan Paul.

Quirk, Randolph & C. L. Wrenn, 1957. *An Old English Grammar*. London / New York: Methuen.

Rickford, John R. 1996. Copula variability in Jamaican Creole and African American Vernacular English: A reanalysis of De Camp's texts. In: Gregory R. Guy, Crawford Feagin, Deborah Schiffrin & John Baugh (eds.): *Towards a Social Science of Language: Papers in honor of William Labov*. Vol. 1. *Variation and Change in Language and Society* [Current Issues in Linguistic Theory 127], 357-372. Amsterdam / Philadelphia: Benjamins.

Rijkhoff, Jan N. M. 1991. Nominal aspect. *Journal of Semantics* 8: 291-309.

Russell, Bertrand 1917. Knowledge by acquaintance and knowledge by description. Revised version in *Mysticism and Logic*. London: Longmans Green & Co. [2004 republication. Mineola, NY: Dover Publications, 165-183].

Sharma, Devyani 2005. Language transfer and discourse universals in Indian English article use. *Studies in Second Language Acquisition* 27: 535-566.

Stewart, Michele M. 2011. The expression of number in Jamaican Creole. *Journal of Pidgin and Creole Languages* 26, 2: 363-385.

Todd, L. 1979. *Some Day been Dey: West African Pidgin Folktales*. London: Routledge & Kegan Paul.

Traugott, Elizabeth Closs & Richard Dasher 2002. *Regularity in Semantic Change*. Cambridge: Cambridge University Press.

Van der Auwera, Johan 2001. On the typology of negative modals. In: Jack Hoeksema, Hotze Rulman & Victor Sanchez-Valencia (eds.): *Perspectives on Negation and Polarity Items*, 23-48. Amsterdam / Philadelphia: Benjamins.

Van der Auwera, Johan & Vladimir Plungian 1998. Modality's semantic map. *Linguistic Typology* 2: 79-124.

Van Rooy, R. 1999. The specificity of indefinites. Ms., University of Amsterdam.

Von Heusinger, Klaus 2002. Specificity and definiteness in sentence and discourse structure. *Journal of Semantics* 19: 245-274.

Yeom, J.-I. 1998. *A Presuppositional Analysis of Specific Indefinites: Common Grounds as Structured Information States*. New York: Garland.

Ziegeler, Debra 2003. On the zero-plural in commercial Singaporean English. In: Deterding et al. (eds.), 48-57.

Ziegeler, Debra P. 2006a. *Interfaces with English Aspect. Diachronic and Empirical Studies* [Studies in Language Companion Series 82]. Amsterdam / Philadelphia: Benjamins.

—. 2006b. Omnitemporal *will*. *Language Sciences* 28: 76-119.

—. 2010a. Semantic determinism and the grammaticalisation of *have to* in English: a reassessment. *Journal of Historical Pragmatics* 11, 1: 32-66.

—. 2010b. Count-mass coercion, and the perspective of time and variation. *Constructions and Frames* 2, 1: 33-73.

—. 2010c. Replica grammaticalisation as recapitulation. The other side of contact. Paper presented at the *Gramis* Conference, Royal Flemish Academy, Brussels, Nov. 11-13, 2010.

PART III:

COVERTNESS IN TYPOLOGY

Covert Patterns of Modality in Typological Comparison

Werner Abraham
Universität Wien und Universität München

Abstract: This brief typological overview compares to what degree different languages have means to give expression to modality (possibility, necessity) without lexical and direct inflectional means. The criterial patterns derive from German and English. They encompass mainly the auxiliaries *HAVE* and *BE* together with either an infinitival embedding of a full verb linked by the infinitival preposition *TO* or other aspectual means. It will be seen that what appear as typical covert modal expressions in the two Germanic languages, and Indo-European in a wider sense, cannot be seen as a recurrent pattern in non-Indo-European languages. Yet, there are recurrent and plausible forms that allow for generalizations.

1. Introduction

Sentences used in communications usually consist of 'propositions' and of 'modality components'. Propositions describe the state of affairs (e.g., what someone does to someone else or, more generally, what happens). Modality gives expression to the concern that the speaker of the utterance of the proposition has towards the proposition itself or to the addressee with respect to his, the speaker's utterance. Modality in the verbal sector is traditionally divided into 'root' (also, but infelicitously, 'deontic') and 'epistemic' types of modality. Root modality in the verbal sector, by itself, can further be subdivided (e.g., the 5-6 modal verbs in the Germanic languages). However, there are other, non-verbal exponents of modality such as the modal particles – a special form of discourse particles like the English sentential tags and weak modal adverbials. There are special particles in South East Asian languages such as Chinese, Thai, and Japanese occurring mostly in sentence-final position. They have similar, but not totally identical discourse functions as the Germanic ones (Abraham 2010, Cardinaletti 2011).

In what follows the focus lies on the verbal modalities of possibility and necessity that are not expressed directly by lexical or grammatical elements, but that come out from certain constructions by implication or implicature. To all appearances, covert modality comes in a number of clear constructions in German and in English. See below (1a-g) for German (see also Holl 2010) and (2a-f) for English (Bhatt 2006). (1b) is not Standard (written) German, but is the only form available in the dialects; there is no simple zu-infinitival embedding in the South German dialects. Notice that zum is the dative fusion of case marking and the preposition. In earlier stages of German, the dative was also marked on the gerundial form of the embedded infinitive thereby yielding a nominal form the the infinitive (capital *Lösen*).

(1) a *Die Aufgaben sind *(zu) lösen*
the tasks are to (be) solve(d)
– indicating obligatoriness or possibility

b *Die Aufgaben sind *(zum) Lösen*
the tasks are to (be) solve(d)
– indicating obligatoriness or possibility;
– gerundial form *zum Lösen*: only South –German dialects

c *die *(zu) lösen- (sei(e)n-)den Aufgaben*
the to solve (being.NUMBER) tasks
– indicating obligatoriness or possibility; gerundive
„the tasks to be solved"

d *Das Buch liest sich gut*
the book reads REFL well
– middle construction indicating possibility

e *Die Farbe ist abwaschbar*
the paint is off-washable
– passive modality of possibility

f *Das Glas ist zerbrechlich*
the glass is breakable
– passive modality of possibility

g *Das Auto fährt 210km/h*
the car rides 210km/hour
– generic reading; indicating possibility
– on the basis of conventional implicature[1]

---

[1] See von Wright's alethic equations < N (*p*) $_{df}$= I (~ p) $_{df}$= ~ P (~ *p*)>, in words: '*p* is necessary' is as much as to say that 'not-*p* is impossible' is again as much as to say 'It is not possible that not-*p*' (VON Wright 1976). The last equation is appealed to by (1g): From 'p is the case' follows that '*p* is possible'. While von Wright's "alethic (modality)" has become to be replaced terminologically by Kratzer's "circumstantial (modality)", von Wright's 'deontic (modality)' appealing to social

It is critical to focus only on the modal meanings denoted in the right margin because we want to exclude other meanings that have nothing to do with the modal ones. See (2a-c).

(2) a *im Kühlschrank ist (da) etwas zu trinken*
in the freezer is (there) something to drink
– no modal reading, just local existential
b **im Kühlschrank ist ein Bier zu trinken*
in the freezer is a beer to drink
c *Hier hast du etwas anzuziehen*
here have you something to put on
– no modal reading, just local existential

Notice the difference with (2a): The local adverbial *im Kühlschrank* "in the freezer" reduces the modality implication to nil the result being just an indication where something to drink is located. The same holds for (2c). (2b) receives no sensical reading because the beer would have to be drunk in the freezer. Obviously, all of this means that any indication of modal obligatoriness or possibility as in (1a) – and, by implication, in (1c) – depends on the agentivity of the subject. The <*x ist zu V*>-construction is a strong subject controller due, to all appearances, to the copula *ist* "is" as a one-place PATIENT adjectival and the preposition *zu* "to" as the passivizer and potential AGENT binder. In the ensuing discussion we want to exclude this interpretation of existential localization, and we know now how to avoid it.

The following utterances are owed to Bhatt as illustrations of silent modality (Bhatt 2006).

(3) a *Tim knows [PRO how to solve the problem]*
– *should*-Deontic, *could*-Possible/Able
b Jane found [a book [PRO to draw cartoons in]] for Sara
– *should*-Deontic, *could*-Poss/Able
c [$_{DP}$ the man [$_{REL}$ PRO to fix the sink]
– *should*-Deontic, *can/could*-Possible/Able

---

laws and human commitments still stands terminologically and conceptually: <O (*p*) df = F (~ *p*) df = ~ P (~ *p*)>, in words identical to the alethic formaltions above (abbreviations: N — necessary, P — possible, permitted, I — impossible, O — ethically necessary, obligatory, F — forebidden, df= defined as, ~ - Negation). See also Table 1.

d Sue went to Torino [PRO to buy a violin]
– *should*-Deontic, *could*-Possible/Able
e Bill has to reach Philadelphia before noon
– *should*-Deontic, *could*-Possible/Able
f William is to leave tomorrow
– *should*-Deontic, $^{(*)}$*could*-Possible/Able
g The stomach is to empty
– *should*-Deontic, **could*-Possible/Able
h The monument is to fall
– *should*-Deontic, **can*/**could*-Possible/Able

Bhatt (2006) focuses mainly upon embedded infinitival questions/EIQs and infinitival relative clauses in English as illustrated in (3a-h).[2]

German has more morphology to serve the encoding of the passive modality readings than English. Notice that also Dutch has abandoned the markings for case and number in comparison to German. However, just like all Germanic and Romance languages, it has to insert the infinitival preposition, *te*.

(4) a De opgaven zijn op *(te) lossen
b de op *(te) lossen opgaven

Dutch *(op)lossen* in attributive function in (3b) has no adjectival inflection, in contrast to German's present participle in attributive function. Compare (1c) above.

As shown below, I will restrict myself to illustrations from Indo-European. Non-Indo-European will be excluded here. This is for several reasons the main one being that modality may be encoded, directly or indirectly, in terms that are quite different from IE, namely: First, one may assume that the type of silent modality syntax illustrated by (1) and (2), with both *HAVE* and *BE* as predicative carriers and the infinitival directional preposition, *TO*, does not generally carry across the genetically related IE languages.

---

[2] Giurgea & Soare (2010) deal with the same constructions in Romance languages, while Gärtner (2009) is concerned with embedded non-finite (i.e., infinitive and participial) interrogatives in general. Grosu (2004) and Šimík (2010a,b), in turn, scrutinize modal existential *wh*-constructions from a typological point of view. Bondaruk (2004) as well as Witkoś (2010a,b) investigate, at least to some extent, the nature and the role of embedded subjects in Polish embedded infinitival questions ('x would like to know how to live there')..

The present chapter is organized as follows. The main body of the ensuing text covers discussions about the samples of covert modal readings in (2) above, partly also by (1), across different IE languages in Europe. Lexical anchors of this survey are IE *HAVE* and *BE* either overtly or covertly represented.

2. Brief exposition of von Wright's modal logic

Von Wright's theory of modal logic (von Wright 1976) comprizes but fundamental definitions. It distinguishes between alethic (natural) and deontic (ethical) modality.

Table 1: von Wright's modal logic – conceptual definitions

Alethic modality – holding under natural circumstances ('circum-stantial modality')	Deontic modality – holding under social laws, commitments, and regulations
$N(p)\ _{df}{=}\ I(\sim p)\ _{df}{=} \sim P(\sim p)$	$O(p)\ _{df}{=}\ F(\sim p)\ _{df}{=} \sim P(\sim p)$
$P(p)\ _{df}{=} \sim I(p)\ _{df}{=} \sim N(\sim p)$	$P(p)\ _{df}{=} \sim F(p)\ _{df}{=} \sim O(\sim p)$
$I(p)\ _{df}{=} \sim P(p)\ _{df}{=}\ N(\sim p)$	$F(p)\ _{df}{=} \sim P(p)\ _{df}{=}\ O(\sim p)$

Legend: (*N(ecessary)* — *P(ossible/ermitted)* — *I(mpossible)* — *O(bligatory)* ethically necessary, obligatory — *F(orbidden)* — df= for "defined as" — ~ for propositional negation)

Quite obviously, the definitions of alethic (natural) and deontic modality are near-convergent. Alethic necessity is analogous with ethical necesssity including both possibilities; Impossibility is on a par with Forbidden. However, there is one important difference: In alethic logic, Existence follows from Necessity, and from Existence follows Possibility, symbolically: $N(p) \rightarrow p$; $p \rightarrow M(p)$. In deontic logic there is no similar chain of implications: Nothing, i.e. no *p,* follows from $O(p)$ and $P(p)$. It has been claimed (ANDERSON 1967) that von Wright's deontic logic has to be extended by the concept of Sanction (‚s') or Punishment much in the following sense: $O(p)\ _{df}{=}\ p \vee (\sim p\ \&\ s)$, in words: ‚obligatory *p* either implies *p* or not-*p* followed by Sanction'; i.e. $F(p)\ _{df}{=} \sim p \vee (p\ \&\ s)$, in words: ‚Forbidden *p* either implies not-*p* or *p* under Sanction', meaning also $P(p)\ _{df}{=}\ p \vee \sim$ p, in words ‚Permission either implies *p* or not *p* — both without Sanction'.

The above shows both the similarity and the difference between alethic and deontic valuations: Alethic utterances with the Necessity operator stand for laws of nature; parallel deontic utterances hold under laws of society (ethical or legislative directives). Such valuations usually have the linguistic form of „If *p*, then *q* must be" (debitive implication), formally <*p* □→ O> (where the symbol □ means 'necessary/obligatory'). The debitive implication does not describe a real, but a prescribed world. It is often expressed by a conditional, whose protasis is the order or the sanction. Tense and mood of the predicate in the protasis may attain different expressive forms.

Often the term *alethic* is taken to refer to the modal ambiguity of *can*, German *können* (Hundt 2003), since it is tough to keep apart their deontic and epistemic denotations. Likewise, *deontic* (from Classical Greek *déon* "that which is obligated") is usually taken in opposition to *epistemic* ("what we know"). We avoid this terminology for the simple reason that it does not reflect the original Greek meaning, which is plausibly reserved for obligatory *must* and *shall*. It is more felicitous to employ the opposition *root modality* vs. *epistemic* (= non-root) *modality*[3] by appealing to the futural implication of root modals (s<e: speech act time before event time) as opposed to epistemically used modals (e≤s: speech act time after, or convergent with, event time).

3. The phrasal prepositional status of infinitivals eliciting modal denotations – in some European languages

In what follows we aim at finding modality readings without lexical items to serve as the source for modality – here: involving infinitivals and gerundials. The goal of the discussion is: peel out the source of modality; detect fine-grained semantic properties and distributional differences and commonalities. [legend: # stands for versions that do not employ infinitival embeddings, but, rather, use biclausal finiteness – it thus marks versions that are no direct syntactic mappings of the English infinitivals. Lexical modals appear boldened. POSS, ABIL, DEONT = possibility, ability, obligating modality].[4]

The illustrations below follow the pattern in (3a-h) (Bhatt 2006).

---

[3] There is an infelicitous implication to the term 'root' modality in that it invites the conclusion that it is the historically original status, whereas the epistemic notion develops later by grammaticalization (e.g., by 'subjectification'). See, on this, Abraham (2012, in this volume).

[4] On drafting the examples in the different language, I had the support of the following native speakers: Marco Coniglio, Michail L. Kotin, Leonid Kulikov, Odleif Leirbukt, Ole Letnes, Pierre-Yves Modicom, Jadwiga Piskorz, and Maria Movsesian-Schröder. Their cooperation is highly appreciated.

3.1 Subject relative infinitive/embedded infinitive question

ENGLISH 1 (embedded infinitive question/EIQ)

1 *Tim knows [PRO how to solve the problem]*
– monoclausal infinitival =
= Tim knows how one/he could/should solve the problem
– POSS, ABIL, DEONT

STANDARD GERMAN 2 (no gerund licensed by infinitival P *zu*)

2a *T. weiß, wie das Problem zu lösen *(ist)*
T. knows how the problem to solve is
– biclausal finite

b *T. weiß wie das Problem (*zu) lösen*
– monoclausal (*P-)infinitival

c *T. weiß wie das Problem lösen*
T. knows (how) the problem to solve

d *T. weiß/hat ein Problem zum Lösen*
– monoclausal gerundial
T. knows/has a problem to.DAT solving

SOUTH GERMAN 3 (gerund/V- nominal licensed by infinitival P *zum* "to-the.DAT.SG.NEUT")

3 *T. weiß wie das/(so) ein Problem lösen/zum Lösen*
T. knows how the/such a problem to.DAT solving
– infinitive embedding without *zu*/ gerundial *zum*+[$_N$ V]

NORWEGIAN 4 (German asdded for direct comparison)

4a **T. vet hvordan problemet er å lose.*
– *finite!

b *T. weiß, wie das Problem zu lösen ist*
"T. knows how the problem is to be solved"
– monoclausal

c **T. vet (hvordan) å løse problemet.*
– *non-finite!
T. weiß/hat ein Problem zum Lösen
– monoclausal
"T. knows/has a problem to solve"

d *T. vet/har et problem å lose.*
– non-finite embedding
T. knows/has a problem to solve

e *T. weiß wie das(/ein) Problem zum Lösen*
"T. knows how this problem to-the.DAT solving"
– South German; monoclausal

f *T. vet hvordan det/et problem å lose.*
T. knows how this/a problem to solve
– *non-finite HOW-embedding!

ITALIAN 5

5a *Tim sa come (*di) risolvere il problema.*
T. knows how (*to) solve the problem
– no infinitival preposition like *to*

b *Tim sa come (*di) risolvere il problema.*
– with or without *come*

c **Tim sa (come) il problema (di) risolvere.*
– ungrammatical on all counts

d *Tim ha un problema *(da) risolvere.*
T. has a problem to solve.GERUND NOMINAL
"T. has a problem to solve"
– ungrammatical without *da*
– cf. the South German gerundial in 3
– deontic reading

e *Questo problema è da risolvere.*
this problem is to solve.GERUND NOMINAL
"This problem is to (be) solve(d)
– cf. the South German gerundial in 3
– deontic reading

f *Ho un problema da risolvere.*
I-have a problem to solve.GERUND NOMINAL

FRENCH 6

6a *T. sait (comment) résoudre le/un problème .*
T. knows (how) solve the/a problem
– monoclausal

b *T. sait (*comment) le problème est à résoudre.*
T. knows (*how) the problem is to solve
– biclausal

c *T. sait/*a résoudre un problem.* = 6d
T. knows/*has solve a problem

d *T. a un problème à résoudre*
"T. has a problem to solve"

RUSSIAN 7

7a *Tom znaet kak rešit´ zadaxu.*
Tom knows how solve.INF.**PERF** (the) problem.ACC.SG
– no infinitival preposition like *to*
– definite reading for DO
"Tom knows how to solve the problems"

– covert deontic reading: stronger than 16b
"…how problems must be solved"

b *Tom znaet kak reš**at**′ zadaxi*
Tom knows how solve.**IMPERF** problems.ACC.PL
– indefinite reading for DO
– generic reading
"Tom knows how to solve problems"
"…how problems must be solved"
– covert deontic reading: weaker than 16a

c *Timofej znaet rešenie zadaxi.*
T. knows solution.ACC problem.GEN
– monoclausal (no modality
"Tom knows how to solve the problem"

d *Tom znaet kak **nado** rešit′ problemu.*
Tom knows how (one) must solve problem
– overt deontics due to MV *nado*
"Tom knows how one **must** solve the problem."

POLISH 8

8a *Tim wie jak rozwiązać (ten) problem*
T. knows how solve.**PERF** this problem.ACC.SG
– covert possibility reading
– no deontic reading
'Tim knows how to/one/he can/could solve the/this problem.'

b *?? *Tim wie jak rozwiąz**yw**ać (ten) problem*
T. knows how solve.**IMPERF** this/the problem.ACC.SG
– no modal reading

c *Tim wie jak rozwiąz**yw**ać problemy.*
T. knows how solve.INF.**IMPERF** problems.ACC.PL
– covert possibility reading
– indefinite plural-DO
– generic reading
"Tim knows how to/one/he can/could solve problems."

Viewing the possibilities of German and its spoken variant one may expect infinitival indirect wh-question embeddings after factive predicates such as *KNOW*, possibly also gerundial object complements as in 3 above. Spoken South German even provides the very idiomatic P-less infinitival complement as in 3. However, the view from German is by no means replicable in other IE languages, quite obviously for various reasons. For one, we do not know what the exact syntactic status of the complement VP is: Under nominalship without TO we do not expect a silent modality reading, as in (dialectal South German) 3b against (Norwegian ungrammatical) 4 above – if the probability reading in German 2b is not due to the how-question in the first place and, thus, is not a true case of covert modality. The same applies to Russian 7. In Polish 8a the perfectivity, or telicity, of the embedded infinitive triggers modal possibility of the entire construal – much in the sense of aspectual event telicity doing the same job as the directional preposition, *TO*. An imperfective verb instead of the perfective one renders the sentence ungrammatical. Embedding an imperfective infinitive is possible only with an indefinite reference of the *DO* – which co-occurs with reference switch to indefiniteness of the direct object under genericity; see 8c as opposed to 8b. Russian *rešit′* in 7a confirms the conclusion about Polish 8: it is telic, while the imperfective embedded infinitive is in 8b. The definite effects are clear, and so is the interrelation with aspects (for Slavic as well as older stages of German see Abraham 1997, Leiss 2000).

Table 2: Covert modality in adjunct-object complement infinitive embedded by factive *know/ wissen*: Tim knows [PRO how *(to) solve the problem] ≈ *should*-Deontic, *could*-Possible/Able.

Germanic				Romance		Slavic	
Engl VO	StGerm OV	S. German OV	Norw VO	Ital VO	French VO	Russ VO	Polish VO
+	–/– gerund	+ gerund	– gerund	+	+	–	–

In the IE languages listed above there is no syntax of (P-)infinitival embedding except for English and dialectal erundial in German. A complement-object infinitive is partly possible in: German, Norwegian. The syntax of infinitival embedding is alright for Slavic, but there is no implied modality – modality is achievable only via a finite predicate, if at all. The crucial factor appears to be that there is no direct equivalent to the directional preposition operating on the non-finite em-bedding (cf. *TO*).

There is reason to assume that, since the respective construals without *HOW* (<*x HAS TO* V>) do indeed give rise to a modal meaning in all IE languages – see next to all Germanic patterns also 12d for Italian and 15b for French –, modality in the English embedded *wh/ how*-construals is a typological loner and is due to the nominal status of English *wh/how+to* +V unshared by any of the other languages looked at here. One may assume that there is an implicature of existential possibility to any direct *how*-question: from <factive-V_1-*how-to*-V_2> → "V_2 is possible". This is strongly reminiscent of the conventional implicature in (1g) above: from generic declarative p → possible p (see also Fn. 1 above).

As to the perfective trigger, instead of the directive infinitival preposition, Russian is a good example next to Polish. As in Polish, there is no correspondent of Germanic/Romance *TO* in Russian. However, a directive vs. indirective-stative meaning is expressed by INF. PERF vs. INF.IMPERF, as in 16a-b.

(20) a *mne* ***nado*** *poiti* *v park.*
me.DAT necessary go.INF.PERF into park
"Ihave togo into the park"
b *mne nado xodit po hasu kajdii den.*
me.DAT necessary go.INF.IMPF for one hour every day
"I must take a walk every day for one hour"

The directionality expressed by the aspectual perfective is reflected also temporally as well as modally in that the perfective relates to both futurity and modal deontics; see (21a). Negation deprives the verbal lexical of its perfectivity as in (21b). The same holds for genericity readings (without any futurity implied) as in (21c).

(21) a *eto* ***nado*** *sdelat'.*
this necessary finish.INF.PERF
"This is to be finished".
b *etogo ne* ***nado*** *delat'.*
this not necessary finish.INF.IMPERF
"This does not have to be finished".
c *eto* ***nado*** *delat' ostorojno.*
this necessary finish.INF.IMPERF carefully
"This must be completed with great care".

The fact that possibility is implied in (20a,b) (in (20a) somewhat more weakly than in 7b) has also to do with the marix verb *znaet* "knows", which denotes ability. This bears out as an important factor for covert possibility in (20a,b), both without the deontic verb *nado*. See the respective generalizations on the affinity between aspect and modality ('perfectivity implying root modality' vs. 'imperfectivity triggering epistemicity') in Abraham (1989, 1991, 2001, 2005). Another generalization that appears to be confirmed by the latter Thai observations is that modal possibility is derived by (conventional) implicature from (generic) declaratives (Holl 2010, Abraham 2012 (in this volume)). See (22) where typically such potentiality triggering declaratives appear negated.

(22) kin may long
eat NEG descend
"I cannot eat (= swallow)"

3.2 Object relative infinitive/ORI

English 1 (modality assignments due to BHATT 2006)
1a *Jane found [a book [PRO to draw cartoons in]] for Sara*
– *should*-Deontic
b = J. found a book for Sara one could/should draw cartoons.
– *could*-Poss/Able
Standard German 2
2a **J. fand ein Buch für Sarah Skizzen rein zu zeichnen*
J. found a book for S. sketches into to draw
– *zu/to*-infinitive
b *J. fand ein Buch, um Skizzen (rein/drinnen) zu zeichnen*
– *um zu/for to*-infinive
– possibility just by implication
South German 3
3 *J. fand ein Buch zum Skizzen einzutragen/reinzeichnen*
– gerundial *zum*+$[_N$ V]
– possibility just by implication
Norwegian 4
4a *J. fant ei bok å tegne skisser i for Sara.*
J. found a book to draw sketches in for S.
*J. fand ein Buch für Sarah Skizzen rein zu zeichnen
b *J. fant ei bok til å tegne skisser i.*
J. found a book for to draw sketches in
J. fand ein Buch für Sarah, um Skizzen (rein/drinnen) zu zeichnen
c *J. fant ei bok til å tegne skisser i.*
J. found a book for to sketch in
$^?$J. fand einBuch zum Skizzieren drin
d **J. fant ei bok til å tegne skisser*
Italian 5
5 $^{(?)}$Jane ha trovato (per Sara) un quaderno dove fare degli schizzi (/dei disegni).

French 6

6a **J. a trouvé un livre pour (*y) faire des dessins.*
J. has found a book for (PART) do of designs
– incorrect in Standard French

b *??un livre à (*y) faire des dessins.*
a book to (PART) do of designs
– incorrect in Standard French

c *Ceci n'est pas un livre pour faire du pain…*
there not is not a book for make of bread

Russian 7

7a *Džein našla knigu čtoby narisovat' karikatury dlya S.*
Jane found book.ACC with which draw.INF cartoons for S.

b *Zhanna našla knigu dlya risovaniya.*
Zh. found book.ACC for drawing.GEN
– modality not obvious

c *Jein nashla knigu, čtobi Sara v nei risovala komiksi.*
Jein found book with which Sara in there drew cartoons
J. fand ein Buch, damit Sara (drinnen) Skizzen zeichnete.

d *Jein nashla knigu v kotoroi Sara mogla risovat komiksi.*
J. found book in which Sara could draw cartoons
"J. found a book in which Sara could sketch."

Polish 8

8 *znalazła książkę w której S. może rysować kreskówki*
J. found book in which S. can draw cartoons
'Jane found a book for Sara in that she can draw cartoons.'
'Jane found a book for Sara in that she is allowed to draw cartoons.'
– impossible to use an embedded infinitival question in this case; instead finite relative clause …
– polyfunctionality of *móc* ([i] 'can', [ii] 'to be allowed to', [iii] 'may')

Table 3: Covert modality in object relative infinitive constructions: *Jane found [a book[PRO to draw cartoons in]] for Sara = = J. found a book for Sara one could/should draw cartoons. – should*-Deontic, *could*-Poss/Able

Germanic			Romance		Slavic	
Engl VO	Germ OV	Norw VO	Ital VO	Fre VO	Russian VO	Polish VO
+	–/#ge-rund	–/no gerund	–/ (?) dove	–	no covert modality	no covert modality
Syntax of infinitival embedding alright for Slavic, but no modality implication – modality only via finite predicate, if at all.						

3.3 Subject relative infinitive/SRI

English 1 (modality assignments for English according to Bhatt 2006)

1 *[The man [PRO to fix the sink]] is here*
– *should*-Deontic, *can/could*-Possible/Able

German 2

2 = The man whose purpose it is to fix the sink is here
a *Der Mann *(um) die Abwasch *(zu) reparieren, ist hier*
the man (for) the sink (to) fix is here
b *Der Mann, der die Abwasch reparieren will/soll, ist hier*
the man who the sink fix wants is here
c *Der Mann zum die Abwasch Reparieren ist hier*
the man to.THE sink fix is here

Norwegian 4 (German versions added below)

4a **Mannen for å reparere vasken er her*
the man (for) to fix the sink is here
Der Mann *(um) die Abwasch *(zu) reparieren, ist hier
b *Mannen som vil/skal reparere vasken, er her*
the man who the sink fix wants is here
c **Mannen til reparere vasken er her*
man.the to fix sink.the is here
Der Mann zum die Abwasch Reparieren ist hier

Italian 5

5 # *L'uomo che deve.*FIN *riparare il lavandino è qui*
The man who must fix the sink is here

French 6

6a ** L'homme pour réparer l'évier est là*
the man for fix(ing) the sink is here

b *L'homme qui doit réparer l'évier est là*
The man who must fix the sink is here

c ??*L'homme à réparer l'évier est là*
The man to fix the sink is here

pour réparer in the first example is gerundial with the verb infinitive functioning as a nominal dependent on the preposition *pour* (English "for fixing"). French does not link the preposition *à* with modality at all. The object *(à réparer) l'évier* in the last illustration had better be indefinite and plural to render such a construal possible – therefore better with machines:

6d *la machine à percer des trous*
the machine to drill holes with which to do something
– no modal semantics; just medium
"the machine for drilling holes"

Russian 7

7a *?*Čelovek, kotoromu činit' rakovinu zdes* ACC
man who.DAT fix.INF sink here
– highly dubious for rendering (covert) modality

b *Čelovek, kotorii remontiruet rakovinu, nahoditsya zdes*
man who.REL repair.3SGPRES sink.ACC is here
"The man who fixes the sink is here."

c *Čelovek, kotorii dolzhen remontirovat rakovinu,nahoditsya zdes.*
man who.REL must.3SG.PRES reparieren sink.ACC be.3SG.PRES here
"The man who wants/must fix the sink is here."

d *Čelovek nahoditsya zdes, čtobi remontirovat rakovinu.*
man is here, with whom fix sink
"The man is here to fix the sink is here."

Russian shows no equivalent without an overt modal verb; in other words, no covert modality is expressed.

Polish 6

6 *Człowiek,który ma naprawić zlew, jest tutaj*
man who has fix.INF.PERF sink is here
– no infinitival relatives;

Table 3: Covert modality in subject relative infinitive/SRI: *[The man [PRO to fix the sink]] is here – should*-Deontic, *can/could*-Possible/Able

Germanic			Romance		Slavic	
Engl VO	German OV	Norw VO	Italian VO	French VO	Russian VO	Polish VO
+	+/? *umzu*/ gerund	–/no gerund	–/(?)dov-	–	no covert modality	no covert modality
No syntax of infinitival embedding for Slavic, Romance, Norwegian (German infinitival P alone insufficient – required: *um zu*/gerund, none of which exists in Norwegian)); in the finite clauses no modality implication						

3.4 Subject relative purpose infinitive after directional/SRPI

English (modality assignments for English according to BHATT 2006)

1a *Sue went to Torino [PRO to buy a violin]*
– *should*-Deontic

b = "Sue went to Torino so that she could buy a violin"
– *could*-Possible/Able

German

2a *S. fuhr nach Turin, um eine V. *(zu) kaufen*
S. went to Torino for a violin (to) buy
– purposive infinitive
– *ability/possibility* only by implication

b *S. fuhr nach Turin eine Violine (zu) kaufen*
S. went to T. a violin (to) buy

Norwegian (German added for direct comparison)

3a *S. dro til T. for *(å) kjøpe en fiolin*
S. drove to T. for (to) buy a violin
– purposive infinitive
– *ability/possibility* only by implication
*S. fuhr nach Turin, um eine V. *(zu) kaufen*

b *S. dro til T. kjøpe en fiolin*
S. drove to T. buy a violin
S. fuhr nach Turin eine Violine kaufen

Italian

4 *Sue è andata a Torino per/a comprare un violin*
S. went to T. for/to buy a violin
– purposive infinitive
– *ability/possibility* only by implication

French

5 *S. a été à Turin (pour) acheter un violon*
S. has been to T. (for) buy(ing) a violin
– purposive infinitive
– *ability/possibility* only by implication

Russian

6a *S'u poxala v Turin kupit′ skripku*
Sue went to Torino.ACC buy.INF violin.ACC
– purposive infinitive
– *ability/possibility* only by implication

b *S. poxala v Turin kupit‘ skripku*
S. went to T. buy.INF violin.ACC

c *Sue poehala v Turin, chtobi kupit skripku.*
Sue went to Turin, therewith buy violine.ACC
≠ *S. fuhr nach Turin um eine V. *(zu) kaufen*

d *Sue poehala v Turin kupit skripku.*
Sue went to T. buy.INF violin.ACC
□ *ability/possibility* only by implication
= S. fuhr nach Turin eine Violine kaufen

Polish

7 *S. pojechała do Turyn-u (aby) kupić sobi wiolonczeę*
S. went.PERF to Torino.GEN (for) buy.PERF REFL violin.ACC
'Sue went to Torino to buy herself a violin.'

Polish 7 is possible due to the matrix verb *jechać* 'go' without the infinitival preposition ('to' or 'for (to)'); the whole structure has a clear purposive reading, but at best an implied possibility reading – Polish verbs of motion allow for embedded infinitival complements; a pure purpose clause introduced by the conjunction *aby* 'in order' is possible as well, and the reflexive pronoun *sobie* may be added for valence bounding.

Table 4: Covert modality in Subject relative purpose infinitive after directional: *Sue went to Torino [PRO to buy a violin]* ≈ *should*-Deontic, *could*-Possible/Able

Germanic			Romance		Slavic	
Engl VO	Germ OV	Norw VO	Italian VO	French VO	Russian VO	Polish VO
+	+	+	–/ (?)*dov-*	–	no covert modality	no covert modality
German: infinitival embedding acceptable on all varieties (*um zu/* (?)*zu/* DO-incorporation); Norwegian: *for *(å)* or DO-incorporation just *å* is not sufficient; modality implication as in English.						

3.5 Subject raising infinitival/SRI

English (modality assignments for English according to BHATT 2006)

1a *Bill has to reach Philadelphia before noon*
– *should*-Deontic, *could*-Possible/Able

b = Bill must reach Ph. before noon

German

2a *B. hat vor Mittag in Ph. *(zu) sein*
B. has before noon in Ph. to be
– *ability/possibility* by implication

b *B. muss/soll vor Mittag in Ph. sein*
S. drove to T. for (to) buy a violin /
/B. must before noon in Ph. Be
– lexically expressed modality

Norwegian (German added for direct comparison)

3a *B. har *(å) være i Ph. før middag*
B. has (to) be in Ph. before noon
B. hat vor Mittag in Ph. *(zu) sein

b *B. må/skal være i Ph. før middag*
B. must/shall be in Ph. before lunch time
B. muss/soll vor Mittag in Ph. sein

Italian

antiquated (was perhaps possible a hundred years back) :

4a **Bill ha da raggiungere Filadelfia prima di mezzogiorno (/pranzo?).*
However, idiomatic in dialects such as in Margherotto (Coniglio p.c.):

b *Bill ga da rivar a Filadelfia par pranso.*

French

5a *ˀB. a à être à Ph. avant midi*
B. has to be in Ph. Before noon
– cacophony: „*a à*“; better with other person subjects, tenses, or moods as in:

b *Nous avons à être à Ph.*
we have to be in Ph.

c *Il avait à être ...*
he had to be …

d *bien qu'il ait à être...*
nice that he had to be

Russian

In Russian modality needs to be expressed overtly:

6a *Bil namerevaetsya byt′ v Filadelfii do poludnya.*
Bill intends be.INF in Ph. before noon.GEN

b *Billu nužno byt' v Filadel'fii utrom*
B.DAT needed be.INF in Ph.LOC in.the.morning

Modality has no covert expression linked to lexical *HAVE* – Russian has no lexical *HAVE*.

6c *Bilu sleduet/ dolzhel dobratsya do Philadelphii do poludnya.*
Bil.DAT must.3SGPRES come to Ph.GEN before noon. GEN
“Bill has to be in Ph. before noon.”

Polish

In contrast to Russian, Polish has *HAVE* and thus would appear to be a candidate for the expression of covert modality if it also haD an equivalent of the infinitival preposition *TO*. However, despite the fact that directional *TO* is missing Polish appears to develop the deontic reading which goes with *HAVE* so often cross-linguistically as shown above.

7 *Bill ma być w Filadelfii przed południem*
B. has be to Ph.LOC before noon.INS
Readings:
(i) ‘Bill is claimed to be in Ph. before noon’
(ii) ‘Bill is supposed to be in Ph. before noon’
(iii) ‘Bill has to be in Philadelphia before noon.’

The English translations reflect the complex modal shadings of Polish: The quotative/evidential readings, (i)-(ii), come closest to the original as in the following context: "Bill called me before his plane took off, and he told to me that he will reach Ph. before noon". Note that this reading does not result from the aspect of the embedded predicate, in the present case of the imperfective infinitive; rather, one just does not have any control over the embedded state of affairs. Nevertheless, the structure indicating deontic modality, (iii), is appropriate too due to the polyfunctionality of *ma/mieć* 'has/to have', most prominently its possessive denotation which gave rise to the deontic reading in most European languages (see also Jedrzejovsky 2011).

Table 5: Covert modality in subject infinitival: *Bill has to reach Philadelphia before noon* ≈ *should*-Deontic, *could*-Possible/Able

Germanic			Romance		Slavic	
Engl VO	Germ OV	Norw VO	Italian VO	French VO	Russian VO	Polish VO
+	+ *(*zu*)	+ *(*å*)	–/ $^{(?)}$*da*	+ *à*	no covert modality	no covert modality
German: infinitival embedding acceptable on all varieties (*um zu*/$^{(?)}$*zu*/DO-incorporation); Norwegian: *for* *(*å*) or DO-incorporation-just *å* not sufficient; modality implication as in English; Slavic: no *HAVE,* no infinitival embedding; modality has to be encoded overtly.						

3.6 Subject raising infinitive on iV/SRI-iV

The embedded predicate is an intransitive verb like *leave* "go away".

English (Bhatt 2006; see patterns (3a-h) above)

1a *William is to leave tomorrow* !≠! a'
a' To leave/Leaving has been commissioned
b = Will is scheduled/supposed to/should leave tomorrow
– no possibility implied
c W. *ist/hat morgen zu gehen !≠! c'
c' W. ist für morgen zu erwarten
d W. muss/soll morgen gehen

to leave alone does not do the modal job – see (a'): it has to be *has-have/ is-are+to* V; thus: finiteness + directional *to*. However: in order to take *to* (infinitival P) as a necessary component of the modality composition, it has to have valuable content features; this, in turn, requires a selection potential, which can only be directed to N (not to V): thus, [*has/is to* V] requires gerunds (=nominalized verbals; [$_{PP}$ *zu* [$_{N}$ V]), from which again the concept (and terminology) <infinitival P> turns out to be ill-conceived. Despite all of that, *has-have+to* V cannot be quite the same as *is-are+to* V: see the clearly dichotomous German or Norwegian on (c). *BE* selects a predicative nominative (as a subject property or identity), whereas *HAVE* selects a direct object accusative. Comparison of (c) and (c') shows that the embedded üredicates have to be transitive; in other words, what we see are different basic diatheses: the subject in (c') for *erwarten* "await" is a basic DO (internal argument), that for (c)für *gehen* "leave", on the other hand, is a basic subject (external argument). We conclude: in the cases, of *HAT,*the German *zu+ V*–construction, *zu* is a diathesis changer applying to transitive verbs; for *IST,* the German *zu+ V*–construction tries in vain to execute this diathetic role: intransitives do not undergo passivization (in the true sense of the "semantic transfer hypothesis" – see Abraham 2009). Norwegian heeds this diathetic constraint as does German, English, however, does not (for reasons undisclosed so far).

Norwegian (German added for direct comparison)
2a *W. *er/har å reise i morgen*
W. is/has to depart tomorrow
*William *ist/hat morgen zu gehen*
b *W. må/skal reise i morgen*
W. must/shall leave tomorrow
W. muss/soll morgen gehen
– *skal*: denoting will of third person or (relatively)
– neutral future marker)

Italian
3 #*Will deve partire domani.*
W. must leave tomorrow

French
4a **W. est à/pour partir demain.*
W. is to/for leave tomorrow
b *W. est censé partir demain.*
W. is thought leave tomorrow
– deontic reading, slight evidential coloring: 'scheduled to/supposed to/said to; also with W. as source of information
c *W. doit partir demain.*
W. must leave tomorrow

Russian

Russian only with overtly expressed modality:

5a *Billu nužno uexat' zavtra*
B.DAT needed leave.INF tomorrow
– no modal equivalent without overt modal verb

b *W. dolžen zavtra uehat.*
W. must:3SG.PRES tomorrow leave

c *Willi nužno zavtra uehat.*
W. must.3SG.PRES tomorrow leave

Polish

6 *W. ma jutro wyjechać*
W. has tomorrow leave.INF.PERF
'Will has to leave tomorrow.'
'Will is supposed to leave tomorrow.'
'Will is claimed to leave tomorrow.'
– translation from Polish highly context-sensitive, compare remarks on Russian

Table 6: Covert modality in subject raising iV-infinitival *William is to leave tomorrow ≠ To leave/Leaving tomorrow has been commissioned* = Will is scheduled/supposed to/should leave tomorrow ≈ *should*-Deontic, (*)*could*-Possible/Able

Germanic			Romance		Slavic	
Engl VO	Germ OV	Norw VO	Italian VO	French VO	Russian VO	Polish VO
+	–iV/ +tV	–	–	–	no covert modality	no covert modality
German infitival syntax only for tV – in contrast to English, with both deontic and optional modality implication. Romance: no *BE*-infinitivals. Slavic: no infinitival embedding; modality has to be encoded overtly.						

Question: Given the option of infinitival embedding, why does *IST/HAT* + *zu* V imply just obligatoriness, not, however, possibility? What makes German <*IST zu* tV> take exception to the above generalization, even as opposed to English? Which of the two modalities is the more basic one winning out in default situations? Why would the present <*IST zu* tV> such a default situation? Is syntactic structure behind it, is semantics, or is it just pragmatics? And again: What is behind the typological constraints of <*IST zu* tV> as opposed to <*HAT zu* itV>?

Any <XP *ist zu* iV> forces a transitive reading (which often is not possible: ??*Sie ist zu gehen* wittily "she needs to be ousted"). This strengthens our conclusion that the so-called P-infinitive *zu* (the second verbal status, according to Bech 1955) functions as a true passivizer: [$_{DP}$ N_{SU} [$_{DP}$ N_{DO} [$_{VP}$ tPRED]]] passivize→ [$_{DP}$ N_{DO} [$_{VP}$ iPRED]]] – where < passivize → amounts to CP-reduction by the external theta role (= Agent, in German). Notice that passivization, in this particular context, is subject to the semantic transfer condition (Abraham 2009) – in other words, intransitive passivization is excluded, which is obvious from the fact that iV does not allow the infinitival *zu*-embedding (**XP ist zu gehen*$_{iV}$ vs. ^{OK}*XP ist zu erwarten*$_{tV}$). In the following chapter the valence criterion is further specified to include unaccusatives, uV.

3.7 Object infinitive – decausV(decausative iV)/OI-decaus

English (following BHATT'S 2006 illustrations for English)

1a *The stomach is (/has) to empty/to be emptied*
– *has to empty* with decausV

b = The stomach must be emptied

German

2a **Der Magen muss entleeren*
the stomach must empty.iV
– *decausV

b *Der Magen *ist/hat entleert zu werden*
the stomach is/has emptied to be
– German restricts valence shift from tV to iV without morphological indication to few verbs

Norwegian (German added for direct comparison)

3a *Magen må bli tømt/tømmes*
stomach must be emptied/empty.REFL-PASSIVE
– *s*-passive more common
Der Magen muss entleert werden

b **Magen er å tømmes*
stomach is to empty.REFL-PASSIVE
– no case marking on *magen*

c ??*Magen er å bli tømt/tømmes*
stomach.the is to be emptied/empty.REFL-PASSIVE
**Der Magen ist geleert zu werden*

Italian

4 *Lo stomaco è da svuotare*
the stomach is of empty(ing)
"The stomach has to empty/to be emptied"

French

5a *L'estomac est (/*a) à purger*
the stomach is (has) to purge

b *L'estomac a (/*est) à être purgé.*
the stomach has (is) to be purged
– more idiomatic with raising verb *il faut* entailing deontic reading *il faut que* +Subj":

c *il faut que W. parte demain,*
EXPL must that W. leave tomorrow

d *il faut que l'estomac soit purge*
EXPL must that the stomach be purged

e *il faut purger l'estomac*
EXPL must purge the stomach
– *il faut* +Inf

Russian

6a *Želudok nužno opustošit'*
stomach.ACC needed empty.INF
– only overt modality expression

b *Želudok nužno oporožnit'*
Stomach.ACC needed empty.INF

c *Zheludok nužno promit'*
stomach.ACC need.3SG.PRES empty
"The stomach must be emptied"

d *Zheludok neobhodimo promit*
stomach.ACC necessary be empty
„The stomach must be emptied"

Polish

7 *Żołądek ma być opróżniony*
stomach.NOM has be.INF emptied
– interestingly enough, no ambiguity reading
– highly context-sensitive
'The stomach has to be emptied.'

Table 7: Covert modality in object infinitive – decausV(decausative iV): *The stomach is (/has) to empty$_{uV}$ / to be emptied$_{iV}$* →intransitive predicate ≈ *should*-Deontic,could*-Possible/Able**

Germanic			Romance		Slavic	
Engl VO	Germ OV	Norw VO	Italian VO	French VO	Russian VO	Polish VO
+	–iV/ +tV	–	–	–	no covert modality	no covert modality
In German there is an infitival syntax only for tV – in contrast to English with both deontic and epistemic implication. Romance: no *BE*-infinitivals. Slavic: no infinitival embedding; modality has to be encoded overtly.						

3.8 Covert modality in subject infinitive – unaccusative verb / uV

English (illustrations following Bhatt 2006; see patterns (3a-h) above)

1a The monument is to fall

b The monument has to fall

c = The monument must fall

German

2a **Das Denkmal ist zu fallen*
the monument is to fall

b *Das Denkmal hat zu fallen*
the monument has to fall

Norwegian (German added for direct comparison)

3a **Monumentet er å falle*
monument.the is to fall
**Das Denkmal ist zu fallen*

b ? *Monumentet har å falle*
the monument has to fall
Das Denkmal hat zu fallen
– problematic; however, good with humans:
Du har å komme 'you have to come'

Italian

4a #*Il monumento deve cadere.*
the monument must tumble (similar to German)
– possible, but meaning different from English

b   #*El monumento ga da cascar*
the monument arrives of tumble(ing)
– only in Venetian dialect, different meaning

French

5a   * *Le monument est à tomber*
the monument is to tumble
– possible only with different semantics

b   *Ce monument est à tomber*
this monument is to (be) turn(ed) over
– only transitive use
"one should turn over this monument"
– passive of tV; deontic *should*
or:
"the m. is just so beautiful to make you fall over"
– purposive; no modal reading
compare German:
Das Denkmal ist zum Kotzen/zum Entzücken aller Touristen
– gerundial; no modal reading, just purposive

c   *Le monument a à tomber*
the monument has to tumble
– natural-empirical necessity constraint

d   *Il faut que le monument tombe*
EXPL must that the monument tumbles

Russian: no modal equivalent without overt modal verb

6a   (?) *Pamyatniku*   *past'*
monument.DAT   fall.INF
– sounds archaic/poetic style, not every-day language

B   * *Pamyatnik*   *dolžen*   *upast'*
monument.NOM   must.3SG.PRES   turn over/tumble.INF.PERF
– unaccusative V = telic iV

c   *Pamyatnik*   *nužno*   *snesti*
monument.NOM   must.3SG.PRES   pull over.PERF
"the monument needs to be pulled over"
– perfective infinitive of imper-fective tV *snosit'*

Polish

7a   ?*Pomnik*   *ma*   *upaść*
monument.NOM   has   fall.INF.PERF
'The monument has to fall.'
– sounds odd; better: passive with the verb
– sounds odd; better: passive with the verb *zniszczyć* 'to destroy'

b	*Pomnik*	*ma*	*zostać*	*zniszczony*
	monument.NOM	has	become.INF	destroyed

Table 8: Covert modality in subject infinitive – unaccusative verb/uV
a The monument is to fall ≠ XP is about to fall/go
b The monument has to fall ≈ *should*-Deontic, **can*/could*-Possible/Able**

Germanic			Romance		Slavic	
Engl VO	Germ OV	Norw VO	Italian VO	French VO	Russian VO	Polish VO
+	*–ist/* *+hat*	*–er/* $^{?}$*har*	–	–	no covert modality	no covert modality
German infinitival syntax only for *hat*, with – in line with English – only deontic modality implication. Romance: no *BE*-, no *HAVE*-infinitivals. Slavic: no infinitival embedding; modality has to be encoded overtly in finite clauses.						

3.9 Covert modality in infinitival DP relatives

English (after BHATT 2006)
1 *[$_{DP}$ the man [$_{REL}$ to fix the sink]]* = the man who is to fix the sink – deontic *should*

German
2a **der Mann die Abwasch zu reparieren*
the man the sink to fix
b *die Abwasch ist zu reparieren*
the sink is to fix
c **der die Abwasch zu reparieren- (seien)-de Mann*
the$_i$ the sink$_j$ to fix.- (being$_i$)-SG.M.NOM man$_i$
c‘ $^{??\#}$*dem die Abwasch zu reparieren seienden Mann*
the.DAT.M$_i$ the sink$_j$ to fix being$_i$.DAT.M man$_i$
c‘‘ $^{??\#}$*für den die Abwasch zu reparieren *sei-/habend-en Mann*
for the$_i$.M.ACC the sink$_j$ to fix *being$_i$.M.ACC /having$_i$.M.ACC man$_i$
d *der die Abwasch zu reparieren habende Mann*
e **der Mann die Abwasch zum Reparieren*
the man the sink to-the.DAT fix(ing)
f $^{(??)}$ *der die Abwasch zum Reparieren habende Mann*
the$_i$.NOM the sink$_j$.ACC to-the.DAT fix(ing) having$_i$.NOM man$_i$
“the man having the sink for fixing”

The construals from d onwards are all grammatically possible and transparent on second, scrutinous thought; nevertheless, they will not be employed for stylistic reasons, probably mainly for reasons of tough parsing. The parsing impediment lies in the fact that the directions of parsing and of verbal valence run counter to each other: online parsing from left to right, verbal valence (in German OV) from right to left.[5]

Norwegian (compare the German formal equivalents)

3a * *mannen å reparere vasken*
man.the to fix sink.the
* *der Mann die Abwasch (um) zu reparieren*

b * *vasken er å reparere*
sink.the is to fix
Die Abwasch ist zu reparieren

c * *den vaskenreparerende (*værende) Mann*
the sinkfixing (being) man
* *der die Abwasch zu reparieren- (seien)-de Mann*

d ? *den vaskenreparerende havende man*
the sinkfixing having man
– understandable, but no one would ever say that
der die Abwasch zu reparieren habende Mann

Italian – no direct parallel – compare with French (4b,c)

French

4a *l'homme ayant à réparer l'évier*
the man having to fix the sink

b **l'homme étant à réparer l'évier*
the man being to fix the sink

c *l'homme **à réparant l'évier*
the man to fixing the sink

d *l'homme qui va réparer l'évier*
the man who will fix the sink

Russian

5a *čelovek kotoromu činit' rakovinu*
man who.DAT.SG.M fix.INF sink.ACC
'(the) man to/for whom (is) fix(ing) the sink'
– Russian does without a copula

---

[5] English (VO) does not produce, and conceive of, anything the like because it takes the licensor left of its complements. Notice that German brackets complements inside bracketing DPs.

b *čelovek remontiruyushii rakovinu*
man.NOM repair having.PARTICIPLE.M.NOM sink.ACC
'man having to repair the sink'

c *čelovek kotorii dolžen remontirovat rakovinu*
man.NOM who.RELPRON must.3SPRES repair sink.ACC
the man, who will/shall repair the sink

d * *čelovek, čtobi remontirovat rakovinu*
man.NOM for repair sink.ACC
'man for to repair the sink'

Polish

6a **człowiek naprawić zlew*
man.NOM fix.INF.PFV sink.ACC

No such structures exist in Polish; instead a finite relative clause is used:

b *człowiek, który ma naprawić zlew*
man.NOM who has fix.INF.PERF sink.ACC

Table 9: Covert modality in infinitival (subject-)DP relatives (see also Table 3 above): *[$_{DP}$ the man [$_{REL}$ PRO to fix the sink]]* ≡ the man who is to fix the sink ≈ *should*-Deontic, *can/could*-Possible/Able

Germanic			Romance		Slavic	
Engl VO	German OV	Norwegian VO	Italian VO	French VO	Russian VO	Polish VO
+	–	–	–	–	–	–

No syntax of infinitival relative for German, Norwegian, Slavic, Romance. They all require finite relative clauses. The English form is enigmatic in itself: the claim that it should be a relative infinitive is a forced correspondence to the finite option; any *to*-infinitive in postposition to the nominal head should rather be taken as an apposition – i.e. an attribute postponed to its constituent head. In other words, the *PRO* is misleading: the form is mono-constituent, *[$_{DP}$ the [$_{ADJ}$ (having) to fix the sink] man]]* → *[$_{DP}$ the [man [$_{ADJ}$ to fix the sink]] ~~man~~];* see German dialectal ??*der die Abwasch zu reparieren/zum Reparieren habende Mann*, which is out only for stylistic-normative reasons. English has no such complex attributes for lack of case and number declensional morphology, more concretely: for the reason that verbs like *fix* or its participle form have no declension to agree with the nominal head, *sink*. Both probing and validation mechanisms fail. In general line with extraposition, in the above postposition the requirements of agreement with the nominal head are suspended – a generalization holding for Germanic throughout (probably under the impact of fundamental head finality in DP-complexes).

Structural distinction between (i) *zu reparieren- (seien)-d-* vs. (ii) *zu reparieren- (haben)-d-*: *(zu* $V_{infinitival}$*) seiend* marks an adjectival passive, and, thus, can only be predicated of a basic object to the verb; (*zu* $V_{infinitival}$) *habend,* by contrast, marks an active participle and, consequently, predicates over an agent subject of the verb. This means that te second verb status (in the sense of Bech 1949, 1955) is ambiguous dependent of the type of auxiliary and its selection: *haben* selects a basic external argument, *sein* selects an internal argument (coherent, therefore, for passive and unaccusative subjects): cf. *Mann* in 9e vs. *9d as well as *der *(zu) fällende*$_{\text{tV}}$ *Baum* "the tree to fell" vs. *(*zu) fallende*$_{\text{uV}}$ *Baum* "the <falling> tree". The fact that <*the tree to fall*> is grammatical as opposed to all other languages under inspection (above) is due to the fact, to the best of my insight, that, unlike German *zu,* Norwegian *å,* French *à*, Italian *a,* the English infinitival marker *to* bears no lexical prepositional denotation and consequently unfolds no directional meaning – the latter selecting N and A, but not V. In German *zu V-end-* two structural properties link together: N/A-selecting directional *zu* and the present participle, in adjectival-attributive functionto the basic internal argument if linked to *sein-* and to the basic external structural argument if linked to *haben-*. Thus, it is not the theta role that matters for such a constituent to crash or be safe, but the diathetic status of the verbal arguments appearing as heads to the participles in attributive position. English *to* has a grammaticalizing status that is beyond that of the other languages: it is truly an infinitival marker (rather than 'preposition') with only selctional properties, but without the lexical direction feature.

Notice that the direction feature of *zu* is confirmed also by the gerundial, case(neuter-dative) -governing usage as in German-dialectal 9e,f above. In the gerund the nominal status of the verb is more than evident. Directional *zu* is considered to function like a perfective/telic/ completive aspect: it lays the event denotation into the future (phase) of the verbal event, much in line with the Germanic modal verbs (older preterit presents and, thus, in a resulative event status). Reconsidered in Bech's (1955) status system, the 3rd status, past participle, applied to verbals in Gothic and OHG with the perfectivizing prefix *ga-/gi-* (Modern German participial *ge-,* without such perfectivizing function) is equivalent to the second status of the infinitive with *ze/zi/zuo*: Both predicate the verb of the event time phase to follow the speech act phase $(\lambda ts,\lambda te,\lambda V)((s<e) \wedge t(e) \wedge e(V))$. Expectably, in aspectually active Gothic and Old High

German perfective verbs prefixed by *gi-* would not be linked by *zu(o)/ze* for the sake of redundancy expressed by the verbal prefix and the infinitival directional marker. See LEISS (2000) for a discussion of such links.

3.10 Covert modality in infinitival (object-)DP relatives/IOR

English (following Bhatt 2006)
Cf. English infinitival DP-relatives vs. German attributive present participles 2b or prepositional gerundials 2c (regio-/dialectal) below.

1a *[$_{DP}$ the book$_i$ [$_{REL}$ PRO$_i$ to read e$_i$]]* ≡
b ≡ *[$_{DP}$ the book$_i$ [$_{REL}$ PRO$_i$ to be read]]*
– non-finite: deontic *should*

German

2a *das Buch *(ist) zu lesen*
the book is to read
– only finite construal has a modal reading:
"kann/muss gelesen warden"– may/must be read
zu lesen ungrammatical in attributive position
b *das zu lesen- (seien)-de Buch*
the to read(ing) (being) book
– modality: "*können-müssen/may-must*" based on prepositional telicity with *zu* "to" before non-finite verb
c *das Buch zum Lesen*
the book to.the reading
– modality: *können-müssen/may-must* based on prepositional telicity

Norwegian

3a **boka er å lese*
bokk.the (is) to read
b ** den å lesende boka*
the to read(ing) book
das zu lesen- (seien)-de Buch
c **boka til lesning*
book.the to reading
das Buch zum Lesen

Italian

4a # il libro da leggere (as in Section 3.9)
the book of read(ing)
b *il libro è da leggere*
the book is of read(ing)

c *il libro da esser letto*
the book of being read

French

5a *le livre à lire*
the book to read

b **le livre à être lu*
the book to be read

c *Le livre est à lire*
the book is to read

d **Le livre est à être lu*
The book is to be read
– alternative: deontic, purporting to rhematize the Agent:

e *C'est à Willy de partir demain*
it is upon W. of leaving tomorrow"
"It is Willy who must leave tomorrow"
– alternatively: elevated style, absolutely admissible

f *C'est à Willy à partir demain*
it is up to W. to leave tomorrow
– for forms of the type:

g *Bill a à être à Philadelphie avant midi*
B. has to be to Ph. Before noon
– there is an alternative iff tV:

h *Tim a [à résoudre un problème]*
T. has to solve a problem
– possessive+telic preposition *à*

i *Tim a [un problème [à résoudre]]*
T. has a problem to solve
– possessive+telic preposition *à*

For the change of *HAVE*-possessive+telic preposition in OE to the deontic reading in Early Modern English see Ziegeler (2010).

Russian

6a *kniga dlya čteniya*
book for reading.GEN
– no modality reading, just in the sense of "to use for"

B *kniga dlya čteniya*
book for reading.ACC

c *kniga kotoruyu nužno prochitat*
book which.RELPRON.ACC must.PRES read.PERF

Polish: must use a nominalized complement as German does

7 *książka* *do* *czytani-a*
book.NOM to reading-GEN
"book for reading"

No modality reading in Polish: The sentence doesn't mean that you must read this book; rather, it means that there is a book that you can read on the basis of its very declarative status: "existential modality" in the sense claimed by Šimík (2011). [Present Part(iciple].

Table 7: modality in infinitival (object-)DP relatives/IOR: infinitival DP-relatives vs. German attributive present participles (2b) or prepositional gerundials (2c) (regiolectal, dialectal): ***$[_{DP}$ the book$_i$ $[_{REL}$ PRO$_i$ to read e$_i$]] ≡ $[_{DP}$ the book$_i$ $[_{REL}$ PRO$_i$ to be read]]*** **- non-finite: deontic *should***

Germanic			Romance		Slavic	
Engl VO	German OV	Norw VO	Ital VO	French VO	Russian VO	Polish VO
+	+ on attributive Pres. Participle	–	–	–	–	–

No syntax of infinitival relative for German, Norwegian, and Slavic: The English form is enigmatic in itself: the claim that it should be a relative infinitive is a forced correspondence to the finite option; any *to*-infinitive in postposition to the nominal head should rather be taken as an apposition – i.e. an attribute postponed to its constituent head. In other words, the *PRO* is misleading: the form is mono-constituent, *$[_{DP}$ the $[_{ADJ}$ (having) to fix the sink] man]]* → *$[_{DP}$ the [man $[_{ADJ}$ to fix the sink]] ~~man~~];* see German dialectal $^{??}$*der die Abwasch zu reparieren/zum Reparieren habende Mann* 'the-the-sink-to-fixing-man', which is out only on stylistic-normative grounds. English has no such complex attributes for lack of case and number declensional morphology, more concretely: for the reason that verbs like *fix* or its participle form have no declension to agree with the nominal head, *sink*. Both probing and validation mechanisms fail. In general line with extraposition, in the above postposition the requirements of agreement with the nominal head are suspended – a generalization holding for Germanic throughout (probably under the impact of fundamental head finality in DP-complexes).

English infinitival DP-relatives vs. German attributive present participles 2b or prepositional gerundials 2c (regio-/dialectal).

General unifying feature: <no modal reading unless the infinitival preposition *to* is involved>. Let us take *to* as a directional triggering a telic interpretation with respect to the fulfillment of the meaning of the infinitival V:

(23) $\lambda x \lambda t\ (is(x) \wedge fall(x) \wedge t' < t$, but it does not denote $\lambda x\ (\square fall(x))$.

Where does the necessity operator come from if not from the futural indication of the preposition *to*? Is it by conventional implicature – certainly not an ordinary implication or entailment? We shall return to these questions.

4. Overt modal form, but no modal meaning

4.1 Environments inverse to (24a) – modal word in the structure, but not in the interpretation as in (24b)

According to Thalberg (1969) there is also the inverse to covert modality – non-modal reading on modal verbs:

(24) a In those days, Brown was **able to/could** hit the bull's eye three times in a row.
– modal reading
b Brown was **able to/could** hit the bull's eye three times in a row.
– non-modal reading

Non-modal reading under the following specific context for (24b):

c Yesterday, B. hit three bull's-eyes in a row. Before he hit three bull's eyes, he fired 600 rounds without coming close to the bull's eye; and his subsequent tries were equally wild.

What is the role of environments in (24a) vs. (24b): In (24a) the environment involves a non-trivial mapping between the structure and interpretation. How is it possible that (24a) is modal when (24b) is non-modal? Our analysis of this environment analyzes the difference between (24a) and 2b in terms of a bi-implicative reading of von Wright's (1976) covert modal, namely $P\ (p)\ {}_{df}{=} \sim I\ (p)$. In other words, from 'what is/if *p* must also be possible/follows possible-*p*' follows 'what is possible/if possible-*p* follows must also be/*p*'. Compare our illustration under (1g), a generic declarative indicating possibility on the basis of conventional implicatures.

4.2 Anaphoricity and modality (D/EMV = deontic-root/epistemic modal verb)

There appears to be a dichotomy of root vs. epistemic readings dependent upon (in)definiteness in the antecedent clause. This appears to bear out in other languages as well. [riMF=right middle field, leMF=left middle field; D/EMV=deontic/root/epistemic modal verb]

(25) **German**

a *Du [$_{C'}$ musst [$_{VP}$ [$_{riMF}$* ***ein*** *BUCH [$_{V'}$ kaufen]]]]. Es soll/muss$_{DMV/*EMV}$*
you must a BOOK buy. it must be intellectual.
intellektuell sein. DMV/*EMV

b *Du [$_{C'}$ musst [$_{leMF}$* ***das*** *Buch [$_{VP}$ KAUFEN]]]. Es soll/muss$_{*DMV/EMV}$ intel-*
you must the book BUY. it must be intellectual.
lektuell sein. *DMV/ EMV

Due to the different positions of the (in)definite direct object, *ein/das Buch* (inside (a) vs. outside (b) of VP), in the German clausal structure, the default prosody and accentuation changes obligatorily (Cinque 1993, Abraham 1994).

Norwegian (same dependency on antecedent (in)definiteness)

(26) a … . *Den skal/må$_{DMV/*EMV}$ være intellektuell*
… . it must be intellectual DMV/*EMV
b … . Den skal/må$_{*DMV/EMV}$ være intellektuell
… . it must be intellectual *DMV/ EMV

Russian

(27) a *Ti dolžel kupit' knigu. Ona dolžna bit' intellektualnoi.*
you need.2SG buy book it need.3SG be intellectual
"You have to buy a book. It must$_{DMV/*EMV}$ be intellectual."
DMV/*EMV
b *Ti dolžel kupit' etu knigu. Doljno bit' ona intellektualnaya.*
you need buy this book must.3SG be it intellectual
"You must buy the book. It is said $_{*DMV/EMV}$ to be intellectual."
*DMV/EMV

OR

c *Ti dolžel kupit' etu knigu. Ona dolžna bit' intellektualnoi.*
you need buy this book it need.3SG be intellectual
"You need to buy this book. It is said$_{*DMV/EMV}$ to be intellectual."
*DMV/EMV

Table 11: Covert modality triggered by (in)definites across single clauses: Du musst ein Buch kaufen. Es soll/muss$_{DMV/*EMV}$ intellektuell sein. Du musst das Buch kaufen. Es soll/muss$_{*DMV/EMV}$ intellek*tuell sein.*

Germanic			Romance		Slavic	
English VO	German OV	Norwegian VO	Italian VO	French VO	Russian VO	Polish VO
+	+	+	–	–	+	–

In a way, the outcome is utterly plausible: The indefinite article, but not the definite article in the protasis, sets the common ground such that there is still room for defining the property of the predicate (*book to be bought*). No such CG-room is provided by the definite reference: therefore all that can be implied from the protasis is an estimate by the assessor of the apodosis.

Account (arguing at the level of C(ommon) G(round)):

Ad (27a): In the protasis indefinite DO, *knigu* "a book", whose property is unknown – the apodosis establishes the grounding the property – therefore the modal D-reading specifies the book property on the basis of the CG-status achieved.

Ad (27b): In the protasis definite DO, etu *knigu* "the/this book", whose property is known – the apodosis inherits the property achieved already – therefore only the modal E-reading is possible due to the CG-match (Speaker knows the book buyer and her preferences as well as her prejudices) – E-reading saves CG without prejudicating what has been determined already.

4.3 Summary

In what follows the single tables 2-9 from above are repeated under one another for easier comparison.

Table 2: Covert modality in adjunct-object complement infinitive: factive *know/wissen* as in *Tim knows [PRO how to solve the problem]* ≈ *should*-Deontic, *could*-Possible/Able

Germanic			Romance		Slavic	
English VO	German OV	Norwegian VO	Ital VO	Fr VO	Russ VO	Pol VO
+	–/?gerundial	–/no gerundial	+	+	–	–

No such syntax of (P-)infinitival embedding except for English and dialectal gerundial in German; complement-object complement infinitive partly possible: German, Norwegian. Syntax of infinitival embedding alright for Slavic, but no modality implication - modality only via finite predicate, if at all.

Table 3: Covert modality in Subject relative purpose infinitive after directional: *Sue went to Torino [PRO to buy a violin]* ≈ *should*-Deontic, *could*-Possible/Able

Germanic			Romance		Slavic	
Engl VO	German OV	Norw VO	Italian VO	French VO	Russian VO	Polish VO
+	+	+	-/(?) dove	–	no covert modality	no covert modality

German: infinitival embedding acceptable on all varieties (*um zu*/(?)*zu*/DO-incorporation); Norwegian: *for *(å)* or DO-incorporation- just *å* not sufficient; modality implication as in English.

Table 4: Covert modality in subject infinitival: *Bill has to reach Philadelphia before noon* ≈ *should*-Deontic, *could*-Possible/Able

Germanic			Romance		Slavic	
English VO	German OV	Norw VO	Italian VO	French VO	Russian VO	Polish VO
+	+ *(*zu*)	+ *(*å*)	-/(?) *da*	+ *à*	no covert modality	no covert modality

German: infinitival embedding acceptable on all varieties (*um zu*/(?)*zu*/DO-incorporation); Norwegian: *for *(å)* or DO-incorporation- just *å* not sufficient; modality implication as in English; Slavic: no *HAVE,* no infinitival embedding; modality has to be encoded overtly.

Table 5: Covert modality in subject raising iV-infinitival: *William is to leave tomorrow* ≠ *To leave/Leaving tm. has been commissioned* = *Will is scheduled/supposed to/should leave tomorrow* ≈ *should*-Deontic, (*)*could*-Possible/Able

Germanic			Romance		Slavic	
Engl VO	Germ OV	Norw VO	Italian VO	French VO	Russian VO	Polish VO
+	–iV/ +tV	–	–	–	no covert modality	no covert modality

German: infinitival syntax only for tV, with – in contrast to English – both deontic and epistemic modality implied. Romance: no *BE*-onfintivals. Slavic: no infinitival embedding; modality has to be encoded overtly.

Table 6: Covert modality in object infinitive – unaccusative V(decausative iV): *The stomach is (/has) to empty$_{uV}$ / to be emptied$_{iV}$* → iPRED ≈ *should*-Deontic, **could*-Possible/Able

Germanic			Romance		Slavic	
Engl VO	Germ OV	Norw VO	Italian VO	French VO	Russian VO	Polish VO
+	–iV/ +tV	–	–	–	no covert modality	no covert modality

German: infitival syntax only for tV, with – in contrast to English – both deontic and optionality modality implication. Romance: no *BE*-infinitivals. Slavic: no infinitival embedding; modality has to be encoded overtly.

Table 7: Covert modality in subject infinitive – unaccusative verb/uV: *The monument is to fall* ≠ *XP is about to fall/go The monument has to fall* ≈ *should*-Deontic, **can/*could*-Possible/Able

Germanic			Romance		Slavic	
English VO	German OV	Norwegian VO	Italian VO	French VO	Russian VO	Polish VO
+	*–ist/ +hat*	*–er/?har*	–	–	no covert modality	no covert modality

Table 8: Covert modality in infinitival (subject-)DP relatives (see also Table 3 above): *[$_{DP}$ the man [$_{REL}$ PRO to fix the sink]]* ≡ the man who is to fix the sink ≈ *should*-Deontic, *can/could*-Possible/Able

Germanic			Romance		Slavic	
English VO	German OV	Norwegian VO	Italian VO	French VO	Russian VO	Polish VO
+	–	–	–	–	–	–

No syntax of infinitival relative for German, Norwegian, Slavic, Romance. They all require finite relative clauses. The English form is enigmatic in itself: the claim that it should be a relative infinitive is a forced correspondence to the finite option; any *to*-infinitive in postposition to the nominal head should rather be taken as an apposition – i.e. an attribute postponed to its constituent head. In other words, the *PRO* is misleading: the form is mono-constituent, *[$_{DP}$ the [$_{ADJ}$ (having) to fix the sink] man]]* → *[$_{DP}$ the [man [$_{ADJ}$ to fix the sink]] ~~man~~];* see German dialectal $^{??}$*der die Abwasch zu reparieren/zum Reparieren habende Mann,* which is out only for stylistic-normative reasons. English has no such complex attributes for lack of case and number declensional morphology, more concretely: for the reason that verbs like *fix* or its participle form have no declension to agree with the nominal head, *sink.* Both probing and validation mechanisms fail. In general line with extraposition, in the above postposition the requirements of agreement with the nominal head are suspended – a generalization holding for Germanic throughout (probably under the impact of fundamental head finality in DP-complexes).

Structural distinction between (i) *zu reparieren- (seien)-d-* vs. (ii) *zu reparieren- (haben)-d-*: *(zu $V_{infinitival}$) seiend* marks an adjectival passive, and, thus, can only be predicated of a basic object to the verb; *(zu $V_{infinitival}$) habend,* by contrast, marks an active participle and, consequently, predicates over an agent subject of the verb. This means that te second verb status (in the sense of Bech 1949, 1955) is ambiguous dependent of the type of auxiliary and its selection: *haben* selects a basic external argument, *sein* selects an internal argument (coherent, therefore, for passive and unaccusative subjects): cf. *Mann* in (9e) vs. *(9d) as well as *der *(zu) fällende*$_{tV}$ *Baum* „the tree to fell" vs. *(*zu) fallende*$_{uV}$ *Baum* „the <falling> tree". The fact that <*the tree to fall*> is grammatical as opposed to all other languages under inspection (above) is due to the fact, to the best of my insight, that, unlike German *zu,* Norwegian *å,* French *à,* Italian *a,* the English infinitival marker *to* bears no lexical prepositional de-notation and consequently unfolds no directional meaning – the latter selecting N and A, but not V. In German *zu V-end-* two structural properties link together: N/A-selecting directional *zu* and the present participle, in adjectival-attributive function to the basic internal argument if linked to *sein-* and to the basic external structural argument if linked to *haben-*. Thus, it is not the theta role that matters for such a constituent to crash or be safe, but the diathetic status of the verbal arguments appearing as heads to the participles in attributive position. English *to* has a grammaticalizing status that is beyond that of the other languages: it is truly an infinitival marker (rather than 'preposition') with only selctional properties, but without the lexical direction feature.

Notice that the direction feature of *zu* is confirmed also by the gerundial, case(neuter-dative)-governing usage as in German-dialectal (2c) above. In the gerund the nominal status of the verb is more than evident. Directional *zu* is considered to function like a perfective/ telic/completive aspect: it lays the event denotation into the future (phase) of the verbal event, much in line with the Germanic modal verbs (older preterit presents and, thus, in a resulative event status). Reconsidered in Bech's (1955) status system, the 3rd status, past participle, applied to verbals in Gothic and OHG with the perfectivizing prefix *ga-/gi-* (Modern German participial *ge-*, without such perfectivizing function) is equivalent to the second status of the infinitive with *ze/zi/zuo*: Both predicate the verb of the event time phase to follow the speech act phase $(\lambda ts, \lambda te, \lambda V)((s<e) \wedge t(e) \wedge e(V))$. Expectably, in aspectually active Gothic and Old High German perfective verbs prefixed by *gi-* would not be linked by *zu(o)/ze* for the sake of redundancy expressed by the verbal prefix and the infinitival directional marker. See Leiss (2000) for a discussion of such links.

Table 9: Covert modality in infinitival object-DP relatives: *[$_{DP}$ the book [$_{REL}$ to read]] = [$_{DP}$ the book [$_{REL}$ to be read]]≈ should*-Deontic, *can/could*-Possible/Able

Germanic			Romance		Slavic	
English VO	German OV	Norw VO	Italian VO	French VO	Russian VO	Polish VO
+	+ on attributive Present Participle	–	–	–	–	–

No syntax of infinitival relative for German, Norwegian, Slavic, Romance. They all require finite relative clauses. The English form is enigmatic in itself: the claim that it should be a relative infinitive is a forced correspondence to the finite option; any *to*-infinitive in postposition to the nominal head should rather be taken as an apposition – i.e. an attribute postponed to its constituent head. In other words, the *PRO* is misleading: the form is mono-constituent, *[$_{DP}$ the [$_{ADJ}$ (having) to fix the sink] man]]* → *[$_{DP}$ the [man [$_{ADJ}$ to fix the sink]] ~~man~~];* see German dialectal $^{??}$*der die Abwasch zu reparieren/zum Reparieren habende Mann*, which is out only for stylistic-normative reasons.

Summary: English infinitival DP-relatives vs. German attributive present participles (2b) or prepositional gerundials (2c) (regio-/dialectal): English has no such complex attributes for lack of case and number declensional morphology, more concretely: for the reason that verbs like *fix* or its participle form have no declension to agree with the nominal head, *sink*. Both probing and validation mechanisms fail. In general line with extraposition, in the above postposition the requirements of agreement with the nominal head are suspended – a generalization holding for Germanic throughout (probably under the impact of fundamental head finality in DP-complexes).

Table 10: Modality triggered by (in)definites across clauses: Du musst ein Buch kaufen. Es soll/mussDMV/*EMV intellektuell sein. vs. Du musst das Buch kaufen. Es soll/muss*DMV/EMV *intellektuell sein.*

Germanic			Romance		Slavic	
English VO	German OV	Norwegian VO	Italian VO	French VO	Russian VO	Polish VO
+	+	+	–	–	+	–

In a way, the outcome is utterly plausible: The indefinite article, but not the definite article in the protasis, sets the common ground such that there is still room for defining the property of the book to be bought. No such CG-room is provided by the definite reference: therefore all that can be implied from the protasis is an estimate by the assessor of the apodosis.

There appears to be a class of futuralizing, and by that property equally modalizing, morphological elements. See the following points of generalization, (28a-g):

(28) a. the directional 'infinitival preposition', English *to*, German *zu*, Romance *a*

b. the auxiliary *HAVE* denoting a property of the subject of *HAVE*

c. the auxiliary, or copula, *BE* denoting a property of the subject of *BE*

d. directional 'infinitival preposition' and *HABE / BE* cooperate in achieving the futural, and modality, denotation.

e. the modality meaning achieved by conditions (28a-d) remains ambiguous, or vague, between NECESS and POSSIB, in ways further unclear. We might want to speak about the basic modality categories constituting in the evolutional-diachronic "modal proto-soup/modale Ursuppe" (Abraham 2010), from which all subclasses of today's modality distinctions, as represented in the paradigm of German modal verbs and the inventory of modal particles emerged in the course of time and by mutual dissociation.

f. Transitive HAVE(x,y) is composed of, and lexically equivalent to, intransitive BE(y)-WITH(x), where x carries the prototypical attributing-to-dative (case) theta role (Kotin 2011: 'something is (to/for) him.dat (for/to) do(ing)').

g. All of the considerations in (28a-g) are totally independent of the embedding constraints of prepositional infinitivals in the different languages discussed here. One suggestion for such constraints is the failure of a variety of languages to relate infinitival form to gerundial, i.e. by nominal, function of verbal form. Recall that exactly this relation is apparent in German dialects, but not in the standard language.

5. Covert modality in diachronics: How did the modal reading evolve?

The grammaticalization of a zero stage of lexically encoded modality to clear possibility and, then, further to obligation is a puzzle. It is a clear case of covertly signaled modality. However, once modal possibility is ectablished, the grammaticalization path from possibility to obligation which describes the development of *haben* to a marker of modality is well-established (cf. Heine& Kuteva 2002). Careful study of Notker's writings (Jäger 2012) reveals evidence of modal '*haben* + *zu*-infinitive' as early as in Old High German. Four stages of grammaticalization of haben with *zu*-infinitive may be identified.

5.1 Modality in non-finite contexts: root infinitives and infinitival relatives from Old High German to Modern German

The development of *HAVE*, German/English *haben/have,* to a marker of deontic modality is cross-linguistically established and widely described (cf. Heine & Kuteva 2002). This development is shared by Old High German/OHG (Ebert 1976, Jäger 2012), Old English/OE (Fischer 1994, Harris & Campbell 1995, Ziegeler 2011), and Latin (Coleman 1971, Adams 1991). Furthermore, the early development of modal verbs out of the inventory of preterit presents both in OE and in OHG appears to be firmly established. Modal verbs/MVs express modal meaning on the embedded bare full verb in infinitival form. All other verbs, expressing modality or not, have to formalize infinitival mebedding with the help of a preposition: *to* in English, the etymological relative *zu* in German, and *a* in Romance. There is no exception to this generalization: only the MVs select a bare infinitive; equally preterit presents such as *wissen* "know" (etymologically related to Latin *vidēō* "see") have no modal shading and need a preposition for embedding an infinitive: *Wir wissen *(zu) warten* "We know to wait". In Gothic, however, other near-inchoative (and, by this token, preterit present) verbs such as *sokjan* "seek" embedded complement infinitives without a bridging preposition, but, to all appearances, always require the selection of a perfective verb. See below (29) (from Leiss 2002; her (15) on p. 77; the preterite present verb and the perfective prefix morpheme on the embedded full verb are boldened).

(29) *jah* ***sokida ga****saihvan Jesu, hvas wesi, jah ni mahte faura managein, unte wahstan leitils was.* [Luke 19,3]
„and (he) desired (to) see Jesus, who he were, and …"

In fact, according to Streitberg (1910), inchoatives such as Gothic *sokjan* always took perfective verbs prefigated with *ga-*. This suggests that the prefix is functionally related to the originally directional preposition used as a construal bridge for embedded infinitivals.

Another argument in this context is the following. Neither *HAVE/BE* by themselves trigger any modal meaning, nor does the root infinitive. Only the construal *HAVE/BE*+preposition+verbal infinitive elicits modal meanings dangling between possibility and obligatoriness. By contrast, MVs achieve the same without the directional-prepositional bridge. This leads to the conclusion that MVs contain as an internal, invisible component that non-MVs have to bring in by external composition. Our conclusion is that the integrated MV-component is futurality, the main diagnostic component for inchoatives and preterit presents. See (30a-h) for the generalizations.

(30) a MV: futural component + modal component
b Preterite presents & inchoatives: only futural component (2nd phase of perfective event: incremental phase + resultative phase)
c embedded infinitival: no modal meaning without preposition bridge in the form of directional *to/zu/a*
d embedded gerundive: gerundive has deontic meaning (Latin): *tamen spernendus est* 'yet-(to-)reject.GERUNDIVE-is' = "yet to be rejected".
e German gerundial (dialects): aligns with prepositional directional according to nominal selection: $[_{PP}$ P $[_{DP}$ V-gerund]]; no modal meaning by itself. No other language appears to have this extra morphology carrying case as selected by the 'infinitival' preposition (DATIVE licensed by German directional *zu*).
f Gothic lexical *ga*-perfective: *ga-* encodes direction toward the resultative function; see (29) above
g infinitival P: encodes direction toward the 'infinitival' (= gerundial) function (Abraham 2006:125)
h the futural component can be encoded either by aspectual Gothic *ga-* or the 'infinitival' (= gerundial) preposition.

All of this suggests that the modal meaning is a component by itself, one that has futurality as a necessary, but not satisfactory, property. Such futurality is encoded by perfective aspect (Gothic *ga-*; lexical perfectives such as the inchoatives or preterit presents) and / or the directional preposition. Where perfective aspect is lexically encoded (such as with MVs), the construing bridge element is missing – in fact, is not only redundant, but is ungrammatical: viz. *this may*.MV *(*to) be true* – German *das darf*.MV *doch nicht wahr (*zu) sein* vs. *this seems *(to) be true* – German *das scheint wahr *(zu) sein.*

5.2 *BE-TO-* and *HAVE-TO*-infinitive

There is a clear division of abor between *HABEN* / *HAVE*+P-infinitive and SEIN / BE +P-infinitive (Ziegeler 2010, Jäger 2011): See (31a,b), where (i)t = (in)transitive.

(31) a λxλy [*haben(*x,y*)* + (DP(y)) + *zu*+ i-tV(x)]
b λy [*sein (*y*)* + *zu*+*i-tV(y)]

Given the decausativelike distribution between the two arguments in (31a,b), the *SEIN / BE*-construal is the unaccusative configuration of the transitive-unagentive *HABEN / HAVE*-construal. This explains why English *is-to-V* is equivalent to the passive form *is-to-be-done*. The German passive infinitive *ist-zu-geschaffen zu werden* is just out for stylistic reasons.

From the above, particularly (30a,f), follows that *haben(*x,y*)+* DP(*y*)+*zu*+tV(x) is fundamentally non-modal. The reason is that the original possession meaning is firmly supported by the direct object DP. See the Latin (32) (illustration due to Jäger 2012) which is not only bare of any modal shade, but whose word order – particularly the order IO-DO-$V_{infinitive}$ – reflects a highly coherent (= non-extraposing) infinitival construction. By contrast, see the extraposed clause in German (33b).

(32) *Simon, habeo tibi aliquid dicere.* (T 238.16)
Simon, (I) have (to) you something (to) tell

(33) a Ich habe [$_{vp}$ Dir [$_{vp}$ etwas [$_{vp}$ zu sagen]]].
→ possessive, deontic
b Ich habe [$_{vp}$ Dir [$_{vp}$ t [$_{vp}$ zu sagen]] [$_{cp}$ dass Du kommen sollst]$_t$
→ $^?$possessive, deontic

It is by no means obvious that the *zu*+infinitive, purely on the basis of its lexical directional meaning, inevitably elicits a modal reading. The same appears to hold for English (cf. Krug 2000:80; Mitchell 1985:402). What it implies beyond doubt is a future reading (Abraham 2006:125). Haspelmath (1989:298) argues that the grammaticalization of the infinitive reaches modal readings in line with the following grammaticalization path in (34).

(34) Semantic changes involved in the grammaticalization of the infinitive (according to Haspelmath 1989:298; somewhat imaged differently): {benefactive, allative, causal} > purposive > irrealis- directive (complements of manipulative and desiderative verbs) > irrealis-potential (complements of evaluative predicates and modal predicates) > realis- non-factive (complements of verbs of cognition or of evaluative predicates) > (realis factive)

The pivotal step on the grammaticalization path toward modal meaning is the transition from irrealis directive to the irrealis-potential. If Haspelmath (1989:299) is to be believed the infinitive is used in complement clauses with irrealis-potential modality. Notice that this excludes directional *zu* "to". In other words, *haben* is said not appear in conjunction with the *zu*-infinitive in Old High German texts. Possibly even, there should not be any modal shade involved. However, first, it is easy to find passages, here from Tatian, as modal readings including '*haben* + *zu*-infinitive'. See (35), secondary quote from Jäger (2012; Jäger's illustration (4)):

(35) *simon, ih haben thir sih uuaz ciqued-an-ne* (T 238.16)
Simon I have.1SG you.DAT something tell.GERUND.DAT
'Simon, I have to tell you something'
„Simon, ich habe dir etwas zu sagen" (Demske 2001:70)

Whether Latin (32), construally in line with (33a), bears a modal shade is not certain. If we are to believe Coleman (1971:216-217) and Adams (1991), the grammaticalization path reaches out from 'purpose/destination > possibility > obligation/ necessity > future > future-in-the past > conditioned unreality'. But the central inclusion of the modal passages 'possibility > obligation/ necessity' before the futural steps is far from self-evident. The least one can say is that Germanic does not tread in the same pace as Latin (and the Romance languages? Why would they have taken to use the directional preposition *a* today?)).

The emergence of the modal meanings can be traced by looking once more at the different types of appearances for '*haben* + *zu*-infinitive' in (36) (somewhat modified after Jäger 2012: 13).

(36) The four stages of grammaticalization of haben with *zu*-infinitive:
Stage 1: [*haben* + [DP-complement (ACC)
(+*zu*-infinitive]]
Stage 2: [*haben* + [DP-complement (ACC) + *(+*zu*-infinitive)]]
Stage 3: [*haben* + [[DP- complement (PARTITIVE/DAT)]
+*zu*-infinitive]]
Stage 4: [*haben* + *zu*-infinitive]

Cf. our (33a,b) above – Jäger's original genitive in Type 3 is replaced here by 'partitive', because such object complements refer only to quantified mass objects – such mass nominals are no different functionally from accusative objects. This makes Type 3 superfluous next to Type 2. Type (1) is no example for '*haben* + *zu*-infinitive'. But, depending on the noun in the position of the object, sentences of this type may encode weak modal meanings. Type (2) is structurally and semantically ambiguous. Since the object may depend from *haben* or from the *zu*-infinitive, the irrealis-prospective and the irrealis-potential readings both offer equally sound interpretations. Type (3) involves '*haben* + *zu*-infinitive' in combination with a complement in the genitive or dative case. Due to the case requirements of *haben*, the nominal complement must depend on the *zu*-infinitive. This evokes a reading of necessity or obligation. Type (4) is not attested in Notker's Old High German texts, yet. It involves *zu*-infinitives of intransitive verbs that are used without any nominal complements. Examples of this type possess a strong reading of necessity or obligation and are unambiguously modal. The pivotal point in the process of grammaticalization is reached as soon as '*haben* + *zu*-infinitive' appears without nominal complements. But this is not where ambiguity ends and where *haben* is on its way to an auxiliary turning into a marker of modality (Jäger 2012: 13).

5.3 Old High German '*sein* + *zu*-infinitive'

According to Jäger (2012), *haben* is not the only Old High German verb that develops modal meanings when it is combined with *zu*-infinitives. The same happens with *sein* ('*to be*'), but at a much faster pace. For example, Notker's writings already offer quite a collection of examples for '*sein* + *zu*-infinitive'. In *De consolatione philosophiae* for example, there are as many as 48 instances of '*sein* + *zu*-infinitive' just in 3rd person singular present indicative (Sehrt/Legner 1955; Tax 1986-90). Many of these appear as translations of Latin '*sum* + gerundive', but they are also quite often used without Latin prompting. Compare: Latin '*sum* + gerundive' and Old High German '*sein* + *zu*-infinitive'. Cf. (37)-(38).

(37) *Quorum quidem exercitus tametsi numerosus est. tamen spernendus est.*
Téro hére nîo sô míchel ne=íst. íz ne=sî zeuerchîes-en-ne.
their army never so mighty NEG=is. it NEG=be.SUBJ to reject-INF-DAT (P. 20,29)
"Their army is never so mighty, that it could not be rejected."

(38) Latin:
Sed quoniam descendunt in te iam fomenta mearum rationum ! puto vtendum esse paulo ualidioribus . s . remediis.
Old High German translation:
Uuánda dîh tóh îu ingân-t mîn-e réd-â . mít tîen
Since you then already enter.3PL my speeches with ART.DAT.PL
íh tíh únz nû fâscô-ta . sô îst nû zeuáhenne uuâno îh
I you until now soothed.1SG so is now to turn think.PRES.1SG I
zestárch-er-en réd-ôn. (P. 87,29)
to strong.DAT.PL speech.DAT.PL
"Since my speeches, with which I have soothed you until now, are now sinking in, we should now turn to stronger arguments, I think."

See an original Old High German '*sein* + *zu*-infinitive' in (39):

(39) *Tára nâh íst táz zeuuîz-en-ne . táz status únde constitutio . ál éin íst*
Thereafter is that to know.DAT that status and constitutio all one is
"Furthermore, one must know that *status* and *constitutio* are one and the same.'

It is important to note, that the *zu*-infinitive in these cases is no longer confined to irrealis-prospective meanings, but takes on irrealis-potential meanings as well. In fact, '*sein* + *zu*-infinitive' is already established as a means for expressing necessity in Notker's writings (cf. Näf 1979: 180-181). This is further proof of the fact that the Old High German infinitive is not restricted to irrealis-prospective meanings, and it indicates where '*haben* + *zu*-infinitive' is headed.

5.4 Summary: Form and morphologically explicit modality early on: *HAVE/BE(*+DP)+*zu*-infinitive

It can hardly be claimed that the P+infinitve by itself denotes, or implies/implicates, a modal shade. As shown by Jäger (2012) on Latin, Old High German/OHG, and Old English/OE, the *HABEN*+complement construction denoted possession already in Latin – a construal which was copied in form and in meaning by OHG authors and translators. However, since Latin, but not the two Germanic languages, had the formal gerundive expressing obligatoriness the Germanic P-inifinitive had to serve two purposes: expressing possession as well as deontic modality. Clearly, the two readings had prototypical construal forms: *HAVE/BE*+DP +P-infinitive had the preferred reading of possession, whereas *HAVE/BE*+P-infinitive was modal by preference. See examples (22)-(24) above for the deontic-only *SEIN*-construal.

The pivotal point is reached as soon as '*haben* + *zu*-infinitive' is combined with nominal complements in the genitive or dative case. These are clearly modal in meaning, and Notker's Old High German texts contain several instances of this use. Finally, the comparison with the original texts demonstrates that '*haben* + *zu*-infinitive' does not descend from Latin, but rises independently in Old High German.

References

Abraham, Werner 1989. Syntaktische Korrelate zum Lesartwechsel zwischen epistemischen und deontisch/volitiven Modalverben. *Groninger Arbeiten zur Germanistischen Linguistik* 30: 145-166. [see also: http://gagl.eldoc.ub.rug.nl/FILES/root/1989-30/04/GAGL-30-1989-04.pdf. last download: May 5, 2012].

—. 1991. Modalverben in Germania. In: Eijirō Iwasaki (ed.): *Begegnung mit dem Fremden: Grenzen – Traditionen – Vergleiche, Akten des VIII. Internationalen Germanisten-Kongresses, Tokyo1990*. Band 4, Sektion 4: *Kontrastive Syntax*, 109–118. München: Iudicium.

—. 1994. Fokusgrammatik und Indefinitheit. In: B. Haftka (ed.) *Was determiniert Wortstellungsvariation? Studien zu einem Interaktionsfeld von Grammatik, Pragmatik und Sprachtypologie,* 235-245. Opladen: Westdeutscher Verlag.

—. 1997. The interdependence of case, aspect, and referentiality in the history of German: the case of the genitive. In: A. van Kemenade & N. Vincent (eds.). *Parameters of morphosyntactic change*, 29-61. Cambridge: CUP.

—. 2001. Modals: toward explaining the ‚epistemic non-finiteness gap'. In: R. Müller & M. Reis (eds.) *Modality und Modalverben im Deutschen*, 7-36. [Linguistische Berichte Sonderheft 9]. Hamburg: Buske.

—. 2004. The grammaticalization of the infinitival preposition – toward a theory of 'grammaticalizing reanalysis'. *Journal of Comparative Germanic Linguistics* 7/2: 111-170.

—. 2005. Event arguments and modal verbs. In: C. Maienborn & A. Wöll-stein (eds.) *Event arguments: Foundations and applications*, 243-276. [Linguistische Arbeiten 501]. Tübingen: M. Niemeyer.

—. 2010. Diskurspartikel zwischen Modalität, Modus und Fremdbewusst-seinsabgleich. In: T. Harden & E. Hentschel (eds.) *40 Jahre Partikelforschung*, 33-77. Frankfurt/M.: P. Lang.

—. 2012a. Sprecherdeixis und Merkmaldistributionsdifferential deutscher Modalitätselemente. *Deutsche Sprache 40*: 72-95.

—. 2012b. Satzabhängigkeit und Fremdbewusstseinsabgleich. In: In: J. Brandtler, St. Huber, D. Håkansson & E. Klingvall (eds.) *Discourse and Grammar. Essays in Honor of Valéria Molnár*, 200-231. Lund: University of Lund, Sweden.

Abraham, Werner & Elisabeth Leiss (eds.) 2008. *Modality-aspect interfaces. Implications and typological solutions.* [Typological Studies in Languages 79]. Amsterdam-Philadelphia: John Benjamins.

Abraham, Werner & Elisabeth Leiss (eds.) 2012. *Modality and Theory of mind elements across languages.* Berlin: Mouton de Gruyter.

Adams, J. N. 1991. Some neglected evidence for Latin *habeo* with infinitive. The order of the constituents. *Transactions of the Philological Society* 89: 131-196.

Anderson, Curtis Anthony 1967. *The logic of decision and action.* Oxford: OUP.

Bech, Gunnar 1949. Das semantische System der deutschen Modalverba. *Travaux du Cercle Linguistique de Copenhague* 4: 3-46.

—. 1955. *Studien über das deutsche verbum infinitim.* Band 1. Copenhagen: Munksgaard.

Behaghel, Otto 1923-32. *Deutsche Syntax. Eine geschichtliche Darstellung.* 4 volumes, [Germanische Bibliothek 1. Sammlung germanischer Elementar- und Handbücher 10]. Heidelberg: Winter.

Bhatt, Rajesh 2006. *Covert modality in non-finite contexts*. [Interface Explorations 8]. Berlin: Mouton de Gruyter.

Birkmann, Thomas 1987. *Präteritopräsentia. Morphologische Entwicklungen einer Sonderklasse in den altgermanischen Sprachen.* [Linguistische Arbeiten 188]. Tübingen: Niemeyer.

Bondaruk, Anna (2004. *pro and control in English, Irish and Polish – a Minimalist analysis.* Lublin: Wydawnictwo KUL.

Cardinaletti, Anna & Michael Starke 1999 The typology of structural deficiency: a case study of the three classes of pronouns. In: H. v. Riemsdijk (ed.) *Clitics in the languages of Europe*, 145–233. Berlin: Mouton de Gruyter.

Cinque, Guilgelmo 1993. A null theory of phrase and compound stress. *Linguistic Inquiry* 24(2), 239-298.

Coleman, Robert 1971. The origin and development of Latin *habēō* + infinitive. *The Classical Quarterly* 21: 215-232.

Coniglio, Marco 2009. Deutsche Modalpartikeln in Haupt- und Nebensätzen. In: W. Abraham & E. Leiss (eds.) *Modalität. Epistemik und Evidentialität bei Modalverb, Adverb, Modalpartikel und Modus*, 191-

221. [Studien zur deutschen Grammatik 77]. Tübingen: Stauffenburg Verlag.
—. 2011. *Syntax der deutschen Modalpartikeln. Ihre Distribution und Lizensierung in Haupt- und Nebensätzen.* [studia grammatica 73]. Berlin: Akademieverlag.
Demske, Ulrike 2001. Zur Distribution von Infinitivkomplementen im Althochdeutschen. In: R. Müller & M. Reis (eds.) *Modality und Modalverben im Deutschen*, 61-86. [Linguistische Berichte. Sonderheft 9]. Hamburg: Buske.
Dentschewa, Emilia 1986. Finalität des Infinitivkomplements. Dargestellt am Beispiel des althochdeutschen Tatian. *Zeitschrift für Phonetik, Sprachwissenschaft und Kommunikationsforschung* 39: 318-338.
Ebert, Robert Peter 1976. Infinitival complement constructions in Early New High German. [Linguistische Arbeiten 30]. Tübingen: Niemeyer.
Fischer, Olga 1994. The development of quasi-auxiliaries in English and changes in word order. *Neophilologus* 78: 137-164.
—. 1997. On the status of grammaticalisation and the diachronic dimension in explanation. *Transactions of the Philological Society* 95: 149-187.
Gärtner, Hans-Martin 2009. More on the indefinite-interrogative affinity: The view from embedded non-finite interrogatives. *Linguistic Typology* 13: 1-37.
Haan, Ferdinand de 2011. Typology of tense, aspect, and modality. In: J. J. Song (ed.) *The Oxford Handbook of Linguistic Typology*, 445-464. Oxford: OUP.
Haspelmath, Martin 1989. From purposive to infinitive. A universal path of grammaticalization. *Folia Linguistica Historica* 10: 287-310.
Heine, Bernd & Tania Kuteva 2002. *World lexicon of grammaticalization.* Cambridge: CUP.
Holl, Daniel 2010. *Modale Infinitive und dispositionelle Modalität im Deutschen.* [studia grammatica 7]. Berlin: Akademieverlag.
Hundt, Markus 2003. Zum Verhältnis von epistemischer und nicht-epistemischer Modalität im Deutschen. Forschungspositionen und Vorschlag zur Neuorientierung. *Zeitschrift für germanistische Linguistik* 31: 343-381.
Iwasaki, Shoichi 2002. *Japanese.* [London Oriental and African Language Library]. Amsterdam: John Benjamins.
Iwasaki, Shoichi & Preeya Ingkaphirom 2005. *A reference grammar of Thai.* Cambridge: CUP.
Jäger, Anne 2012. The emergence of modal meanings from *haben* with *zu*-infinitives in Old High German. In: G. Diewald, L. Kahlas-Tarkka & I.

Wischer (eds.) *Comparative studies in early Germanic languages: with a focus on verbal categories.* [Companion Series of Studies in Language]. Amsterdam: John Benjamins.

Jędrzejowski, Łukasz 2012. What is it that keeps the rein on quotative modals so tight? In: W. Abraham & E. Leiss (eds.) 2012 *Modality and Theory of mind elements across languages,* 425-454. Berlin: Mouton de Gruyter.

König, Ekkehard 1997. Zur Bedeutung von Modalpartikeln im Deutschen: ein Neuansatz im Rahmen der Relevanztheorie. *Germanistische Linguistik* 136: 57-75.

Kotin, Michail 2008. Aspects of a reconstruction of form and function of modal verbs in Germanic and other languages. In: W. Abraham & E. Leiss (eds.) *Modality-aspect interfaces. Implications and typological solutions,* 371-384. [Typological Studies in Languages 79]. Amsterdam: John Benjamins..

—. 2012 (in this volume). Impersonal dative constructions as covert root-modality patterns.

Kratzer, Angelika 1981. The notional category of modality, in: *Words, Worlds, and Contexts. New Approaches in Word Semantics* ed. by H.-J. Eikmeyer & H. Rieser. [Research in Text Theory 6]. Berlin: de Gruyter, pp. 38-74.

—. 1991. Modality. In: A. v. Stechow & D. Wunderlich (eds.) *Semantik: Ein internationales Handbuch zeit-genössischer Forschung*, 639-650. Berlin: de Gruyter.

Krug, Manfred G. 2000. *Emerging English modals. A corpus-based study of grammaticalization.* [Topics in English literature 32]. Berlin: de Gruyter.

Landau, Idan 2000. *Elements of control. Structure and meaning in infinitival constructions.* [Studies in Natural Language and Linguistic Theory 51]. Dordrecht: Springer.

—. 2006. Severing the distribution of pro from case. *Syntax* 9: 153-170.

—. 2007. Movement-resistant aspects of control. In: W. D. Davies & S. Dubinsky (eds.) *New horizons in the analysis of control and raising*, 293-325. [Studies in Natural Language and Linguistic Theory 71]. Dordrecht: Springer.

—. (2008. Two routes of control: evidence from case transmission in Russian. *Natural Language & Linguistic Theory* 26: 877-924.

Łecki, Andrzej M. 2010. *Grammaticalisation paths of* have *in English.* [Studies in medieval language and literature 24]. Frankfurt a. M.: Lang.

Lubańska, Maja 2005. *Focus on* wh-*questions*. Frankfurt am Main: Peter Lang.
Leiss, Elisabeth 2000. *Artikel und Aspekt.* Berlin: de Gruyter.
—. 2002. Explizite und implizite Kodierung von Deontizität und Epistemizität: Über die grammatische Musterbildung vor der Entstehung der Modalverben. *Jeziko Slovlje* 3/1-2: 69-98.
—. 2008. The silent and aspect-driven patterns of deonticity and epistemicity: a chapter in diachronic typology. In: W. Abraham & E. Leiss (eds.) *Modality-aspect interfaces. Implications and typological solutions,* 15-42. [Typological Studies in Languages 79]. Amsterdam: John Benjamins.
—. 2012 (in this volume). Aspectual patterns of covert coding of modality in Gothic and Old High German.
Mitchell, Bruce 1985. *Old English syntax*. Vol. 1. *Concord, the parts of speech, and the sentence*. Oxford: Clarendon Press.
Müller, Reimar & Marga Reis (eds.) 2001. *Modality und Modalverben im Deutschen.* [Linguistische Berichte – Sonderheft 9]. Hamburg: Buske.
Näf, Anton 1979. *Die Wortstellung in Notkers Consolatio. Untersuchungen zur Syntax und Übersetzungstechnik.* [Das Althochdeutsche von St. Gallen 5]. Berlin: de Gruyter.
Narrog, Heiko & Bernd Heine (eds.) 2011. *The Oxford Handbook of Grammaticalization.* Oxford: OUP.
Öhlschläger, Günther 1989. *Zur Syntax und Semantik der Modalverben des Deutschen.* [Linguistische Arbeiten 144]. Tübingen: M. Niemeyer.
Pittner, Karin 2011. Anmerkungen zur (Un-)Integriertheit von Konditionalsätzen mit Verberststellung. *Zeitschrift für Sprachwissenschaft* 30: 75-105.
Portner, Paul & Rafaella Zanuttini 2000. The force of negation in *wh* exclamatives and interrogatives. In: L.R. Horn & Y. Kato (eds.) *Negation and polarity. Syntactic and semantic perspectives*, 193-231. Oxford: OUP.
Reis, Marga & Angelika Wöllstein 2010. Zur Grammatik (vor allem) konditionaler V1-Gefüge im Deutschen. *Zeitschrift für Sprachwissenschaft* 29: 111-179.
Šimík, Radek 2011a. Modal existential wh-constructions. Ph.D. dissertation, Rijksuniversiteit Groningen.
—. 2011b. Covert modality in modal existential *wh*-constructions. Paper read at the Annual SLE Meeting in Logroño, Workshop 'Covert patterns of modality'.
Streitberg, Wilhelm 1910. *Gotisches Elementarbuch.* Heidelberg: C. Winter.

Thalberg, Irving 1969. Austin on abilities. In: K.T.Fann (ed.) *Symposium on J.L. Austin*, 182-205. New York: Humanities Press.

Witkoś, Jacek 2010a. Movement theory of control and CP-infinitives in Polish. In: N. Hornstein & M. Polinsky (eds.) *Movement theory of control*, 45-66. [Linguistik Aktuell/ Linguistics Today 154]. Amsterdam: John Benjamins.

—. 2010b. On the lack of case on the subject of infinitives in Polish. *Folia Linguistica* 44: 179-238.

Wright, Georg Henrik von 1976. *Handlung, Norm und Intention*. Berlin: Walter de Gruyter.

Ziegeler, Debra 2010. Semantic determinism and the grammaticalization of *have to* in English. A reasessment. *Journal of Historical Pragmatics* 11,1: 32-66.

Zimmermann, Malte 2004. Zum Wohl: Diskurspartikeln als Satztypmodifikatoren. *Linguistische Berichte* 199: 1-35.

—. 2005. Discourse particles in the left periphery. In: Ph. Cook, W. Frey, C. Maienborn & B. Shaer (eds.) *Dislocated elements in discourse*, 200-231. Oxford: Routledge.

Primary sources

[P] = Piper, Paul (ed.) 1882/3. *Die Schriften Notkers und seiner Schule*. 3 volumes. *Schriften philosophischen Inhalts*. [Germanischer Bücherschatz 8-10]. Freiburg/Br.-Tübingen: Mohr

Sehrt, Edward H. & Wolfram K. Legner 1955 (eds.) *Notker-Wortschatz. Das gesamte Material zusammengetragen von Edward H. Sehrt und Taylor Starck*. Halle (Saale): Niemeyer.

Sievers, Eduard (ed.) 1966. *Tatian. Lateinisch und altdeutsch mit ausführlichem Glossar*. [Bibliothek der ältesten Deutschen Literatur-Denkmäler 5]. 2nd edition. Paderborn: Schöningh

[T] = Masser, Achim (ed.) 1994. *Die lateinisch-althochdeutsche Tatianbilingue Stiftsbibliothek St. Gallen Cod. 56*. [Studien zum Althochdeutschen 25]. Göttingen: Vandenhoeck & Ruprecht.

Tax, Petrus W. (ed.) 1986-90. *Notker der Deutsche. Boethius, »De consolatione Philosophiae«*. 3 volumes. Buch I-V. [Altdeutsche Textbibliothek. Die Werke Notkers des Deutschen 1-3]. Tübingen: Niemeyer.

—. (ed.) 1979. *Notker der Deutsche. Der Psalter. Psalm 1-50*. [Althochdeutsche Textbibliothek 84. Die Werke Notkers des Deutschen 8]. Tübingen: Niemeyer.

SUBJECT INDEX